D0209548

Anabolic Steroids and the Athlete

SECOND EDITION

WILLIAM N. TAYLOR, M.D.

McFarland & Company, Inc., Publishers
Jefferson, North Carolina, and London

Library of Congress Cataloguing-in-Publication Data

Taylor, William N.
Anabolic steroids and the athlete / William N. Taylor—
2d ed.
p. cm.
Includes bibliographical references and index.
ISBN 0-7864-1128-7 (softcover : 50# alkaline paper) ∞
1. Doping in sports. 2. Anabolic steroids. I. Title.
[DNLM: 1. Anabolic steroids. 2. Sports medicine.]
RC1230.T39 2002
362.29'088'796—dc21 2001044927

British Library cataloguing data are available

©2002 William N. Taylor. All rights reserved

No part of this book may be reproduced or transmitted in any form or by any means, electronic or mechanical, including photocopying or recording, or by any information storage and retrieval system, without permission in writing from the publisher.

Cover images ©2001 Digital Stock

Manufactured in the United States of America

McFarland & Company, Inc., Publishers
Box 611, Jefferson, North Carolina 28640
www.mcfarlandpub.com

To the two most important people in my life:
my son, William N. Taylor, III (Nathan),
and my wife, Judith Jones Taylor.

Life without them
would be just going through the motions.
Their support of my efforts in writing this book
has been invaluable.

Acknowledgments

I would like to thank the following people for their major contributions and encouragement:

Robert O. Voy, M.D., former chief medical officer for the United States Olympic Committee Drug Control Program, for choosing me to serve as physician crew chief under his direction and guidance during the 1985–1988 quadrennial, and for his decision to be the first medical doctor to support my proposal to have anabolic steroids reclassified as Class III narcotics under federal law. These drugs were the first class of drugs ever added to the Federal Controlled Substance Act since its inception in 1970. His continued courageous insight and inspiration have contributed to helping countless athletically inclined people who have never set foot in his medical office.

Robert W. Brown, M.D., former president of the American League of Professional Baseball Clubs, for his courage in promoting my lectures in the late 1980s that I presented to most of the major league baseball teams during the Grapefruit League spring training schedule and to the November 1990 meeting of team owners, managers, and league officials. What an opportunity it was to educate people and to discuss this topic with the nation's professional baseball players.

The countless pharmaceutical representatives, district managers, and regional managers of Pfizer Pharmaceuticals, who promoted and supported my lecture series "Drug Issues in Sports Medicine" for the continuing medical education of the nation's physicians. Thanks for showing me the best of America's landscape in every state.

Dewey and Bea Liston for their financial and other forms of support of this project.

Table of Contents

Preface

This book is the second edition of one that I wrote 20 years ago. I never intended to write a second edition, but so much has happened with the topic over the past two decades that I felt that a new edition could be more instructive to a readership of expanded numbers and expanded interest.

In the original edition, I attempted to strike a balance between the athlete's use and the physician's knowledge. For the most part, I succeeded. For instance, the athletes felt that the book was a valid representation of their steroid use and provided physicians knowledge of the results of this use. Moreover, many physicians felt that the book educated athletes as to the risks of anabolic steroid abuse. The original edition was well received by both the athletic and medical communities.

The continuing controversies and mistakes that have plagued the scientific advancements associated with anabolic steroids are perhaps unparalleled in medical history. Testosterone and other anabolic steroids are powerful hormones, both for medical applications and for abuse by athletes who are searching for ways to enhance muscle mass and strength. Describing both the medical applications and the athletic abuse is one of the major goals of this book; distinguishing between the two is another.

Like the first edition, this new version also contains a chapter on the athletic abuse of human growth hormone. This updated version reveals the major problem of athletic use of growth-stimulating hormones in competitive sports. Detailed in this chapter are the reasons behind my continued efforts to have all growth-stimulating hormones reclassified as controlled substances.

Historical Perspectives

I first became interested in anabolic steroids around 1979 when I was in my second year of medical school. My medical training had taught me that anabolic steroids were mere placebos when used by athletes. The consensus among athletes, however, was that anabolic steroids were powerful muscle-building drugs. These two views were diametrically opposed. My review of the scientific literature and observations with strength-training athletes quickly convinced me that medical school had failed me on this issue. The athletes were correct, and their view was actually supported by the scientific studies conducted on experienced weightlifters.

Medical school also taught me that anabolic steroids had little or no use as drug therapy in patients. After an extensive review of the scientific literature, I felt certain that anabolic steroid therapy could be useful to many patients. Again, my formal medical education seemed to have failed me.

As I pondered this situation, it was difficult for me to accept that conflicting views about anabolic steroids had created this quandary. I could envision new medical modalities that focused on rehabilitating ill patients by prescribing anabolic agents to help them return to an independent lifestyle. Yet I could also see the athletic and bodybuilding abuse of anabolic steroids escalating. Many athletes knew more about anabolic steroids than the majority of the physicians did. How could I help stop the abuse of anabolic steroids and still help promote and preserve their future medical uses?

I developed a plan. The first step was to try to bring anabolic steroid–using athletes together with physicians to reexamine the scientific literature indicating that anabolic steroid use combined with adequate dietary protein intake and strength training did indeed enhance muscle mass and strength. I illustrated this concept in my 1982 book *Anabolic Steroids and the Athlete*. I was the first medical doctor to speak out with such a bold premise and support it using the scientific literature. The first step was accomplished in 1984 when my input help revise the official position of the American College of Sports Medicine on anabolic steroids.

The second step would take a congressional act to accomplish: reclassification of anabolic steroids as controlled substances under federal law. My 1985 book, *Hormonal Manipulation: A New Era of Monstrous Athletes*, helped launch the public and professional momentum to accomplish this goal. When Congress held hearings in the late 1980s on the subject, this book was submitted into the Congressional Record by Henry A. Waxman, who chaired the hearings in the House of Representatives. On November 30, 1990, President George Bush signed the bill that reclassified anabolic steroids as Schedule

III narcotics under the 1970 Federal Controlled Substance Act. A history of this step is detailed in my 1991 book *Macho Medicine: A History of the Anabolic Steroid Epidemic*. Major medical opponents of this reclassification claimed that it would thwart the research with anabolic steroids for medical uses. This has not been the case.

The final step is actually an ongoing process, involving research into the medical uses of anabolic steroids. My 1996 book, *Osteoporosis: Medical Blunders and Treatment Strategies*, describes some of my work and research with anabolic steroids in this area.

Currently, I hope to be a part of the renewed efforts to help define the use of anabolic steroids in physical medicine and rehabilitation. After all, these drugs were first developed over 50 years ago to help rehabilitate patients with acute, chronic and disabling conditions. To that end, I hope that this book will help patients who can benefit from anabolic steroid therapy prescribed with medical supervision. I have certainly looked forward to this exciting opportunity for many years.

Introduction: The Two Faces of Anabolic Steroids

Drugs have a major influence on society. They can be used to benefit society or abused causing detrimental effects. Many drugs, including anabolic steroids, possess the inherent capability to be a benefit or a detriment depending on how they are used. This produces a dilemma, use or abuse, or the two faces of anabolic steroids.

Well over a million people (athletes and physique enthusiasts) illegally obtain anabolic steroids for muscle building. Each year, tens of thousands of graduating 12th-grade males do so. Sixty-five percent of them become heavy users who become addicted with no definite plans to stop using.[1] They begin using anabolic steroids when they are young, otherwise healthy, and are not in need of them. They engage in self-experimentation with these steroids without medical supervision. In addition, it has been shown that heavy anabolic steroid use greatly increases the likelihood to use an array of other dangerous drugs. Thus, the dark face is the abuse of anabolic steroids.

The original intent of anabolic steroids use *was* to treat illness. This is the positive face of these drugs — a face meant to help a larger group of people whose health is declining from diseases such as osteoporosis, severe burns, acquired immune deficiency syndrome (AIDS), andropause, menopause, dementia, cancer, systemic lupus, rheumatoid arthritis, depression, and other disabling conditions. Anabolic steroids were originally made clinically available for these individuals and have been available for over 40 years. Unfortunately, most physicians don't prescribe them for these conditions in spite of the fact that these drugs are safe and effective when used in clinically approved doses with physician supervision. Anabolic steroids have become the "forgotten steroids" in too many medical formularies.

A growing specialty in medicine deals with the decline of systems seen in aging. It is nearly impossible to discuss aging without understanding the roles that testosterone and anabolic steroids, such as dehydroepiandrosterone (DHEA), play. Most aging individuals die from atherosclerosis, cancer, or dementia; but in the oldest old, loss of muscle and bone strength is *the limiting* factor for an individual's chances of living an independent life until death.[2] This age-related loss of musculoskeletal strength primarily brought about by a decrease in anabolic steroids and growth hormones within the body has been called *sarcopenia.*[3] This name is derived from the muscle cell units called sarcomeres and the reduction in their number ("penia") with aging. Sarcopenia is a consequence of aging, and does not require a disease to occur, but can be greatly accelerated by a variety of chronic illnesses. Sarcopenia is a major cause of disability and frailty in the elderly. Estimates of the health care dollars spent dealing with this condition are easily in the hundreds of billions of dollars annually.

There are many candidate mechanisms leading to sarcopenia, including age-related declines in production of anabolic steroids, growth hormones, and reduced physical activity. Other hormonal systems decrease with age and play roles in the dramatic declines seen within the musculoskeletal system, such as human growth hormone (GH), insulin-like growth factor-1 (IGF-1), and estrogens. Sarcopenia can be reversed with high-intensity progressive resistance exercise coupled with the replacement of the declining anabolic steroids and other anabolic hormones. Therefore, a major challenge in preventing an *epidemic* of sarcopenia-induced frailty in the future is developing public health interventions that deliver an anabolic stimulus to the muscle and bones of elderly adults on a mass scale.

States of subnormal anabolic hormone concentrations are seen in both elderly men and women. Therefore, the potential roles of anabolic hormone replacement in aging men and women should parallel each other. The goal of anabolic hormone replacement would be to improve body composition, increase muscle and bone mass, improve the quality of life, and reduce cardiovascular risk factors, thereby reducing mortality and morbidity.[4] Although the data are limited, recent studies of anabolic steroid and other anabolic hormone therapy for sarcopenia have demonstrated considerable improvements,[5–17] especially when combined with strength training.[18–24]

Abuse: The Dark Face of Anabolic Steroids

When most people think about anabolic steroids they think about muscularity for good reasons. Almost every imposingly muscular body that exists today is a product of heavy and prolonged anabolic steroid use. Nevertheless, there is much more to anabolic steroids than the muscles that they build. Most people don't think about the potential addiction, denial of such addiction, violent behavior, hostility, aggression, likelihood of promoting narcotic abuse, suicidal behavior, premature death, and the heightened sexual appetite that the abuse of anabolic steroids can cause. Fewer still comprehend the multifaceted degree of anabolic steroid abuse or *anabolic steroid charisma* that has captured a significant portion of Americans.[25]

By most accounts, America's youth are more aggressive, violent, foulmouthed, and less respectful than in generations past. Many factors play a role, but many experts feel that the media plays a large role through its coverage and portrayal of television, movies, and sports heroes exhibiting aggressive, hypersexual, and violent behaviors, including drug abuse. Drug abuse is certainly a factor in violent and criminal behavior, and one class of drugs that escalates overly aggressive, violent, and hypersexual behavior is anabolic steroids. The heavy users of anabolic steroids are provided a huge amount of media coverage through their participation in sporting events, magazine pictures, television programs, "gangsta rap" music videos, and motion pictures.

To understand the phenomenon of anabolic steroid charisma, it is important to understand the degree to which anabolic steroid use has infiltrated professional sports, acting, and other professions. Perhaps the most objective measure that has dealt with the prevalence of anabolic steroid use was conducted on college football players in the spring of 1988. Drug testing officials from the National Collegiate Athletic Association conducted a national, unannounced drug test on football players from 25 colleges and universities during the off-season. Their results showed that nearly *one-third* of the players in Division I tested positively for anabolic steroid use.[26] This contrasted sharply to the announced testing prior to the bowl games in the fall of 1987 when only 1.3 percent of the 1,589 athletes tested positive for drug use of any type.[27] My best estimates of current anabolic steroid use in selected professional sports and other professions are shown in Table 1. This information suggests that the prevalence of anabolic steroid use is not accurately obtained from information published as a result of drug testing or league or organizational sanctions.

My estimates are based on 20 years of studying the anabolic steroid issue. Sources of these estimates include information gained from my scientific publications, congressional testimonies, personal communications with athletes and sports officials, expert witness testimonies, clinical observations, sports medicine symposia participation, work with the United States Olympic Committee, lectures provided to Major League Baseball, teaching graduate courses in exercise physiology, judging bodybuilding competitions,

TABLE 1. ESTIMATES OF ANABOLIC STEROID USE BY MEN IN VARIOUS SPORTS AND PROFESSIONAL ORGANIZATIONS

Occupation	*% Steroid Use**	*Testing***	*Sanctions****	*Comments*
Professional bodybuilding	95–100	none	none	steroid addiction is the rule; violent behavior is common
Professional wrestling	95–100	none	none	steroid addiction is the rule; violent behavior is common
Professional boxing (heavy wt)	95–100	none	none	promotes violent and criminal behavior
Professional football	65–70	annual	rare	factor in off-field violence; long-term use common
Professional basketball	20–25	none	none	use is increasing; factor in off-court violence
Professional baseball	20–25	none	none	use is increasing among power hitters and pitchers; factor in new records and career extension; factor in on-field violence
Professional acting	10–15	none	none	promotes violence and sex
Olympic athletes	30–40	random, post-event	few	strength sports, sprinters, swimmers, cyclers, track and field competitors
Police officers	10–15	none	none	factor in police brutality[28,29]

*Estimated percentage of individuals with anabolic steroid use within the previous year
**Accurate anabolic steroid testing program which is executed and enforced
***Disciplinary actions are enforced

numerous lectures provided to the medical profession, work with power-lifting organizations, analysis of black market sources, locker room histories, longitudinal studies of anabolic steroid users, and personal observations.

The temptation to start anabolic steroid use can be magnified by peer pressure, encouragement from older users, pressure applied by coaches or parents for athletic success, ready availability of the drugs, or the hope of a college athletic scholarship. For many youths, watching muscular men acting violently, seemingly without consequences, can leave a lasting "macho" impression. An adolescent male may develop an attitude resting on the belief that, "If I were that big and strong, then I wouldn't have to take any punishment from anybody. No one could tell me anything!" That attitude, coupled with the fact that anabolic steroid use can deliver that type of body, attract girls, and lead to fame, fortune, and stardom, can be overwhelming. Anabolic steroid use offers the lure of "trying to be the best that I can be and have the best body that I can have." Perhaps strongest of all is the lure of great financial rewards that are offered to some of the most prominent anabolic steroid users. Thus it becomes easy to see the seduction of "anabolic steroid charisma."

Preventing a Second Anabolic Steroid Epidemic

Anabolic steroid charisma fueled an epidemic of anabolic steroid abuse that reached its peak in 1990. At that time, as many as 11 percent of the country's adolescent males were using these steroids.[30] In 1990, these drugs were added to the 1970 Controlled Substance Act (CSA) as Schedule III narcotics.[31] This law had a major influence on reducing the supply of anabolic steroids that were available for non-medical uses. The result was that, during the 1990s, teen anabolic steroid use dropped significantly, rapidly, and leveled off to a male teen usage rate of about 4 percent. However, disturbing results from recent studies indicate that anabolic steroid abuse is on the rise again.

Much of the increase in teen anabolic steroid use can be attributed to the Internet. Flagrant abuses of the CSA are not uncommon to find online. Several Internet sites have advertised anabolic steroids for sale along with a wealth of information (much of it incorrect) on how to use them. These Internet sites are fueling a new type of anabolic steroid black market that is adding to the anabolic steroid charisma in America.

Thus, with abuse fueled by easy attainability, some experts feel that we may be on the verge of another anabolic steroid epidemic. Perhaps it is time for the United States Congress to reassess the original 1989 bill. This bill, proposed by Senator Joseph Biden, chairman of the Senate's Committee on the Judiciary, would have reclassified anabolic steroids under Schedule II of the CSA.[32] This classification would have allowed for national quotas to be placed on anabolic steroid production by the pharmaceutical industry based on medical use only. It would have ensured stricter enforcement and penalties for illegal anabolic steroid importation for non-medical uses. Most importantly, it would have continued to allow specific quantities to be made available for continued medical research.

Funding Needed for Expanded Medical Applications

Traditionally, much of the money for clinical research for drug applications has come from the pharmaceutical industry. However, once the patent protection expires, as with anabolic steroids, there is little financial support forthcoming from that industry to further fund research. Therefore, it is time for national legislators to promote anabolic steroid research efforts through congressional actions.

During the 1990s there was a new enthusiasm for investigating medical uses for anabolic steroids. Some of these medical uses are the same ones that anabolic steroid therapy was intended for decades ago, such as for osteoporosis, immune deficiencies, and the rehabilitation from disabling conditions that contribute to a significant reduction in the activities of daily living. The medical research for expanded medical applications must continue at an accelerated pace. An extensive chapter has been included in this book to focus on these important medical therapy issues.

Summary: The Continuing Controversy

The major purpose of this book is to address both of the faces of the anabolic steroid dilemma. It *is not* intended to be a guide or "how to" book for athletic-oriented users.

Over one million Americans are experimenting with these steroids without medical supervision. The non-medical use of anabolic steroids by athletes and fitness buffs continues to be a controversial phenomenon that has expanded to become an international, interdisciplinary, and intergenerational predicament with heavy financial and political overtones.[33] The widespread use of anabolic steroids in sports has become a sort of national conspiracy of denial. Self-experimentation with anabolic steroids by athletes can be very dangerous to the health of the user and to others around the athlete. The non-medical use of anabolic steroid use should be curbed as much as possible. It is hoped that the information provided in this book will be used to promote the appropriate legislative changes and educational efforts to achieve that end.

The medically supervised uses of anabolic steroids for a variety of disease conditions have not been fully appreciated. The medical history of anabolic steroids has been loaded with controversy, ups and downs, and twists and turns. This book details this medical history of these steroids, including the variety of clinical conditions for which they are useful for and some areas for which further medical research is indicated. As more and more medical applications of anabolic steroids are being explored, one hopes that clinical research and medical use will expand to offer hope to those suffering from conditions that will respond in a positive manner with the use of anabolic steroids.

1

Description of Anabolic Steroid Compounds

Introduction: Nomenclature Begins with Testosterone

The traditional definition of anabolic steroids is that these molecules are synthetic derivatives of the natural male sex steroid hormone, testosterone. This definition is only partially true. Anabolic steroids *are* synthetic derivatives or analogs of testosterone, but testosterone is *not* a male sex hormone. Therefore, in order to accurately define anabolic steroids, it is important to describe what testosterone is and what basic influences it has on body functions.

Testosterone was originally synthesized in 1935 by biochemists who later received the Nobel Prize for their work.[1,2] It has had a checkered and controversial medical history that was initially fueled by nomenclature mistakes that called it "the male hormone."[3] Testosterone's molecular structure and physiological functions are complicated, and like any drug it can be harmful and dangerous when it is abused. Shortly after it was made clinically available in the late 1930s, testosterone was abused by the American public. It was available without a prescription and sold over-the-counter in the nation's drug stores. Many people took testosterone supplements to enhance sexual desire and longevity, all without medical supervision.[4] Then in the early 1950s, athletes began taking testosterone supplements to enhance muscle mass, strength, and athletic performance.[5] This non-medical use by athletes remains a major problem.

Today, much of the information about testosterone made available to the public is incorrect, conflicting, and confusing. Therefore, in this chapter, some basic physiological facts regarding testosterone will be presented. It is important that the reader utilize this information as a basis for understanding the material presented in the rest of the book.

Facts About Testosterone

TESTOSTERONE IS PRODUCED BY BOTH SEXES

Testosterone is a steroid hormone that is produced by specific glands in both sexes. It influences or regulates both sexually related and non-sexually related mechanisms. Testosterone exhibits these influences by binding to receptors in several tissues of the body. Receptors for testosterone are located in the brain, heart, lungs, muscles, bones, skin, sexual organs, and other tissues and organs.

In men, the primary production sites for testosterone are the testicles. These glands synthesize over 95 percent of a man's testosterone. The adrenal glands, non-sexual tissue located along upper aspects of the kidneys, produce most of the remaining quantity of testosterone in men.

In women, the primary production sites for testosterone are the ovaries and the adrenal glands. In general, the ovaries synthesize approximately 85 percent of a woman's testosterone with the adrenal glands producing the remaining 15 percent.[6] However, the ovarian to adrenal production ratio may vary significantly in any given woman over time and in response to stressful situations. During times of stress, the adrenal glands increase their production of testosterone. *Testosterone plays such an important role in a woman's biochemistry that two primary sources contribute to its total production.*

Thus, testosterone is a steroid hormone that is produced by specific glands in both sexes. It plays an important metabolic role in both men and women. Although its production is much greater in men than in women, testosterone is *not* the male sex steroid hormone.

TESTOSTERONE PRODUCTION VARIES WITH THE STAGES OF LIFE

Prior to puberty, testosterone production is low in males. During puberty and thereafter, testosterone production reaches its peak. It remains near its peak levels until the fourth decade of life. Testosterone production begins a steady decline and approaches the pre-puberty levels at about the eighth decade of life. This reduction of testosterone production is caused by a slow involution of the testicles.

Prior to puberty, testosterone production in females is low. During puberty and thereafter, testosterone production reaches its peak. It remains near its peak levels until the fourth decade of life. During the perimenopause, about a decade prior to menopause, testosterone production by the ovaries declines significantly. After menopause, ovarian production of testosterone essentially ceases. Adrenal gland production of testosterone continues in the postmenopausal woman, but at a low level. The adrenal glands' ability to increase testosterone production is severely restricted, so that in the post-menopausal woman, testosterone production declines and approaches her pre-puberty levels. This reduction of testosterone production is caused by the involution of the ovaries.

Testosterone Production Varies Among Males

Daily testosterone production in adult men varies considerably. Its average production can vary four-fold. In other words, one man can produce four times the daily testosterone of another man. This definition for the normal ranges of testosterone levels in men was established decades ago. In general, men with high normal ranges of testosterone tend to be more muscular and have more aggressive personalities. Men on the low end of the normal range tend to be less muscular and have less aggressive personalities. Men produce 30 to 100 times the amount of testosterone that women produce.

Testosterone Production Varies Among Females

Daily testosterone production in adult women varies to a greater degree than in men. Its average production can vary ten-fold. In pre-menopausal adult women, the daily testosterone production is associated with the menstrual cycle. Its production is greatest during the five days prior to and after ovulation.[7] It is this increased production of testosterone that is responsible for a woman's enhanced sexual desire during this period of her menstrual cycle.[8]

Testosterone Is a Steroid

Testosterone is classified as a steroid due to its molecular structure. A *steroid* is *any* chemical that possesses the specific four-ring molecular structure depicted in Figure 1-1. The four rings of a steroid molecule are designated as either the A,B,C or D ring and each of the carbon atoms numbered. Utilizing this naming system, testosterone's chemical name is 17-beta-hydroxyandrost-4-en-3-one. Testosterone's specific chemical structure is shown in Figure 1-2.

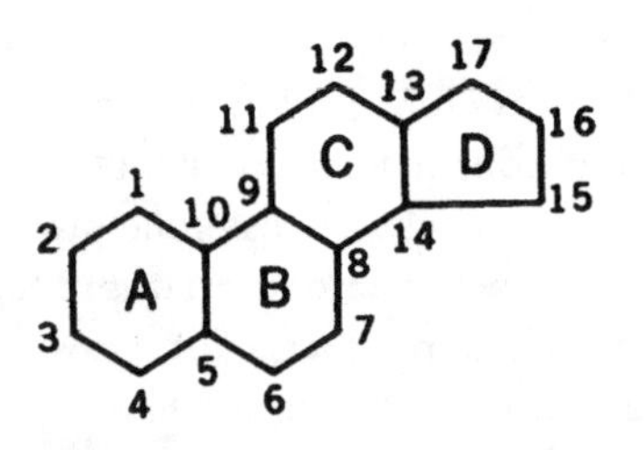

Figure 1-1. Basic steroid molecular structure.

The human body produces dozens of different steroids. Examples of steroids that are made by both sexes include estradiol, progesterone and testosterone (see Figure 1-2). Notice the similarity in the molecular structures of the major sex steroids: testosterone, estrogen, and progesterone.

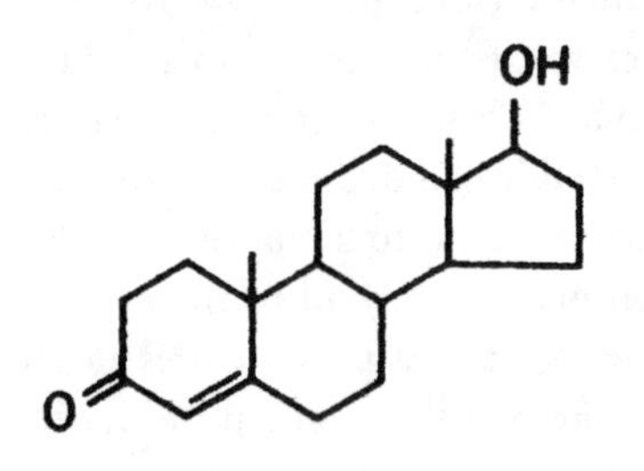

Testosterone

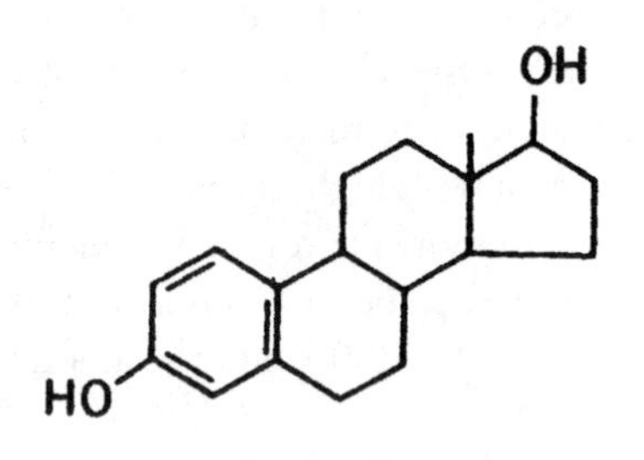

Estradiol-17β

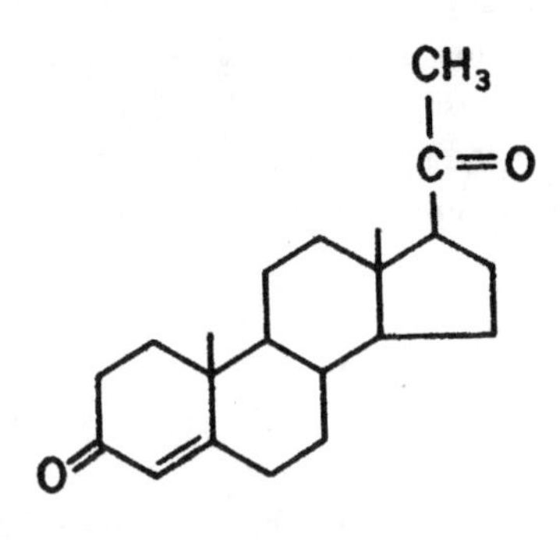

Progesterone

Figure 1-2. Molecular structures of testosterone, estrogen, and progesterone.

TESTOSTERONE IS AN ANDROGEN

An *androgen* is defined as a sex hormone that is produced by the gonads (testicles or ovaries) and adrenal glands and possesses the capability of inducing male characteristics. Testosterone meets these criteria in the male. However, under normal physiologic conditions, the amount of testosterone produced by these glands in the female does not induce male characteristics. In exceptionally large doses, testosterone does produce male characteristics in women. This can be seen in women bodybuilders. Examples of other physiologic androgens common to both men and women are dihydrotestosterone (DHT), dehydroepiandrosterone (DHEA), and androstenedione ("andro"). These molecular structures are shown in Figure 1-3.

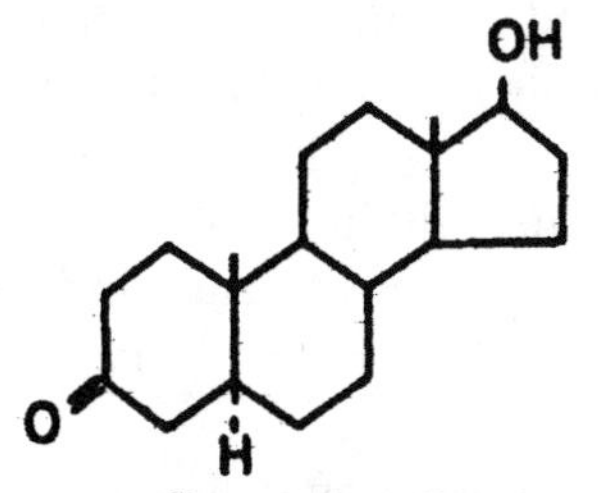

17β-Hydroxy-5α-androstan-3-one (DHT)

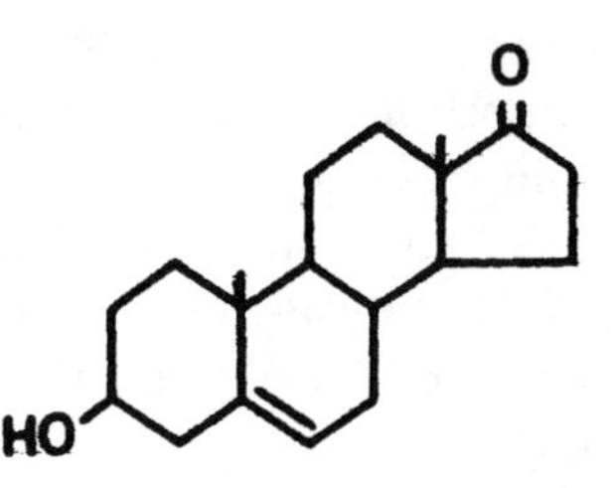

Dehydroepiandrosterone (DHEA)

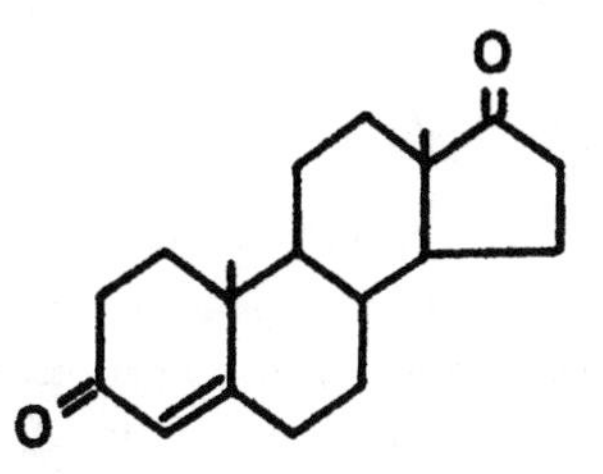

Androst-4-ene-3, 17-dione ("Andro")

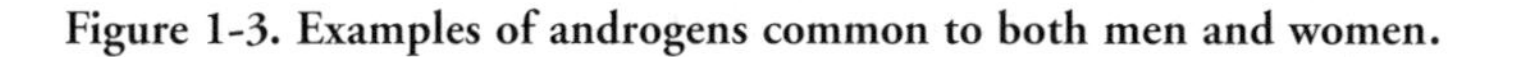

Figure 1-3. Examples of androgens common to both men and women.

TESTOSTERONE IS A HORMONE

A *hormone* is defined as a substance that is produced by an endocrine gland and regulates metabolism, growth, and reproduction through specific chemical processes within the body. Hormones also serve to coordinate the function of various groups of organs. Hormones that have the molecular structure of a steroid are called *steroid hormones.* Not all hormones are steroids, that is, they do not have the specific four-ring structure that defines a steroid. Examples of non-steroid hormones are peptide hormones and polypeptide hormones.

Testosterone Is an Anabolic Steroid

Testosterone causes considerable anabolic or "building" effects on the body. Its anabolic influences are due to its ability to bind to receptors contained in many tissues throughout the body. Some examples of testosterone's anabolic effects are listed below.

In skeletal muscle tissue, testosterone binds to receptors within the cytoplasm of the muscle cells. The testosterone/receptor complex enters the muscle cell nucleus and stimulates genetic material to begin the process of protein synthesis within muscle cells. Prolonged protein synthesis can result in enhanced muscle mass and strength, especially when combined with athletic and weight training.[9]

In bone tissue, testosterone binds to receptors within osteoblasts (bone-forming cells). The osteoblast is stimulated to incorporate calcium and other proteins to form new bone tissue. This increases bone mineral density and strength of bones.

In red blood cells, testosterone binding results in an increased hemoglobin concentration. It also works synergistically with erythropoietin to increase red blood cell formation and total blood volume.

Testosterone Has Anabolic and Androgenic Properties

Several body functions are under either direct or indirect control of testosterone. It has a direct stimulatory effect on a number of tissues and organs, including skeletal muscle, bone, visceral organs, stem cells, and the immune system. Within the brain, testosterone acts as a direct and indirect neurotransmitter to influence behavior, including the enhancement of libido in both men and women. Testosterone also affects secondary sexual characteristics.

As we have seen, testosterone's effects on the body can be placed into two basic categories: anabolic (constructive metabolism, or simply "to build") and androgenic (characteristics that are man-like). Some of the androgenic and anabolic functions are listed in Table 1.[10]

Basic Description of Anabolic Steroids

Anabolic steroids are synthetic derivatives of testosterone. They were originally synthesized to retain and magnify testosterone's anabolic effects

Table 1-1. Basic Comparison of the Androgenic and Anabolic Functions of Testosterone

Androgenic Functions

Initial growth of the penis (men) and clitoris (women)
Growth and development of the seminal vesicles (men)
Growth and development of the prostate gland (men)
Increased density of body hair
Development and pattern of pubic hair
Increased density and distribution of facial hair
Deepening tone of the voice
Increased oil production of the sebaceous glands
Increased libido and awakening of sexual interest (both sexes)
Certain "male" personality characteristics

Anabolic Functions

Increased skeletal muscle mass
Increased bone density
Increased hemoglobin concentration
Increased red blood cell mass
Enhancement of the immune system, especially T-lymphocytes
Influence on the distribution and quantity of body fat
Increased nitrogen retention and protein synthesis
Increased visceral organ size
Increased retention of several electrolytes
Increased height during puberty (synergism with growth hormone)

while reducing or alleviating some of the androgenic effects. However, the "perfect" anabolic steroid, one that enhances testosterone's anabolic functions while eliminating the androgenic functions, has never been developed. Nearly every conceivable alteration to testosterone's steroid molecular structure has been synthesized and studied in attempts to find the perfect anabolic steroid. Each of these anabolic steroids has a unique molecular structure that is similar to testosterone. Because all of the anabolic steroids retain some androgenic potential, they are often referred to as *anabolic-androgenic steroids*. By the mid–1960s, the attempts to find the perfect anabolic steroid resulted in over a dozen anabolic steroids used as medicinal drugs.

Anabolic steroids are not "true" hormones since they are not made by glands within the human body. However, within the body, they function as steroid hormones. Different anabolic steroids have different effects on the body. This is due to the androgen receptors and their location throughout the body. Anabolic steroids seem to have different affinities for binding to these receptors. For instance, one anabolic steroid may tend to bind more to muscle cell receptors than to brain cell receptors. Another anabolic steroid may tend to bind more to osteoblast receptors in bone than to hair cell receptors, and so forth. This concept of "selective receptor binding" has been used to determine the anabolic-to-androgenic ratio of a particular anabolic steroid. This will be further discussed in the next chapter.

Summary: Testosterone Is the Parent Compound for Anabolic Steroids

Testosterone is the most potent, anabolic-androgenic steroid hormone produced by the human body. It is produced by both sexes and has many powerful, anabolic and androgenic influences. It is not simply a male hormone.

Testosterone was the first hormone ever synthesized. From the time of testosterone synthesis in 1935, dozens of anabolic steroids, produced by altering one or more aspects of testosterone's molecular structure, were developed to promote the anabolic properties over the androgenic properties. Anabolic steroids have become drugs of both use and abuse, demonstrating the two faces of anabolic steroids.

Testosterone and other anabolic steroids are the drugs of choice for many athletes and body image obsessed Americans. These groups of people use them in both supratherapeutic doses and over extended periods of time. This abuse or dark face of testosterone and anabolic steroids will be discussed in detail in other chapters of this book.

Anabolic steroids have been available for medical use since the mid–1960s. It was hoped that anabolic steroids would play a major role in the treatment of a variety of diseases and debilitating conditions, but, for various reasons, if physicians have used them they have done so sparingly. In the near future, anabolic steroids are likely to play a significant role in the rehabilitation of patients from a variety of conditions that require tissue rebuilding and building for recovery. This is the positive or other face of anabolic steroid use. These uses will be discussed in detail in other chapters in this book.

2

Anabolic-to-Androgenic Ratio (Therapeutic Index)

Introduction

Testosterone and anabolic steroids exert both anabolic and androgenic influences on the body. The anabolic and androgenic functions of a particular steroid are often arbitrarily set apart even though there can be considerable overlap of these influences. These influences are very complex and to date, scientific research has not been able to completely sort out these issues.

Anabolic steroids tend to have the ability to promote anabolic functions to a greater degree than testosterone while, at the same time, reducing or alleviating androgenic functions. As mentioned, precisely determining both the anabolic and androgenic effects of these steroids in humans has not been possible. Except for the self-experimentation by athletes and bodybuilders, humans have not been used as subjects for modern scientific studies dealing with anabolic steroid use. What is known has been determined through research utilizing animal subjects. However, results from controlled human studies are needed, especially since these steroids are prescribed to patients and misused by athletes. For the most part, these studies have not been done. Therefore, a discussion of the available animal studies is appropriate.

Following this review, sections pertaining to the molecular structures of anabolic steroids, the mechanisms that lead to their enhanced anabolic activities, and the categorization into a therapeutic index will be presented. Finally, a brief summary will introduce some of the frustrations felt by the medical profession when anabolic steroids were made clinically available without sufficient medical research.

The presentation of the material in this chapter is technical by its nature. Some previous knowledge of chemistry, biochemistry, and human physiology would be helpful. However, the material will be presented in such a way that understanding can be gained without an extensive scientific background.

A Review of the Animal Literature

Historically, the androgenicity of a particular steroid compound has been defined in terms of the growth it stimulates in the sex glands of rodents. The glands that have been studied are the prostate and the seminal vesicles of selected male rodents when anabolic steroids are given after castration. The post-castration growth of these glands has provided an accurate, objective measurement of the androgen influences of various anabolic steroids, at least in rodents. Similar studies of these compounds on the growth, size, and function of the sex organs in male humans after castration have not been conducted. Similarly, definitive studies of the effects of these steroids on the size and function of the external genitalia of human females have not been conducted. Therefore, extrapolating the results of the rodent studies to human use is limited but provides the best available information.

Like androgenic potential, the anabolic potential of a particular anabolic steroid is also difficult to study. Again, animal studies have been utilized, specifically using rodents to investigate the anabolic effect of various anabolic steroids. The changes in various rodent muscle groups or organs, before and after anabolic steroid administration, are used to evaluate the anabolic effects of a particular steroid. Major problems arise when the rodent results are extrapolated to human use. First, rodents don't lift weights or participate in goal-oriented exercise programs. Second, some of the muscle groups that have been selected for scientific studies in rodents are muscles that are involved with sexual activity. The study of these muscle groups, which were selected to help delineate the anabolic versus androgenic effects, have only further confused the distinction. In other words, the muscles rodents used for sexual activities enlarged when they were treated with anabolic steroids. Was the muscle enlargement a product of anabolic potentials alone, or was it a composite of anabolic and androgenic factors?

Numerous studies have been conducted to investigate the anabolic versus androgenic effects of testosterone and synthetic anabolic steroids in rodents. Although various methods have been used to study the genital and extragenital responses to selected anabolic-androgenic steroids, they can be categorized into four areas:

a) sexual organ growth[1–4]
b) renotrophic (kidney growth) versus androgenic response[5–10]

c) myotrophic and levator ani muscle growth versus androgenic response[11–17]
d) nitrogen balance versus androgenic activity[18–41]

Although these animal studies have been shown to have many imperfections, they served as a starting point for evaluating the numerous anabolic steroid compounds that were synthesized.

During the 1950s and 1960s there was worldwide enthusiasm for the development of anabolic steroid compounds. Almost every major pharmaceutical company developed one or more synthetic anabolic steroids for clinical or veterinary use. Through chemical reactions, scientists made minor alterations to testosterone's molecular structure by adding a methyl group here, a hydroxyl group there, a carbon group over there, and so forth. The result was a plethora of anabolic steroids. Primarily, crude laboratory assays and animal testing were utilized to evaluate these steroids and over a dozen of these compounds became patented anabolic steroids. However, not all of these patented molecules proved to be clinically viable anabolic steroids.

Basic Modifications of the Testosterone Molecule

Minor alterations to the testosterone molecule have major effects on the physiological nature of the resultant anabolic steroid compound. These major effects can alter the anabolic potential, the duration of the steroid's action within the body, the effective dose of the steroid, the most effective route of administration (e.g., orally, by injection, or by transdermal patch or gel), and so forth.

To gain a basic understanding of the effects of these modifications, it is important to present testosterone's chemical structure with the carbons numbered as shown in Figure 2-1. The alpha and beta denotation refers to the stereochemistry of the hydroxyl and hydrogen groups at carbon 17.

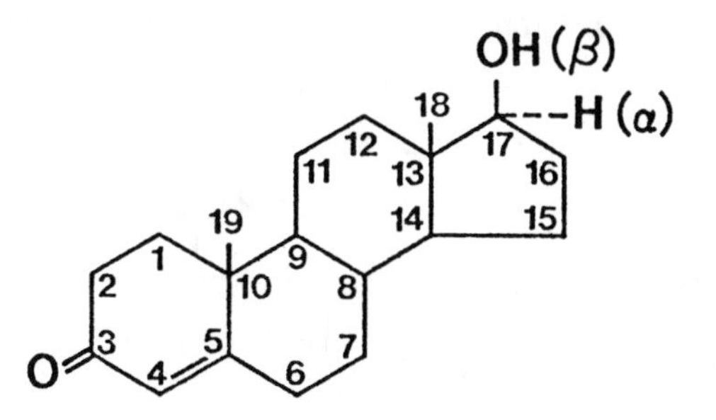

Figure 2-1. Nomenclature of the testosterone molecule. The numbers refer to carbon atoms. β and α refer to the stereochemistry of the hydroxyl and hydrogen groups at carbon 17.

Modifications at the 17-alpha Position

Testosterone is not very biologically active when it is consumed orally because it is poorly absorbed from the stomach and small intestines. Molecular testosterone that survives the strongly acidic conditions and absorption by the gastrointestinal tract is rapidly degraded by the liver. However, if alterations are made at the 17th carbon, in the alpha position, the resultant anabolic steroid becomes biologically active when consumed orally. The addition of a methyl or ethyl group to the 17th carbon in place of the hydrogen atom results in the 17-alpha-alkylated anabolic steroids.

The efficacy of methyltestosterone is approximately four times that of testosterone when taken orally and is of sufficient magnitude to make oral or sublingual therapy practical. For this reason, substitution of a 17-alpha-methyl or ethyl group is a common feature of many orally active anabolic steroids.[42–44] It has been shown that 17-alpha-alkylated anabolic steroids bind directly to androgen receptors. Excretion and degradation products have been shown to contain the 17-alpha-alkyl groups intact.[45,46]

The enzymatic removal of the methyl or ethyl group at the 17-alpha position does not occur prior to binding to androgen receptors as once thought.[47] Therefore, the modifications at the 17-alpha position of testosterone molecule result in biologically active anabolic steroids different from testosterone itself. Examples of these modifications are shown in Figure 2-2.

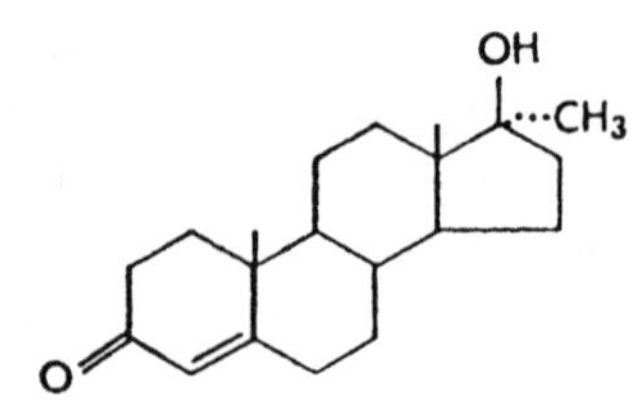

methyltestosterone

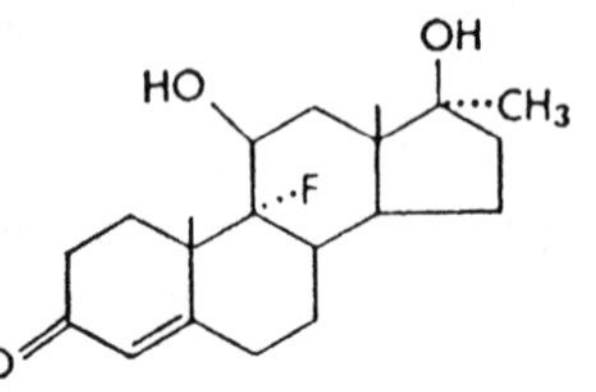

fluoxymesterone

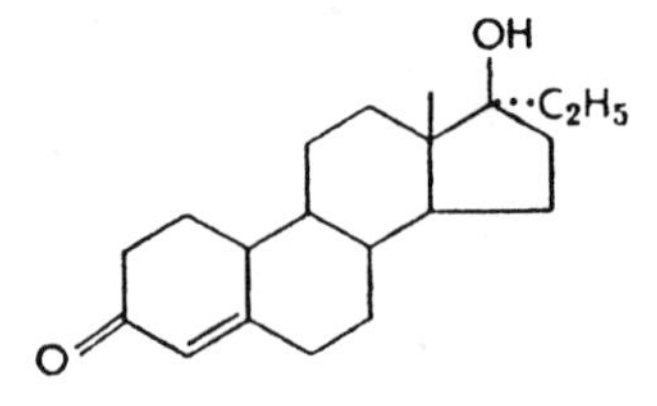

norethandrolone

Figure 2-2. Modifications of the testosterone molecule at the 17-alpha position.

MODIFICATIONS AT THE 17-BETA POSITION

Alterations of the testosterone molecule at the 17-beta position include esterification of the hydroxyl group with various carboxylic acids. Esterification decreases the polarity of the molecule and increases its solubility in lipid solutions. Most of the esterified versions of anabolic steroids are dissolved in lipid solution vehicles (oils) for intramuscular injection. Since esterification at the 17-beta position increases the anabolic steroid's affinity for lipids, once they are injected there is a slow release of the steroid from the muscular site into the circulation.[48,49] Esters of all anabolic steroids are removed by enzymatic reactions (hydrolyzed) before the steroid is active within the body.[50]

In general, the more carbon molecules in the added acid group that are esterified, the more prolonged the action the steroid has on the body.[51] Increasing the number of carbons subsequently increases the affinity of the anabolic steroid for the lipid carrier solvent that prolongs the release of the steroid from the injection site. Examples of these ester modifications that have resulted in commonly used, injectable anabolic steroids are contained in Figure 2-3.

If the 17-beta esterification contains a large enough number of carbons, then it can be effective as an oral preparation. These anabolic steroids are hydrolyzed very slowly by the liver making them effective when taken orally. An example of this type of modification is testosterone undecanoate.[52] It is absorbed into the lymphatic system and slowly released into the bloodstream where it becomes biologically active after enzymatic conversion to testosterone.[53,54]

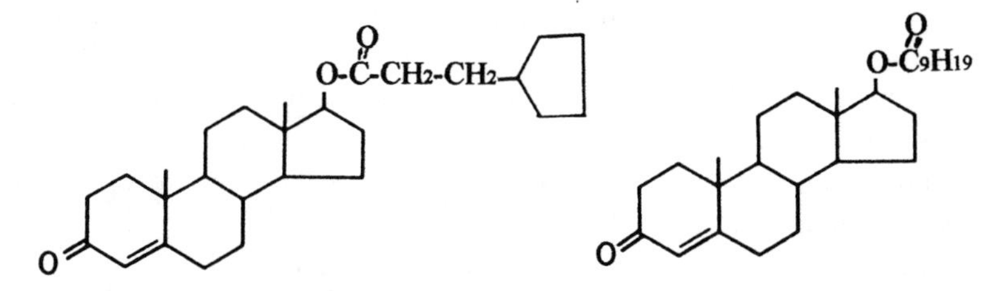

Figure 2-3. Modifications of the testosterone molecule at the 17-beta position.

Modifications at Various Other Positions

A variety of chemical alterations at the 2, 9, 11, and 19 carbon positions have been made and cause an increase in the anabolic activity of the steroid. A number of complex mechanisms have been proposed to account for the enhanced anabolic activities of anabolic steroids with these modifications. These include the alteration's ability to:

a) slow the rate of degradation of the anabolic steroid-receptor complex within the target cells' nucleus resulting in prolonged stimulation of cell's genetic anabolic machinery.[55]
b) slow the rate of inactivation of the anabolic steroid within cytoplasm of the target cells resulting in prolonged availability of the steroid for receptor binding.[56]
c) increase the steroid's affinity for receptor site binding in specific tissues. In many tissues, a variety of steroids, including androgens, estrogens, corticosteroids, and others, compete for receptor sites.[57] Some alterations to the molecular structure of testosterone may result in a competitive advantage over other steroids attempting to bind to a receptor site. This competition of steroids attempting to bind to receptor sites varies with the type of target cells involved.
d) alter the steroid's stereochemistry which "flattens" the molecular structure. This phenomenon may increase anabolic activities by inhibiting the anabolic steroid's enzymatic conversion to weaker androgens or estrogens.[58] Testosterone is degraded within the body by several enzymatic conversions. It can be reduced by enzymatic reactions to dihydrotestosterone (DHT) in certain tissues.[59] DHT is considered a weak androgen. Testosterone may also undergo an enzymatic aromatization to estrogens in certain tissues. Therefore, alterations made to the testosterone molecule may prevent these enzymatic conversions and enhance its anabolic activities.
e) alter the steroid's binding affinity for sex hormone binding globulin (SHBG), which may result in more "free" anabolic steroid molecules to bind to various target cells. Steroid hormones circulate in the bloodstream and are predominately bound to a large globular protein, SHBG. Approximately 99 percent of the steroid is bound to SHBG and in this form is not available to stimulate the target cells. The other 1 percent of the steroid that is not bound to SHBG, available in the "free" form is bioactive.[60,61] Sex hormone binding globulin serves as a "sponge-like" reservoir for steroid hormones that circulate in the bloodstream. If an anabolic steroid has a molecular alteration that *reduces* its binding to SHBG, then more than 1 percent of it would be in the active form.

f) alter the testosterone production by the gonads. Normally, administering testosterone supplementation causes a reduction in gonadal testosterone production. The molecular configuration of other anabolic steroids may not reduce gonadal testosterone production to the same degree that testosterone supplementation does.[62–65]

g) enhance the synergism with other anabolic hormones, including human growth hormone (GH), insulin-like growth factor-1 (IGF-1), and erythropoietin (EPO). Testosterone normally has stimulatory and synergistic influences on anabolic functions that coordinate with other anabolic hormones. Molecular alterations of testosterone may further enhance these effects.[66–68]

Any given modification at these sites may alter the steroid's anabolic activities by one or more of these mechanisms. However, further research utilizing the most current laboratory techniques are necessary to further delineate these or other mechanisms responsible for the enhanced anabolic activities of the numerous clinically available anabolic steroids.

A number of anabolic steroids have a combination of site modifications. For instance, a steroid may have an alteration to make it orally effective (17-alpha alkyl modification) and an alteration to enhance its anabolic activities (2, 9, or 11 modifications). Another steroid may have an alteration to make it long acting (17-beta esterification) and an alteration to enhance its anabolic activities (2, 9, or 11 modifications). Some examples of these anabolic steroids are shown in Figure 2-4.

The Therapeutic Index

Anabolic steroids were originally developed to alter the testosterone molecule to increase the anabolic functions while decreasing the androgen

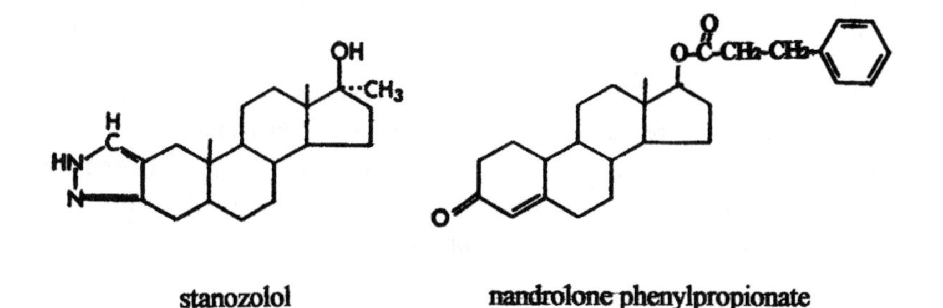

Figure 2-4. Modifications of the testosterone molecule both at the 17-alpha and 2,3 carbon positions (stanozolol); both at the 17-beta and 19 carbon positions (nandrolone phenylpropionate).

functions. The ratio of anabolic to androgenic functions has been termed the *therapeutic index.* The therapeutic index was developed in an attempt to measure and classify the anabolic and androgenic effects of anabolic steroids. The reference point for the therapeutic index is testosterone, which is assigned a therapeutic index of 1. Anabolic steroids would generally have a therapeutic index of greater than 1 since they tend to magnify the anabolic functions and reduce the androgenic functions. A comparison of the therapeutic index range for a number of anabolic steroids has been published,[69] and an adapted version[70] is presented in Table 2-1.

TABLE 2-1. THERAPEUTIC INDEX FOR SELECTED ANABOLIC STEROIDS

Trade Name	*Generic Name*	*Original Manufacturer*	*Therapeutic Index*
Testoderm	testosterone	Alza	1
Androderm	testosterone	Smith-Kline	1
Depo-Testosterone	testosterone cypionate	Upjohn	1
Methandren	methyltestosterone	Lilly	1–4
Dianabol	methandrostenolone	Ciba	2–7
Halotestin	fluroxymesterone	Upjohn	2–6
Myagen	bolasterone	Upjohn	2–5
Nivelar	norethandrolone	Searle	3–7
Adroyd	oxymetholone	Park-Davis	3–8
Oranabol	oxymesterone	Farmitalia	4–7
Nortestonate	nandrolone	Upjohn	5–16
Durabolin	nandrolone phenylpropionate	Organon	11–12
Deca-Durabolin	nandrolone decanoate	Organon	11–12
Winstrol	stanozolol	Winthrop	5–20
Primobolan	methenolone	Schering A-G	7–16
Anavar	oxandrolone	Searle	13
Maxibolin	ethylestrenol	Organon	8
Genabol	norbolethone	Wyeth	22
Dostalon	dimethazine	Richer	14–22

The list in Table 2-1 is by no means an exhaustive one and does not list *all* the anabolic steroids that have been commercially available for human use over the decades. Even with this abbreviated list, it is easy to see that the pharmaceutical industry was banking heavily on the medical future of anabolic steroids for treating disease conditions.

Summary

Understanding the effect anabolic steroids have on the body begins with knowledge of the biochemistry and physiology of steroid hormones. While inherently technical in nature, a basic understanding of these biological pathways is important.

Anabolic steroids are derivatives of testosterone, meaning that the molecular structure of testosterone has been altered through chemical reactions. An overview of these chemical alterations has been presented in order that the reader may obtain a scientific basis for the "hows" and "whys" behind the regimes of anabolic steroid use by athletes and bodybuilders. Some of these anabolic steroid regimes are based upon sound scientific knowledge, while others are based on locker room hearsay. The understanding of anabolic steroid use by athletes will be important to later understanding clinical use.

The therapeutic index of an anabolic steroid is an estimate of the steroid's ability to promote anabolic activities relative to its androgenic activities. The estimates are based primarily on decades of animal research and then extrapolating this information to human use. This has left us with a substantial gap in knowledge. This contributes to the frustration seen in the medical community as it treats patients with the promise of great benefits from anabolic steroids, but with little medical research to substantiate the promises. An example of this frustration can be seen in the statements published in the 1970 edition of a major medical pharmacology textbook. This came after most of the animal research had been concluded:

> Most of the newer [anabolic] steroids used for their anabolic effects have not been so carefully studied, and their anabolic potency compared to testosterone in man is largely unknown. Furthermore, their androgenic activity in man has not been determined with any degree of accuracy. The problem would be simplified if there were some simple indicator of the action short of waiting for the growth of facial hair, for example.[71]

For years, medical science did not provide any simple indicators for the anabolic or androgenic activities of anabolic steroids in human patients or research subjects. Therefore, the frustration regarding the clinical use of these steroids not only continued, it intensified. Research enthusiasm declined and dogmatic statements filled medical journals and textbooks. Although these issues will be discussed in detail in other chapters in this book, statements published in 1980 in a major review article will be presented to portray the blend of frustration and incorrect dogma that had arisen:

> Androgens have been used in a variety of clinical situations ... in the hope that benefits to be expected from non-virilizing actions of the agents (such as increase in nitrogen retention and muscle mass, increase in hemoglobin levels, increased skeletal growth, increased levels of plasma proteins, etc.) would outweigh any deleterious actions of the drugs. In general, these expectations

> have proved to be illusory for two reasons. One, pharmacologic doses of androgens do little if anything in men beyond the normal testosterone androgen.... Two, no androgen derivative has been devised that exhibits only the nonvirilizing effects of the hormone.... Of the current forms of androgen abuse, the most pervasive is their administration to male athletes in the expectation that muscle development and athletic performance will be improved. Whether such improvement does result is dubious.[72]

The anabolic steroid epidemic began in the United States shortly after these statements were published. One result of this epidemic was that the athletes who experimented with large doses of anabolic steroids *proved* what the medical profession refused to admit: that these drugs built muscle mass and strength, thus improving athletic performance. Imposingly muscular male and female bodies, fueled by anabolic steroids and strength training, were not "illusory." The bodybuilding industry had become a burgeoning reality. This phenomenon will be discussed in detail in later chapters.

3

Basic Principles of Muscle Building

Introduction

Most athletes and bodybuilders use anabolic steroids for the muscle building properties that these steroids possess. The use of supratherapeutic doses of anabolic steroids in conjunction with strength training and adequate dietary protein intake is known to enhance muscle mass and strength. To understand the mechanisms of how this phenomenon occurs, it is important to present the basic principles involved with protein synthesis within the skeletal muscle cells.

Three basic ingredients are necessary for optimal muscle building. These are: use of anabolic steroids, overloading of skeletal muscles through strength training, and dietary intake of protein above the normal daily requirements.

Adequate Dietary Protein Intake

Under normal physiological conditions, the recommended daily allowance (RDA) of protein intake in adult men is approximately one gram per kilogram of body weight. Protein intake in this quantity generally maintains the body's protein turnover requirements and necessary balance between anabolic and catabolic functions. Protein requirements during illness, prolonged exercise or exertion are higher than under healthy or sedentary conditions. If dietary protein intake is much greater than can be utilized, then much of is converted to carbohydrate for storage as muscle or liver glycogen. After the carbohydrate storage capacity has been achieved, additional dietary protein can be converted to body fat.

Anabolic steroid use by strength-trained athletes allows the body to utilize a greater quantity of dietary protein for conversion to skeletal muscle. Under these conditions, dietary protein intake of 1.5 grams or more per kilogram of body weight may be utilized prior to conversion of the excess protein intake into carbohydrates or fats.

If anabolic steroids are used in conjunction with a strength-training program, but dietary protein is not increased, then there will be very little resulting muscle mass enhancement. In other words, the stimuli for muscle growth have been provided, but the necessary dietary building blocks for muscle synthesis has not.

Even with heavy anabolic steroid use along with an optimum strength-training program, there is a limit to the daily dietary protein that can be incorporated into manufacturing skeletal muscle. Science has not provided the answer to what this limit is under these conditions. However, it is known that some bodybuilders can consume two grams or more of protein per kilogram of body weight prior to conversion of the excess protein into glycogen or body fat.

Strength Training as a Stimulus

The *use* of a specific muscle group is the basic stimulus for protein synthesis that results in skeletal muscle growth above the body's maintenance level. However, the exact stimulus on a cellular level is not known at this time. On a training basis, there are many regimens that scientists and athletes employ to stimulate the growth of skeletal muscles. It is beyond the scope of this book to discuss strength-training programs. To date, the *best* regimen for the stimulation of skeletal muscle growth is unknown.

Weight training turns on the genetic machinery in the skeletal muscle cells.

Anabolic steroids have been shown to enhance this genetic machinery and keep it stimulated for a much longer period of time. In rodents treated with supratherapeutic doses of anabolic steroids, overloading selected muscle groups has resulted in the genetic machinery being stimulated four times stronger and up to 10 times longer than with overloading alone.

Basics of Protein Synthesis

The basic flow of information within the genetic machinery of the muscle cell is from DNA (deoxyribonucleic acid) to RNA (ribonucleic acid) to protein formation. All of the information in a particular cell is contained in its DNA, which is the genetic substance of the cell. Different areas on the DNA molecule may be transcribed to eventually cause the synthesis of different proteins. The transcribed copy of a portion of the DNA molecule occurs within the cell's nucleus and results in a strand of genetic material called messenger RNA (mRNA). This messenger RNA then combines with another form of cytoplasmic RNA called ribosomal RNA (rRNA) that is specific for a particular amino acid.

The amino acids are joined together in a particular order as determined by the initial copy of DNA that was transcribed. This gives rise to a variety of proteins that the cell may need. Some of these proteins are then used for the increased size of the stimulated skeletal muscle cells.

Enhancement of Protein Synthesis by Anabolic Steroids

Anabolic steroids play a major role in the process of protein synthesis. The mechanism begins when the anabolic steroid molecule enters the muscle cell through the cell membrane. The steroid then binds to an intracellular receptor molecule within the cell's cytoplasm forming a steroid-receptor complex. This complex then enters the muscle cell's nucleus as schematically depicted in Figure 3-1.

Once the steroid-receptor complex is in the cell nucleus, it binds to the DNA, and the process of transcription is enhanced by *increasing the amount of mRNA that is formed.* This increased quantity of mRNA leaves the muscle cell's nucleus and binds to rRNA within the cell's cytoplasm. Then, translation of the mRNA takes place allowing for protein synthesis to occur within the golgi apparatus of the cell. The additional proteins are then incorporated to increase the size of the muscle cell.

Estimates of Muscle Mass Gains

A rigorous strength-training program combined with an adequate dietary protein intake can add muscle mass and strength for most people. However, these gains tend to occur slowly over time. Adding anabolic steroids, after strength training for at least three months, can substantially reduce the amount of time required for increasing muscle mass and strength gains.

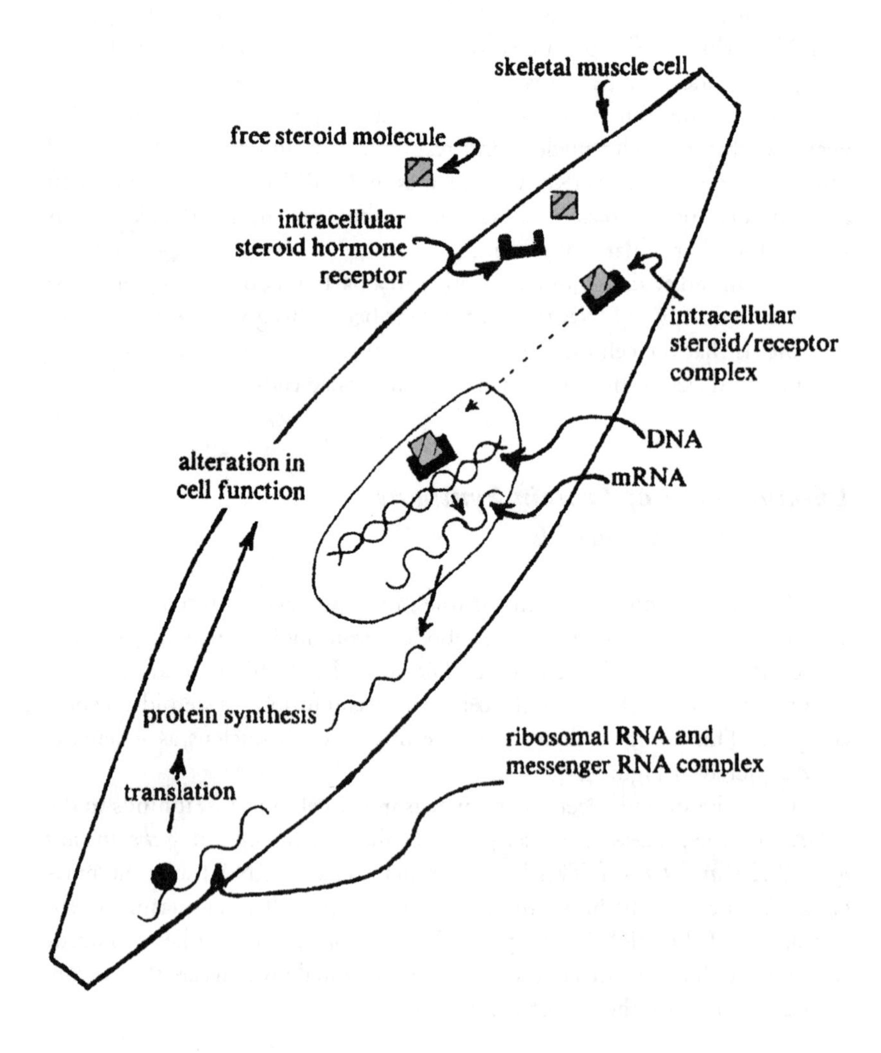

Figure 3-1. Schematic of anabolic steroid's role in skeletal muscle cell protein synthesis.

Let's put this into perspective. In order to compare two variables (dietary protein intake with and without anabolic steroid use) the third variable (strength training) must be held constant. Assume a rigorous strength-training program for a 70 kg, 25-year-old man. The time required to gain 10 pounds of muscle mass with differing dietary protein intakes, with and without anabolic steroid use, can be estimated as shown in Table 3-1.

TABLE 3-1. THE EFFECTS OF DAILY DIETARY PROTEIN INTAKE AND ANABOLIC STEROID USE ON THE ESTIMATED MUSCLE MASS GAINS ACHIEVED WITH A RIGOROUS STRENGTH-TRAINING PROGRAM

Subject: 25-year-old man, experienced in strength training, with a 70 kg body weight and no previous anabolic steroid use.

Daily Dietary (% RDA)	*Protein Intake (Grams)*	*Anabolic Steroid Use*	*Muscle Mass Gain (Grams/day)*	*Days for 10# Muscle Mass Gain*
100	70	none	5–10	450–900
100	70	moderate*	5–10	450–900
100	70	heavy**	5–10	450–900
150	105	none	5–20	225–300
150	105	moderate	30–35	130–150
150	105	heavy	30–35	130–150
200	140	none	15–20	225–300
200	140	moderate	60–70	65–75
200	140	heavy	60–70	65–75
300	210	none	15–20	225–300
300	210	moderate	60–70	65–75
300	210	heavy	100+	30–45
400	280	none	15–20	225–300
400	280	moderate	60–70	65–75
400	280	heavy	100+	30–45

*moderate anabolic steroid use of 2–3 times the recommended clinical doses
**heavy anabolic steroid use of 5 or greater times the recommended clinical doses

As illustrated in Table 3-1, it takes about two months for a young man to add an additional 10 pounds of muscle mass by combining 200–300 percent RDA of daily dietary protein intake and moderate anabolic steroid use when combined with a rigorous strength-training program. With the same dietary protein intake without anabolic steroid use it can take 8–10 months to add 10 pounds of muscle mass. Following the RDA for daily dietary protein, with or without anabolic steroid use, it can take years to add 10 pounds of muscle mass.

The apparent importance of these estimates can be illustrated by an example. All too often a high school football player is told by his coach that he needs to put on 20 pounds of muscle mass to make the team or to play a certain position. How can 20 pounds of muscle mass be added in just a few months? It can't, unless anabolic steroids are used. Since the player doesn't have two or three years to achieve this 20-pound muscle gain, the temptation to use anabolic steroids becomes paramount.

Summary

Anabolic steroid use can promote the formation of additional muscle mass and strength gains when combined with adequate dietary protein and a rigorous strength-training program. On a cellular level, the basic mechanism of action is to turn on the muscle cell's genetic machinery by increasing the production of mRNA within the cell's nucleus. If adequate protein is available, the increased mRNA is translated and protein synthesis is enhanced. Anabolic steroids provide a stronger and prolonged stimulus to the muscle cell's genetic machinery, resulting in significant gains in muscle mass over a short period of time.

When anabolic steroid use is discontinued, even though adequate dietary protein and strength training is continued, there is loss of muscle mass from its peak level. In other words, there is loss of some of the gained muscle mass that occurs during the anabolic steroid withdrawal period. This loss of muscle mass can be a strong influence on the user's decision to rapidly return to anabolic steroid use. This influence can be the first step toward anabolic steroid addiction that is described in detail later in this book.

4

Current Anabolic Steroid Preparations

Introduction: Unsupervised Hormonal Manipulation

Athletes and bodybuilders who use anabolic steroids usually do so without medical supervision or guidance. This hormonal manipulation becomes a major focus as they seek to obtain anabolic steroids and find the most effective regime for maximizing the effects. To build muscle dietary habits, nutritional supplements, weightlifting protocols, and anabolic steroid protocols becomes a major part of life. Many users become obsessed with this lifestyle and the quest to find the "magic" combination of anabolic steroids and behavior that will produce the greatest muscle-building effects. No matter how muscular they are, they perceive themselves as not muscular enough. This can result in a complex and dangerous addiction to anabolic steroids and other drugs.

Most anabolic steroid users minimize the potential adverse effects that these drugs can cause. They often feel that these adverse effects won't happen to *them*, especially if they use the drugs correctly. After months and years of anabolic steroid use, most users become "shade tree" pharmacologists and exercise physiologists. They learn to treat some of the more pesky side effects with other prescription (including narcotics) drugs. For instance, they take antibiotics for the anabolic steroid-induced acne, anti-hypertensive medication for the anabolic steroid-induced hypertension, human chorionic gonadotrophin (HCG) for the anabolic steroid-induced testicular atrophy, estrogen receptor blocking drugs, such as tamoxifen, for the anabolic steroid-induced gynecomastia, and so forth. It is not uncommon for heavy anabolic steroid users to use many other drugs to treat adverse conditions brought on by the steroids. Anabolic steroid black market dealers stock up on a variety of prescription drugs to sell to their anabolic steroid-using "clients." This polypharmacy effect will be discussed in further detail in a later chapter.

In this chapter, classes of anabolic steroid preparations will be discussed. Most of these preparations are prescription drugs classified as controlled substances and manufactured by pharmaceutical companies. Others, perhaps weaker versions, are commercially available as over-the-counter "nutritional supplements." Anabolic steroid preparations are also produced by the veterinary industry to treat conditions in diseased animals and as food additives to enhance growth in livestock.

Classifications of Anabolic Steroid Preparations

Currently, there are 10 major classes of anabolic steroids. They are grouped in classes based on the route of administration, the type of carrier solvent used to introduce the steroid into the body, or the over-the-counter (OTC) availability of the steroid. These 10 classes are:

(1) oral preparations;
(2) injectable oil-based preparations;
(3) injectable water-based preparations;
(4) patch and gel preparations;
(5) aerosol propellant preparations;
(6) sublingual preparations;
(7) "home-made" transdermal preparations;
(8) androgen-estrogen combination preparations;
(9) counterfeit anabolic steroid preparations; and,
(10) over-the-counter (OTC) anabolic steroid preparations.

Each class of anabolic steroids has a variety of characteristics that will be discussed. All of the prescription anabolic steroid preparations are classified as Schedule III controlled substances, including the counterfeit ones. When misused or abused, prescription steroids, as well as veterinary grade anabolic steroids, and OTC (over-the-counter) anabolic steroids can produce adverse effects. The veterinary and OTC steroids create a dilemma for practicing physicians, lawmakers, and the public as they are not regulated like their prescription counterparts.

Oral Anabolic Steroid Preparations

As previously discussed, to produce oral anabolic steroids, testosterone is modified by the addition of a side chain at the 17-alpha position. Oral anabolic steroids are synthesized in such a manner as to increase the protection for the molecule when it is exposed to strong stomach acid and degradation by the liver.

An oral anabolic steroid preparation has the following characteristics:

(1) Its molecular structure must be altered to withstand acidic gastric secretions without being rendered ineffective by degradation.
(2) It must have the capability of being absorbed in the gastrointestinal tract, usually in the stomach or the proximal small intestine.
(3) It must be capable of avoiding total degradation by the liver. After absorption from the gastrointestinal tract, the drug is carried through the bloodstream to the liver where some of it is degraded to inactive metabolites by various enzymes contained within the liver. Enough of the drug must survive this initial pass through the liver to be effective.
(4) It must retain the capacity to bind to receptors within the target cells. If the target cells are skeletal muscle cells, enhancement of protein synthesis and muscle mass is promoted.
(5) It must be consumed on a regular basis. Within the body, oral preparations of anabolic steroids have short half-lives, generally on the order of a few to several hours. The half-life of a drug can be defined as the amount of time during which the blood level of it is reduced to one-half of its original blood concentration. In order to maintain an effective blood level, oral anabolic steroids are clinically prescribed to be taken one or more times daily.

Anabolic steroid users usually start first with the oral preparations. Examples of commonly used oral anabolic steroid preparations include methyltestosterone, Anavar, Winstrol, Dianabol, Halotestin, Maxibolin, and Adroyd.

In addition to the 17-alpha modification, oral anabolic steroids may have been modified at one or more molecular sites. As previously discussed, most of these additional modifications enhance the activity of the steroid to promote the anabolic over androgenic functions, thus altering the steroid's therapeutic index.

Injectable Oil-Based Preparations

Injectable oil-based anabolic steroid preparations do not have modifications at the 17-alpha position of the testosterone molecule and are not effective when taken orally. They are not able to survive the hostile, acidic environment of the stomach or avoid rapid degradation occurring with the first pass of the liver. Injectable oil-based anabolic steroids are modified at the 17-beta position of the testosterone molecule. These modifications generally involve ester side chains that make them more soluble in lipids and oils. In general, the larger the ester side chain, the longer the steroid remains in the body. Characteristics of injectable oil-based anabolic steroid preparations are as follows:

(1) They are intended for intramuscular (IM) use only. They are injected deep into large muscle groups such as the buttocks or deltoid areas. They should not be injected into arteries, veins, or joints.
(2) They tend to have much longer half-lives than oral anabolic steroids. Generally, the half-lives of these steroids are on the order of several days. This means that the intramuscular injection of these drugs can be spaced over several days without appreciably decreasing the blood level of the steroid. Once injected, the absorption rate from the injection site is a logarithmic process. Urinary excretion of their detectable metabolites continues over several weeks or even months.[1]
(3) They are dissolved in a lipoid carrier solvent that is usually a mixture of a vegetable oil and an alcohol.
(4) The anabolic steroid concentration in oil-based preparations ranges from 25 to 250 mg/cc. They are usually packaged in 1, 2, 5, or 10-milliliter vials, except for Equipoise, which is packaged in 50 or 100-milliliter vials. Equipoise is intended for use in animals and is manufactured by pharmaceutical companies for sale to veterinarians. However, Equipoise is commonly used by anabolic steroid users.
(5) They are slowly absorbed into the bloodstream from the intramuscular injection site. Considerable individual variations in blood levels may occur, especially if the injection quantity is 2 cc or greater. Users often divide 2–5 cc doses into two injections at different injection sites.

The pharmacokinetics and pharmacodynamics of the use of *single* oil-based anabolic steroids are complex. However, a discussion of some of these complexities will be provided to help understand the dynamics of self-experimentation by anabolic steroid users without medical supervision. It should also provide insight into the difficulties in attempting to study the various anabolic steroid regimens (presented in the next chapter) used by athletes.

There are several variables that can influence the actions of a particular preparation, such as the side-chain ester chemistry, injection technique, site of injection, volume of the injection, and type of oil used as the carrier solvent. Some of these variables have been recently studied with the popular oil-based injectable anabolic steroids nandrolone phenylpropionate (Durabolin) and nandrolone decanoate (Deca-Durabolin).[2]

(a) **Side-chain ester chemistry.** Variations in side-chain ester chemistry are important to the pharmacokinetics of anabolic steroids in an oil vehicle.[3] After injection, absorption rates can be estimated by the affinity of the steroid to the oil vehicle. In general, the oil vehicle is absorbed more slowly from the injection site than the anabolic steroid.[4] Short linear esters, such as propionates (three carbon esters), have much shorter duration of action and lower lipid affinities than esters with longer linear side chains and higher lipid affinities.[5] As the linear side chain is lengthened from seven to 10 carbons, the subsequent changes in the durations of action are only slightly increased.[6] Similarly, linear ester side chains containing aromatic rings have increased duration of action that increases with the number of linear carbons.

(b) **Injection technique.** Variations in action can depend on where the anabolic steroid is injected at a given injection site. This variable tends to correspond to the amount of fat at the tissue injection site.[7] In general, the greater the fat content of the injection site, the longer the duration of action. This is a factor that contributes to sex differences (as women tend to have a higher percentage of body fat than men) in absorption and anabolic dynamics, especially for buttocks and deltoid injection sites.[8]

(c) **Injection site.** The site for anabolic steroid injection plays a role in the dynamics of action due to both the differences in tissue composition and the blood flow to the site.[9] Since the deltoid muscles receive more blood flow and generally have less fat content than the gluteal muscles, anabolic steroid absorption is more rapid.[10]

(d) **Injection volume.** The bioavailability and physiological effects of anabolic steroids in an oil vehicle are affected by the volume of the injection and the concentration of the anabolic steroid. Greater effects have been shown when small (1 cc vs. 4 cc) volumes are injected. For example, 100 mg of nandrolone decanoate in a 1 cc oil vehicle volume has greater anabolic activities than 100 mg of nandrolone decanoate in a 4 cc oil vehicle volume.[11] Additional injections at a site, before all of the preceding injection volume is absorbed, may also affect bioavailability and physiologic actions.

(e) **Type of vehicle oil.** It has been shown that the type of oil vehicle used for injections affects the action of anabolic steroid ester pharmacology.[12] The lipid affinity of an anabolic steroid may be different in various oil vehicles and affect the onset and duration of action. Caution must be used when attempting to extrapolate from research with one anabolic steroid ester in different oil vehicles. For example, nandrolone decanoate in sesame seed oil may not have the same anabolic activities as nandrolone decanoate in arachis oil.[13]

Anabolic steroid users usually do not start with injectable oil-based anabolic steroids. They tend to use oral anabolic steroids for a few months before using injectable oil-based preparations. Initially, injections are usually given to a user by a workout partner, personal trainer, or friend. Most users eventually learn to self-administer these injectable anabolic steroid preparations. Improper injection site selection or technique may cause a temporary or permanent nerve palsy, infection, hematoma, or sterile abscess that may require surgical drainage.[14] There have been reports of transmission of serious bacterial, viral (hepatitis and AIDS), and fungal infections among anabolic steroid users who share needles or multi-dose vials.[15–17]

Examples of injectable oil-based anabolic steroid preparations having only 17-beta modifications are Depo-Testosterone (testosterone cypionate), Delatestryl (testosterone enanthate), and Oreton (testosterone propionate). In addition to the 17-beta modification, injectable oil-based steroids may have modifications at two or more sites of the testosterone molecule. In particular, the modification at the 19-position tends to increase the therapeutic index. These anabolic steroids, as a group, are commonly referred to as the 19-nor-testosterone derivatives. Examples of these include Deca-Durabolin (nandrolone decanoate) and Durabolin (nandrolone phenylpropionate).

Injectable Water-Based Preparations

Water-based (aqueous) anabolic steroid preparations make up only a small percentage of the steroids that are available for human use. These steroids are usually dissolved in a water and alcohol solution for intramuscular use. Characteristics of these steroids include the following:

(1) They have half-lives of several hours resembling that of the oral preparations. Clinically, they are injected two or more times weekly in patients requiring androgen therapy who are unable to take oral preparations.
(2) They are associated with much less discomfort at the injection site due to being much less viscous compared to the oil-based preparations.
(3) Their molecular structures can be identical to the oral preparations. The unmodified testosterone molecule can be effectively delivered in a water-based preparation.
(4) They are rapidly released into the bloodstream since they have little lipid affinity.
(5) They do not undergo a first pass liver degradation since they do not require absorption by the gastrointestinal tract.

(6) They are often used by competitive bodybuilders who believe that these preparations help them to "cut up" or burn extra body fat in the days or weeks prior to a competition.
(7) They are available in veterinary grades and strengths that are commonly used by athletes and bodybuilders.

Site-dependent differences in absorption rates and physiological effects have been described for a variety of drugs in aqueous solutions.[18] These are analogous to the mechanisms of anabolic steroids in oil vehicles and will not be further discussed here.

Testosterone, methandriol, and stanozolol (Winstrol-V) are examples of anabolic steroids available in water-based preparations. Winstrol-V is an example of an aqueous anabolic steroid manufactured by pharmaceutical companies for veterinary use. It comes in 10, 30, and 50 milliliter vials with a concentration of 50 mg/cc. This concentrated dose (2 mg is the concentration for oral human use) is intended for large animals, such as horses and other types of livestock.

Patch and Gel Preparations

Testosterone patch and gel preparations have recently become available for transdermal delivery of testosterone into the body. Currently, no other anabolic steroid has been approved for transdermal delivery; however, such preparations may be forthcoming.

Androderm, a testosterone patch preparation, is designed to provide a 24-hour continuous delivery when applied to the skin. Testosterone is dissolved in an alcohol-based gel that is contained in a five-layer laminate adhesive patch. For clinical use, the patches come in 2.5 mg and 5 mg strengths and are applied daily. Athletes and bodybuilders use testosterone patches with and without other anabolic steroid preparations.

Androgel, a testosterone gel preparation in a tube, is applied directly to the skin. The gel carrier solvent is designed to provide a slow release of testosterone and is applied daily. In June 2000, Androgel received FDA approval for clinical use.

Testosterone gel and patch preparations have a high potential for abuse by anabolic steroid using athletes and bodybuilders. Testosterone delivered via gel or patch is difficult to detect (urine drug testing techniques are discussed in a later chapter). Since detection is so difficult, these preparations are expected to be used by both male and female Olympic athletes in the 2000 summer games.

Aerosol Propellant Preparations

A variety of steroids, including anabolic steroids, can be administered via aerosol propellant dispensers. For instance, danazol has been shown to be effective when dissolved in various hydrofluoroalkane (HFAs) mixtures, with and without ethanol.[19] The effects from inhaled anabolic steroid preparations are rapid. Since the detection period is short these preparations may become popular for competitive athletes who will be subjected to urine drug testing.

Sublingual Preparations

Sublingual preparations (dissolved under the tongue) contain testosterone molecule modifications that enhance their absorption into the body. They do not need molecular structure modifications to survive the hostile stomach environment. These preparations act rapidly and may pose special detection problems when used by athletes.[20] Testosterone cyclodextrine is an example of this type of clinically available preparation.[21]

"Home-made" Transdermal Preparations

The transdermal use of solutions of dimethylsulfoxide (DMSO), hydrocortisone, and anabolic steroids to treat soft tissue and muscle injuries was proposed over 30 years ago.[22] DMSO is an aprotic solvent which dissolves many hormones, including anabolic steroids,[23–25] progesterogenic steroids,[26,27] estrogenic steroids, corticogenic steroids,[28] and insulin.[29] DMSO enhances permeation to deliver high drug concentrations across the skin into the tissues and systemic circulation.[30] When ethanol is combined with DMSO, drug delivery is improved.[31]

Recent studies have indicated that anabolic steroids may aid in the healing processes of sports-related muscle injuries.[32] They have been shown to aid in the healing of muscle contusion injury by speeding the recovery of the muscle's force-generating capacity.[33] This information has increased the popularity of "home-made" preparations by athletes to treat their injuries.[34] An example of this type of preparation is a combination of DMSO, ethanol, lidocaine, Winstrol-V, hydrocortisone and a drop of wintergreen oil. (Wintergreen oil helps alleviate the "raw oyster" odor and taste of DMSO.) The solution is applied to the skin over an injury and a hair dryer is used to hasten absorption. Anecdotal evidence claims pain is relieved and healing hastened. This preparation is not an approved medical use of either DMSO or anabolic steroids.

Currently, research on a variety of transdermal techniques for administration of medicines is being conducted. The use of transdermal administration of anabolic steroids to alleviate pain and hasten healing in muscle injuries in athletes and non-athletes is also an area that warrants investigation.

Androgen-Estrogen Combination Preparations

Androgen-estrogen combinations are available in oral and injectable oil-based preparations. In the oral preparation (Estratest) the androgen component is methyltestosterone and the estrogen component is a mixture of esterified estrogens consisting of 75–85 percent estrone sulfate.

Androgen-estrogen combinations have been clinically available for decades. They are used to treat a variety of conditions in women, such as osteoporosis and hormone replacement therapy (HRT) for menopausal symptoms. The athletic use of these drugs has been confined to female athletes because of the estrogen component.

Counterfeit Anabolic Steroid Preparations

The supply of black market anabolic steroids in the United States decreased after their reclassification as controlled substances under federal law in 1990. As a result, black market anabolic steroid dealers responded by importing more of the drugs from other countries. Some dealers developed a supply of fake or counterfeit anabolic steroid preparations to sell. It was during this time that several black market dealers were prosecuted for supplying both "real" and "fake" anabolic steroid preparations.

To make these "fake" or counterfeit anabolic steroids look authentic, a number of methods are employed. Some of the methods used by counterfeit dealers include:

(1) stealing, purchasing, or counterfeiting reproductions of anabolic steroid labels which were adhered to vials containing very dilute solutions of anabolic steroid preparations or just plain sesame seed oil;
(2) stealing or purchasing vial tops, vials, and rubber stoppers identical to those used by the pharmaceutical industry;
(3) replicating package inserts of the same size and quality of the original package insert that accompanies authentic anabolic steroid preparations;
(4) stealing, purchasing, or counterfeiting the pill bottles of authentic anabolic steroid preparations;
(5) stealing or purchasing tablet manufacturing equipment, dyes, and

ingredients to make sugar pills which resemble the size, shape, and color of authentic anabolic steroid tablets; and,

(6) stealing, purchasing, or counterfeiting packaging materials which resemble authentic anabolic steroid packages. Black market dealers, who are often gym owners or personal fitness trainers, tend to pick and choose whom they sell the "fake" steroids to. For instance, if a user purchases several types of preparations to use in an upcoming regimen, the dealer sells the buyer a combination of "real" and "fake" anabolic steroids. The user will probably not be able to tell that the Depo-Testosterone was "real," but the Deca-Durabolin was "cut" or "fake" when they were used together.

The degree to which counterfeit anabolic steroid preparations have infiltrated the anabolic steroid black market is difficult to assess. Non-sterile production techniques and "doctoring" of these "fake" anabolic steroid preparations could pose major health concerns. Another concern is that the "fake" anabolic steroid could be "doctored" with another, easily detected substance banned from athletic competition. This would result in a positive drug test for a drug the athlete was unaware of taking.

In 2000, the prevalence of counterfeit anabolic steroids was assessed by obtaining anabolic steroid preparations from the black market and testing them with state-of-the-art analysis equipment. The results of these analyses found that 37.5 percent of these preparations *were not anabolic steroids* and that some preparations contained other types of drugs.[35]

Based on external packaging, differentiating between authentic and fake drugs was impossible. A German study indicated that almost 40 percent of anabolic steroids purchased on the black market are "fake."[36] Counterfeit anabolic steroid preparations not only contribute to the credibility gap between athletes and physicians, they are potentially health hazards.

Over-the-Counter Anabolic Steroid Preparations

Over the past decade, the nutritional supplement industry has burgeoned. Most of the nutritional supplements do not qualify as either foods or drugs. Therefore, the FDA has little or no direct regulatory powers to ensure that these supplements are safe or even effective products.

Nutritional supplements have blurred the line between what is considered a drug and what is considered a supplement. Some currently available nutritional supplements would have previously been classified as drugs. Examples of such products used by athletes include: ephedrine, dehydroepiandosterone (DHEA), and androstenedione ("Andro"). Both DHEA and "Andro" are marketed and promoted as muscle building supplements. Both are steroids similar in molecular structure to testosterone.

The Andro Controversy

INTRODUCTION

Few sports enthusiasts will forget the 1998 baseball season that hosted the epic home run derby between Mark McGwire and Sammy Sosa. Both sluggers shattered the single-season home run records of Babe Ruth (60 homers in a 154 game season) and Roger Maris (61 homers in a 162 game season). McGwire finished the magical season with 70 homers and Sosa had 66 round-trippers. Soon after a reporter snooped into McGwire's locker and found a bottle of androstenedione, "andro." McGwire admitted that he had used the anabolic steroid. A columnist for the *Denver Post* found andro in the locker of Colorado Rockies slugger Dante Bichette. (The Baseball Writers Association of America revoked the columnist's press credentials after he admitted to "finding" the andro.) Since andro is not a banned substance in Major League Baseball, McGwire, Bichette, and others faced no sanctions. In addition to taking andro, McGwire admitted using creatine, a supplement promoted for muscle-building. Sammy Sosa also stated that he uses the supplement creatine.

The sports supplement industry is big business. An estimated 18 million people worldwide are currently taking creatine, at a cost of over $350 million. Andro sales currently around $15 million are expected to soar to over $100 million on the wings of McGwire's record.[37]

Andro is an oral anabolic-androgenic steroid drug first used in the 1970s as a nasal spray preparation by East German Olympic athletes. The Dietary Supplement Health and Education Act of 1994 exempted nutritional supplements from FDA jurisdiction. This act allows manufacturers to sell and promote drugs like andro and others directly to the public if they are labeled nutritional supplements. Thus over-the-counter sales of andro cause problematic medical, legal, and societal implications.[38] In addition to andro promotion for building muscle, andro is also being touted as an over-the-counter sexual stimulant,[39] similar to testosterone's sales promotion in the 1940s.[40]

IS ANDRO AN ANABOLIC STEROID?

Testosterone and andro are in equilibrium within various body tissues. In other words, they can be converted from one to the other as shown in Figure 4-1.

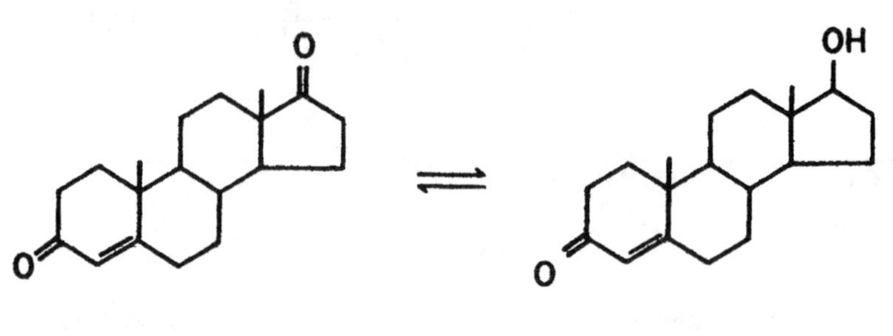

Figure 4-1. Interconversion of testosterone and "andro."

Androstenedione is an immediate precursor to testosterone production. In theory, taking andro supplements could increase the production of testosterone, either in the bloodstream or within various target cells, including skeletal muscle cells. Furthermore, if andro causes such an increase in testosterone production, then it could cause an enhancement of muscle mass and strength when combined with strength training. By definition, then, andro is an anabolic steroid and as such, should not be sold as a nutritional supplement. It should be reclassified as an anabolic steroid and regulated under Schedule III of the CSA.

According to the federal government's definition, androstenedione, andro is an anabolic steroid. The Steroid Trafficking Act of 1990 states:

> The term "anabolic steroids" means—
>
> (A) any drug that is chemically and pharmacologically related to the male hormone testosterone and that promotes or purports to promote muscle growth, including any amount of the following chemical designations and their salts, esters, and isomers ... [the naming of 27 anabolic steroids follows].
> (B) any substance which is purported, represented, or labeled as being or containing any amount of any drug described in subparagraph (A), or any substance labeled as being or containing any such drug.[41]

Andro:

(a) is a drug that is chemically and pharmacologically related to testosterone. In fact, under physiological conditions, andro and testosterone are enzymatically converted to each other.
(b) is purported to promote muscle growth.

Therefore, according to definition (A) of the Steroid Trafficking Act of 1990, androstenedione — andro — is an anabolic steroid and should be considered a controlled substance.

In March 2000, the Blue Cross and Blue Shield Healthy Competition Foundation urged the federal government to ban over-the-counter sales of andro. The foundation cited "an alarming growth in the use of anabolic steroids in recent years" and called for the FDA and DEA to stop andro sales both online and in health food stores.[42] As of this writing, the federal government has taken no action to reclassify andro from a nutritional supplement to an anabolic steroid.

Is Andro a Banned Substance in Sports?

Andro is allowed by professional baseball, but it is banned in the NFL, Olympics, the NCAA, and the Association of Tennis Professionals.[43,44] However, no sanctions have been levied on any athletes in these associations.

Does the Use of Andro Increase Testosterone Levels and Build Muscle Mass?

There have been very few studies conducted to determine whether or not andro increases testosterone levels in the blood. The results of these few studies have been mixed, confusing, and contradictory as shown in Table 4-1. Future studies should be forthcoming to evaluate andro's potential as a performance-enhancing supplement. The anecdotal evidence strongly suggests that andro is bioactive and can promote muscle growth when combined with adequate dietary protein intake and vigorous strength training. Anecdotal evidence also strongly suggests that heavy andro use promotes a side effect profile similar to that seen with other anabolic steroids. Use of andro can cause a positive test for anabolic steroid use.[45]

Table 4-1. Studies of Andro Use, Testosterone Levels, and Athletic Performance

Research Group & Date	*Subjects*	*Dose*	*Testosterone Elevation*		*Muscle Mass and Strength Gains*	*Study Design*
			Total	*Free*		
King, et al. (1999)[46]	10 men (age 19–29)	300 mg/day (8 weeks)	no	no	no	with exercise; placebo; untrained men
Wallace, et al. (1999)[47]	40 men (avg. age 48) weight trained	100 mg/day (12 weeks)	no	–	yes (NS)	with exercise; double-blind; placebo

Research Group & Date	*Subjects*	*Dose*	*Testosterone Elevation*		*Muscle Mass and Strength Gains*	*Study Design*
			Total	*Free*		
Rasmussen, et al. (2000)[48]	6 men	100 mg/day (5 days)	no	–	–	no exercise; placebo
Earnest, et al. (2000)[49]	8 men (mean age 24)	200 mg/day (1 day)	yes (S)	yes (S)	–	no exercise; double-blind; cross-over; placebo; AUC*
Leder, et al. (2000)[50]	15 men (age 20–40)	100 mg/day (7 days)	yes (NS)	–	–	no exercise; placebo; AUC*
	14 men (age 20–40)	300 mg/day (7 days)	yes (S)	–	–	
Ballentyne, et al. (2000)[51]	10 men	200 mg/day (2 days)	no	–	–	with exercise; double-blind cross-over; placebo

(S) = statistically significant
(NS) = not statistically significant
*AUC = area under the curve analysis for testosterone levels above baseline levels

SUMMARY

According to the definition of anabolic steroids, andro is an oral anabolic steroid and should be reclassified as a controlled substance. Instead it is sold over-the-counter as a nutritional supplement. For the discussions presented in this book, andro will be considered an anabolic steroid. That it is sold without a prescription does not mean it is a safe drug when taken without medical supervision. Although the pharmaceutical industry has known about andro for decades, it has never been marketed as a drug. The reasons for this remain unclear.

The DHEA Controversy

INTRODUCTION

Dehydroepiandrosterone, DHEA, is an endogenous anabolic-androgenic steroid hormone that exhibits an age-related decline in both adult men and women.[52] The serum level of DHEA reaches its peak at about 25 years of age.[53] Secreted by the adrenal glands, DHEA and its sulfate, DHEA-S, are converted first to androstenedione and then to testosterone, dihydrotestosterone, and estrogens in peripheral tissues. The age-related reduction in the formation of DHEA causes a dramatic fall in the formation of active sex steroids in peripheral target tissues. This reduction is thought to be associated with age-related conditions such as insulin resistance, osteoporosis, cardiovascular diseases, sarcopenia, cancer and other diseases.[54,55]

Dehydroepiandrosterone is sold nationally as an over-the-counter nutritional supplement. The sale of DHEA has been made possible by The Dietary Supplement Health and Education Act of 1994, allowing its manufacturers to classify it as a nutritional supplement. Shortly after the passage of this act, DHEA became available over-the-counter and sales have been brisk. Some scientists view the commercial availability of DHEA, which is outside the United States pharmaceutical-medical network, as creating a real public health problem.[56] Their view is that use of DHEA is simply hormonal manipulation without medical supervision. Others view it as a product that fuels human desire to preserve youthful vigor and delay aging.[57]

It is not hard to see why significant medical attention and media hype have been paid to the alleged benefits of DHEA.[58] Because DHEA raises testosterone levels when consumed orally, it is also promoted as able to build muscle and enhance sexual performance and desire. Indeed, some scientific studies support these notions.

Clinical Uses of DHEA

Unlike andro, DHEA is viewed as a drug with significant medical applications. Like other anabolic steroids, DHEA's potential therapeutic value extends to many areas of medicine, because of its ubiquitous presence in so many tissues and organs.[59] A number of scientific studies have shown benefits of DHEA therapy in a variety of medical conditions. Studies indicate therapeutic benefits in:

a) patients with systemic lupus erythematosus, SLE,[60]
b) patients with Addison's disease,[61]
c) patients with senile dementia and Alzheimer's disease,[62–65]
d) patients with acquired immune deficiency syndrome, AIDS,[66,67]
e) patients with postmenopausal symptoms,[68–72]
f) patients with spinal cord injury, SCI,[73]
g) patients with congestive heart failure, CHF,[74]
h) patients with osteoporosis,[75–77]
i) patients with sarcopenia,[78–80]
j) patients with erectile dysfunction, ED,[81,82]
k) patients with depressed immune systems,[83] and
l) patients with low libido.[84–86]

The results of early studies indicate that DHEA, like anabolic steroids, exhibits influential effects on many organs and tissues. Results are seen with both glandular secretion of DHEA or oral consumption of DHEA. DHEA has various actions in the body:

(1) It is a neurosteroid. Scientific studies have shown that DHEA can act as a neurotransmitter. It is enzymatically converted to testosterone and estrogens within brain cells in several regions of the brain. As a neurotransmitter, DHEA affects a variety of receptors that influence sense of well-being, libido, aggression, and personality.
(2) It is an antioxidant. Scientific studies have shown that DHEA has a neuroprotective effect as an antioxidant in the brain. By inhibiting oxidation, DHEA has anti-aging effects on the brain. It may be helpful in reducing the risk for Alzheimer's disease and senile dementia. When DHEA is given as a therapeutic agent, beneficial effects on the cognitive mechanisms in older people have been demonstrated. When DHEA levels remain at "youthful" levels, older people have better mental capacities.
(3) It is an osteoblast stimulator. DHEA, through its conversion to testosterone, stimulates bone-forming cells to combine dietary calcium with bone proteins to regenerate bone structure and strength. It has been shown to have therapeutic benefits for people with osteoporosis.
(4) It is an osteoclast inhibitor. DHEA, through its conversion to estrogens, inhibits bone-dissolving cells so that bone homeostasis remains in check.
(5) It is an anabolic steroid precursor. DHEA can be enzymatically converted to testosterone, raising serum testosterone levels, especially in postmenopausal women.
(6) It is an anabolic steroid. Besides elevating testosterone levels, DHEA can elevate the levels of other anabolic molecules, including androstenedione, growth hormone, and insulin-like growth factor-1. DHEA has been shown to play a beneficial role in sarcopenia and other muscle-wasting conditions.
(7) It is an immunosteroid. DHEA has been shown to have a positive influence on the immune system in both healthy older people and in people with diseases where the immune system is depressed, including AIDS, lupus, and rheumatoid arthritis.
(8) It is a vasodilator. DHEA has been shown to have vasoactive effects on the erectile tissues of sex organs to improve erectile dysfunction.
(9) It is an insulin agonist. DHEA has been shown to lower insulin resistance to promote improved glucose balance.
(10) It is a cardiosteroid. DHEA plays a role in maintaining the integrity and contractility of cardiac muscle.

Does DHEA Increase Testosterone Levels and Increase Muscle Mass and Strength?

Under normal physiologic conditions, DHEA is a precursor for testosterone production. Study results indicate that DHEA supplementation can elevate testosterone levels in people, especially women, with reduced serum levels of testosterone. The results of the few studies that have examined muscle mass and strength changes with DHEA supplementation indicate that it may enhance muscle mass and strength. Most of these studies *do not* address whether or not DHEA supplementation can enhance the anabolic mechanisms in strength-trained athletes. However, when testosterone levels and other anabolic markers are studied, results indicate DHEA has the potential to enhance the anabolic mechanisms within the body. The studies looking at DHEA's influence on testosterone levels, muscle mass, muscular strength, and other anabolic markers are shown in Table 4-2. From these few studies, it appears that DHEA has the potential to enhance anabolic mechanisms to increase muscle mass and strength. However, to fully address this issue, properly designed, long-term studies are necessary.

To answer the question of whether or not DHEA enhances anabolic mechanisms in strength-trained athletes, the study design should utilize experienced weight-trained subjects with adequate dietary protein intake. Several doses of DHEA should be used, from replacement doses to a few times the replacement dose. The study should also evaluate endocrine responses, body composition changes, strength, and psychological parameters. Until these studies are conducted, it is assumed that DHEA is an anabolic steroid with all of the effects and potential side effects of other anabolic steroids.

Summary and Discussion

According to the definition of anabolic steroids as legislated by the United States Government in the Steroid Trafficking Act of 1990, DHEA is an anabolic steroid. DHEA should be classified as a controlled substance under federal law. The use of DHEA is hormonal manipulation. It is an anabolic steroid that is also a precursor for other anabolic steroids via enzymatic conversion within the body's tissues and organs. It is not clear how andro, DHEA, and other nortestosterone "nutritional supplements" became "non-drugs."

The use of DHEA appears to be safe when it is used short-term and at recommended doses. DHEA alters the endocrine and other body systems, perhaps to their betterment, especially in aged users. But that is not the real issue. The real issue deals with the hormonal manipulation without

Table 4-2. Studies of DHEA Use and Testosterone Levels, Muscle Mass, Strength, and Other Anabolic Markers

Research Group (year)	*Subjects*	*Dose*	*Increased Testosterone*		*Increased Muscle Mass*	*Increased Strength*	*Other Increased Anabolic Markers*	*Study Design*
			Total	*Free*				
Morales, et al. (1994)	13 men (aged 40–70)	50 mg/day (6 months)	no	-	-	-	IGF-1, A	no exercise; placebo; cross-over
	17 women (aged 40–70)	50 mg/day (6 months)	yes	-	-	- DHT	IGF-1, A,	
Wolf, et al. (1997)	40 men & women (mean age 69)	50 mg/day (2 weeks)	yes	-	-	-	A	no exercise; placebo; cross-over; double-blind
Morales, et al. (1998)	9 men (aged 50–65)	100 mg/day (6 months)	no	-	yes	yes	IGF-1	no exercise; placebo; cross-over; double-blind
	10 women (aged 50–65)	100 mg/day (6 months)	yes	-	no	no	IGF-1, A	
Brown, et al. (1999)	9 men; untrained (mean age 23)	150 mg/day (8 weeks)	no	-	yes (NS)	yes (NS)	A	strength training protocol; placebo
Wallace, et al. (1999)	13 men; trained (mean age 48)	50 mg/day (12 weeks)	no	-	yes (NS)	yes (NS)	-	strength training protocol; double-blind; placebo
Barnhart, et al. (1999)	60 perimenopausal women	50 mg/day (3 months)	yes	-	-	-	-	no exercise; placebo; double-blind protocol
Stomati, et al. (1999)	8 postmenopausal women	50 mg/day (3 months)	yes	-	-	-	GH	no exercise; placebo; double-blind protocol
Baulieu, et al. (2000)	280 men & women (age 60–79)	50 mg/day (1 year)	yes	-	-	-	-	no exercise; no control group

NS = not statistically significant, A = androstenedione, GH = growth hormone, IGF-1 = insulin-like growth factor-1, - = not studied, and DHT = dihdrotestosterone.

medical supervision. This is a Pandora's Box which must be addressed. The question becomes: Is the general public informed enough to manipulate its own endocrine systems with positive, worthwhile results? The anabolic steroid epidemic in the past suggests this is not the case.

Anabolic Steroid Residuals in Meat Products

Introduction

Meat consumed by Americans contains anabolic steroids. The United States government allows anabolic steroids to be added to feed of the nation's livestock. Cows, pigs, chickens, and sheep are all fed diets with anabolic steroid additives. Examples of these animal feed products include Ralgro, Synovex-S, and Revalor.[87] The information on feed packages indicates that it contains an anabolic agent that stimulates growth. These anabolic steroid additives allow the animals to grow faster, larger, leaner, and more muscular. These steroid-fed animals become the meat products consumed by Americans. The animal feed products are eaten by some bodybuilders and strength athletes because they are able to obtain anabolic steroids exempt from controlled substance status![88] This illustrates the "winning-at-all-cost" mentality that is often seen in many anabolic steroid users.[89,90]

For over 30 years, anabolic steroid implants have been used extensively in beef production.[91] Anabolic steroids have also been added to chicken feed for over 30 years.[92] Today, implants have become almost "designer" products with various doses and combinations of estrogenic and androgenic steroids.[93–95] Anabolic steroid implants are cost-effective for beef production. Recent studies have shown that increasing potency in succession allows for the greatest animal lifetime weight gain of up to 150 pounds. The implants accomplish an additional 23 percent to feed efficiency[96] and an additional increase in daily body weight gains of 3–5 percent.[97] Using three anabolic steroids (one in the feed, and two administered by implants) with an estrogenic steroid implant in beef cows has been shown to produce the greatest ultimate lean body mass.[98] Steaks from anabolic steroid-implanted cows have been shown to be statistically superior in flavor intensity, improved marbling, myofibrillar tenderness, overall tenderness, and overall higher quality grade.[99]

In 1999, an evaluation of the lipid composition of beef steer steaks showed a statistically significant increase in total cholesterol with beef produced with anabolic implants compared to the steaks produced without implants.[100] The combined atherogenic effects due to consuming meat with an increased total cholesterol, may have had a dramatic impact on the health of Americans over the past few decades. The health consequences from eating meat with both anabolic steroid residue and higher cholesterol levels should be revisited by both scientific and legislative communities.

The task of enforcing the quantity limits of anabolic steroids fed or administered to livestock falls to the United States Department of Agriculture. Federal health officials know that health problems can occur when people eat meat with high levels of residual anabolic steroids. However, enforcing anabolic steroid quantities in livestock feed is both difficult and expensive.

The Puerto Rican Catastrophe

In the early 1980s, an epidemic of premature puberty occurred in children living in Puerto Rico and the Caribbean islands. A documentary on the program *60 Minutes* reported that over 2,000 young girls were going through puberty before their 8th birthdays.[101] A large number of these girls showed signs of precocious puberty (premature thelarche) as young as two years of age! Growth of pubic hair, onset of menstruation, breast enlargement, and advanced bone development were noted. The island endocrinologist evaluating these girls suspected that this early puberty was the result of anabolic steroids. She traced the source to meat from livestock and milk from dairy cows given feed with anabolic steroids. She sent a feed sample to be evaluated by an independent laboratory. Their results indicated that steroid levels in the meat and milk were well above the allowed limits. The livestock feed was manufactured in America. Shortly after she made her findings public, her car was fire-bombed.[102]

When health officials from the United States were sent to test the meat and milk, they found no significant steroid levels in either the meat or milk. Other laboratory experts became involved to solve this mystery. It turned out that high steroid levels were found in the lipid extractions of the meat and milk, just as the physician suspected. The U.S. officials found little or no steroids because they had tested only the aqueous extracts. These officials eventually admitted that they should have tested the lipid extractions as outlined by their own protocols.

The Italian Epidemics

In November 1977, an outbreak of breast enlargement was reported in girls and boys attending a district school in Milan. Nearly 30 percent of boys (aged 3–14 years) and 22 percent of girls (aged 3–5 years) had pronounced breast development.[103] Steroid contamination of the meat and poultry was suspected and shown. However, similar problems persisted in Italy for over a decade.

In the mid–1980s Italian physicians reported that an epidemic of gynecomastia (abnormal breast development in males) and premature thelarche was occurring in two northern Italian cities. Breast enlargement was observed in nursery school children (37 percent of girls and 30 percent of boys below two years of age). Gynecomastia occurs when certain anabolic steroids are enzymatically converted to estrogens or when estrogen levels are high. Again, high content of steroid additives in livestock feed was suspected. The Italian government continues to struggle with this issue. Commercial kits to test for anabolic steroids in meat products have recently been used by Italian scientists. But, overzealous use of steroids in the livestock and poultry industries continues.[104]

European Bans on Anabolic Steroids for the Growth-Enhancement of Livestock

Reaction from these incidents illustrating the health risks involved with anabolic steroid use in livestock and poultry products spread throughout Europe. Officials from various countries began to address this issue, with meat wars becoming a result of the controversy. In addition to the health risks, athletes began testing positive for anabolic steroids after eating anabolic steroid tainted meat. The doping control in sports that had been meticulously devised was being threatened. As a result, an international industry was formed to devise better tests for anabolic steroid detection in meat, poultry, and milk products.

In the late 1980s, politics played a large part in this controversy. As an early consequence, countries banned meat products from other countries fearing meat contaminated with anabolic steroids. In 1987, despite demonstrated, dramatic, and severe epidemics of health risks, the World Health Organization (WHO) concluded that use of anabolic steroids in animal production poses no consumer health risks.[105] But in Europe, unscrupulous farmers, ranchers, and veterinary pharmaceutical manufacturers continued to experiment illegally with high doses of anabolic steroids in their animals for years.[106] Then in 1988, on the heels of the Puerto Rican and Italian fiascoes, the European Union banned the use of anabolic steroids as growth-promoting agents[107] by Directives 96/22/EC and 96/23/EC.[108] The United States government, however, refused to ban anabolic steroids as a growth-stimulator in the meat production industry. Officials from the Department of Agriculture stated that if the United States chose to ban these anabolic agents, then an estimated reduction of 2.1 billion pounds of beef would occur. Estimated financial losses at the farm and feedlot levels would exceed $3 billion annually.[109]

Enforcement of the European Ban

Enforcement of the European ban has been plagued by inaccurate detection methods. As a result, the illegal use of anabolic steroids in the European meat and milk industries escalated. In 1998, a major symposium was held on surveillance techniques that could help enforce the European ban on the use of anabolic steroids in livestock, poultry, and dairy industries. Scientists presenting research came from several countries, including the Netherlands,[110–114] Belgium,[115–122] France,[123–125] United Kingdom,[126–129] Ireland,[130] Spain,[131] Northern Ireland,[132–134] and Italy.[135] The consensus from the meeting indicated that major improvements in a variety of detection techniques have been made, however, the search for improved surveillance techniques is ongoing.[136,137] Meanwhile, the growth of the black market supplying multiple high-dose anabolic steroid cocktails[138,139] has proven to be difficult to control.[140] Publications by European consumer magazines continue to fuel health concern issues, especially in underdeveloped countries lacking the resources to investigate or control the problems.[141]

Currently in the United States, anabolic steroid and growth hormone use for growth-stimulation in livestock is legal. Officials from other countries have become aware that America's meat industry has become dependent on anabolic steroids to increase the size and muscularity of livestock. Many countries have recently placed bans on meat products from the United States.

Positive Drug Tests for Athletes Consuming Anabolic Steroid Treated Animals

Athletes consuming meat from anabolic steroid-fed livestock may have an additional problem unrelated to health concerns. A number of studies have shown that consuming meat from anabolic steroid-treated animals can cause positive test results for anabolic steroid use in competitive athletes.[142–145] These studies have shown that the detectable levels of anabolic steroids can last for about 24 hours after the consumption of the tainted meat. This brings the testing for anabolic steroid use by athletes under a cloud of uncertainty. A detailed discussion of anabolic steroid testing will be presented in a later chapter in this book.

Athletic Animals and Anabolic Steroid "Therapy"

Anabolic steroid "therapy" in animals has several illicit uses. Some of these include:

(1) animal shows. County fairs have become experimental bodybuilding contests for animals on anabolic steroids. The largest and most muscular animals receive blue ribbons. Breeders and owners take significant pride in winning these local, regional and national contests.
(2) horse racing. Anabolic steroids have been employed extensively in horse racing over the past 30 years. Steroids are used to increase muscle mass and strength. Anabolic steroids are also used in the raising of yearlings and in the training and racing of horses for improving performance.[146–150] Risks can be encountered if large doses are used and the horse can become difficult to manage due to increased aggressiveness. Reproductive efficiency may be temporarily impaired, but is usually reversible following cessation of treatment.[151] Surveys of doping studies have revealed positive tests for as much as 20 percent of the racehorses in some countries.[152] Urine drug testing has played a role in detection of anabolic steroids in racing horses. Diuretics and other masking drugs and techniques have been shown to be popular methods of tricking drug testing efforts.[153] International efforts to refine the detection techniques, similar to those employed in the Olympics, continues.[154–156]
(3) dog racing. Anabolic steroids have been used for many years in dogs that compete at racetracks. Forensic drug testing for anabolic steroids in racing dogs is performed at some tracks because of the potential use and abuse of these drugs.[157]
(4) animal fighting. Anabolic steroids have been used for many years in fighting dogs and cocks. These drugs enhance muscle mass, strength, and aggressive behavior. Often these animals are allowed to fight until one of the animals dies. Overly aggressive behavior plays a role in winning animals. Anabolic steroids have been shown to induce overly aggressive and fighting behavior in a variety of animals.[158–164]

Summary: Anabolic Steroids Are Anabolic Steroids

The information in this chapter has shown the many ways that anabolic steroid preparations can be introduced into the human body. But, no matter how anabolic steroids get into the body, once they are there, they act like anabolic steroids. Physiologically, anabolic steroids are ubiquitous and influence, directly or indirectly, many organs and tissues.

Anabolic steroids are simple molecules that carry out very complex, intertwined actions within the body. There are several endogenous anabolic steroids which can be enzymatically converted to one another as the body needs them. For example, in the brain, anabolic steroids are neurosteroids that can act as direct or indirect neurotransmitters and protect the brain from oxidation. In bone, anabolic steroids act as direct osteoblast stimulators that influence the formation of new and dense bone. In immune cells, anabolic steroids are immunosteroids that can influence the manner in which the immune system wards off infection or disease. In the skin, anabolic steroids are dermatosteroids that can influence hair growth, skin characteristics, tanning ability, and skin blemishes. In the heart, anabolic steroids are cardiosteroids that can influence the strength and quality of cardiac muscle. Along these same lines, anabolic steroids influence muscle mass and strength, voice tone, libido, sense of well-being, insulin resistance, aggression, personality, healing from injury, nutrient utilization, aspects of puberty and aging, and on and on. Anabolic steroids also can directly influence the production of other anabolic and growth factors. In short, anabolic steroids act as powerful hormones within the body and are powerful drugs that are used for medical and non-medical applications.

The use of anabolic steroids is hormonal manipulation and can have far-reaching effects and consequences. Anabolic steroids have dramatic effects on growth and development as well as influences on the brain. Their use can produce beneficial results, while abuse can result in adverse effects. Most anabolic steroids are available only with a prescription and are regulated under the Controlled Substance Act. In the United States, anabolic steroids, like DHEA and andro, are available as over-the-counter "nutritional supplements." The discussion regarding anabolic steroid tainted meat products should underscore the importance of reclassifying *all* anabolic steroid preparations as controlled substances under federal law. After all, an anabolic steroid is an anabolic steroid.

5
Anabolic Steroid Regimes Used by Athletes

Introduction: Locker Room Hearsay with a Smattering of Science

Most athletes who use anabolic steroids do so based on information obtained in locker rooms, underground "how to" anabolic steroid books, Internet sites, or by trial and error. Studies have shown that most, if not all, anabolic steroid users lack accurate information about the drugs they are using. This lack of knowledge is not surprising since, without a prescription, possession of anabolic steroids is illegal in the United States.

For decades, athletes and bodybuilders have utilized various methods and regimes in their anabolic steroid usage. All of these have contributed to the body of knowledge on which anabolic steroid users rely. Fellow users talk shop during workouts or when they socialize. They compare notes on which steroids to take, where to get them, how much to take, how long to take them, and so forth. Information obtained from the most muscular users and dealers is trusted over others, because this is the look other users want to achieve.

In previous chapters, we saw examples of the scientific complexities involved with the use of a single anabolic steroid preparation. One can imagine how complex it becomes when many different anabolic steroids are used, and often they are combined with other drugs. There are simply too many variables and not enough scientific knowledge available to adequately describe such use. This, however, does not stop the "knowledge" about regimes that is shared by anabolic steroid users.

In this chapter, many of the common anabolic steroid regimes used by athletes will be presented and discussed, including stacking, alternating, pyramiding, stacking the pyramid, and cycling. Where appropriate, these regimens will be evaluated utilizing the most current scientific information available about such practices.

None of the practices discussed in this chapter are meant as an endorsement. The information is provided solely to illustrate the informational gaps that exist between anabolic steroid users and the scientific community.

The First Cycle

The Anabolic Steroid User's Regime

Most first-time anabolic steroid users begin with a single oral preparation. Based on information obtained from other more experienced users, they take anabolic steroid pills in moderate doses (2–5 times greater than a clinically recommended dose) for 6–8 weeks. Then the pills are discontinued for an equal amount of time in order to give their bodies a rest. Significant gains in muscle mass and strength are seen in users who have previously weight trained. When they compare this increase obtained with the use of anabolic steroids to the increase they experienced after a period of strength training, the results are dramatic. First-time anabolic steroid users usually experience a significant increase in muscle mass and strength and report psychological changes such as improved body image and increased self-esteem. At the very least, they conclude that anabolic steroids are harmless supplements.

During the period of anabolic steroid withdrawal, first-time users experience some loss of muscle mass and strength gains even though their workouts continue. Workout intensity and amount of weight lifted decreases. Minor injuries heal more slowly. Many experience some level of depression. They become impatient for the next cycle, and often cut short their rest periods.

The Science Behind the Regime

Studies have shown that low to moderate supratherapeutic (larger than clinically prescribed) doses of anabolic steroids can significantly enhance muscle mass and strength in previously trained, otherwise healthy, athletes over and above the effects of weight training alone.[1–11] The duration of anabolic steroid use in these studies varied from 4–24 weeks. Thus, scientific evidence supports significant muscle mass and strength gains with anabolic steroids during the first cycle. There is little scientific evidence to validate the user's practice of a rest phase for either safety or effectiveness of the next anabolic steroid cycle.

A recent study showed that after three months' cessation, much of the muscle mass and strength gains attained with anabolic steroid use remained. This study also reported that some of the biochemical abnormalities, including blood pressure, lipoprotein profiles, and liver enzymes, seen while on anabolic steroids return to normal range upon cessation.[12]

The Second Cycle

The Anabolic Steroid User's Regime

A second cycle is started because users are convinced that anabolic steroids have delivered the desired effects and will deliver desired effects again. They believe the same anabolic steroid taken at the same dose will again provide the same muscle mass increases.

Heavier anabolic steroid use begins when the second cycle gains are not as dramatic as the first cycle gains. In an effort to regain the dramatic increases experienced in the first cycle, they turn to experienced users who suggest more is better, longer is better, and other methods of administration are better. They begin to read black market anabolic steroid literature in search of the answer. Many users keep diaries, plotting their gains in an attempt to determine which, how and what works best for them.

The Science Behind the Regime

Anabolic steroid use causes an increase in levels and or activity of liver and other tissue enzymes that degrade and convert the anabolic steroid into non-effective molecules. The enzymes tend to return to their normal level and activities when anabolic steroid use is discontinued. There is little or no scientific evidence to indicate that reintroducing a previously taken anabolic steroid, after a lengthy rest period, will cause an even greater induction of these enzymes to higher activity levels. It may occur, but it remains unproven.

Recent scientific studies have shown that anabolic steroid use causes a statistically significant increase in skeletal muscle cell numbers, muscle cell nuclei, and androgen receptors within these nuclei.[13,14] A specific number of anabolic steroid molecules must bind to all of these receptors to optimize the stimulation of the genetic machinery. When the same anabolic steroid at the same dose is reintroduced, the steroid molecules are binding to more androgen receptors than they did previously. Thus, to continue significant increases in muscle mass and strength, a greater dose of the anabolic steroid may be required to activate the genetic machinery and manufacture new nuclei and androgen receptors to attain a higher level of protein synthesis again. Muscle mass has been shown to be tightly controlled by the quantity of the genetic machinery within skeletal muscle.[15] It is likely that this mechanism is the reason that increases in the dose of anabolic steroids are required to extend muscle mass gains. However, this theory needs further investigation. Recent developments in scientific tools and modalities have made this a viable area for research and it is hoped that accurate information will be forthcoming.

The Third through Fifth Cycles

The Anabolic Steroid User's Regime

By the third cycle, anabolic steroid users expand their use with regimes varying considerably. Availability of anabolic steroids, peer pressure, and inaccurate information accelerate their expanded use. Some users increase the dose of the same oral anabolic steroid previously taken. They may also take the higher dose schedule for a longer period of time. Other users begin a cycle with moderate doses, increase the weekly dose for several weeks, and then reduce the weekly dose for several weeks. This practice is called *pyramiding*. Athletes believe that pyramiding helps alleviate withdrawal symptoms. The muscle mass and strength gains associated with dose and duration increases are usually considerable. Rest periods usually become shorter.

Some users switch oral anabolic steroids, using steroid X for one cycle, steroid Y for the next cycle, back to steroid X again, and so on. This regimen is called *alternating cycles*. Alternating cycles are believed to help alleviate tolerance to a particular anabolic steroid. The muscle mass and strength gains are usually modest with this practice. Rest periods become shorter.

Other users take two or more oral anabolic steroids during a cycle. This practice is called *stacking*. Combining stacking and pyramiding is the practice called *stacking the pyramid*. Stacking the pyramid is believed to increase the effects of both anabolic steroids.

It is during the third cycle that some anabolic steroid users begin to experiment with injectable preparations. "You can't grow if you are afraid of the needle" is heard through locker rooms. Initially, another person administers the injectable preparation, but soon the user becomes a self-injector.

Another practice is that of stacking oral and injectable anabolic steroids. This practice is believed to increase the total anabolic steroid concentrations and their effects on the body while reducing the toxic effects on the liver.

During the third cycle and beyond, users become more aware of the adverse side effects associated with anabolic steroid use. In an attempt to deal with adverse side effects, users often begin taking prescription drugs, with or without medical supervision, in an attempt to counter these effects.[16] They can usually obtain these prescription drugs through black market steroid dealers.

The Science Behind the Regime

Alternating anabolic steroids may have some basis in science. If anabolic steroids, which are alternated, have different molecular structures, then they may be degraded by different enzymatic mechanisms within the target tissues. For instance, the oral anabolic steroid, 7-alpha-methyl-19-nortestosterone (MENT), has a molecular alteration that creates a steric hindrance and it is not reduced by the enzyme 5-alpha reductase.[17–20] Another oral anabolic steroid, stanozolol (Winstrol), has a molecular alteration that creates a steric hindrance that makes it non-aromatizable via enzymes to estrogens.[21] Alternating these types of oral anabolic steroid preparations in cycles may further potentiate anabolic actions by changing the body's enzymatic conversion of them. However, there is no direct scientific evidence to support this practice.

Stacking multiple anabolic steroids together may have additive or synergistic influences on the total anabolic effects. However, there are no medical studies that have been conducted on humans to investigate these effects. The available scientific evidence to support stacking is derived from research conducted on livestock animals.[22–26] The reader is reminded that these anabolic steroid regimes have little or no scientific support and more research is needed before definitive conclusions can be reached.

Beyond the Fifth Cycle

During this period, which may go on for years or decades, users continue many of the practices used in their previous cycles. Anabolic steroid doses escalate, more types are stacked, and self-injections of multiple anabolic steroids become common practices. Experimentation with other anabolic agents is the rule. Diaries are often abandoned as users realize that there so many variables to their regimens that keeping workout records has become a worthless endeavor. Cycles become long periods of anabolic steroid use with little or no rest periods. In some users, rest periods become short periods of lower anabolic steroid use.

Abrupt withdrawal from heavy anabolic steroid use can have devastating consequences. Continued heavy anabolic steroid use can also have devastating consequences. Drugs believed to enhance the effects of anabolic steroids, and drugs used to treat the adverse effects from anabolic steroid use become common. Some of heavy users may be on a dozen or more various drugs at the same time.

Many heavy anabolic steroid users become anabolic steroid dealers in order to support their own habits. Heavy users experience physiological and psychological consequences. Many begin to realize their experimentation has become a biochemical and psychological nightmare with no end in sight.

Summary: The Blind Leading the Blind

Studies indicate that anabolic steroid users know more about the effects of the drugs than non-users, but limited knowledge is not enough. First-time anabolic steroid users enter into a type of drug use that seems safe enough to them, especially if they follow the patterns of use recommended by other users. They deny that any side effects will happen to *them*. They underestimate the addiction potential and withdrawal behaviors. They know little or nothing about the altered neurochemical effects. Over half of the first-time users will go into the fifth cycle and beyond with no real plans of quitting.

Many of the components of anabolic steroid use have been discussed. The applicable and available research that supports or refutes these components has also been presented. But, after all is said and done, the use of anabolic steroids is still not much more than a "blind leading the blind" proposition.

Without a prescription and medical supervision anabolic steroid use is both illegal and dangerous. The heavy anabolic steroid usage by over a million users during the 1980s and 1990s has had a plethora of both pesky, serious, and lethal medical health risks and consequences. Later chapters in this book will detail both the mental and physical health risks associated with the non-medical use of anabolic steroids.

The prescription use of anabolic steroids in clinical doses and medical supervision is a safe and effective method for treating a number of diseases and debilitating conditions. Medical research has attained renewed enthusiasm for these purposes. A detailed chapter on the medical applications of anabolic steroid use appears later in this book.

6

How Anabolic Steroids Enhance Athletic Performance

Introduction: Are Modern-Day Athletes Born or Made?

Over the years we have all heard remarks that claim that the best athletes are the ones with the best pharmacists. Perhaps so, but is there absolute proof that anabolic steroids or other drugs enhance athletic performance? Is an athlete born or made?[1] Or are potentially good athletes born and then hormonally manipulated to become elite athletes?[2]

It has been proven that anabolic steroid use, combined with weight training and adequate dietary protein intake, can build muscle mass and strength over and above weight training alone. It seems obvious that increased muscle mass and strength could enhance performance in many sports. Perhaps it is a moot point that is not so obvious to some purists. A few of the statements addressing this issue, published in the 1990s, should illustrate this point.

"Although there is no definite proof of a performance enhancing effect of anabolic steroids, evidence suggests that steroids may increase muscular strength in some subgroups of athletes."[3]

"Many athletes believe that they must take steroids in order to compete, even though scientists are divided on the question of whether steroids increase strength."[4]

"The widespread use of anabolic steroids in male athletes to increase their physical performances poses the question of whether these compounds are active in the presence of normal circulating levels of testosterone.... It is still not clear whether anabolic steroids are able to improve athletic performance."[5]

"Warning: Anabolic steroids have not been shown to enhance athletic ability."[6]

There must be a continued disconnection in the logic of these authors' thinking. Doesn't it seem obvious that increased muscle mass and strength would enhance the athletic performance of Olympic weight lifters, shot putters, and wrestlers? What about football players and baseball players? Enough said.

Let us design a prospective study to prove that anabolic steroids enhance athletic performance. Our design would include selecting identical male twins (we can't use cloned humans) who play baseball in high school. We would put them on identical weight training programs for one year and evaluate them with comprehensive medical and athletic measurements. Then we would administer anabolic steroids to one and placebo to another over the next few years. We would again evaluate them with the same comprehensive measurements. Assuming that both young men would go on and play professional baseball, we could evaluate their athletic performances. What if one player hit 50 homers every year and had 100+ RBIs while the other only hit 15 round-trippers with 50 RBIs? Would that be proof of enhanced athletic performance? Even so, the doubters would claim that anabolic steroids only enhance performance in baseball, wouldn't they?

In this chapter, the mechanisms of action of anabolic steroids that could be translated to improved athletic performance will be presented. Besides increased muscle mass and strength, anabolic steroids have been shown to alter a variety of ingredients, both physiologic and psychological, that involve athletic performance.

Overview of Potential Performance-Enhancing Mechanisms

In 1984, the first comprehensive listing of the potential performance-enhancing effects of anabolic steroids was published.[7] These potential effects were based on human and animal research, clinical observations, and theory. These mechanisms are listed in Table 6-1. Over the past 15 years, these potential mechanisms have been further studied and understood. Each of these mechanisms will be presented, with the available science, to illustrate how it contributes to the performance-enhancing effects of anabolic steroids.

Table 6-1. Mechanisms of Anabolic Steroids That Enhance Athletic Performance

1. Stimulates skeletal muscle machinery to increase protein synthesis to increase muscle mass and strength over and above weight training alone
2. Increases blood volume and hemoglobin concentration
3. Increases bone mineral density and bone strength
4. Hastens rehabilitation from muscle, tendon, and "overuse" injuries
5. Increases pain tolerance
6. Induces a "psychological high," mental intensity, and aggressiveness
7. Decreases body fat
8. Reduces reflex time
9. Other major anabolic effects

Enhanced Muscle Mass and Strength

Anabolic steroids have been proven to enhance muscle mass and strength when combined with strength training and proper diet over and above training alone. The scientific studies on weight-trained athletes and a detailed discussion of the cellular mechanisms have been presented in previous chapters and will not be further commented on in this section.

Enhanced Blood Volume and Hemoglobin Concentration

Numerous studies have shown that anabolic steroids increase total blood volume and hemoglobin concentrations.[8] A recent study has shown that anabolic steroids can significantly increase hemoglobin and hematocrit over and above the effects of physiologic levels of testosterone.[9] Anabolic steroids also increase the vascular supply concomitant with the increase in muscle mass over and above the effects of weight training alone,[10] thereby expanding both the vascular bed and total blood volume. Increased blood volume and hemoglobin concentrations have been shown to enhance athletic performance, especially in endurance competitions.

Enhanced Bone Mineral Density and Bone Strength

Anabolic steroids increase bone mineral density (BMD) and bone strength, especially when combined with weight training. They directly bind to osteoblast receptors and stimulate the genetic machinery in bone tissues.

As a result, increased calcium and protein bone matrix are formed. However, there are no studies available that have been conducted with BMD increases with healthy people using anabolic steroids combined with weight training. Strong and dense bones are important aspects for contact sports. A detailed discussion of osteoblast stimulation by anabolic steroids is contained in Chapter 13 of this book.

Hastened Healing of Muscular Injuries

Recent studies have indicated that anabolic steroids may aid the healing processes of sports-related injuries.[11] Anabolic steroids may have an ethical clinical application in helping heal muscle injuries.[12] Athletes have known for years that anabolic steroids assist healing of injuries, and further research is definitely needed in this important area of rehabilitation.[13]

In sports medicine circles there has been a prolonged debate about whether or not anabolic steroid use predisposes an athlete for tendon rupture. Tendon rupture has been linked with anabolic steroid abuse on the basis of a small number of published case reports. Recently, ultrastructural evidence has shown that anabolic steroid abuse *does not* induce collagen or tendon changes that might predispose to tendon rupture in humans.[14] Another recent report has shown that anabolic steroid treatment enhances the capacity to regenerate muscle tissues in animals.[15] Further research is indicated with anabolic steroid therapy for skeletal muscle and soft tissue injuries, with or without physical therapy. Results of these studies could revolutionize the treatment and management of these injuries.

Increased Aggressiveness, Euphoria, Mental Intensity, and Pain Tolerance

Anabolic steroids have a direct effect on the brain. They act as neurosteroids that can be both direct and indirect neurotransmitters, thereby altering the brain's neurochemistry.

Numerous studies have shown that anabolic steroid use is associated with increased aggressiveness, euphoria, and mental intensity. A detailed presentation of the effects and consequences of anabolic steroids' influences on the brain's neurochemistry is contained in Chapter 8 of this book.

The ability of anabolic steroids to increase pain tolerance is likely via the effects on the opioid receptors in the brain.[16,17] It has been postulated that anabolic steroid abuse may also be a gateway drug to opioid dependence due to the effects on the opioid receptors in the brain.[18] It has also been shown that withdrawal from anabolic steroids has many opioid-like features, including reduced pain tolerance.[19] A recent animal study has shown that various neurosteroids have analgesic effects via central nervous system activities.[20]

High pain tolerance and mental aggressiveness are important factors that can enhance athletic performance in a variety of sports. They are also important parameters in vigorous athletic training.

Decreased Body Fat

Numerous studies have shown that anabolic steroid use is associated with decreased body fat percentage. Recent studies show significant reductions in body fat when anabolic steroids are used in conjunction with weight training. These anabolic steroid-induced reductions in body fat were over and above the effects of weight training alone in young athletes[21] and athletic men over age 65 years.[22] Anabolic steroids can also increase the loss of body fat over and above dieting alone.[23]

Low body fat is an important factor in athletic performance. Most athletes have lower body fat percentages than non-athletes.

Reduced Reflex Time

Over 50 years ago, anabolic steroid therapy was shown to reduce the central nervous system reflex time in normal older men.[24] Since that time, very little formal research has been conducted to follow up on this finding. However, athletes have known for years that anabolic steroid use makes them quicker in their reflex response and neuromuscular reactions to athletic movements. Athletes have also felt that anabolic steroid use contributed to the vague area of "muscle memory."

It has been shown that anabolic steroid use enhances isometric fast force production over and above weight training alone in strength-trained athletes.[25] It has also been shown that anabolic steroids can enhance certain reflex components in athletes.[26] Little research has been conducted to determine whether the improved reflex components are solely due to anabolic steroids' effect on the central nervous system. It is possible that enhanced reflex effects are due to both the central and peripheral nervous systems.

Evidence that anabolic steroids directly affect motoneurons has been lacking on a cellular level. However, a recent study in animals has shown that chronic exposure to supraphysiological levels of anabolic steroids significantly increases the choline acetyltransferase messenger RNA levels in motoneurons in several spinal cord tracts.[27] The results of this study have demonstrated that anabolic steroids can affect the levels of specific messenger RNAs in motoneuron populations throughout the spinal cord. It also has suggested that motoneuronal characteristics are modulated by anabolic steroid levels regardless of the purported "androgen sensitivity" model of the neuromuscular system. This study could help explain the beneficial effects of anabolic steroids on central nervous system reflex time.

Scientific evidence on the effects of anabolic steroids on the reflex components of the peripheral nervous system is scarce. An animal study has shown that anabolic steroid administration can improve electromyographic (EMG) performance.[28] Further research should be conducted on anabolic use with trained and untrained people with respect to this issue. The results of these studies could reveal benefits of anabolic steroid therapy for many rehabilitative conditions.

Enhanced reflex responses are important factors that can improve performance in many sports. In some sports, the ability to anticipate body movements and move rapidly on those anticipations are elite ingredients for enhanced performance.

Other Major Anabolic Effects

Numerous recent studies have shown that anabolic steroids have a beneficial interaction on the growth hormone–growth factor–binding protein (GH-IGF-IGFBP) axis in various disease conditions. The GH-IGF-IGFBP axis is complex and powerful.[29] In general, anabolic steroid therapy has been shown to increase levels of IGF-1 (insulin-like growth factor-1) and to decreased levels of IGF-binding proteins. Increases in IGF-1 and increased bioavailability of IGF-1 via reduced IGF-1 binding proteins provides a powerful anabolic effect in many tissues, including skeletal muscles. The intertwined mechanisms involving anabolic steroids and growth hormones and factors is very complex and will be presented in a later chapter in this book.

Let us simplify this complex endocrinology and put it into athletic perspective. It has been shown that increased IGF-1 levels and IGF-1 bioavailabilities are a direct anabolic effect of supratherapeutic anabolic steroid administration in otherwise healthy men. Testosterone enanthate (300 mg IM each week for six weeks) administration has been shown to double growth hormone (GH) secretion and significantly increase IGF-1 levels. Nandrolone decanoate (300 mg IM each week for six weeks) administration raised GH secretion mildly, reduced the levels of IGF-binding proteins, and increased the levels of bioavailable IGF-1.[30]

Insulin-like growth factors have anabolic influences on cell growth and tissue repair.[31] These growth factors promote anabolic and growth actions through binding to IGF-1 receptors.[32] The presence of IGF-1 receptors in skeletal muscle cells indicates that IGF-1 acts independently of the androgen receptors to stimulate protein and glycogen synthesis.[33] IGF-1 receptor stimulation results in increased levels of IGF-I messenger RNAs that translates into increased protein synthesis[34] and inhibition of catabolism.[35]

Anabolic steroids increase IGF-1 levels and bioavailabilities. Therefore, anabolic steroids have both direct (via androgen receptors) and indirect (via IGF-1 receptors) anabolic effects on two types of genetic machinery. This double receptor effect probably acts in a synergistic manner to enhance skeletal muscle mass, strength, and repair; these are all important for performance enhancement, especially with vigorous athletic training.

Inhibited Catabolic Responses to Training

Anabolic steroids can enhance athletic training by several mechanisms, especially when vigorous exercise induces an initial catabolic effect on skeletal muscle. Exercise-induced skeletal muscle damage results in a remarkable number of localized and systemic changes. These changes include the release of catabolized intracellular proteins, delayed onset muscle soreness, and increased skeletal muscle protein breakdown and turnover. These exercise-induced adaptations appear to be integral to the repair of damaged muscle and may be essential for muscle growth. They also can be part of an injury mechanism.

Anabolic steroids, directly, and indirectly via increased IGF-1 levels and bioavalibility, inhibit the catabolic responses to vigorous athletic training. They may play a role in preventing "overuse" injuries and stress fractures.[36]

Since anabolic steroids increase the repair responses, they allow an athlete to train harder and more often. In this manner, anabolic steroids allow an athlete to optimize the beneficial stimuli of training. This factor can add to the overall anabolic influence that anabolic steroids provide.

Summary: Anabolic Steroids Can Enhance Athletic Performance

Anabolic steroids can enhance athletic ability. They can enhance athletic ability through a number of mechanisms that have been presented in this chapter. Anabolic steroids can enhance athletic ability to such a degree that athletes in many sports cannot compete without them. Elite caliber athletes have known this for years as illustrated by the various following statements provided in hearings held before the United States Senate in 1989.[37]

"[On anabolic steroids] I was able to train longer and harder, which ultimately improved my performance.... I was a woman who suddenly became strong like a man.... Forty percent of the United States team of 1988 had used anabolic steroids." Diane Williams, former national track and field champion.

"I believe that steroid use is rampant among the NFL, and that includes my own team. It is rampant in colleges, and it is rampant in high schools. Everybody is blind to it because they choose to ignore what is happening in the world of steroids.... Steroid use in football represents a vicious cycle. I know that there are many players in high school, college, and the NFL who want to stop using steroids, but they cannot or will not because they do not believe that they can be competitive without them." Bill Fralic, former Atlanta Falcon football player.

"Dianabol was the first entry in 1958 of anabolic steroids in American sports. It was not long afterward when this chemical started spreading throughout the various athletic institutions and weight rooms in America.... Here we have the beginning of an escalating chemical warfare. After 25 years, there are new drugs which created a dilemma, not only for the sports world, but for society. Most sports medicine experts all agree that steroid use in strength sports is epidemic." Steve Courson, former Pittsburgh Steelers football player.

Many modern-day athletes *are made* through hormonal manipulation. Anabolic steroids are just one class of drugs that hormonally manipulated athletes use to make them the athlete they want to become. Often, other anabolic and growth-stimulating hormones are used. This will be the topic of Chapter 10.

7
Adverse Physical Effects Associated with Anabolic Steroid Abuse

Introduction: Anabolic Steroid Abuse: A Dangerous "Breakfast of Champions"

Clinical doses of anabolic steroids for medically supervised patients are as safe and effective as any other prescription drug. This is strongly emphasized, *anabolic steroids when taken in clinically approved doses under medical supervision are both effective and safe!* However, the prolonged abuse of anabolic steroids in doses well above the clinically acceptable is a dangerous "breakfast of champions."[1]

Since the peak of the anabolic steroid epidemic in the early 1990s, evidence of the adverse physical effects of anabolic steroid abuse by athletes and bodybuilders has been mounting. The available information has come from cross-sectional, short-term longitudinal, and case studies. To fully investigate the adverse physical effects the needs are: a) to develop a comprehensive battery of sensitive and specific markers of the adverse effects, particularly ones able to detect the onset of adverse reactions; and, b) to conduct controlled and long-term longitudinal studies designed to understand the mechanisms involved in the doses and duration regimes athletes employ that cause adverse physical effects.[2]

Anabolic steroids function as hormones, and when abused have potentially detrimental effects on many of the body's systems, including the hepatic (liver), endocrine, cardiovascular, reproductive, neuroendocrine, and immune systems.[3-5] There is a wide range of concomitant temporary and permanent adverse effects that can occur with high-dose anabolic steroid use. Several adverse reactions may develop rapidly, within several weeks or less, while others require several years of anabolic steroid intake. Recent case studies of athletic anabolic steroid users indicate a plethora of adverse physical effects.

Anabolic Steroid–Induced Risk-Taking Behaviors

There are over 50 prescription drugs that pose potential adverse drug interactions when taken simultaneously (and unknowingly to the physician) with anabolic steroids.[6] This can place both medical care providers and anabolic steroid users in danger. A recent study reported that among patients who receive frequent medical care and are prescribed an assortment of prescription drugs, less than one-third of anabolic steroid users inform their physicians about their anabolic steroid use.[7] The anabolic steroid users who are prescribed prescription drugs and do not inform their physicians may be making a deadly mistake.

It is impossible to discuss the potential risks associated with anabolic use without discussing anabolic steroid–induced risk-taking behaviors. Anabolic steroid abuse promotes the use of a variety of prescription drugs without medical supervision in an attempt to treat the pesky anabolic steroid–induced side effects.[8] Anabolic steroid users also use non-prescription drugs and substances, both legal and illegal ones. This polypharmacy behavior is practiced by over 80 percent of anabolic steroid users.[9] Anabolic steroid users also consume dramatically more alcohol and demonstrate higher rates of binge drinking than do non-users. In addition, anabolic steroid users are more likely to use tobacco products, marijuana, cocaine, amphetamines, sedatives, hallucinogens, heroin and other opiates, inhalants, and designer drugs.[10,11] Recently it has been reported that anabolic steroid use can be a gateway to opioid dependence, including heroin.[12]

For anabolic steroid users, experimentation with other drugs can be a lethal mixture. Of great concern is the use of gamma-hydroxybutyrate (GHB) as a "bodybuilding supplement" and rave party drug. A number of deaths and near-deaths have occurred when anabolic steroid users took GHB.[13] Homicides, suicides, and lethal poisonings have been implicated, due to disinhibited behavior, in the deaths of dozens of anabolic steroid users.[14]

The out-of-control aggressive behavior seen in some anabolic steroid users can result in negligent homicide, especially when a user exhibits this behavior in an automobile.[15] Police officers on anabolic steroids act in aberrant, erratic, and bizarre manners when engaged in automobile chases and brutality excursions, some of which end with lethal consequences.[16,17] Imagine the disastrous results occurring from the combination of anabolic steroid–using police officers attempting to apprehend anabolic steroid–using assailants.

Another potentially lethal form of anabolic steroid–induced risk-taking behavior is the spread of life-threatening and often lethal infections. Needle and multi-dose vial sharing have been reported among anabolic steroid users resulting in the transmission of viral hepatitis, AIDS, bacterial, and fungal infections.[18,19]

Perhaps the most common result of the risk-taking behaviors of anabolic steroid users is incarceration. America's prison system is overloaded with anabolic steroid users who have acted in risky and violent manners. Child sexual abuse and murder has a high correlation with anabolic-androgenic steroid use.[20,21]

A recent study evaluating high-risk behaviors of high school students found that anabolic steroid use was associated with all the high-risk categories studied. These high-risk behaviors included risky sexual behavior, suicidal behaviors, not wearing a passenger seat belt, riding a motorcycle without a helmet, driving and drinking, fighting, and carrying a weapon.[22]

Underreporting of Anabolic Steroid–Induced Adverse Effects

Anabolic steroid users eventually seek medical attention. However, the true incidence of adverse physical effects due to anabolic steroid self-use is unknown. This has resulted in an underreporting by physicians and researchers. The reasons for this phenomenon include:

a) the fact that nearly two-thirds of anabolic steroid users do not inform their primary physicians of their use;
b) the fact that over 80 percent of anabolic steroid users take other drugs along with their anabolic steroid use;
c) the fact that many anabolic steroid users deny their use;
d) the fact that local, regional and state laboratories, including those used by coroners and medical examiners, do not have the means to test for anabolic steroids;
e) the fact that many physicians do not ask their patients about anabolic steroid use;

f) the fact that some physicians are unaware of some or all of the potential health risks of anabolic steroids and do not know how to recognize use in their patients. This is illustrated by reports indicating "no side effects"[23] with prolonged anabolic steroid use, or "the incidence of serious health problems associated with the use of androgens by athletes has been overstated";[24] and,
g) the fact that there is still a substantial "credibility gap" between anabolic steroid users and physicians. Some physicians still believe that anabolic steroids are just placebos or "fool's gold" for athletes.

Despite these shortcomings, considerable progress has been made in identifying the adverse physical effects associated with anabolic steroid use. In this chapter, these adverse physical effects will be arbitrarily divided into categories even though some of the adverse effects are more of a continuum of factors that may take years to fully develop. These categories include: lethal, serious and life-threatening, serious but not life-threatening, and less serious adverse physical effects.

Lethal Adverse Physical Effects

A number of adverse anabolic steroid–induced effects are lethal. Most of these lethal effects have involved the cardiovascular system and have been reported in case studies. The cases that have occurred in young (ages 20–39) anabolic steroid users include:

a) sudden death from myocardial infarction (heart attack),[25–33]
b) sudden death from pulmonary embolism (blood clot in the lungs),[34,35]
c) sudden death from cerebral edema and cerebellar hemorrhage (stroke),[36,37]
d) sudden death from intra-abdominal hemorrhage,[38] and,
e) sudden death from suicides, homicides, and accidental drug overdoses.[39,40]

These published reports probably represent just the tip of a huge iceberg. When anabolic steroid users die of cardiovascular insult, suicide, homicide, or accidental drug overdose, it is usually very difficult to obtain an accurate history. Since anabolic steroid users tend to hang out together, the surviving users deny anabolic steroid use as a possible factor, especially if the survivors are dealing anabolic steroids, since an admission could implicate them in murder, practicing medicine without a license, or dealing in controlled substances.

There is no doubt that some anabolic steroid users have died and will die of heart attacks caused by the drugs. Some will die early from a sudden death from myocardial infarction while others will die later due to the acceleration of atherogenic effects.

There are at least five hypothetical mechanisms of anabolic steroid–induced adverse cardiovascular effects. These include:

a) an atherogenic (plaque-forming) model involving the effects of anabolic steroids on lipoprotein concentrations in the blood;
b) a thrombus (clot) model involving the effects of anabolic steroids on clotting factors and platelets;
c) a vasospasm (spasm of the arteries) model involving the effects of anabolic steroids on the vascular nitric oxide system;
d) a direct myocardial injury model involving the effects of anabolic steroids on myocardial cells; and,
e) a combination of all of the above models.[41]

Besides the acute nature of the adverse lethal conditions, anabolic steroid users also show an increase in premature mortality rates. A recent study compared mortality rates of non-users to elite anabolic steroid–using powerlifters from Finland. A 12-year follow-up study was conducted on 62 of the powerlifters. The study results showed that the premature death rate of the anabolic steroid–using powerlifters was 12.9 percent compared to 3.1 percent of non-users. Eight of the 62 anabolic steroid users died before the age of 40 years. The causes of the premature death among the anabolic steroid users were: suicide (3), acute myocardial infarction (3), hepatic coma (1), and non-Hodgkin's lymphoma (1).[42]

Evidence is mounting that indicates a strong correlation between anabolic steroid abuse and premature death. Some of these serious and life-threatening adverse physical effects leading to premature death are discussed in the next section.

Serious and Life-Threatening Adverse Physical Effects

Liver Conditions and Other Cancers

It has been known for decades that patients who have been treated with high-dose prolonged anabolic steroid therapy have been at a greater risk for liver cancer and other serious liver conditions. These include peliosis hepatitis, hepatomas, hepatocellular carcinomas, hepatitis, severe cholestasis, hepatic angiosarcoma, and fatal hepatic coma.[43–47]

Long-term anabolic steroid use is the fourth leading cause of a highly lethal form of liver cancer, hepatic angiosarcoma.[48,49] Peliosis hepatitis is a condition that describes the presence of blood-filled sacs or spaces within the liver.[50] Documented case reports of severe liver abnormalities and other types of cancers suggest that these conditions occur in anabolic steroid users. These conditions, while currently considered rare, include:

a) hepatocellular carcinoma (liver cancer),[51,52]
b) severe cholestasis (bile build up in the liver),[53]
c) renal cell carcinoma (kidney cancer),[54]
d) intratesticular leiomyosarcoma (rare form of testicular cancer),[55] and,
e) adenocarcinoma of the prostate (prostate cancer).[56]

Some argue that the underlying diseases and not anabolic steroids are responsible for these conditions.

Serious Cardiovascular Conditions

As previously presented, anabolic steroid use can cause lethal cardiovascular events. It can also cause other cardiovascular conditions that can be life threatening. Documented case reports of these cardiovascular events in young anabolic steroid users include:

a) severe coronary artery disease,[57]
b) severe cardiomyopathy (weakening of the heart muscle),[58]
c) congestive heart failure and ventricular fibrillation (irregular heart beating),[59]
d) cardiac tamponade (blood that accumulates in the space between the heart muscle and the outer heart lining preventing the heart from properly beating),[60]
e) ascending aortic dissection (tearing of the muscle lining of the aorta).[61]

These life-threatening cardiovascular events occur in some young anabolic steroid users, and are currently considered rare events.

Serious, Non-Life Threatening Adverse Physical Effects

A number of anabolic steroid–induced conditions are serious and may even require surgical intervention and rehabilitation. Others, such as serious viral infections, may require prolonged medical care and may lead to premature death.

Over the past decade a number of serious, non–life threatening conditions have been reported in case studies of anabolic steroid users. These serious, non–life threatening conditions include:

a) avascular necrosis of the femoral heads.[62,63] Avascular necrosis means that the blood supply to a region (in these cases the head of the femur) has been disrupted resulting in tissue (femoral head) death. Treatment is usually a surgical hip replacement. Avascular necrosis of the femoral head has been associated with high-dose corticosteroid therapy and trauma. Bo Jackson, a college Heisman Trophy winner, NFL and MLB player, had this condition. After receiving an artificial hip, he continued to play professional baseball for a short while, but his athletic career was both limited and shortened by avascular necrosis.
b) spontaneous rupture of the anterior cruciate ligament of the knee.[64] This is a condition almost always associated with significant trauma. The anterior cruciate ligament provides major support for the knee joint. Even with surgical intervention, a ruptured anterior cruciate ligament can be a career-ending injury for an athlete.
c) atrial fibrillation (a non-lethal heart beat abnormality).[65]
d) systemic lupus erythematosus (SLE)[66] This disease can affect nearly every system in the body. It is thought to be initiated by a disruption of or abnormality in the immune system. Patients with SLE usually have severely abbreviated life spans.
e) multi-compartment syndrome following surgery.[67] In several areas of the body, muscles are contained by fibrous tissue, thus compartmentalized. When large muscles swell, usually due to trauma, there is very little room available for the swelling processes to occur. Blood and nerve supply to the compartment may be compromised due to the mounting pressure within the compartment. This is a condition that may require emergency surgical intervention.
f) spinal epidural lipomatosis with radiculopathy.[68] This is a rare condition in which excess fat tissue is deposited circumferentially about the epidural space in the spinal cord. It is most commonly seen in patients on chronic corticosteroid therapy for a variety of medical conditions. This condition can cause muscle weakness and chronic pain.
g) neuropathies of the upper extremities.[69] This condition (in these cases) is probably caused by excessive muscle enlargement squeezing the nerves to the muscles in the upper extremities. This condition can cause muscle weakness and chronic pain.

These case studies represent areas where physicians have linked anabolic steroid use with adverse physical conditions. It is likely that these studies represent only a small portion of the adverse physical effects caused by anabolic steroid use. The true incidence of these conditions is unknown.

Less Serious Physical Health Risks

Anabolic steroid use can cause alterations in almost every system within the body because cellular receptors for these drugs are in almost every tissue in the body. Therefore, it should not be surprising that many of these alterations appear as qualitative or quantitative adverse effects. Some of these adverse effects are seen only in male users or are more prevalent in males than females.

In general, the less severe anabolic steroid–induced adverse effects are dose and duration related. However, there is a wide variance to this generality. Less severe adverse effects may occur in one user and not another. These side effects may occur in moderate doses in some users but require larger doses in others. In short, anabolic steroid abuse is a form of self-experimentation with controlled substances.

There are hundreds of scientific articles that report adverse effects of a less serious nature in anabolic steroid users. Many of these are listed in Tables 7-1 and 7-2.[70–98]

Table 7-1. Minor Abnormalities Due to Anabolic Steroid Use in Men

Hypertension	Disturbances in sleep cycles
Acne	Increased appetite
Fluid retention	Gynecomastia
Abnormal liver function tests	Deepening of the voice
Reduction in testicular size & function	Increased sebaceous gland size and secretion
Psychological disturbances	Viral illness after steroid cessation
Penile enlargement	Increased energy level
Increased libido	Cessation of mental depression
Changes in hair growth & distribution	Rebound resetting of hormonal balance
Epistaxis (nose bleeds)	Increased aggressiveness
Alterations in coping mechanisms	Withdrawal reduction in libido
Withdrawal depression	Atherogenic lipoprotein profiles
Altered thyroid function tests	Altered immune system tests
Altered healing capacity for injuries	Increased bone mineral density
Reduced inhibitions for risky behaviors	Abnormal blood clotting tests
Increased risk for drug abuse	Increased hemoglobin concentration
Benign prostate enlargement	Heart enlargement

TABLE 7-2. MINOR ABNORMALITIES DUE TO ANABOLIC STEROID SELF-USE IN WOMEN

Hypertension	Disturbance in sleep cycles
Acne	Increased appetite
Fluid retention	Reduction in body fat
Abnormal liver function tests	Menstrual disturbances
Psychological disturbances	Increased energy level
Reduction in breast tissue	Deepening tone of the voice
Clitoral enlargement and sensitivity	Cessation of mental depression
Epistaxis (nose bleeds)	Increased aggression
Changes in hair growth and distribution	Increased sebaceous gland size and secretion
Viral illness after steroid cessation	Withdrawal depression
Ruddiness of the face	Rebound estrogenization
Increased muscle vascularity	Withdrawal reduction in libido
Abnormal liver function tests	Atherogenic lipoprotein profiles
Altered thyroid function tests	Altered immune system tests
Reduced inhibitions for risky behaviors	Abnormal blood clotting tests
Altered endocrine function tests	Increased risk for drug abuse
Altered healing capacity from injuries	Increased hemoglobin concentration
Increased libido and orgasmic responses	Increased bone mineral density
Heart enlargement	

Summary: Anabolic Steroid Abuse Is "'Roid" Roulette

In this chapter the adverse physical effects that anabolic steroid users can and have experienced have been presented. No other form of drug abuse has such a wide variety of associated adverse physical effects. Some of these effects can be lethal and some of them, while chronic, are life shortening nonetheless. Other side effects are more benign, subtle, or minor irritations. No one can predict which adverse physical effects will happen to any given user.

Anabolic steroid use is endocrine experimentation. No qualified endocrinologist would ever perform such experimentation with patients. Every anabolic steroid user is participating in an experiment that could lead to lethal and or legal consequences. The fallout of these experiments is accumulating. Some of the health consequences of these self-experiments will not be known for a decade or more.

The use of anabolic steroids is unsafe. It sets bad examples for society. For a select few lucky users, anabolic steroids *are* the breakfast of champions.[99] For the rest, their abuse is a health hazard, a "'roid roulette." Have body image and athletic fame, fortune, and glory reached the point in society that we must continue to bet our health and futures on the "'roid" roulette wheel? Sadly, for many, it is probably so.[100]

8

Mental Health Risks Induced by Anabolic Steroid Abuse

Introduction: "'Roid Rage" Is Real

This author was the first to describe the explosive temper, short fuse, overly aggressive, and violent behavior seen in anabolic steroid users.[1–4] The term for these behaviors, labeled "'roid rage," was first used in the mid–1980s.[5] "'Roid rage" describes the behaviors associated with moderate-to-heavy anabolic steroid use which was emphasized in a Food and Drug Administration (FDA) drug bulletin in 1987.[6] These negative behaviors, coupled with the addictive qualities of anabolic steroids, are why this author was so persistent in pushing for the controlled substance reclassification.

In 1984, this author published the earliest reports describing the array of psychological changes experienced by anabolic steroids users. A description of these personality changes is shown in Table 8-1[7] and Table 8-2 below.[8]

TABLE 8-1. PSYCHOLOGICAL ALTERATIONS SEEN WITH ANABOLIC STEROID SELF-USE (1984)

Increased hostility, mental intensity, anger, aggressiveness
Increased desire to excel
Increased libido
Probable enhancement of mental alertness
Psychological dependence and withdrawal symptoms
Decreased inhibition to use other medications or drugs
Tendency toward "one-track mindedness"
Tendency toward violence

TABLE 8-2. PSYCHOLOGICAL CHANGES INDUCED BY THE SELF-USE OF ANABOLIC STEROIDS (1985)

While on Anabolic Steroids	*After Cessation of Anabolic Steroid Use*
Increases in self-esteem, sex drive, explosive hostility and violence, mental intensity, energy level, tolerance of pain, desire to train	Increases in depression, listlessness, apathy, desire for steroids
Decreases in ability to accept failure or poor performance, general tolerance, inhibitions about other drug use	Decreases in self-esteem, sex drive, hostility and violence, desire to train intensely
Other changes, including sleeping disturbances and nightmares	Other changes, including a return to normal sleep patterns and ability to control violent behavior

The most prevalent of the adverse conditions brought on by anabolic steroids use is due to psychoactive effects on the limbic system in the brain. The *limbic system*, a term applied to a group of brain structures which include the hippocampus, septum, and hypothalamus, is thought to control human emotion, behavior, and influence personality. Testosterone and anabolic steroids, which bind to receptors in the limbic system, tend to influence several aspects of human behavior through a variety of mechanisms.[9] First, testosterone and anabolic steroids can act as direct neurotransmitters binding to certain brain receptors. Second, in supraphysiologic doses, these steroids can alter both the function of these brain receptors, as well as increase the number of these receptors. Third, anabolic steroids can modulate or alter the function of other neurotransmitter receptors within the brain, which include dopaminergic, serotonergic, GABAergic receptors.

Even though the absolute mechanisms of testosterone and anabolic steroids on the brain are unknown, there is little doubt that these steroids are strong psychoactive chemicals. On a biochemical level, the psychoactive influences of these steroids are complicated, interrelated, and multifactored. High doses of these steroids over a prolonged period of time produce both psychotoxic and neurotoxic effects.

Testosterone's influence is manifested in several interrelated physiological and psychological ways. First, as we know, testosterone increases body size, muscle mass, and strength. Second, testosterone plays a role in male-female social dominance. Third, testosterone influences the way men react to stress. A male is more likely to respond to stress with a "flight or fight" reaction, while women typically reduce stress through verbal communication. These "macho" influences indicate the significant role testosterone plays in the differing reactions seen in men as compared to women.

When testosterone is secreted in higher amounts (as seen during adolescence) or when testosterone or anabolic steroids are abused, a number of these "macho" patterns can become aberrant. Some of these aberrant behaviors include manic or hypomanic episodes, delusions, aggressive, violent, sexually violent, and criminal behavior. Abuse of testosterone and anabolic steroids also can cause addiction and a condition called "megorexia," "bigorexia," or the "Adontis Syndrome." Withdrawal from heavy anabolic steroid use can cause depression, suicidal ideation, and suicide.

Aggression and Violence

INTRODUCTION

The ability of testosterone and anabolic steroids to induce aggression and violence is not confined to humans. In animal studies, treatment with testosterone and anabolic steroids has long been known to cause overaggressive and violent behavior. High serum testosterone levels and androgen treatments in rodents, hooved mammals, and primates have been shown to exert a major influence on social rank and dominance, which are often related to physical fighting.[10–17]

One of the earliest clinical trials utilizing testosterone therapy revealed a tendency for the steroid to induce aggression and violent behavior when the doses were large.[18] Several other researchers have found positive correlations between high testosterone levels and aggressive, violent, criminal and sexually criminal behavior.[19–24] In 1980 a study with normal adolescent males linked high serum testosterone levels to certain personality traits. The study, which utilized a dozen different personality inventories, showed that these normal 16-year-old males exhibited statistically significant increases in bouts of verbal and physical aggression, and potential for violence, especially in response to provocation or threat. These findings correlated significantly with elevated serum testosterone levels.[25]

In the mid–1980s, this author published early reports that linked the use of testosterone and anabolic steroids to overly aggressive and violent behavior.[26–31] In 1987 two psychiatrists (Dr. Pope and Dr. Katz) reported that 12 percent of 33 regular anabolic steroid users exhibited psychotic symptoms, and many others exhibited near-psychotic symptoms, mania and withdrawal depression.[32] In their follow-up study, Pope and Katz reported the following behaviors to be attributable to anabolic steroid use: aggression, violent episodes, paranoia, depression, and hallucinations.[33] Other studies published in 1990 echoed the findings of many of the earlier reports.[34–37]

Selected Criminal Court Cases

Case One In 1988 this author, along with Harvard psychiatrists Drs. Pope and Katz, testified as expert witnesses in one of the first federal court cases involving anabolic steroid-induced criminal violence and murder. NBC aired the case in a television documentary entitled "On Trial." The case involved a brutal murder committed by Horace K. "Ace" Williams. Ace was a former high school football player turned bodybuilder. He was a high school graduate and the son of a minister, and spent much of his time as a youth minister. He had no known history of violence, conduct disorder, or other psychiatric problems. At 18 years of age, with hopes of playing college football, he became interested in weight training to help him achieve this goal. He quickly saw that the use of anabolic steroids resulted in rapid and significant weight gains. Unfortunately, Ace never played college ball; instead he spent the next three years using anabolic steroids as a bodybuilder.

One day Ace and a friend stopped at a phone booth to determine the location of a party they were to attend. Ace received a busy signal and that was enough to cause him to fly into a rage. He hugged the phone booth, uprooted it from the concrete, and tossed it into the parking lot about 50 feet away. He and his friend left and while driving along I-95 in south Florida, picked up a hitchhiker. They drove to a deserted field. There Ace undressed the hitchhiker, beat him to death with a board and a lead pipe, scalped him, shave the hair off his body, hung him with a rope, and then repeatedly ran over him with his vehicle. After hiding for hours, he turned himself in at the police department. His friend, also a heavy anabolic steroid user, later admitted that during this time, even he was afraid of Ace. Ace only remembered bits and pieces of the events. His account was consistent with an anabolic steroid psychosis. Although he escaped the death penalty, Ace received a prison sentence of 40 years.

During the trial, this author testified that Ace's anabolic steroid use, addiction and "'roid rage" fit the classic pattern. The three phases of anabolic steroid use which led to Ace's "'roid rage" and ultimately murder, were presented to the jury. These phases will be utilized for illustrative purposes and compared to Ace's own recollections. These findings illustrate the psychotoxic effects of anabolic steroids when they are used in unregulated amounts.

Typical early phase of anabolic steroid use:

a) Oral anabolic steroids are used in low to moderate amounts;
b) Significant muscle mass and strength gains are noted with weight training; and,

c) Major personality changes include euphoria, increased self-esteem, sense of well-being, sex drive, appetite, aggressiveness, desire to train, and desire for further anabolic steroid use leads to greater doses.

Ace's early phase of anabolic steroid use:

a) Oral Dianabol (methandrostenolone) of 5 mg per day for two weeks, then increasing to 25 mg per day over the next five weeks;
b) Significant muscle mass and strength gains with weight training; and,
c) Major personality changes included "felt great ... more confidence ... able to ask any girl for a date ... always hungry ... would challenge anybody ... spent more time in the gym training."

Typical middle phase of anabolic steroid use:

a) "Stacking" both oral and injectable anabolic steroids with increased doses and total anabolic steroid burden;
b) Further increases in muscle mass and strength; and,
c) Major personality changes include major mood swings, sleeping disturbances, irritability, easily provoked to display temper and violence, grandiosity, use of recreational drugs, manic episodes, increased desire for more anabolic steroids, withdrawal depression, and distorted body image.

Ace's middle phase of anabolic steroid use:

a) "Stacked" Dianabol and Anadrol-50 orally and injections with testosterone cypionate;
b) Further increases in muscle mass and strength; and,
c) Major personality changes, included "felt special powers ... had nightmares ... got mad real easily ... hit the wall with my fists ... pulled telephones off of the wall ... threatened people ... used cocaine occasionally ... stopped steroids for two weeks and I was so depressed that I thought that I might kill myself if I didn't get back on steroids ... felt like a wimp off steroids."

Typical late phase of anabolic steroid use:

a) "Stacking" several anabolic steroids together orally and by self-injection, further increasing the total anabolic steroid burden;
b) Further increases in muscle mass and strength; and,
c) Major personality changes, including manic episodes, grandiose delusions, paranoia, "'roid rage," narcissistic behavior, psychotic symptoms,

criminal activity, full-blown steroid psychosis and violent sexual criminal behavior.

Ace's late phase of anabolic steroid use:

a) "Stacked" four or more steroids together without any particular schedule; began to inject himself daily;
b) Further increases in muscle mass and strength; and,
c) Major personality changes: "Had rushes of energy and power ... could pound the earth with my fists and feel the earth vibrate ... everyone was watching me ... everyone was afraid of me ... everything pissed me off ... most of my friends stopped being my friends ... I was in several fights ... all I thought about was building my body to compete in bodybuilding ... I was arrested for possession of cocaine ... I once turned over fifteen cars ... I pulled a phone booth out of the cement and threw it ... I beat up that hitchhiker real bad for no reason ... out in that field with the hitchhiker I felt like I was alone ... everybody was in the shadows ... all I could hear was my head buzzing."

This author examined and interviewed Ace in his prison cell. As I entered the cell, Ace was sitting in shackles and cuffs. I asked for the officers to remove the restraints. With the restraints off, no one, not even his own attorney, would go into the cell. Anabolic steroids are often available in prison, but it appeared to me that he was not on them at that time and thus not a threat. I spent over an hour with him obtaining the history and performing a physical exam. I was convinced after talking with Ace that he had been a heavy anabolic steroid user, one who had experienced the horror associated with such abuse.

Case Two In 1987, this author testified in another case where anabolic steroid use was implicated in a death. In this case, I was testifying for the state of Indiana regarding the role that police brutality might have played in the death of a star Indiana University (IU) football player, Denver Smith.

Denver had been an All-American offensive linemen at IU and was drafted by the Cincinnati Bengals. During his senior year at IU he sustained a knee injury and spent the remainder of the year rehabilitating his injury. Denver was 6'1", weighed over 260 pounds and could bench press 500 pounds. Shortly after his death, his family instigated a wrongful death suit against the police department and the state of Indiana. They were suing for millions of dollars for inappropriate lethal force resulting in the death of Denver.

On the day of his death, Denver had just returned from a Bengals preseason football camp. He was sent home because he had failed the physical exam due to his knee injury. He was seen walking down Main Street with a tire tool in his hand, jumping on cars and bashing windows with the tire tool. He was enraged. As the police arrived, he ran and hid behind a convenience store. Six police officers cornered him and attempted to talk him down. He was asked to drop the tire tool but he refused. He attacked the police officers with the tire tool and was shot in the leg and chest. A skirmish developed with Denver maintaining the upper hand even after sustaining the initial gunshot wounds. Several officers were injured. One officer ran to call for more help while the other five officers continued attempts to restrain Denver. He was eventually shot several more times. When one bullet struck his heart, he died.

The autopsy photos of Denver Smith showed a very muscular man with the following characteristics:

- acne on his back
- several bruises in his upper buttocks region from probable anabolic steroid injections
- striae (stretch marks) across the anterior shoulder areas
- testicular atrophy.

A review of the records indicated he exhibited significant increases in bench and leg press since his freshman year. Testimony from his anabolic steroid suppliers indicated that Denver had a long history of anabolic steroid use. The police officers testified that Denver was enraged and "exhibited superhuman strength."

Lethal force was used against Denver, but this author testified that it was necessary because of his size and steroid psychosis. The jury agreed and the police officers and state were found not guilty.

This case and that of Ace Williams are real life examples of "'roid rage." It is a real phenomenon and is a factor that continues to be responsible for the overwhelming number of violent crimes seen in high school, college, and professional strength athletes today.

Clinical Studies Showing Anabolic Steroid–Induced Aggression and Violence

One result of placing testosterone and anabolic steroids on the Federal Controlled Substance Act of 1970 (CSA) was that research grants became available to study these drugs. Since 1992, there have been numerous studies showing a strong relationship between testosterone and anabolic steroid use and major personality changes, including aggression, violence, and criminal acts. A historical listing of these studies appears in Table 8-3.

TABLE 8-3. STUDIES WHICH SHOW THAT TESTOSTERONE AND ANABOLIC STEROIDS INDUCE AGGRESSIVE AND VIOLENT BEHAVIOR

Author and Date	*Type of Study*	*Steroid-Induced Personality Changes*
Taylor (1984)[38]	anabolic steroid users	hostility, aggression, anger, violence, addiction, polypharmacy, withdrawal depression
Taylor (1985)[39]	anabolic steroid users	aggression, violent behavior, addiction, withdrawal depression, suicidal ideation
Freinhar (1985)[40]	patients treated with anabolic steroids	hypomania
Taylor (1987)[41]	anabolic steroid users	aggression, violence, "'roid rage," increased energy level and libido, addiction, polypharmacy, withdrawal depression
Barker (1987)[42]	patients treated with anabolic steroids	aggresssion
Pope (1987)[43]	anabolic steroid users	mania, psychoses, withdrawal depression
Taylor (1988)[44]	anabolic steroid users	aggression, violence, "'roid rage," addiction, polypharmacy, withdrawal depression
Pope (1988)[45]	anabolic steroid users	aggression, violent episodes, paranoia, hallucinations, withdrawal depression
Kashkin (1989)[46]	anabolic steroid users	psychological and physiological addiction
Choi (1990)[47]	anabolic steroid users	aggression, hostility, anger, anxiety
Lefavi (1990)[48]	anabolic steroid users	aggression, hostility, anger, anxiety
Perry (1990)[49]	anabolic steroid users	anger, hostility, aggression
Taylor (1991)[50]	anabolic steroid users	aggression, "'roid rage," addiction, polypharmacy, "megorexia," withdrawal depression, suicidal ideation
Uzych (1992)[51]	review	aggression in response to provocation, psychosis, mania, hypomania, withdrawal depression
Isacsson (1993)[52]	review	aggression, paranoid psychoses, violent behavior, polypharmacy
Schulte (1993)[53]	anabolic steroid users	high incidence of domestic violence
Su (1993)[54]	low-dose and high-dose Methyltestosterone administration to normal male volunteers	euphoria, increased energy level, sexual arousal, irritability, violent feelings, mood swings, hostility, confusion, distractibility, mania, hypomania
Burnett (1994)[55]	adolescent anabolic steroid users	anger, vigor, mood swings, depression

Author and Date	*Type of Study*	*Steroid-Induced Personality Changes*
Choi (1994)[56]	anabolic steroid users	fights, verbal aggression domestic violence
Pope (1994)[57]	anabolic steroid users	mania, hypomania, mood swings, irritability, aggression, depression, polypharmacy
Parrott (1994)[58]	anabolic steroid users	aggression towards objects, verbal aggression, alertness, anxiety, irritability, suspiciousness, negativism
Kouri (1995)[59]	male volunteers given supraphysiologic dose of testosterone cypionate	aggression
Nakatani (1995)[60]	review	aggression, violence, rage, grandiosity
Peet (1995)[61]	review	mania
Cooper (1996)[62]	chronic anabolic steroid users (DSM3-R) criteria	abnormal personality traits, violence aggression, mania
Corrigan (1996)[63]	review	violent murders, aggression, violent behavior, psychiatric disorders
Dukarm (1996)[64]	anabolic steroid users	weapon carrying, violent behavior
Rubinow (1996)[65]	review	psychotoxic effects, aggression
Isacsson (1998)[66]	prison inmates	violence
Porcerelli (1998)[67]	review	pathological personality traits, aggression, violence
Wilson-Fearon (1999)[68]	A Mr. Universe competitor	aggression, polypharmacy, negativism, mood swings
Thiblin (1999)[69]	anabolic steroid users who committed suicide	hypomania, acts of violence, withdrawal depression, suicide
Pope (2000)[70]	normal male volunteers given supraphysiologic testoserone doses	mania, hypomania
Thiblin (2000)[71]	deaths of 34 male anabolic steroid users	increased risk of violent death, violence, aggression, withdrawal depression, violent rages, mood swings, disinhibited behavior, polypharmacy, suicide, cardiac events

Results from these studies, show that supraphysiologic doses of testosterone and anabolic steroids induce overly aggressive and violent behavior. However, there have been a few studies that have not shown this type of psychopathology.[72,73]

In 1999, in a controlled, double-blind design study researchers administered testosterone to normal men. The authors concluded:

> All doses of testosterone demonstrated only minimal effects on measures of mood and behavior during acute and withdrawal phases for all study completers. There were no effects on psychosexual function. There was no evidence of dose-dependent effect on any measure.... Doses of testosterone up to five times the physiologic replacement dose appear to have a minimal risk of adverse psychosexual effects in the majority of normal men; however, beginning at around five times the replacement dose a minority of normal men may experience significant adverse psychological effects. Because illicit anabolic steroid users may use larger doses of multiple drugs under less restrictive conditions, our study may significantly underestimate the psychological effect of steroid use in the community.[74]

While it is not unusual for medical researchers to report conflicting findings, an *overwhelming* number of scientific reports and review studies have found one or more aspects of psychotoxic or neurotoxic effects induced by supraphysiologic doses of testosterone and anabolic steroids. Overly aggressive and violent behavior patterns are the results of some of these effects.

Is the Anabolic Steroid–Induced Rage Phenomenon Permanent?

There is concern that the possibility of prolonged, high dose use of testosterone and anabolic steroids may have some permanent influences on brain neurochemistry. Scientific studies on non-humans have indicated that there are alterations to the testosterone receptors in the brain caused by supraphysiologic doses of androgens. Several studies also show that a variety of other neuroreceptors are altered as well.[75–82] These results indicate direct effects of anabolic steroids on the function of central nervous system receptor complexes. Also, these studies suggest that the behavioral and psychological effects of anabolic steroid use result from the interaction of these steroids with multiple regulatory systems in the brain. The effects of anabolic steroids on the hippocampus, septum, and hypothalamus have been suggested to be involved with the mechanisms responsible for the aggressive and defensive behavior associated with anabolic steroid abuse.[83]

Perhaps the most bothersome alterations in the brain's neuroreceptors are both an increase in the number of androgen receptors and an increased binding capacity of these receptors.[84] How long these receptor changes persist after cessation of androgen use is unknown. If these alterations are permanent or persist for years, the following theories may help explain some of the anecdotal reports that have been voiced over the years.

After prolonged, high-dose use of testosterone and anabolic steroids, the user's brain may experience a permanent or persistent increased density of androgen receptors with increased binding affinities. When steroid use is discontinued and the androgen levels eventually return to the normal range, these receptors are "hungry" for elevated androgen levels again. Androgens modulate the functions of other neurotransmitters and their receptors. Brain levels of dopamine, serotonin, GABA, and other neurotransmitters may remain low without the previous influence of elevated androgen levels. In short, these receptors may "see" a decreased androgen level similar to that described in male andropause. This phenomenon may result in chronic depression and loss of self-esteem. These anabolic steroid induced changes may also have altered the brain's neurochemistry to cause a prolonged or permanent tendency toward episodic displays of anger, anxiety, panic attacks, and rage continuing years after steroid use has stopped. These theories require further study.

In summary, despite a few studies that have indicated otherwise, supratherapeutic doses of testosterone and anabolic steroids have dramatic effects on the human brain. There are mechanisms by which alterations in brain receptors account for the aggressive and violent behavior seen with heavy anabolic steroid use. There has been a plethora of scientific information published that shows aggression and violent behavior can be induced by the unregulated use of these steroids. Supraphysiologic doses of androgens over a prolonged period of time are psychotoxic and neurotoxic. These drugs also cause danger for spouses and significant others since they may become the victims of the aggressive outbursts. There is some evidence suggesting that a variety of these psychotoxic effects may be long lasting or more permanent in nature.

It is easy to see why Congress placed these powerful drugs under the CSA. Without this action, the anabolic steroid epidemic would have accelerated, resulting in countless numbers of users suffering from the drugs' psychotoxic and neurotoxic effects.

Addiction and "Megorexia"

Addiction to Anabolic Steroids

Initial reports in the mid–1980s indicated that anabolic steroids became addictive for some users.[85] To rank the addictive potentials of anabolic steroids, they were reported to be "more addicting than amphetamines."[86] By 1990 almost every leading expert in the anabolic steroid field agreed that anabolic steroids are potentially addictive drugs.[87]

Drug addiction may be defined as habituation to the use of a drug to the extent that deprivation gives rise to symptoms of distress, withdrawal symptoms, or an irresistible impulse to take the drug again. With some drugs, the addiction process has been well documented. In many cases, the irresistible impulse to use the drug again can be initiated by a familiar experience the user associates with prior use of that drug. For, example, with cigarettes, the impulse to smoke may be most intense after meals. With cocaine, a strong desire impulse may occur at a party where others are using the drug. The impulse to use a drug varies with the user's experience. In this manner, addiction to a drug can be triggered by an event where the user previously used the drug. For some people, taking prescription narcotics to ease the pain from extensive dental work is enough to propel the person into a reoccurrence of a previous narcotic addiction. Others become addicted to narcotics after surgery or after prolonged anxiolytic therapy. Often, physicians resist prescribing narcotics due to their inability to determine which patients are likely to become addicted to a particular medication.

The addiction to anabolic steroids is a complex addiction as these drugs alter the entire neurochemistry of the brain. Aspects of this addiction involve the traditional psychological and physiological parameters of addiction. But, anabolic steroid addiction differs from the more traditional views because of the effect anabolic steroids have on body image. Some of these alterations are subtle and others more obvious. The heavy user becomes obsessed with body image and can become wrapped up in the "steroid image." Anabolic steroid users caught up in the steroid image continually compare their bodies to others, often seeing themselves fit and others fat. Anabolic steroid users can spot other users. They compare themselves before and after using anabolic steroids, and conclude that anabolic steroid use is a necessity. Everywhere users go they are confronted with the "macho image" of other anabolic steroid users. No other drug addiction has been so intertwined with psychological, physiological, and body image factors. This is why this author believes that anabolic steroids may be more addicting than cocaine for many users.[88]

Megorexia

Once an anabolic steroid user is in the grasp of these drugs, the users's perception of body image can become very distorted. The user is never large, lean, or muscular enough. For many users, these steroids induce an almost unquenchable thirst to achieve a fat-free muscular body image. The user may spend hours posing in front of a mirror; posing and assessing, posing and assessing. The net result is that the user perceives that what is in the mirror is either too small or too fat. This facet of anabolic steroid addiction has been termed "megorexia."[89,90] Megorexia is the body image distortion often associated with prolonged, high-dose anabolic steroid abuse. It describes a distorted body image associated with an unquenchable desire to be more muscular and leaner than anyone else, a voracious appetite for protein, and a continual comparison of the megorexic's body image. It becomes a disease process highlighted by obsession and narcissism. Megorexia is associated with a voracious appetite and a distorted body image associated with both cognitive and affective disorders.[91] Descriptions of this body image distortion are listed in Table 8-4.

TABLE 8-4. MEGOREXIA AND OTHER BODY IMAGE DISTORTIONS ASSOCIATED WITH ANABOLIC STEROID ADDICTION

Scientist and Date of Study	*Applied Name or Description Given*
Taylor (1985)[92]	Bodybuilder's syndrome
Taylor (1988)[93]	Megorexia
Taylor (1991)[94]	Megorexia
Pope (1993)[95]	Reverse anorexia
Porcerelli (1995)[96]	Narcissism
Blouin (1995)[97]	Eating disorder
Schwerin (1996)[98]	Body image disorder
Wroblewska (1997)[99]	Body dysmorphia
Gruber (2000)[100]	Muscle dysmorphia

Other researchers described this condition as reverse anorexia or muscle dysmorphia.

Adolescent Traits and Testosterone Levels

Testosterone and anabolic steroids can be addictive hormones. They are powerful psychoactive chemicals that induce strong impulses especially when used in supratherapeutic doses. During adolescence, when testosterone levels are at their physiologic peak, some of these impulses manifest themselves. These impulses are generally "socialized" through time and adherence to the social mores of the times. One simply does not act and react on impulses. Social skills, coping skills, and social mores must be learned. Often, this is a difficult process.

During adolescence in both boys and girls, serum testosterone levels are known to be at their peak. These elevated testosterone levels direct many of the mental and physical changes associated with puberty and adolescence. The elevated testosterone levels help provide for accelerated growth and development, awakening of sexual desire, secondary sexual organ maturation, and a variety of brain impulses that must be "socialized" into acceptable behavior. Three of the more prominent brain impulses that high testosterone levels regulate are anger, aggressiveness, and libido.

In the United States, the adolescent period is longer than in any other country. This maturation period is often accompanied with a difficult socialization period. Adolescents make many mistakes during this socialization period, and they often act on impulse. These mistakes may take the form of poor control of sexual desire that may lead to sexual promiscuity and unwanted pregnancies. When the teenager is unable to control angry and aggressive impulses that are enhanced by peak testosterone levels, criminal and or violent behavior may result.

When adolescents experiment with testosterone and anabolic steroids, elevating the total androgen burden on the brain, their brain impulses may become difficult or impossible to socialize and control. This can give rise to personality traits and behavior that may be different from what has previously been established. Even seemingly minute stresses can provoke an anabolic steroid-using adolescent into abnormal and aberrant behavior. An anabolic-steroid using adolescent feels invincible. Drug education efforts fall on deaf ears as users feel adverse effects from anabolic steroids only happen to others. They are prone to use other drugs and engage in risky behaviors or endeavors.

A young adult who begins using anabolic steroids is faced with brain impulses that in many ways resemble a second adolescent period. These heightened brain impulses increase libido, anger, aggressiveness, energy, and self-esteem. These brain impulses and their resulting feelings can become very addictive. They can induce behaviors such as mania, hostility, grandiosity, and moodiness. Withdrawal from these steroids can cause depression, loss of libido, low self-esteem, and low energy level. Returning to anabolic steroid use can alleviate all of these negative feelings. But, by returning to anabolic steroid use again, the user may become insidiously addicted.

Prescribing sex steroid therapy for adolescents raises some important issues. The usual requests by adolescent females for sex steroids to prevent pregnancy result in a prescription for oral contraceptives or other sex steroid preparations. These requests have been considered appropriate medical therapy for decades. There have even been recent FDA discussions to consider removing oral contraceptives from the prescription drug classification and making them over-the-counter medications. In contrast, an adolescent male who requests testosterone or anabolic steroids to enhance his sexuality or athletic performance will have this request denied. The request is considered unethical by the medical profession. Is there a difference in prescribing sex steroids to female adolescents for preventing pregnancy or sex steroids to male adolescents for enhancing muscle mass, strength, libido, and athletic performance? For this author, the deciding difference has been the ability of anabolic steroids to induce overly aggressive and violent behavior in male adolescents who often already have naturally occurring high testosterone levels.

To date, there are no findings to refute the fact that extra doses of testosterone and anabolic steroids induce major psychological changes.

The "Steroid Spiral" and "Steroid Charisma"

The initial description of the mechanisms for anabolic steroid addiction was coined "the steroid spiral" in the mid–1980s.[101] For the overwhelming majority of anabolic steroid users, this spiral is downward in terms of steroid addiction, multiple drug use, deterioration of interpersonal relationships, and trouble with the law. Unfortunately, for a very few users, their addiction to anabolic steroids has led them to fame and fortune on the athletic field, in their acting careers or both. Most Americans are fascinated by these users, even if they are aware that these sports and cinema "heroes" are anabolic steroid addicts. Ironically, most anabolic steroid users feel that the steroid spiral as an uphill ride to the top because their "heroes" made it that way. Their perceptions of this uphill trek may persist even though their anabolic steroid use is causing their own lives to rapidly decline into chaos. This form of the "pied piper" phenomenon has been termed "steroid charisma."[102] This type of denial seen with anabolic steroid use and addiction is similar to many other forms of drug addiction.

The traditional first step along the steroid spiral usually involves a six-week "cycle" of a single anabolic steroid. The user takes the steroids orally on a daily basis at a few times greater than the medically recommended dose. Significant improvement in muscle mass and strength is seen. Body mass gains can range from 20 to 30 pounds. Weight training sessions usually become more intense with regular weekly increases in the maximum weights that can be lifted for a given exercise. The psychological and physiological adverse effects are generally mild and may be reversible. The typical psychological alterations include increased libido, self-esteem, energy level, aggressive behavior, and a decreased need for sleep. However, even at this stage, some first time users experience more dramatic psychological alterations such as manic episodes and increased hostility. After the six-week "cycle" the user intends to remain free of anabolic steroids for about six weeks. The withdrawal symptoms typically include some loss in the muscle mass and strength which was gained while "on" the steroids even when regular gym sessions are adhered to. Other withdrawal symptoms may include depression, loss of energy level, reduced libido, and a desire to quickly return to anabolic steroid use.

The adolescent user who completes a single six-week cycle has an 87 percent likelihood to go on to use anabolic steroids for five cycles or more.[103,104] Some researchers believe that five cycles mark the beginning of heavy steroid use, because once anabolic steroid users go through five cycles it has been shown that they will continue the use for years afterwards. Approximately 65 percent of the single "cycle" steroid users go on to use for eight or more cycles and 35 percent go on to use for four years or more.[105] Eighty-six percent of the heavy users have reported no plans to stop using.[106]

Typically during the second through fifth anabolic steroid cycle, users become more sophisticated. They begin to "stack" and "pyramid" their anabolic steroid use. They use larger dosages (89 percent), increase the number of different steroids per cycle in a "stacking" fashion (72 percent), lengthen their cycles of use (64 percent), and shorten the time between cycles (65 percent). These anabolic steroid doses *greatly* exceed normal therapeutic levels. Users combine an average of five different steroids in one cycle, and 99 percent inject the drugs.[107] They "pyramid" their steroid use by beginning their cycles with moderate doses of anabolic steroids, progressively increasing the doses to some arbitrary point several weeks or months later, and then begin a prolonged tapering period.

Beyond the fifth cycle, addiction to these drugs is often "full-blown." The majority of users will go on to years of anabolic steroid addiction. The previous cycles become blurred and the user may begin to "cycle" on prolonged periods of high-dose use coupled with short periods of low-to-moderate dose use. In this manner, some heavy users never completely come "off" anabolic steroids.[108] Anabolic steroid addiction becomes similar to the classic syndrome seen in persons suffering from chemical dependency.[109] However, in adolescents some socially acceptable values and life-stage concerns with appearance and peer approval motivate anabolic steroid use. For example:

a) Some researchers characterize anabolic steroid use as a unique substance abuse problem. They describe steroid users, in general, as highly motivated people who are trying to improve themselves or to achieve a positive goal. Some of them want to be better athletes or even champions. Others want to look better and believe that they are health conscious and taking care of their bodies.

b) Unlike other drug users, who frequently have negative or no goals, anabolic steroid users do not seek to escape reality or to attain instant gratification. Whether users are athletes or simply obsessed with their appearance, they know they must train intensely to reach their goals. They are willing to make that effort. Many users see steroids as a way to approach their goal faster or to attain an even higher level of performance.
c) For adolescent males, muscularity and strength are two ingredients of their perceived success and enhanced self-esteem. Nearly two-thirds of anabolic steroid users start the drugs to improve appearance. Others report that monetary rewards, such as athletic scholarships, are the motivation to use anabolic steroids.
d) Many users say they were influenced to begin anabolic steroid use by friends or athletes at the gym where they work out. In most cases, the friend was a user who had achieved the results that the would-be user desired. Moreover, non-using peers rarely discourage anabolic steroid use.
e) Anabolic steroids work, producing physical and other effects that some adolescents desire. Besides improved muscle mass, strength, body image, and athletic performance, users list increased sexual drive, prowess, or pleasure as examples of unexpected benefits of anabolic steroid use.
f) Adults can also influence an adolescent to begin and continue anabolic steroid use. These adults include parents, coaches, athletic trainers, successful athletes and entertainment personalities. Some of these adults are role models for the users. They may indirectly encourage adolescent anabolic steroid use by sending mixed messages. At other times the message is clear: using anabolic steroids to enhance performance is acceptable. Our society praises winning, affords athletes special treatment, and overlooks their transgressions. Famous role models greatly influence adolescent users. More than half of the anabolic steroid users indicated "muscle magazines" and entertainment personalities as playing a major role in influencing their use.[110]

It has been a long time since Charles Atlas "muscled up" from a 90-pound weakling and "strutted his stuff" on the beaches. But, even then, the male muscular body image had a certain charisma. The early *Tarzan* movies featured a muscular Olympic swimmer, Johnny Weismuller. Today's version of *Tarzan* resembles a competitive bodybuilder. The major league baseball slugger of 30 years ago has given way to anabolic steroid–using bodybuilders with bats; and anabolic steroid use in professional baseball is on a runaway course. But, perhaps the greatest impact of "steroid charisma" is seen in professional wrestling. Huge, anabolic steroid–using wrestlers entertain millions of American youths as they strut around the ring each week. In the music arena, muscled-up rock and "gangsta rap" groups exhibit anabolic-induced violence in music videos. In the National Basketball Association "muscle mass under the boards" from anabolic steroid–using basketball players has become the rule and not the exception. In professional football, the field is full of "heavy" anabolic steroid addicts.

In the entertainment and marketing world, GI Joe dolls have put on pounds of muscle mass over the past 40 years. Overly muscular cartoon "heroes" and dolls promote the American ideal to preschoolers. "Bulked up" cinema stars portray graphic violence to the American public. Movie themes are simple ones: anabolic steroids, muscle, sex, and violence, over and over again. The typically rebellious rock music industry has taken on an extremely violent tone in part due to the influence of anabolic steroids. Anabolic steroid users are becoming "porn" stars both on the movie screen and over the Internet. Television's "soap stars" are studs on steroids. America appears to be hooked on "steroid charisma" with little hope of ever turning back.

Polypharmacy and the Gateway Phenomenon

The tendency for heavy anabolic steroid users to take other medications was recognized in the mid–1980s. Their motives include recreation, the belief that other drugs further promote the effects of the steroids, and a desire to combat the adverse effects of heavy steroid use.[111–116] In 1986, drugs were seized from a black market anabolic steroid dealer. Along with the anabolic steroids, several other drugs were found. They are listed in Table 8-5.[117]

Table 8-5. Examples of Other Prescription Drugs Seized by Police from a Black Market Anabolic Steroid Dealer

Generic Name	*Trademark*
Human growth hormone	Crescormin
Human chorionic gonadotrophin	Pregnyl
Furosemide	Lasix
Levodopa	Sinemet
Thyroid hormone	Ticana
Tamoxifen	Nolvadex
Tetracycline	Achromycin
Indomethacin	Indocin
Adrenocorticotrophic hormone	H.P. Acthar Gel

Generic Name	*Trademark*
Cyanocobalamin	Injectable vitamin B-12
Norethindrone with ethinyl estradiol	Ortho-Novum 7/7/7
Carisprodol	Soma
Spironolactone with hydrochlorothiazide	Aldactazide

It has been reported that after starting anabolic steroids, nearly 50 percent of the users used other drugs for performance enhancement or for countering the side effects of steroid use. This report also indicated that 31 percent added estrogen receptor inhibitors, 22 percent used HCG, 17 percent added diuretics, 17 percent used "uppers" including amphetamines, 15 percent used pain killers, and 11 percent started recreational drugs other than ethanol, including marijuana and cocaine. This assortment of drugs was usually obtained from the user's anabolic steroid sources.[118]

Many black market anabolic steroid dealers practice medicine without a medical license. It has been common for adolescent anabolic steroid users to seek medical advice from dealers who are usually heavy users themselves. Several handbooks are available to anabolic steroid dealers and users that suggest ways to counter the side effects of steroid use with other drugs. Examples of prescription drugs used to alleviate anabolic steroid–induced side effects include estrogen receptor inhibitors for gynecomastia, diuretics for fluid retention, and human chorionic gonadotrophin (HCG) to stimulate natural testosterone production. These drugs are available on the black market and through the Internet. This type of polydrug use can be very complex, sophisticated, and dangerous and can lead to addiction of other drugs. A recent report indicated that polypharmacy is practiced by over 80 percent of male anabolic steroid users.[119] Another report compared the drug use of anabolic steroid–using college students (58,625 students from 78 institutions) with non-users. The anabolic steroid users reported consuming dramatically more ethanol with higher rates of binge drinking. In addition, a significantly higher percentage of steroid users reported using tobacco, marijuana, cocaine, amphetamines, sedatives, hallucinogens, opiates, inhalants, and designer drugs such as ecstacy and gama-hydroxybutyrate (GHB) than non-users.[120] In a similar report, 12,272 students (grades 9–12) who used anabolic steroids were significantly more likely to use cocaine, amphetamines, heroin, tobacco and ethanol than non-users.[121] Several other studies have reported on the prevalence and severity of the polypharmacy phenomenon of anabolic steroid abuse.[122–127]

One of the reasons Congress placed anabolic steroids under the CSA was due to the gateway effect of these steroids to induce multiple drug use. Since the act was expanded to include testosterone and anabolic steroids, several studies have reported on this polypharmacy phenomenon. This serious effect seen with anabolic steroid use often results in devastating consequences for the user and those around the user.

Summary: Anabolic Steroids Should Be Reclassified as Schedule II Narcotics Under Federal Law

Anabolic steroids used to build the body can have destructive effects on the mind. In this manner, the term *anabolic*, which means "to build," is a misnomer.

The destructive effects of anabolic steroids (when not used for appropriate medical reasons) include:

a) a complex drug addiction;
b) gateway and polypharmacy phenomena;
c) "steroid charisma" effects;
d) psychotoxic and neurotoxic effects which cause mental health problems including "'roid rage," steroid psychosis, violent behavior, sexually violent behavior, withdrawal depression, suicidal behavior, mania, hypomania, and probable chronic brain neurochemistry alterations; and
e) the megorexia condition of distorted body image and narcissism.

It has been a decade since Congress placed testosterone and anabolic steroids under the CSA as Schedule III narcotics. In the few years following this congressional action, adolescent use of these steroids declined sharply and then leveled off. However, recent government sponsored studies have reported that the illegal use of these drugs is on the rise again. The ability to purchase anabolic steroids through the Internet is one factor accounting for the recent increase in adolescent use.

The original House and Senate versions of the Steroid Trafficking Act of 1990 would have designated testosterone and anabolic steroids as Schedule II controlled substances.

> According to the act, this designation was proposed a crackdown on illegal steroid use in four ways:
> (1) it would increase steroid trafficking penalties to match the penalties for selling cocaine and other dangerous drugs;
> (2) it would impose tight record-keeping and production control regulations to prevent the diversion of legally produced steroids into the illicit market;

> (3) it would give the Drug Enforcement Administration the authority and responsibility to investigate violations involving the illegal production, distribution, or possession with intent to distribute steroids; and,
> (4) the bill would require U.S. agencies to incorporate anabolic steroids in all federally supported drug abuse prevention, education, and treatment programs."[128]

In this author's opinion, it is time for Congress to revisit its original versions of the act. Designating testosterone and anabolic steroids as Schedule III narcotics under the CSA has had a definite impact on adolescent steroid use. However, there are major differences in the enforcement policies and penalty assessments between Schedule III and Schedule II narcotics. Providing or selling anabolic steroids to minors should be considered a major criminal action with devastating consequences. The time has come for the American judicial system to get serious about this pervasive problem that afflicts a unique and very productive portion of our society. History has shown that the most important step in controlling anabolic steroid use is by minimizing the availability of the drugs, especially to minors. This author would encourage Congress to take the necessary steps to further restrict this availability by exercising its original intent of reclassification of testosterone and anabolic steroids as Schedule II narcotics under the provisions of the Controlled Substance Act of 1970.

9

The Reclassification of Anabolic Steroids as Controlled Substances

Introduction: From Placebos to Narcotics

The class of drugs that includes testosterone and anabolic steroids was the first to be added to the Controlled Substance Act of 1970 (CSA). President George Bush signed the Steroid Trafficking Act of 1990 into law on November 29, 1990. Although the original draft of the act recommended that testosterone and anabolic steroids be reclassified as Schedule II narcotics, the final version of the act placed these steroids into Schedule III of the CSA.[1]

In order for the reader to gain a better understanding as to why testosterone and anabolic steroids were reclassified as narcotics under federal law, it is imperative that some historical highlights be presented. Increasingly complex relationships exist among the scientific, economic, and political aspects of drugs or medicines made available to the American public. These relationships have undergone considerable evolution during the past century.

Today's federal drug laws will likely change and become tighter in the future. Various factors played a major role in the federal drug laws that were passed over the last decades. With the reclassification of testosterone and anabolic steroids, there were major factors playing participating roles. Therefore, a historical perspective on these factors will be presented in this chapter.

The reclassification of testosterone and anabolic steroids into the CSA was unique in several ways. First, these steroids had been labeled with some very extravagant claims as well as denials. In the 1940s, testosterone was called "sexual TNT" and "medical dynamite."[2] Prominent sports medicine physicians in the 1970s called anabolic steroids "fool's gold" and "placebos" for athletes.[3] In the 1980s, the United States Food and Drug Administration (FDA) stated in the *Physicians' Desk Reference* (PDR) that "anabolic steroids do not enhance athletic potential." Second, powerful groups and organizations lobbied *against* the incorporation of these steroids into the CSA. Some of these groups included the American Medical Association (AMA),[4] the Drug Enforcement Agency (DEA), the FDA, various sports organizations,[5] and sports medicine groups.[6] Third, other drug laws passed by the United States Congress actually contributed to the widespread availability of anabolic steroids on the black market. The generic drug laws passed by Congress in the early 1980s allowed the generic pharmaceutical industry to mass produce and divert these steroids to the athletic black market, fueling the burgeoning anabolic steroid epidemic.[7] Fourth, major sports medicine organizations had to reverse their official position statements regarding the performance-enhancing effects of these steroids. In 1976, the American College of Sports Medicine (ACSM) issued an official position statement that anabolic steroids *did not* enhance athletic performance.[8] Then, in 1984, the ACSM reversed and revised its official statement to claim that anabolic steroids could enhance athletic performance.[9] Critical reevaluations of the scientific literature support the ACSM's revised position statement.[10–12]

To understand how testosterone and anabolic steroids qualified for controlled substances under federal law it is important to have a basic understanding of major federal laws that have been passed over the decades. After these earlier laws are discussed, several sections that led up to the Congressional hearings regarding anabolic steroids will be presented. Finally, a section that deals with the impact of adding anabolic steroids to the CSA and a summary recommending the enforcement of the law will conclude this chapter.

Early Federal Regulation of Narcotic Drugs

Drugs that are attainable and alter aspects of behavior and body image are likely to be abused by segments of the American public. History tells us that the federal government has spent a significant amount of time debating and passing laws to prevent the use of a variety of such drugs. Laws have been passed which criminalized the possession, use, inappropriate prescription of and distribution of several drugs. There is little doubt that such laws have to some extent curtailed drug use. However, drug abuse in America remains a major concern today.

Drugs that are likely to be abused are those producing desired effects. A person who abuses a certain class of drugs may or may not abuse another class of drugs. For example, there are few if any heroin addicts who use anabolic steroids to enhance their athletic performance. But there may be some heroin addicts who abuse testosterone and anabolic steroids for their libido-enhancing effects. Similarly, few bodybuilders who abuse anabolic steroids become heroin addicts. While they may experiment with heroin at a party they are more likely to abuse ethanol, cocaine, painkillers, and amphetamines.

Drugs of abuse and addiction tend to have specific effects on their users. A list of drugs and their characteristics that may become addictive are contained in Table 9-1.

Table 9-1. Characteristics of Drugs with Abuse Potential

Desired Effects	*Example Drugs*
Heightened libido, enhanced sexual performance or reduced sexual inhibitions	testosterone, anabolic steroids, Viagra, nitrates, human chorionic gonadotrophin, cocaine, ecstasy, marijuana, peyote, heroin, morphine, amphetamines, ephedrine, hypnotics, tranquilizers, anxiolytics, seratonin reuptake inhibitors, ethanol, gama-hydroxy buterate (GHB), opioid pain killers, Dilaudid, Lortab barbiturates, nutritional supplements, ginseng, oral contraceptives
Altered body image, weight reduction, or increase energy	testosterone, anabolic steroids, amphetamines, cocaine, ephedrine, phenylpropanolamine, nicotine, caffeine, serotonin reuptake inhibitors, human growth hormone, growth factors, diuretics, emetics, nutritional supplements, ginseng
Altered mental status	testosterone, anabolic steroids, marijuana, peyote, heroin, cocaine, ecstasy, barbiturates, anxiolytics, hypnotics, nicotine, caffeine, amphetamines, ephedrine, opioid pain killers, morphine, Lortab, serotonin reuptake inhibitors,

Altered mental status *(cont.)*	ethanol, GHB, mushroom hallucinogens, Lysergic acid (LSD), PCP
Enhanced athletic performance	testosterone, anabolic steroids, human growth hormone, erythropoietin, growth hormone releasing hormone, insulin-like growth factor-1, creatine, nutritional supplements, beta-blockers, amphetamines, ephedrine, cocaine, nicotine, caffeine, xanthines, dimethyl sulfoxide (DMSO), GHB, GH-stimulators, clonidine, insulin, glucagon, tamoxifen, opioid pain killers, corticosteroids, non-steroidal anti-inflammatory drugs
Enhanced longevity	testosterone, anabolic steroids, human chorionic gonadotrophin, estrogen, human growth hormone, growth hormone releasing hormone, insulin-like growth factor-1, growth hormone releasers, high-dose vitamins, nutritional supplements.

American legislators have passed laws to regulate narcotic suppliers and prosecute those who sell or illegally or inappropriately provide addictive drugs to others. Therefore, a brief history of the legislative attempts to control narcotic drug abuse in America seems appropriate.

Drug addiction became a major problem in the United States shortly after the Civil War. There were three major contributing factors that led to widespread narcotic addiction in the late 1800s:

a) the invention of the hypodermic syringe in 1856;
b) the importation of Chinese railroad workers who introduced the habit of smoking opium which spread rapidly; and,
c) the widespread legal distribution of patent narcotic medications dispensed by traveling peddlers or by local stores as over the counter medications.

By the end of the 19th century, it was estimated that one person out of every 500 was addicted to some form of opium. Abuse of the elixir combination of opium and ethanol called paregoric (a Greek word which means "soothing") was the narcotic of choice for many Americans. To control the abuse of opium-containing elixirs, Congress passed the Opium Exclusion Act of 1909 that prohibited the importing of opium or its derivatives except for medical purposes. Despite this law, it was estimated that by 1914 one in every 400 Americans was addicted to some form of opium.[13]

The 1914 Harrison Act was passed by Congress in an attempt to make it illegal for narcotic addicts to obtain their opium. For the first time, federal law mandated dealers and dispensers of narcotics to register annually with the Treasury Department's Bureau of Internal Revenue. If registered, physicians, dentists, and veterinary surgeons were named as potential legal distributors for narcotics. The Harrison Act was the narcotics control law in the United States until the 1970 Federal Controlled Substance Act was enacted in May 1971. Soon, violators of the Harrison Act begin to fill the prisons. By the late 1920s narcotic offenders made up about one-third of the prison population.[14] Opium, cocaine, marijuana, and peyote were the major narcotics used by abusers.

In 1930 Congress passed several bills culminating in the formation of a separate Bureau of Narcotics within the Treasury Department. This bureau continued in operation until April 1968, when it was transferred to the Department of Justice and renamed as the Bureau of Narcotics and Dangerous Drugs.

Following World War II the illegal narcotics trade increased dramatically. In 1951 Congress passed the Boggs Amendment to the Harrison Act. This amendment established minimum mandatory sentences for all narcotic offenses. In 1956, a subcommittee of the Senate Judiciary Committee published a document stating that drug addiction was responsible for 50 percent of crime in urban areas and 25 percent of all reported crimes.[15] In response to this report, Congress passed the 1956 Narcotic Drug Control Act that raised the mandatory minimum sentence for violations of the Harrison Act.

In the late 1950s, the abuse of prescription narcotics obtained from physicians increased. In 1960 Congress passed the Narcotics Manufacturing Act in an attempt to monitor the volume of legal narcotics that were prescribed for medical needs. This act licensed all medical narcotic drug manufacturers and made it illegal to manufacture narcotic drugs unless the company was registered. It also allowed for annual quotas to be established for the manufacturing and purchase of narcotic drugs.[16]

During the 1960s the types of narcotics that were abused expanded. Abuse of heroin, amphetamines, barbiturates, marijuana, peyote, cocaine, lysergic acid (LSD), and hallucinogens contained within mushrooms became popular. The abuse of combinations of different types of narcotics was common among heavy narcotic abusers who wished to alter mood or consciousness. Also at this time, a small number of bodybuilders began to experiment with testosterone and anabolic steroids to alter body image. The use of the anabolic steroid Dianabol was becoming popular in Southern California gyms. Bodybuilders wore T-shirts with a logo that read *Dianabol, the Breakfast of Champions.*[17]

In response to the need for improved controls over the manufacturing and distribution of both legal and illegal narcotics, in 1965, Congress passed the Drug Abuse Control Amendments. In 1966, the United States Food and Drug Administration (FDA) developed criteria to determine whether a particular narcotic caused hallucinations, illusions, delusions, or other alterations in personality. The criteria were:

a) orientation with respect to time or place;
b) consciousness, as evidenced by confused states, dreamlike revivals of past traumatic events, or childhood memories;
c) sensory perception, as evidenced by visual illusions, synesthesia, or distortion of space and perspective;
d) motor coordination;
e) mood and affectivity, as experienced by anxiety, euphoria, hypomania, ecstasy, or autistic withdrawal;
f) ideation, as evidenced by flight of ideas, ideas of reference, or impairment of concentration and intelligence; and,
g) personality, as evidenced by depersonalization and derealization or impairment of conscience and of acquired social and cultural customs.[18]

In the late 1960s, prescription use and illegal diversion of amphetamines and barbiturates accelerated despite federal laws. For example, it was reported that eight billion doses of amphetamines were manufactured in the United States annually and that nearly half of these were diverted into illegal distribution markets.[19] In order to gain a tighter control on both legal and illegal narcotic use, Congress passed the Comprehensive Drug Abuse Prevention and Control Act of 1970. This act was renamed the Controlled Substance Act of 1970 and signed into law by President Richard M. Nixon.

The Federal Controlled Substance Act of 1970

This comprehensive federal law dealing with all types of narcotic drugs became effective in May 1971 and continues in effect today. The Federal Controlled Substance Act (CSA) mandated federal enforcement and prosecution for any illegal activity involving controlled drugs.

Under the CSA, enforcement authority was transferred to the Department of Justice (DOJ) from the Treasury Department. This change shifted the emphasis of narcotic control from an excise tax to a powerful direct control the by DOJ. The attorney general became responsible for the administration of the control aspects of the law, and the secretary of Health and Human Services (HHS) was responsible for the final decisions on which drugs were controlled under the provisions of the CSA. The secretary of HHS soon delegated this latter responsibility to the FDA. Before placing a drug into the controlled substance category, the FDA requires the following:

1. Scientific evidence of its pharmacological effect, if known.
2. The status of the scientific knowledge regarding the drug or substance.
3. Potential risks the drug may have on public health.
4. Potential risks for the drug's psychic or physiological dependence liability.
5. Whether the substance was an immediate precursor of a substance previously placed into control under this law.

Five categories defined by the CSA ranked the scheduling of a drug or class of drugs based on its abuse potential and known medical applications. The CSA also outlined penalties for the illegal manufacturing and distribution for each of five categories (Table 9-2). Note that general prescription drugs, such as antibiotics, non-steroidal anti-inflammatory drugs, or corticosteroids are not scheduled under the CSA. Most general prescription drugs do not possess major psychoactive properties or significant abuse potential as outlined by the FDA's criteria listed above.

Some special control provisions mandated by the CSA include the following:

1. No prescription for a Schedule II drug can be filled or refilled over the telephone. Each time the drug is dispensed it requires a new written prescription. In emergency situations only, can a Schedule II drug be dispensed with an oral prescription.
2. Prescriptions for Schedules III, IV, or V cannot be refilled more than six months after the original prescription has been written.
3. The label of a drug in Schedule II, III, or IV must contain this warning: "Caution: Federal law prohibits the transfer of this drug to any person other than the patient for whom it was prescribed."
4. Manufacturing quotas were placed on the drugs classified in Schedules I and II.

TABLE 9-2. SUMMARY OF DRUG SCHEDULES AND PENALTIES FOR VIOLATION OF THE FEDERAL CONTROLLED SUBSTANCE ACT OF 1970

Schedule	*Abuse Potential*	*Medical Uses*	*Examples*	*Maximum Penalties for Illegal Manufacturing or Distribution**
I	very high	none	heroin, LSD, peyote, marijuana, mescaline, hallucinogens, PCP, GHB****	1st offense 15yr/$25,000/3yr**
II	high	yes	morphine, methadone, Ritalin, cocaine, methaqualone, meperidine	1st offense 15yr/$25,000/3yr
III	high-to-moderate	yes	amphetamines, paregoric, codeine, anabolic steroids***	1st offense 5yr/$15,000/2yr
IV	moderate	yes	anxiolytics, chloral hydrate, phenobarbital, anorexics	1st offense 3yr/$10,000/1yr
V	low	yes	dilute narcotic mixtures, dilute opium mixtures	1st offense 1yr/$5,000/none

*Maximum penalties may also include confiscation of property, and the offender may be subject to taxes due to the Internal Revenue Service.
**Maximum prison sentence/maximum fine/mandatory probation after prison release.
***Anabolic steroids were added to Schedule III by the Steroid Trafficking Act of 1990.
****Gama-hydroxybuterate (GHB) was added to Schedule I in February 2000.

One purpose of the CSA was to control the manufacturing and distribution of controlled substances. Violators of its provisions are punished more harshly than those who possess the drugs. Other provisions required monitoring of the prescribing and dispensing of controlled substances by physicians and pharmacists. It required annual or periodic registration with the Drug Enforcement Agency (DEA) of everyone who manufactured, distributed, or dispensed any controlled substances. Scientists involved with research on controlled substances had to also register with the DEA. All registrants are required to keep records of controlled substances. These records are to be made available for DEA inspection.

It is safe to say that since its passage, the CSA has drastically reduced the volume of controlled substances diverted to the black market. At the same time, the CSA has preserved the use of controlled substances for appropriate medical applications. The provisions of the CSA have dramatically reduced the abuse of amphetamines, anxiolytics, and anabolic steroids. This has been especially true when the controlled substances are manufactured by the pharmaceutical industry within the United States.

The CSA has not been as effective in curbing the abuse of drugs made outside of the U.S. pharmaceutical industry. Some of these drugs include heroin, crack cocaine, cocaine, marijuana, and hallucinogenic mushroom extracts obtained from illegally grown plants. Other narcotic drugs such as methamphetamines, ecstasy, gama-hyroxybuterate (GHB), and phencyclidine (PCP) can be readily synthesized in "garage labs." The main impact of the CSA on these drugs is in the investigation and prosecution processes.

It has been shown that abuse of controlled substances can be diminished through educational efforts, law enforcement, judicial efforts, treatment programs, and efforts to restrict the drug supply. As efforts to place anabolic steroids and testosterone under the CSA are examined, it will be important to remember that until recently the effects of these drugs were either underestimated or denied.

The 1975 British Association of Sport and Medicine Meeting

During the period from the mid–1960s to the mid–1970s about 20 scientific studies were published on the potential ability of anabolic steroids to enhance muscle mass, strength, and athletic performance. Half of the studies did not definitively show short-term use of anabolic steroids enhanced muscle mass and strength. However, the other studies showed significant increases in muscle mass and strength.

In February 1975 the British Association of Sport and Medicine (BASM) held a symposium on the topic "Anabolic Steroids in Sport." Sports delegates from Belgium, Denmark, France, Germany, Hungary, Italy, the Netherlands, Romania, Spain, Sweden, the United States, the Soviet Union, and Yugoslavia attended. World-renowned researchers spoke on the subject of anabolic steroid use by athletes. Topics were divided into the following categories: metabolic effects of anabolic steroids, practical experience of anabolic steroid users, detection methods for anabolic steroids, and methods for enforcement of the BASM's forthcoming position statement on anabolic steroids. As a result of this symposium the following conclusions were made:

a) anabolic steroid use was confined to a few "heavy event" athletes;
b) little was known about the beneficial effects of anabolic steroid use by athletes;
c) little was known about the adverse effects of anabolic steroid use by athletes;
d) no current drug testing methods could detect anabolic steroid use; and,
e) there were no mechanisms for enforcement of anabolic steroid regulations.

The BASM's official policy, published after this meeting, held steadfast to its previous policy stating:

1. The only effective and safe way of ensuring optimum athletic performance in any activity is a proper program of training and preparation.
2. No known chemical agent is capable of producing both safely and effectively an improvement in performance in a healthy human subject.
3. It is unethical to experimentally provide moderate to large doses of these steroids to athletes and observe the results.
4. Education is the major tool to prevent anabolic steroid abuse.

In effect, the conclusions of the BASM gave athletes a green light for anabolic steroid use. Their "education" was to acknowledge there were no detection tests and no enforcement measures to prevent the use of anabolic steroids. How can education be an important tool when the BASM conceded that little was known about the benefits or dangers of anabolic steroid use?

In the past, both physicians and sports organizations throughout the world stated that anabolic steroids *did not* enhance performance. But athletes knew differently, and the credibility of sports medicine physicians, scientists, and officials was damaged.

The 1976 American College of Sports Medicine Meeting

The BASM officials were not the only ones promoting the non-effectiveness of anabolic steroids in athletes. During this time, Allan J. Ryan, M.D., a former president of the American College of Sports Medicine (ACSM), stated that anabolic steroids were simply "fool's gold" and a "myth" for enhancing athletic performance.[20] Another sports medicine physician, Dan Hanley, also felt that anabolic steroids were only "placebos." Dr. Hanley was on the executive committee of the United States Olympic Committee (USOC) and a highly ranked medical official for the National Collegiate Athletic Association (NCAA). These two physicians headed the group of those believing that anabolic steroids did not enhance athletic performance.

In 1976, the ACSM at its annual meeting held a symposium on the subject of anabolic steroids in sports. Several experts and medical scientists gave presentations and participated in a lengthy roundtable meeting following the scientific session. The symposium was polarized and two basic groups emerged. The groups were:

1. Physicians and exercise physiologists who believed the scientific literature was not conclusive and supported the stance that anabolic steroids were mere "placebos." Dr. Ryan and Dr. Hanley led this group.
2. Physicians and exercise physiologists whose believed the scientific literature showed anabolic steroids could enhance athletic performance. Leaders of this group were: Dr. Levon C. Johnson (steroid researcher at the University of Oregon), Dr. James E. Wright (steroid researcher at the United States Army Research Institute of Environmental Medicine), and Dr. Arthur Jones (founder of Nautilus Equipment).

Dr. Johnson presented a paper that showed anabolic steroids enhanced strength in weight lifters.[21] After this presentation, Dr. Hanley accused Dr. Johnson of promoting anabolic steroid use in athletes. During the meeting, Dr. Arthur Jones was expelled by the ACSM for supporting the results of Dr. Johnson's research. (As a result of his expulsion, Dr. Jones threatened to take a hundred athletes to South America, and design the definitive study to prove that anabolic steroids enhance athletic performance.) Dr. Wright reported on information he had learned from working with athletes. (This information was later published in a 1978 book.)[22] He stated:

> Information gathered at the 1972 Olympic games indicated that 68% of a large number of athletes interviewed (from: USA, USSR, Egypt, Morocco, Canada, New Zealand, and Great Britain, and who were involved in such diverse activities as throwing, jumping, vaulting, sprinting, and middle distance running to 3000 meters) has used anabolic steroids.
>
> As of 1976, based on personal observations and interviews with numerous athletes in strength related sports, I [Dr. Wright] would estimate that over 90% use steroids on a regular basis.... Why then, since the athletes using the drugs (anabolic steroids) are so overwhelmingly convinced of the efficacy, do the majority of physicians and officials of sports governing bodies insist that steroids are worthless and have no effect on performance?[23]

After the 1976 symposium on the use of anabolic steroids in sports, the ACSM published its official position statement. Their statement was authored by Dr. David Lamb, a former president of the ACSM. Excerpts from this position paper echoed those made a year earlier by the BASM:

> There is no conclusive evidence that extremely large doses of anabolic-androgenic steroids either aid or hinder athletic performance.... Serious and continuing effort should be made to educate male and female athletes, coaches, physical educators, physicians, trainers, and the general public regarding the inconsistent effects of anabolic-androgenic steroids on improvement of human performance and the potential dangers.... Administration of anabolic-androgenic steroids to healthy humans below age 50 in medically

> approved therapeutic doses often does not of itself bring about any significant improvements in strength, aerobic endurance, lean body mass, or body weight.[24]

It seemed that the ACSM believed that anabolic steroids were placebos, and that there were potential side effects caused by using them; however, they were not knowledgeable about the side effects. Furthermore, by making it unethical to study the effects caused by the amounts taken by athletes there would be no answers. Perhaps they thought the anabolic steroid problem would just go away!

The official position statements of the BASM and ACSM regarding the effects of anabolic steroids strongly influenced many people. The statements were incorporated into books used by medical students, physicians, physical educators, athletic trainers, nurses, and exercise physiologists. Their statements also influenced the FDA to publish an italicized warning for testosterone and anabolic steroids in the *Physicians' Desk Reference: "Warning: Anabolic steroids do not enhance athletic ability."*

Building Blocks for the Anabolic Steroid Epidemic

The first major building block accelerating anabolic steroid use in the United States was the position statements and beliefs of the BASM and ACSM. A growing number of athletes and bodybuilders used testosterone and anabolic steroids and knew first hand that these statements were not true. Some coaches and trainers who had used anabolic steroids during their athletic career began promoting anabolic steroid use to their athletes. As a result of their anabolic steroid–enhanced athletic performance, college scholarships were given to thousands of anabolic steroid users. The public believed that all of these huge college and professional athletes were "bulking up" with weight training alone. Physicians, who had been taught that anabolic steroids were placebos, discounted claims that anabolic steroids had muscle-building effects.

The second basic building block in the anabolic steroid epidemic was brought about by the official policies that discouraged further medical research. The lack of funding for studies to address the impact of moderate to large doses of anabolic steroids had a devastating impact. An unprecedented void in the scientific literature persisted for nearly a decade. With little or no research addressing the adverse effects of anabolic steroid use, educational efforts failed.

The third major building block in the anabolic steroid epidemic was the formation and rapid expansion of new industries: the health club, bodybuilding gyms, and professional wrestling organizations. Suddenly, health and weight lifting clubs opened up all over the U.S. In the early 1980s, owners and customers sold anabolic steroids in health clubs (Table 9-3).[25,26] As the fitness craze expanded, so did the number of health clubs. Numerous bodybuilding magazines were found on magazine racks throughout the United States. The new anabolic steroid and weight lifting "macho image" exploded.

Table 9-3. Poll of 100 Strength Athletes in Florida—Sources of Anabolic Steroids

Source of Anabolic Steroids	*Percentage of Athletes*
health club owners	38
fellow athletes	20
licensed medical physicians	15
drug company representatives	7
pharmacists	6
nurses	5
coaches/trainers	4
direct drug company orders	2
health food stores	1
bodybuilding magazine ads	1
forged or altered prescriptions	1

The fourth major building block in the anabolic steroid epidemic was the enactment of the generic drug laws passed by Congress in the early 1980s. Until then, pharmaceutical companies could indefinitely retain patent protection for any drug they initially developed and marketed. The generic drug law contributed to the anabolic steroid epidemic by allowing generic pharmaceutical companies to mass-produce and sell anabolic steroids at much cheaper prices, after the patent had expired. Since most of the anabolic steroids were commercially available by 1962, they all qualified as candidates under the generic drug law 17 years later. Within a year of the patent expiration, dozens of pharmaceutical companies synthesized generic copies of the more than 20 name brand anabolic steroids. Millions of bottles of pills and injectable vials of the generic anabolic steroids were illegally diverted with only a small percentage of this huge increase in production going for approved medical uses. Generic companies offered extensive catalogs of drugs that they had for sale and included their generic anabolic steroids. Some of these catalogs fell into the hands of black market steroid dealers. Extensive networking between health clubs and dealers provided a steady supply for the increasing demand from club members. Although it is illegal to sell prescription drugs, the federal law did little in the way of enforcement. Record keeping of the manufacturing and selling of generic anabolic steroids was not required. In short, the generic drug law fueled the anabolic steroid epidemic by allowing for a dramatic increase in the production and thus availability of these drugs.

The fifth building block in the anabolic steroid epidemic was the popularity associated with having a muscular body, enhanced athletic performance, and enhanced sexual performance. This "macho" image quickly spread, fueled by athletes, movie stars, professional wrestlers, and bodybuilders, all of whom exhibited "bulked up" bodies. This "steroid charisma" filtered down to high school and middle school students. Students signed up for weight training classes. And all used anabolic steroids without medical supervision, for the physicians had lost credibility with these steroid-using athletes.[27]

A Critical Reevaluation of the Anabolic Steroid Literature

One of the first steps needed for the medical profession and sports organizations to regain their lost credibility with the anabolic steroid issue began with a critical reevaluation of the scientific literature. In 1982, available literature was reviewed and studies were divided into two groups, studies performed on weight-trained subjects versus untrained subjects. The results of these two study groups were diametrically opposed.[28] As shown in Table 9-4, studies performed on untrained subjects were not able to differentiate

TABLE 9-4. SUMMARY OF ANABOLIC STEROID STUDIES USING UNTRAINED MALE SUBJECTS

Reference	*Drug & Dose*	*Blind Study*	*Cross-Over Study*	*Placebo Control*	*Statistical Increased Mass or Strength*
Fowler[29] (1965)	Nibal 20 mg/day (16 weeks)	yes	no	yes	no
Johnson[30] (1968)	Dianabol 10 mg/day (6 weeks)	yes	no	no	no
Casner[31] (1971)	Winstrol 6 mg/day (42 days)	yes	no	yes	no
Johnson[32] (1972)	Dianabol 10 mg/day (7 weeks)	yes	no	yes	yes
Fahey[33] (1973)	Deca-Durabolin 1 mg/day (4 injections/9 weeks)	yes	no	yes	no

Reference	*Drug & Dose*	*Blind Study*	*Cross-Over Study*	*Placebo Control*	*Statistical Increased Mass or Strength*
Win-May[34] (1975)	Dianabol 5 mg/day (3 months)	yes	yes	yes	no
Hervey[35] (1976)	Dianabol 100 mg/day (6 weeks)	yes	yes	yes	no

between muscle mass and strength gains achieved by *learning* to lift weights from the muscle mass and strength gains attributable to anabolic steroid use. In contrast, in weight-trained subjects, addition of anabolic steroids showed a statistically significant increase in muscle mass and strength. These studies, listed in Table 9-5, showed that anabolic steroids enhanced muscle mass and strength over and above the effects of weight training alone.[36]

TABLE 9-5. SUMMARY OF ANABOLIC STEROID STUDIES USING TRAINED MALE SUBJECTS

Reference	*Drug & Dose*	*Double-Blind Study*	*Cross-Over Study*	*Placebo Control*	*Statistical Increased Mass or Strength*
O'Shea[37] (1970)	Anavar 10 mg/day (6 weeks)	no	no	no	yes
O'Shea[38] (1971)	Dianabol 10 mg/day (4 weeks)	no	no	no	yes
Bowers[39] (1972)	Dianabol 10 mg/day (5 weeks)	yes	no	yes	yes
Ariel[40] (1973)	Dianabol 10 mg/day (8 weeks)	yes	no	yes	no
Ward[41] (1973)	Dianabol 10 mg/day (4 weeks)	yes	no	yes	yes
Golding[42] (1974)	Dianabol 10 mg/day (12 weeks)	yes	no	yes	no
Stanford[43] (1974)	Dianabol 20 mg/day (4 weeks)	yes	no	yes	yes
O'Shea[44] (1974)	Winstrol 8 mg/day (4 weeks)	yes	no	yes	yes
Freed[45] (1975)	Dianabol 10 mg/day	yes	yes	yes	yes
	Dianabol 25 mg/day (6 weeks)	yes	yes	yes	yes

In 1984, Haupt and Rovere reviewed the anabolic steroid literature using a statistical-analysis method and reported results similar to those found by this author.[46] The literature showed that anabolic steroid use, in low doses for short periods of time, did indeed enhance muscle mass, strength, and athletic performance. But these studies did little to show the true extent of anabolic steroid use in athletes. Athletes tended to take much larger doses of anabolic steroids and for longer periods of time than subjects in the research studies. They tend to "stack" anabolic steroids, using two or more together, which raises the total steroid burden on the body. There were also few or no published reports on the potential adverse effects of high-dose, prolonged, multiple anabolic steroid use.

These critical reevaluations provided information needed for the ACSM to reconsider their position statement at their 1984 annual meeting.

The 1984 American College of Sports Medicine Meeting

The ACSM's annual meeting in 1984 was held in San Diego, California on May 23–26. On Thursday May 24, 1984, a symposium entitled "Drug Use in Sports" was held. Chairpersons for this daylong symposium were John A. Lombardo, M.D., director of sports medicine at the Cleveland Clinic, and Barbara L. Drinkwater, Ph.D., of the University of Washington. This focus of this symposium was anabolic steroid use by athletes. Professionals considered to be anabolic steroid experts gave presentations. A list of presenters and the title of their presentations are shown in Table 9-6.

TABLE 9-6. "DRUG USE IN SPORTS" SYMPOSIUM AT THE 1984 ACSM'S ANNUAL MEETING

Speaker	*Presentation Title*
John A. Lombardo, M.D.	Introduction
Barbara L. Drinkwater, Ph.D.	Introduction
James E. Wright, Ph.D.	"Biological Actions and Potential Uses for Anabolic Steroids"
G. R. Hervey, Ph.D.	"Effects of Anabolic Steroids on Performance and Composition on Men in Athletic Training"
Thomas Fahey, M.D.	"Side Effects and Adverse Reactions of Anabolic Steroids"
Mona M. Shangold, M.D.	"Physiological Consequences of Anabolic Steroids Specific to Women"
William N. Taylor, Jr., M.D.	"Actions and Effects of Growth Hormones"
Laura van Harn	"The Athletes' World"
Richard H. Strauss, M.D.	"Detecting Drug Use in Athletes"
Daniel Hanley, M.D.	"Ethical Implications of Drug Use by Athletes"
Jane Fredricks	"The Female Athletes' Viewpoint"

Speaker	*Presentation Title*
Paul Ward, Ph.D.	"The Male Athletes' Viewpoint"
Richard L. Brown	"The Coaches' Dilemma"
John A. Lombardo, M.D.	"The Clinician's Approach to Athletes on Anabolic Steroids"

After the symposium a post-symposium roundtable meeting was held. Participants included Brown, Taylor, Lombardo, and van Harn. Also in attendance was Robert O. Voy, M.D., director of sports medicine and chief medical officer of the USOC. Following these meetings, the ACSM revised its official position statement to read: "The use of anabolic steroids in combination with weight training and proper diet may result in enhanced athletic performance."[47] This revision offered the chance for sport medicine physicians, athletic trainers, coaches, and sports organizations to regain credibility lost due to their support of the ACSM's previous position statement.

The 1984 National Strength and Conditioning Association Meeting

A month after the 1984 ACSM meeting, the National Strength and Conditioning Association (NSCA) held its symposium on anabolic steroid use in sports. The meeting was held in Pittsburgh, Philadelphia, on June 27, 1984. Six presentations were given followed by a lengthy question and answer session. The presenters included John A. Lombardo, M.D., Mike Stone, Ph.D., Jeff Everson, Bob Goldman, Fred Hatfield, Ph.D., and William N. Taylor, Jr., M.D. Shortly after the 1984 meeting, the NSCA revised its official policy statement to one similar to the revised ACSM's position statement. Like the ACSM, the NSCA agreed that the use of anabolic steroids in combination with weight training and proper diet can result in enhanced athletic performance. This revision also offered the chance for coaches and athletic trainers to regain credibility with athletes.

The 1986 Resolution of the American Medical Association

Following the revisions of the ACSM's and NCSA's official position statements on anabolic steroids and athletic performance the American Medical Association (AMA) held meetings to address this issue. Meetings were held in Chicago in June 1986 to discuss the abuse of anabolic steroids and synthetic growth hormone. This author, sponsored as a medical expert by an AMA Delegate from Missouri, submitted a resolution bill to the AMA. This bill proposed legislation to have anabolic steroids and human growth hormone reclassified as controlled substances. My testimony, along with my book *Hormonal Manipulation: A New Era of Monstrous Athletes* were submitted for inclusion into the record.

Six months after these meetings (December 1986), the AMA published a report of the Council on Scientific Affairs (see Appendix C for the full report). In this report, the AMA failed to support the reclassification proposals and stated that

> Anabolic steroids have been used by athletes for more than two decades in the belief that they increase body mass, muscle tissue, and strength.... Although studies of these agents have not shown uniformly increased muscular strength, certain benefits to athletic performance seem probable.... In a continuing program of intensive exercise coupled with a high protein diet (and anabolic steroids), increased muscular strength may be realized in some individuals.... It should be noted that small, difficult-to-measure increments in muscular performance or psychological benefit may constitute the difference between winning and losing, particularly at a professional or world-class level. Therefore, these changes may be perceived to be critical to an athlete.[48]

So, instead of adopting the proposal to incorporate anabolic steroids into the CSA, the AMA's recommendations to cope with the burgeoning anabolic steroid epidemic focused on other regulatory and educational actions. These recommendations included:

1. Regulatory action: The AMA should continue to endorse current activities of the FDA, FBI, and DOJ directed toward curbing illegal distribution of these drugs. If these efforts are ineffective, the AMA should undertake a study of alternate methods of monitoring and limiting distribution.
2. Educational action: The AMA should endorse educational activities at various levels including sports group administrators, coaches, parents, and athletes. Activities suggested for consideration are:
   a) Preparation and distribution of educational pamphlets on drug abuse in athletes emphasizing the adverse effects and limited benefits of such use;
   b) Development of a nationwide network of physicians who would be available to give presentations on this topic to interested community groups;
   c) Preparation of videotape(s) on drug abuse in athletes for distribution and use by schools, sports programs, parent groups, and community organizations; and,
   d) Judicious use of the news media; editorials and articles in AMA publications to publicize the AMA's interest in and availability to work on this problem.

The followthrough on the educational actions proposed by the AMA was minimal. There is little evidence that the AMA sponsored the preparation and distribution of educational pamphlets. As far as the educational programs are concerned, the AMA neglected the most important aspect of education: reeducating the nation's physicians. (After all, the majority of the nation's physicians were taught that anabolic steroids were mere "placebos" or "fool's gold" for athletes.) Medical knowledge regarding some of the newly discovered adverse effects of these drugs had not been widely disseminated. There is also no evidence that the AMA sponsored any nationwide speakers' bureau on the topic or prepared and distributed any videotapes on anabolic steroid abuse.

The AMA did allow a few editorial articles to be published in its magazine, *JAMA*. One particular article was published in 1987 with the title: "Classifying steroids as controlled substances suggested to decrease athletic supply, but enforcement could be a major problem." While this article seemed to consider that classifying anabolic steroids as controlled substances may decrease the availability to athletes (the article even cited this author), it also seemed to serve as an effort to support the AMA's earlier resolutions opposing the reclassification of anabolic steroids into the CSA.[49] As for the regulatory actions recommended by the AMA, according to its own report they were failing.

As long as anabolic steroids remained in the general prescription category instead of regulated by the CSA, illegal diversion of these steroids would continue to increase. In this author's opinion, the AMA, by not adopting the proposal to have anabolic steroids reclassified as narcotics, lost an opportunity not only to support the preventive side of medicine, but did little to stop the illegal use of these drugs.

Personal Efforts to Push for Controlled Substance Status

From 1984 through 1990 this author made a concentrated effort to push for the reclassification of anabolic steroids as controlled substances. This effort included:

a) publication of scientific articles and books providing information supporting the rationale for anabolic steroids to be included in the CSA;
b) giving over 1,000 continuing medical education lectures regarding the anabolic steroid epidemic and the need to include anabolic steroids in the CSA. The majority of these lectures were sponsored by Pfizer Pharmaceutical Company;
c) serving as a physician crew chief for the USOC's Drug Control and Education Program from 1984 to 1988;
d) serving as an advisor and appearing in several educational videotapes regarding anabolic steroids and high school students. They were funded by both private and governmental agencies;

e) providing expert witness testimony for the FDA in steroid trafficking cases;
f) preparing and providing a proposed legislative packet of information intended to help physicians influence the legislative process in their states;
g) providing oral and written expert witness testimony to Congress addressing the issue of adding anabolic steroids and human growth hormone to the CSA.

In 1987, the debate over adding anabolic steroids to the CSA began to intensify. An informal sampling of 50 physicians attending the February ACSM's Clinical Conference showed that about three-quarters supported the idea.[50] For instance, John Lombardo, M.D., argued that the controlled substance status would pay off: "If steroids were controlled the onus would be on the producer. When large amounts of legitimately produced drugs are found in an illegal distributor's basement during a dealer drug arrest, then you know that it is too easy to divert these drugs. Producing them should carry some responsibility."[51]

Critics of a status change argued that the federal government could handle the problem through existing agencies and laws. However, in 1987 the anabolic steroid problem was just beginning to be discussed at a federal level.[52] Some federal drug officials did not feel that anabolic steroids met the criteria for reclassification. Tom Gitchel, chief of the state and industry section in the Office of Diversion Control of the Drug Enforcement Agency, said that "[Anabolic] steroids probably wouldn't meet the standard of having actual or relative potential for abuse. Just because a drug is used for a nonrecognized purpose does not necessarily denote abuse."[53]

The Anti-Abuse Act of 1998

Due to the growing concern over adverse physical effects of anabolic steroids, the federal government began to adopt regulations and enact legislation to reduce the abuse of these drugs. Congress passed the Anti-Drug Abuse Act of 1988, which included several provisions to control the abuse of anabolic steroids and growth hormone. Violators are subject to imprisonment for up to three years or a fine or both if they (1) distribute anabolic steroids or (2) possess anabolic steroids with the intent to distribute them for any use in humans other than the treatment of disease on the order of a physician.

This federal law, however, was weakened by the fact that anabolic steroids were still general prescription drugs and drug manufacturers were not required to submit production data to the FDA. The generic pharmaceutical industry could manufacture huge amounts of anabolic steroids and divert them without the FDA's knowledge. The FDA could not even determine the amount of anabolic steroids that were used for medical purposes. There was no federal requirement that (1) physicians report prescriptions for medications other than controlled substances or (2) pharmaceutical manufacturers keep records of the number of patients who would use the steroids. Thus, the FDA had no way to correlate steroid distribution with steroid production.

Another provision of the act required the U.S. General Accounting Office (GAO) to obtain information regarding the estimated use of anabolic steroids among high school students, college students, and the adult population. The GAO was also required to include in its report a summary of the health consequences resulting from anabolic steroid use, information on policies and regulations developed by sports organizations to monitor athletes' use of anabolic steroids, and information on the legal and illegal anabolic steroid production and distribution nationally and internationally.

The GAO issued the *Report on Drug Misuse: Anabolic Steroids and Human Growth Hormone* on August 18, 1989, to the Committee on the Judiciary, U.S. Senate. Some of the findings of the GAO are below:

1. Clandestinely manufactured, smuggled, and legitimately manufactured U.S. anabolic steroids have been diverted and are the sources of the anabolic steroid black market. In 1988, Department of Justice officials estimated that the retail sales of these steroids was $300 to $400 million annually. When the estimated number of anabolic steroid users in the United States was one million, the estimated black market sales were about $100 million.
2. In 1988, national and state surveys indicated 7 to 11 percent of 11th and 12th grade boys in American high schools had used or were currently using anabolic steroids. This estimate represented 500,000 users.
3. The manufacturing of anabolic steroids within the United States had increased dramatically since the generic drug law was passed. The annual production consistently increased every year thereafter. During that same period of time (1980–1988), anabolic steroids prescribed by licensed physicians dropped significantly.
4. According to the FDA's state law coordinator, nine states (Alabama, California, Florida, Idaho, Kansas, Minnesota, North Carolina, Texas, and Utah) had reclassified anabolic steroids as controlled substances under state laws.

Hearings Before the Committee on the Judiciary, United States Senate

Senator Joseph Biden, chairman of the Committee on the Judiciary in the Senate, held hearings on the anabolic steroid situation in America on April 3, 1989, and May 9, 1989. The hearings included testimonies from professional sports league officials, professional and amateur coaches and trainers, and Olympic, professional, and amateur athletes. The hearings began with Senator Biden's opening statement:

> The use of steroids in sports is troubling for a number of reasons. First, steroid abuse threatens the mental and physical welfare of thousands of our fittest, healthiest and brightest young people. Second, as experts have told us, and we will hear today and in future hearings, steroids could be another gateway drug, a phrase which is now being used. If young people accept the idea that using steroids to build their body is okay, they may be all the more likely to try other drugs to alter their minds, as well as their bodies. And, third, using drugs to improve athletic performance undermines our most basic notions of honesty, discipline and hard work as a means for achieving. And it also undermines, quite frankly, our value system.... And finally, the words and deeds of athletes are critical because they are role models for all people, not just athletes and young people.
>
> I want to get a clear message to the pushers of the drugs (anabolic steroids), including unscrupulous coaches and doctors who are willing to risk the lives of their athletes and patients in the pursuit of fame and glory, that distributing steroids is wrong and that those who do it face serious penalties.
>
> There is one last message that I would like to get across. We cannot continue the notion of plausible deniability in this country. I am in the process of contacting NFL coaches and major college coaches in the Nation. And guess what? We are having trouble getting them to testify. I want to promise you that if they continue to refuse to come and testify, I will see to it that this committee lets everybody know why.
>
> We cannot continue this notion of plausible deniability—"I do not care how my athlete got so big and got so fast; I am winning with that athlete." They should care.

Compelling testimonies came from elite athletes. Excerpts from the testimonies of three of the athletes are presented below:

"My following athletic achievements were a result of the steroid Dianabol. I am currently a collegiate record holder of the women's 100 meters with a time of 10.94. I was second at the Athletic Congress National Championships in Indianapolis, June 1993. I was a bronze medalist in the first world championships in Helsinki, Finland. [The coach] supplied me with more Dianabol and furthermore, he charged me a fee of 10 cents to 25 cents a pill, depending on whatever he felt was appropriate.... There is approximately 45 to 50 women on a team (who used steroids) ... 40% of the 1988 team had tried it at least." Diane Williams, former national track champion.

"I believe steroid use is rampant among the NFL, and that includes my own team. It is rampant in colleges, and it is rampant in high schools. Everybody is blind to it because they choose to ignore what is happening in the world of steroids." Bill Fralic, NFL player for the Atlanta Falcons.

"Dianabol ... was the first entry in 1958 of anabolic steroids in American sports. It was not long afterward when this chemical started spreading throughout the various athletic institutions and weight rooms in America.... Here we have the beginning of an escalating chemical warfare. After 25 years, there are new drugs that created a dilemma, not only for the sports world, but for society. Most sports medicine researchers agree that steroid use in strength sports is epidemic." Steve Courson, former NFL player for the Pittsburgh Steelers.

With these testimonies in mind, the Committee on the Judiciary (composed of senators Biden, Arlen Specter, Strom Thurmond, and Charles Grassley) acted to propose a federal bill to reclassify anabolic steroids as controlled substances.

Still the AMA refused to support it. They submitted their official position and oral testimony to the Senate. The AMA's policy stated:

> The AMA recognizes that steroid abuse is a significant problem. We must, however, oppose legislation that would schedule steroids under the CSA. *First*, the appropriate method for scheduling a drug is through the established regulatory process. *Second*, anabolic steroids do not meet the statutory criteria for scheduling under the CSA. *Finally*, there are more appropriate approaches to address the problem of steroid abuse. These include enforcement of the recently increased criminal penalty for selling steroids without a prescription, and educating the public concerning the harmful health effects of steroid abuse.[54] [Full statement contained in Appendix B.]

It had been nearly 20 years since the passage of the Controlled Substance Act. The law was written primarily to place psychoactive drugs such as heroin, cocaine, marijuana, amphetamines, barbiturates, LSD, and other hallucinogens under stricter control by the federal government. At that time, no public official, physician, or scientist envisioned the classification of testosterone and anabolic steroids as controlled substances. However, along with their ability to enhance muscle mass and strength, anabolic steroids have powerful psychoactive and psychosexual properties. For many users they can become addictive. In the face of the anabolic steroid epidemic and in spite of information outlining their violence production ("'roid rage") and addictive effects, reclassification of anabolic steroids as controlled substances did not immediately occur. It took congressional hearings to finally make the difference.

The Steroid Trafficking Act of 1990

After House and Senate hearings, the original draft of the Steroid Trafficking Act of 1990 recommended that anabolic steroids be reclassified as Schedule II narcotics under the CSA. The final version of the act reclassified testosterone, anabolic steroids, and related compounds as Schedule III narcotics (see Appendix D for the full act). The provisions of the act included the following:

1. Increased anabolic steroid trafficking penalties to match the penalties for selling other dangerous drugs.
2. Tighter record keeping and manufacturing control regulations to prevent the diversion of legally manufactured anabolic steroids into the illegal black market.
3. The DEA holds the authority and responsibility to investigate violations involving the illegal manufacturing, distribution, or possessing with intent to distribute anabolic steroids.
4. United States demand-reduction agencies are to incorporate anabolic steroids in all federally supported drug abuse prevention, education, and treatment programs.

Impact of the Reclassification of Anabolic Steroids on Anabolic Steroid Use

Classifying anabolic steroids as controlled substances affected the black market dealers by reducing the availability of the steroids. Instead of anabolic steroid use increasing (especially among adolescents), their use decreased. The generic pharmaceutical companies stopped their production of massive quantities, since they had to keep manufacturing and distribution records subject to DEA inspection. Most of these pharmaceutical companies completely stopped making anabolic steroids. "Drug busts" in health clubs increased. Nationwide, health club assets were seized. Steroid dealers were arrested, convicted, and incarcerated. Fewer young potential users had access to anabolic steroids, since users and dealers were forced further underground. Steroid use by "hard-core" users became more clandestine.

Since anabolic steroids were added to the CSA, a number of national and state surveys have been conducted to determine the prevalence of anabolic steroids. A report published in 1997 examined three national surveys investigating the prevalence of anabolic steroid use in adolescents in the United States between 1988 and 1996. These national surveys included: Monitoring the Future (MTF) survey, Youth Risk and Behavior Surveillance System survey, and the National Household Survey on Drug Abuse. Most of the survey respondents were middle school and high school males and females. The results from the MTF survey revealed a statistically significant drop in lifetime steroid use had taken place from 1991 to 1996. Results from the other two surveys indicated that anabolic steroid use had dropped and been generally stable. The overall conclusions of this report indicated:

a) long-term comparison of anabolic steroid use (from 1989 to 1996) among adolescent males and females had a statistically significant decrease;
b) findings of multiyear state-level studies showed a decrease in lifetime anabolic steroid use rates between 1988 and 1994 for male and female adolescents;
c) from 1991 to 1996 the use of anabolic steroids *within the past year* was stable for 10th and 12th grade males and significantly decreased among 8th grade males;
d) since 1991, data from the three national surveys indicated an increase in lifetime anabolic steroid use among females, although only one of these reported increases was statistically significant; and,
e) since 1991, use of anabolic steroids *within the past year* increased in females in a statistically significant manner in the 8th and 10th grades.[55]

Other studies have evaluated the post-legislation prevalence of anabolic steroids among adolescents. The summaries of these regional, state, and city studies are listed in table 9-7 below.

Table 9-7. Recent Regional Prevalence Studies on Anabolic Steroid Use by Adolescents

Region	*Date*	*Group Studied*	*Prevalence of Use in Boys*	*Prevalence of Use in Girls*
Minneapolis[56]	1993	7th graders	4.7%	3.2%
Denver[57]	1995	high schoolers	4.0%	1.3%
Nebraska[58]	1996	7th–12th graders	4.5%	0.8%
Massachusetts[59]	1998	5th–7th graders	2.6%	2.8%
Indiana[60]	1999	HS football players	6.3%	n/a

A 1999 National Institute on Drug Abuse (NIDA) study on the prevalence of anabolic steroid use among high school students found a slight rise in the use of the steroids over the past year. The NIDA reported that the 1999 use of anabolic steroids was:

a) in boys: 8th grade—2.5%, 10th grade—2.5%, and 12th grade—3.1%;
b) in girls: 8th grade—0.9%, 10th grade—0.6%, and 12th grade—0.6%.

These studies indicate that the overall use of anabolic steroids has significantly decreased since these steroids were added to the CSA. As presented previously, the GAO report in 1989 indicated that the use of these steroids was approximately 7–11 percent among high school boys. Studies indicate that the primary reason for this decline has been the decreased availability of anabolic steroids to this age group. A secondary influence on reducing the use of these steroids has been an increase in educational efforts supported by additional monies. The recent slight increase in anabolic steroid use among adolescents may be attributed to the availability of anabolic steroids on the Internet. The slight increase in adolescent female use may be due to the dramatically increased availability of college athletic scholarships offered to females over the past decade.

Summary: Reasons for Enforcement of the CSA

Adding anabolic steroids to the CSA has helped reduce the number of anabolic steroid users, particularly young users. It has lessened the number of young Americans who would eventually experience adverse physical effects and psychological problems, including addiction from their use.

As a result of adding anabolic steroids to the CSA, efforts to educate potential users about the dangers of anabolic steroid use have increased. We know that potential users minimize the adverse physical effects and rarely consider the psychological effects. They are unaware of the potential for addiction or the psychological scars inherent with anabolic steroid use.[61] Several studies have shown that users of anabolic steroids are less likely to believe that anabolic steroids are a threat to health.[62] Another study showed that anabolic steroid users knew less about the steroid-induced effects on the body than non-users did.[63] One study concluded that educational programs warning athletes about the dangers of taking anabolic steroids may have limited value in terms of creating appropriate, responsible attitudes toward this illegal, unethical, and medially questionable practice.[64] On the other hand, intensive educational and intervention programs, especially when they are team-based, have been shown to reduce the factors that encourage the use of anabolic steroids.[65]

Educational programs to prevent anabolic steroid use have mixed results. As with many drug education programs, the potential user may only hear the positive effects of the drugs. However, it is felt that educational programs consistently presented will help discourage anabolic steroid use. Counseling efforts should focus on *psychological* consequences of anabolic steroid use and the significant risk for addiction.[66] Unfortunately, results from a recent study showed that psychologists have neglected prevention programs for anabolic steroid abuse. This may be due, in part, to their lack of knowledge regarding anabolic steroid abuse.[67]

Recent steroid users, whether they participate in sports or not, have been shown to be more likely to use other drugs than other students.[68–70] These studies point to a gateway effect to increase the use of other drugs. Anabolic steroid users are likely to use other drugs to treat or avoid adverse conditions that arise with the use of these steroids.

Enforcement of the CSA laws continues to be met with difficulties. The majority of anabolic steroids obtained for use by American youth come from abroad. This presents another problem for law enforcement officials. However, if we are ever to truly deal with the issue of anabolic steroid abuse, strict enforcement of the provisions in the CSA is necessary.

10

Growth Hormones and Other Anabolic Hormones

Introduction: Hormonal Manipulation Beyond Anabolic Steroids

Over the past 40 years the summer Olympic games have been dominated by gold medal winners who are products of hormonal manipulation. In modern times, the summer Olympic games have been more about endocrine drugs and creative exercise physiology than "clean" athletes competing with elite class skills. This has not been true for every event, but over the years, more and more events have produced hormonally manipulated (with anabolic steroids, growth hormone, and growth factors) champions.[1]

The Games test out international theories of hormonal manipulation techniques just as novelist Peter Lear warned us in 1977. In his novel *Goldengirl*, Lear showed us how sports sponsorship (government or private) and "selective gigantism" (via hormonal manipulation) would change the face of sports forever.[2]

In an attempt to halt or curb this phenomenon, pleas to reclassify growth hormone (GH) as a controlled substance under the Federal Controlled Substance act of 1970 were published.[3–5] By 1985, it was recognized that synthetic GH would become the first controversy in the genetic engineering arena.[6,7] The American Medical Association (AMA) and the United States Congress held hearings to consider these proposals, but both groups took actions falling short of reclassification of human growth hormone as a controlled substance.[8,9]

Government Sponsorship of Hormonal Manipulation of Athletes

For decades rumors were heard claiming rampant anabolic steroid and growth hormone use in East Germany. The East Germans lead the world in anabolic hormone technology. In the 1976 and 1980 summer Olympic games, East German athletes won an unprecedented number of Olympic medals (216, of which 87 were gold medals). We know now that East German athletes used anabolic steroids in *every sport* except sailing.[10]

In 1997, rumors of East German athletes using anabolic steroids and growth hormone became truth with the publishing of an incredible exposé on the scope and magnitude of governmental sponsorship of hormonal manipulation in athletes and children. After the collapse of the German Democratic Republic (GDR) during the mid–1990s, classified documents were obtained that described the *governmental promotion* of drug use, notably anabolic steroids and growth hormones, in high performance sports. Top-secret doctoral theses, scientific grant reports, proceedings from symposia of experts, and reports from physicians and scientists who served as unofficial collaborators for the Ministry for State Security ("Stasi") revealed shocking, almost unbelievable, findings of hormonal manipulation in athletes and children. From 1966 on, hundreds of physicians and scientists, including top-ranking professors, performed hormonal research on athletes. Thousands of male and female athletes were treated with anabolic steroids and growth hormones. These experiments included children chosen to be future athletes. Special emphasis was placed on administering anabolic steroids to women and adolescent girls as this practice proved to be particularly effective for improving sports performance. However, along with enhanced performance, damaging side effects were recorded that required surgical and or medical interventions. In addition, it was learned that several prominent GDR scientists and sports medicine physicians contributed to the development of drug administration methods that would *evade detection by international drug control methods.*[11]

The Aftermath of the East German Experiments

In September 2000, top leaders of East Germany's hormonal manipulation experiments were brought to trial in Berlin. Manfred Ewald, chief of the former East German sports program and 73 years old at the time of the trial, was a member of the Hitler Youth party and later was a member of the Nazi party. He joined the GDR Communist Party's central committee in

1963 and took over the country's Olympic program the following year. He oversaw the East German hormonal manipulation experiments that flourished in the 1970s and 1980s. Manfred Ewald and his former medical director, Manfred Hoeppner, were convicted of being the "driving force" behind the now infamous East German sports program. Both Ewald and Hoeppner received suspended jail terms, not a popular decision in East Germany.

The trial against Ewald and Hoeppner ended the "official" East German sports experiments. None of the East German officials implicated in this doping scheme received more than a small fine and or suspended sentence. No athletes who participated in these experiments relinquished their gold medals. No consideration was ever given the athletes losing out to these East German athletes.

During the trial, women who were subjects in the East German sports program experiments provided dramatic testimonies. Their stories were compelling, and at times, horrifying. However, their stories were not much different from the testimony given a decade earlier before the United States Congress by former female American Olympians.

The Influence of Doping Control Measures

Elaborate drug testing methods introduced at the 1984 Olympic games in Los Angeles were supposed to curb the use of anabolic steroids in Olympic athletes. These tests did not achieve this goal. Fewer than two dozen athletes were disqualified for anabolic steroid use in the 1988, 1992, and 1996 Olympic summer games combined. Yet the use of anabolic steroid and growth hormones was widespread and growing among Olympians. The use of anabolic steroids and growth hormones has become so widespread that Olympic drug testing has become little more than window dressing.[12]

For the last 15 years, the most elaborate and expensive drug testing methods have failed to have a substantial impact on the use of anabolic steroid and growth hormones by Olympians.[13] Dozens of articles have been published on the use of urine testing technologies for detecting anabolic steroid use in competitive athletes. Yet, the application of these testing protocols continues to be encumbered by medical technicalities, international differences in intent, and legal difficulties.[14]

The "Genetic Supermarket"

"Anabolic steroids and synthetic human growth hormones are basically nothing short of being the biochemical 'fertilizers' for human growth and development, which can distort the norms for ultimate height and afford superhuman muscle mass and strength and can be converted into a fortune on the athletic field."[15]

Legal experts admit that nontherapeutic use of GH is likely to be the first of many biotechnology and gene therapy enhancements publicly available at a "genetic supermarket" of performance and cosmetic enhancement products.[16] They warn that current regulations do not adequately address unapproved uses of GH let alone the possibility (probability) of genetic manipulation in a "race to perfection."[17]

Over the past two decades genetic engineering has made monumental advances in providing the chemical "tinker toys" for human growth and muscularity. Many anabolic and growth-stimulating hormones have been produced from the brilliance of recombinant DNA technology. Elite athletes, through personal and collaborative "clinical trials," know that when combined with training, GH is a performance-enhancing drug.[18]

Many genetic engineering researchers promise opportunities for curing diseases and providing beneficial therapies. Others know these products have been and are being abused by both competitive and non-competitive athletes. These recombinant products all have the potential to beneficially influence disease processes and enhance athletic performance. None of these genetically engineered anabolic and growth-stimulating hormones can be detected with current urine drug testing methods and no detection method is on the horizon.

Perhaps the most intensely debated area in genetic engineering concerns the off-label use of GH in children and adolescent athletes. The use of GH to increase height and thereby increase chances of athletic success may be tempting to coaches, parents, athletes, and some physicians.[19] The question becomes, do we use GH to increase the height of these potential athletic children and adolescents? As synthetic GH has become more available through international sources, black market supplies, and off-label use by physicians, ethical as well as scientific questions are raised. In countries where off-label use of GH is widespread, use in children has greatly increased over the past few years.[20] Like it or not, the menu of these newly synthesized anabolic and growth hormones is occurring at such a rapid pace that efforts to control and study these drugs lag behind "clinical trials" of athletes in their quest for gold medals.

As the shelves in the "genetic supermarket" are rapidly expanding, it is urgent that we investigate the issue of athletic and would-be athletic hormonal manipulation. The current and future "shopping list" of synthetic anabolic and growth-stimulating hormones includes:

a) anabolic steroids. Anabolic steroids are the mainstay of performance-enhancing drugs.

b) luteinizing hormone (LH) and human chorionic gonadotrophin (HCG).[21–23] LH is a synthetic polypeptide hormone copy of a hormone manufactured by cells in the anterior pituitary gland. LH stimulates the testicles and ovaries to produce testosterone. Studies on healthy athletes have shown that LH administration produces testosterone levels over and above normal production. Once released into the bloodstream, LH has a short half-life that makes urine detection methods unlikely. It has been available commercially for over two decades. Human chorionic gonadotrophin is an extract version of LH. It is extracted from cadaver pituitary glands and has been commercially available for several decades. Male athletes use these hormones in conjunction with anabolic steroids to stimulate the testicles to produce testosterone, even when total androgen levels are high. They also use these products during anabolic steroid withdrawal to stimulate the testicles and restore testicular function.[24,25] These hormones enhance performance in male athletes by increasing testosterone levels. HCG has been widely used by athletes for many years.

(c) luteinizing hormone-releasing hormone (LHRH), also called gonadotrophin hormone-releasing hormone (GnRH).[26–29] These drugs are copies of the hormone naturally produced by the hypothalamus. They act as neuropeptides and stimulate the pituitary gland to release LH and follicle stimulating hormone (FSH) into the bloodstream. In males, LH stimulates the testicles to produce and release testosterone. In normal males, LHRH has been shown to significantly elevate testosterone levels well above normal ranges. It has been available for nearly two decades in a long-acting nasal spray. LHRH has been widely used by athletes for many years.

d) LHRH analogs.[30] These are long-acting superactive analogs of LHRH. The high action of these analogs increases testosterone levels in normal men for an extended period of time. The abuse potential of these hormone-like drugs is high. Anecdotal evidence from athletes suggests that these drugs have been used for years.

e) GH.[31–34] GH can enhance performance in many ways. However, GH is not a single molecular structure. The commercially available GH is just one of over 100 human GHs with different molecular structures. Human growth hormones are molecules produced by the pituitary gland and released into the bloodstream. The anabolic and growth producing effects of circulating GHs are enormously complex. Each of these 100 or so molecular structures may have specific anabolic effects over and above the present commercially available GH. They possess differential and selective clearance rates and receptor binding affinities. As of now, GH is properly defined as a family of anabolic proteins, many of which fulfill as yet unknown functions within the body. Scientists are synthesizing and experimenting with these GH variants. It should be expected that one or more of the variant GH forms will be proven to enhance anabolic and growth mechanisms over and above that of the commercially available GH. On the commercial horizon are bioactive GHs in nasal spray applicators.[35]

f) GH analogs.[36–38] These derivatives of GH have been made in hopes of selectively increasing the anabolic activities of GH over and above the normal activities. Much as they produced anabolic steroids (analogs of testosterone), scientists are producing GH analogs to selectively enhance and selectively reduce some of the effects of GH.

g) growth hormone–releasing hormone (GHRH).[39] GHRH is a small neuropeptide produced in the hypothalamus. Its function is to drive the entire growth axis by specifically stimulating the release of GH from the pituitary gland. It is available in nasal spray preparations.[40]

h) GH secretagogues (GHS) and GH-releasing peptides (GHRPs).[41–48] Growth hormone–releasing peptides are a group of synthetic hexa, hepta, and octapeptides. They are the most powerful GH-releasing drugs known. Their structures are simple 6, 7, and 8 amino acids that are able to interact in the brain and its various structures. This family of small peptides will soon be part of the rapidly expanding commercially available neuropeptides. GHRPs and GHSs have chemical structures that are very different from GHRH. They are *superanalogs* of a natural GHRP yet to be discovered.

Receptors for GRHPs have been found in both the hypothalamus and pituitary glands of humans.[49] This specific receptor has been cloned and various short peptides (GRHPs) have been discovered that bind to this receptor in vitro.[50] Many of these GHRPs and GHSs are bioactive when taken orally or intra-nasally in non–GH-deficient humans.[51]

GHRPs and GHSs cause a much greater and sustained GH-release than GHRH in normal adults.[52] In fact, when GHRPs and GHRH are taken together, they act synergistically and independently to cause a *massive release of GH* in a dose-related manner.[53,54] Oral GHRPs have been shown to release GH both day and night at supranormal levels in normal adults and children.[55] They also cause GH release even when the GHRH-induced release of GH is inhibited.[56–58] They have been shown to increase GH release *over and above* that produced when GHRH is taken with GH.[59,60]

Combination therapy with anabolic steroids and GHRPs provides a statistically significant elevation of GH in a synergistic manner in both normal children and children with delayed puberty.[61–63] GHRPs also stimulate the hypothalamus to make GHRH in supranormal levels.[64] In normal prepubertal and pubertal children and adolescents, oral GHRP treatment results in a statistically significant higher GH release than GHRH.[65]

The overall anabolic and growth-enhancing effects of these drugs are enormous. The athletic abuse (in children, adolescents, and adults) *may even dwarf the abuse of anabolic steroids.* Clinical availability of GHRPs and GHSs is widespread in some countries. The abuse potential is so high that it will be discussed further in this chapter.

i) insulin-like growth factor-1 (IGF-1).[66–69] Clinical studies with synthetic IGF-1 are ongoing and preliminary results show beneficial effects. It has been shown that enhancement of anabolic effects of GH and IGF-1 occur by using both agents simultaneously.[70] GH and IGF-1 have similar and different anabolic mechanisms.[71] IGF-1 administration in normal adolescent monkeys has been shown to increase ultimate height (crown to-rump length) over normal controls.[72] Already there are documented reports of IGF-1 use by athletes.[73]

j) erythropoietin (EPO).[74] EPO is an endogenous hormone that stimulates red blood cell formation and increases oxygen utilization. Synthetic EPO is a proven performance-enhancing hormone. It is widely used by athletes participating in prolonged aerobic competitions, such as middle and long distance cycling, swimming, and running, due to its ability to increase oxygen utilization. EPO use is so common it no longer offers a competitive edge as it is used by most if not all competitive athletes in some events. In competitive aerobic sports, the formula for success has become EPO plus other anabolic agents. In July 2000, $1 million worth of EPO was stolen from Alice Springs Hospital in central Australia and diverted to the athletic black market prior to the summer Olympic Games in Sydney.

k) selective anti-GH receptor factor vaccines.[75] These vaccines are recombinantly produced peptide regions of the growth hormone DNA. They cause an antibody-induced blocking effect to a portion of the GH structure. Antibody binding to a part of the GH structure can enhance some of the functions of GH by making it incapable of binding to specific receptors. Also, the "blocked" portion may enhance GH's anabolic activities by inhibiting the enzymatic degradation of GH. This technology has the potential to enhance the anabolic effects of GH while reducing negative effects on insulin functions.

l) muscle-specific gene medicines.76,77 The production of peptide hormones by skeletal muscle tissue is a promising area of gene therapy. Gene medicine is composed of a muscle-specific DNA plasmid complex with a protective, interactive non-condensing (PINC) delivery system. After injection of this system into skeletal muscle, the DNA is incorporated into the DNA of skeletal muscle cells. Within the muscle cell, the DNA plasmid complex manufactures the peptide hormone. Muscle-gene medicine provides for long-term secretion of peptide hormones from skeletal muscle into the systemic circulation (GH has been successfully administered in this fashion).

These systems and others, using all of the hormones and factors listed above, are on the horizon. This technology may revolutionize the clinical replacement of hormones; however, as might be expected, athletic abuse potential is extremely high.

A Scientific Dilemma: To Study or Not to Study?

In every case, use and abuse of anabolic agents by athletes has been far ahead of scientific research to prove or deny effects on athletic performance. Generally, medical science has leaned toward efforts to prove that these agents *do not* enhance athletic performance. Although discouraging drug use is commendable, when information is distorted or missing, drug education prevention programs lose credibility, and thus do little to stop drug usage.

The athletic community has and continues to be first in proving anabolic agents effective in enhancing athletic performance. The medical community has eventually confirmed what the athletes have known all along, that anabolic agents enhance athletic performance. Therefore, the question for the medical community becomes, do we investigate the effects of anabolic agents through properly designed studies utilizing athletes as subjects, or do we let the athletes perform their own self-experiments?

Let's look at a few of the properly designed studies.

Studies with Synthetic Human Growth Hormone

In 1984, this author presented information on the performance-enhancing effects of GH to sports medicine physicians and scientists at the American College of Sports Medicine's Annual Meeting. During this lecture, the following performance-enhancing effects of GH were outlined.[78] GH use:

a) causes an increase in protein synthesis, muscle mass, and strength;
b) causes a significant reduction in body fat;
c) inhibits the catabolic effects of athletic training and aids the anabolic responses associated with athletic training;
d) can cause a significant height increase if used in normal children; and,
e) causes a synergistic anabolic effect when used with anabolic steroids.

Results from Properly Designed Studies Using Athletes

There have been very few studies addressing the performance-enhancing effects of GH. To address these effects, the study subjects should be experienced weight-trained athletes in a double-blind study design given sufficient doses of GH with adequate protein intake. Results from studies that have met these criteria conclude that GH can enhance athletic performance in athletes with existing normal or supranormal body composition by:

a) causing a significant decrease in body fat percentage;
b) causing a significant increase in lean body mass;
c) causing an increase in skeletal muscle metabolism;
d) causing an enhanced response-recovery effect from training;
e) causing an increased anabolic effect via elevated IGF-1 levels;
f) causing a synergistic effect with anabolic steroids on the total anabolic hormonal effect of elevating IGF-1 levels or reducing IGFBP (insulin-like growth factor binding protein) levels.[79–83]

Results from Improperly Designed Studies Using Athletes

Studies with design flaws conducted to investigate the anabolic and athletic performance–enhancing effects of GH have either found no evidence supporting the athletic performance enhancing effects, or simply failed to report supporting evidence. One example of a design-flawed study and its misleading conclusions is presented below:

> The purpose of this study was to determine whether growth hormone (GH) administration enhances the muscle anabolism associated with heavy-resistance exercise. Sixteen men (21–34 yr) were assigned randomly to a resistance training plus GH group (n=7) or to a resistance training group (n=9). For 12 weeks, both groups trained all major muscle groups in an identical fashion while receiving 40 micrograms recombinant GH daily or placebo. Fat-free mass (FFM) and total body water increased (P less than 0.5) in both

groups but more (P less than 0.01) in the GH recipients. Whole body protein synthesis rate increased more (P less than 0.03), and whole body balance was greater (P=0.01) in the GH treated group, but quadriceps muscle protein synthesis rate, torso and limb circumferences, and muscle strength did not increase more in the GH-treated group. In the young men studied, resistance exercise with or without GH resulted in similar increments in muscle size, strength, and muscle protein synthesis, indicating that 1) the larger increase in FFM with GH treatment was probably due to an increase in lean tissue other than skeletal muscle and 2) resistance training supplemented with GH did not further enhance muscle anabolism and function.[84]

The subjects in this study were neither weight trained or provided with an adequate protein intake that was documented. The conclusions are misleading and actually contradict the study findings. The results indicated a statistically significant increase in fat-free mass, whole body protein synthesis rate, and whole body protein balance in the GH-treated group *over and above* weight training alone. The authors concluded that GH administration did not enhance skeletal muscle anabolism. If that is true, where did all of this statistically significant fat-free protein synthesis go?

This example was presented to illustrate two points. First, faulty scientific studies provide faulty results and misleading conclusions. Second, this type of study is exactly the type of study performed in the 1970s attempting to show that anabolic steroids *do not* enhance athletic performance. As we now know, the results of these studies have all but been disproved.

Results from Studies on Aging

Aging is associated with a significant decline in secretion of growth hormone.[85] As people age they secrete less and less GH until they are GH deficient. There are several studies that have shown the anabolic effects of GH administration in healthy non–strength trained older persons (with and without documented GH deficiency). These studies have consistently shown:

a) statistically significant increases in lean body mass;
b) statistically significant decreases in body fat percentage;
c) statistically significant improvements in atherogenic lipid profiles;
d) statistically significant elevation of IGF-1 levels; and,
e) statistically significant improvements in physical and psychological well-being.[86–100]

Only one study has evaluated the effects of GH administration (10 weeks) on muscle mass and strength training in older non-deficient GH patients. This study showed:

a) statistically significant increases in muscle mass and strength (24–62 percent depending on the muscle group) over and above weight training effects alone;
b) statistically significant reductions in body fat percentage; and,
c) statistically significant increases in IGF-1 levels.[101]

Another study evaluated the effects of GH administration (three months) in healthy subjects over 60 years old and concluded GH increases muscle mass and strength, but does not restore a completely youthful rate of muscle protein synthesis.[102] GH plays a role in the regulation of body composition in adults through its anabolic and lipolytic actions.[103] GH has direct effects on lipolysis within fat cells and enhances fat utilization as a fuel substrate.[104,105] Many of GH's anabolic and lipolytic effects are mediated through IGF-1.[106]

Reduced muscle mass and strength associated with aging is primarily caused by a reduction in GH and androgen levels.[107] It has been shown that administration of both GH and anabolic steroids have an additive effect on improving body composition, muscle mass and strength, body fat reduction, and improved atherogenic lipoprotein levels.[108] Thus, both GH and anabolic steroids have important roles in body protein synthesis in adults.[109]

Prevalence of GH Use by Athletes

The actual use of GH by athletes is unknown. Fortunately the abuse of GH is limited by its cost and the fact that anabolic steroids are simply more enticing to the athlete.[110] A few review articles, however, have documented that GH use by athletes and bodybuilders is of significant importance and increasing.[111–118]

The growth hormones industry is rapidly expanding due to the enormous potential for use in medical conditions now and in the future. International manufacturers of GH have made large quantities of the hormone available for clinical research worldwide while lawyers have worked to secure patent protection.[119]

However, with increasing quantities of GH available for clinical use and research, supplies to black market dealers also increase. GH is readily available through the Internet. Shipments of GH have been stolen from warehouses, hospitals, and transportation vehicles.[120] Drug busts of anabolic steroid black market dealers have also found GH supplies. A pharmaceutical company employee has been convicted for stealing shipments of GH from a West Coast manufacturer, then selling it to black market dealers. A few physicians are prescribing GH to their athletic patients. Many GH users make trips to Mexico and other countries where physicians will prescribe GH for them.[121,122]

Growth hormone is one of the drugs of choice for Olympians. GH was used by so many athletes during the 1996 summer Olympic Games in Atlanta that the Games were called the "Growth Hormone Games."[123] (Some media members have dubbed the 2000 summer Olympic Games as the "SyDNA games"— Sy for Sydney, and DNA for genetically-engineered hormone products.)

Can GH Use Enhance Human Performance? Yes It Can.

The Human Growth Axis

How does GH enhance athletic performance? To answer that question, it is imperative to look at the biological role of GH on the growth axis. (In the remainder of this book, the term *growth axis* will replace the generally accepted terminology of the GHRH–GH–IGF-1–IGFPB–IGF-1–receptor axis. (The generally accepted abbreviation for this complex axis reveals the general flow of information along the axis.)

It is beyond the scope of this book to delve too deeply into a presentation of growth axis of the human body, but a brief discussion is warranted.

The basic growth axis of the human body is much better understood than it was even a decade ago. In the 1980s, it was known that specific cells in the anterior portion of the pituitary gland produced GH and that it played the commanding role in the growth and development processes. The generally accepted view of the growth axis was that there was one GHRH, one to three GH forms, a few growth factors, and a few receptors for GH and IGF-1 in various tissues. Physicians were taught that there were distinct feedback mechanisms in the growth axis. These feedback mechanisms were felt to prevent "tampering" with the growth axis. Physicians knew that administering GH to GH-deficient children helped them grow taller than they would have otherwise. Most physicians felt that administration of GH to healthy people would have little or no effect. Only a few molecules were thought to play a direct role in the growth axis.

With the aid of biotechnology, scientists have begun to understand the enormous complexities of the human growth axis. Researchers have discovered that the more molecules they find the more there are to find. Although the number of molecules that contribute to the growth axis is not infinite, it is much larger than originally thought.

Hundreds of molecules are now known to be involved with the growth axis, with each having specific bioactivities and specific roles. For instance, there are over one hundred versions of GH alone.

There are many versions of GHRH and GH binding proteins that all play important roles. There are many GH receptors located throughout the body, each possessing individual characteristics.

There are many versions and forms of IGF, all with different roles. Versions of IGF binding proteins (IGFBPs) that carry circulating IGFs have been identified. There are different binding affinities associated with the IGF binding proteins. There are a variety of IGF receptors each playing different roles based on their locations throughout the body.

All these factors play a part in the growth axis and further research will help sort out the enormous complexities yet to be understood. *The strict feedback mechanisms once believed in simply do not exist.* The growth axis can be driven and overridden by a number of mechanisms and chemicals.

Factors That Influence the Growth Axis

There are many factors that influence the function of the growth axis. These include a variety of exogenous and endogenous factors and variables that can drive the growth axis in either a positive or a negative direction. Some scientists believe that each person has one's own set of growth axis molecules. Although there are strong similarities, no two people will have the exact same number or types of molecules. This heterogeneity may account for the different effects of drugs on the growth axis of different people.

Drugs can influence the functions of the growth axis. Prescription drugs, over-the-counter drugs and supplements can all interact with the growth axis. Some drugs and supplements are consumed expressly for the purpose of stimulating the growth axis.

Besides drugs and over-the-counter medications and supplements, there are many non-drug factors involved in the growth axis equation. Some of these factors involve day-to-day living habits and nutrition. Modifications in diet, exercise, illness, stress, perceived stress, aging, and the biological stages of life all can have major impact on the growth axis. Sleep patterns, both quality and quantity, have also been shown to influence the human growth axis that affects aging, responses to body repair, and the immune system. "Graveyard" workers and shift workers often have sleep disturbances that negatively affect the growth axis that promotes premature aging.

Endogenous hormones and other molecules play a role in the growth axis. Examples are insulin, corticosteroids, sex steroids, and other peptide hormones such as prolactin, thyroid hormones, epinephrine, norepinephrine, somatostatin, and dozens of neuropeptides. It is likely that each of us has one's own set of steroids and hormones, with no two people having identical levels and actions of these hormones.

Every individual is a unique biochemical machine, with a set of growth axis molecules and receptors. Every person also has unique endogenous and exogenous factors acting in response to stimuli that influence the growth axis.

GH Enhances Athletic Training Effects

Now let us add exercise and athletic training to the mix. There are hundreds of researchers investigating the impact of exercise on the growth axis and athletic performance. Even the exercise variables seem infinite with huge variations in the recovery response of the growth axis.

In general, exercise performed with moderate intensity (greater than just walking) increases GH secretion. Increased GH secretion aids in all of the physical, anabolic, and some of the mental adaptations to exercise training. These responses are dependent on the amount of GH that is released, thus adding more GH may enhance responses to exercise.

So, does growth hormone use enhance athletic performance? Will it make my children grow taller so that they can excel in sports? Will GH use help *me* live longer and better? In general, the answer to these questions is YES! But a strong word of caution is added: until we fully understand the mechanism of growth axis, the potential dangers and risks of adding GH to this process cannot be ignored.

"Selective Gigantism"

In 1984, I presented a lecture at Harvard Medical School to a group of sports medicine physicians. My lecture was entitled "The Philosophical Aspects of 'Selective Gigantism.'" It dealt with the concept of creating man-made giants through hormonal manipulation. After I finished my lecture, the room was quiet. It seemed my listeners were in disbelief over such a theory. However, today through genetic engineering and hormonal manipulation, the "theory" is rapidly becoming reality. Today, some gigantic athletes may have already been made this way.[124]

Philosophical Aspects of "Selective Gigantism"

"Selective gigantism" simply refers to the selection of persons to become giants by utilizing anabolic hormonal manipulation.[125,126] These anabolic and growth-stimulating drugs may include combinations of those available at the genetic supermarket. This concept was outlined over a decade ago:

> Selecting the proper drugs for this monstrous undertaking is part of the process, and so are the people who will ultimately do the selecting. Who will choose the children and adolescents to be inflicted with this method of making human giants? Will the minor child decide? Or will it be the parents of the child, or perhaps a group of sporting officials and physicians under the auspices of governmental nationalism? Will it be the government who selects the children, maybe even children of yours? And, if not in this country, how about in the countries where human rights are engulfed in the sea of dehumanization? And if the Eastern Bloc countries practice the ludicrous art of "selective gigantism" to beat our American athletes, will we begrudgingly follow their lead and allow our children to be *nationalistic pawns* to promote athletes, winning, and the democratic style of life? Indeed, these are heavy questions to answer. In my opinion, it is doubtful that anyone will be able to accept the liability of "selective gigantism."[127]

Making Human Giants

The overproduction of human growth hormone during puberty in normal boys and girls results in *gigantism.* This is, however, an extremely rare biological phenomenon.

For decades, endocrinologists believed that the growth axis could only be driven in GH-deficient children. Administration of GH to these children increased their ultimate height. Today we know that driving the growth system through the addition of GH can make almost *any* child taller. If the growth axis is chronically driven, then gigantism or near-gigantism will result. Prolonged GH use, and especially prolonged GHRPs use by normal children, just prior to and during puberty, can produce giants. If anabolic steroids along with weight training are added, then overly muscular giants will be "made." However, no ethical medical scientist would knowingly set out to make a human giant.

Studies on Constitutionally Tall People

Near-giants or *constitutionally tall* people according to medical science are much more prevalent than true giants. The mechanism by which otherwise normal sized humans become constitutionally tall is nearly the same as it is for giants. In reality, the differences are just a matter of semantics and degree.

Relatively few studies have been published on the growth process of constitutionally tall people, such as NBA players. Many of us would consider these athletes to be giants. However, the little amount of information that has been published is not only convincing, but also somewhat frightening.

Research over a decade ago showed that, during puberty, constitutionally tall adolescents had increased levels of GH in response to a GHRH stimulus. In fact, tall girls had more of an elevated GH response to the GHRH stimulus than tall boys.[128] Another study indicated that tall stature stemmed from one of two mechanisms: hypersecretion of GH, hypersensitivity of IGF-1 or a combination of both.[129] Of 75 adolescents evaluated for tall stature, two-thirds were documented to hypersecrete GH with response to known stimuli, such as GHRH administration.[130]

A 1996 study showed a significant variation in GH secretion for pubertal boys. This variation was greater from boy to boy than variations within one boy.[131] This means that, if everything else is equal, then the boys on the higher end of GH secretion scale will be taller than those who secrete less GH. Boys that do not produce high-end GH levels are not likely to do so on a day-to-day basis given their set of growth axis molecules.

In 2000, a study showed that in normal children, a given set of growth axis molecules can be *driven* by GHRP administration alone or by combined GHRP + GH administration, providing GH levels once thought unlikely or even impossible. (These levels had previously been seen only in giants and acromegalics.) The GH elevations were statistically higher after the combination treatment of GHRP + GH than treatment with GH alone.[132]

It is now known that GHRP administration overrides the negative feedback mechanisms that had been believed to limit GH production. These findings leave little doubt that the growth axis molecules can be manipulated and enhanced to add inches to the height of normal children and adolescents.

Discussion: Pandora's Box Is Wide Open

For those of us involved in sports medicine, the secret documents that surfaced after the fall of the Berlin Wall proved our worst fears: hormonal manipulation of athletes with government support and sponsorship. While the East German "experiments" are officially over, the records of those experiments remain for the world to see.

It was during the time of Hitler's reign that a hormone was first synthesized. That hormone was testosterone.[133] History tells us that unethical experiments using anabolic steroids were conducted on prisoners, Gestapo members, and Hitler himself.[134] German scientists synthesized anabolic steroids and human experiments were carried out. For Americans, it is relatively easy to condemn Germany for its athletic experiments and childhood hormonal manipulations, but let us not cast stones too quickly.

Drugs that are stocked in the "genetic supermarket" will fuel the next era of hormonal manipulation. This new era may take place in any country. In 1985, I predicted this occurrence with my book, *Hormonal Manipulation: A New Era of Monstrous Athletes*. In this book, I recommended that all of these anabolic products be classified as controlled substances. Today, it seems even more important for this to occur.

With the easy availability of anabolic agents through the black market and on the Internet, and with the ever-increasing numbers of anabolic agents due to genetic engineering, Pandora's box is wide open. Curtailing all illegal and unethical use of anabolic agents is unlikely, but progress can be made if Congress will reclassify these anabolic agents as Class II controlled substances under the Federal Controlled Substance Act of 1970. Again, I say:

> I think, in summary, it is better to study all of the ramifications of growth hormone in a controlled setting versus self-use and social experimentation, which is what is the case with anabolic steroids. It is difficult for anyone to fully assess the steroid charisma that is afflicting our youth, and the emphasis on body image that is afflicting our youth. I support with all of my efforts, courage, and heart the proposal to place human growth hormone into the Class II controlled substance category. I do not see any other mechanism that I feel will work at this time.[135]

11
Limits of Urine Drug Testing

Introduction: From the "Sink Method" to Sophistication

In an ideal situation, drug testing for performance-enhancing drugs would detect such drug abuse by athletes under most, if not all, circumstances. Such detection techniques would play a dominant role in discouraging the abuse of the wide variety of performance-enhancing drugs. And, as a result of this role, competitive athletics would become a drug-free area of human endeavor that could be further utilized to persuade the athletic American youth to refrain from cheating by the abuse of performance-enhancing drugs. By examining the limits of urine drug testing of elite amateur athletes, it can be shown that this ideal concept has fallen far short of its best intentions. Use of performance-enhancing drugs is far more widespread than drug-testing data indicates.[1]

One purpose of this chapter is to inform the reader as to the basic principles of urine testing for anabolic and growth hormones. These agents include synthetic anabolic steroids and testosterone preparations. They also include various anabolic and growth-stimulating hormones that are synthesized via genetic engineering techniques, such as recombinant human growth hormone (GH), erythropoietin (EPO), insulin-like growth factor-1 (IGF-1), growth hormone releasing hormone (GHRH), growth hormone releasing proteins (GHRPs), and other recombinant synthetic growth factors.

Another purpose is to provide insight as to what role drug testing of athletes for these anabolic agents has today and in the future. It is likely that drug testing of competitive athletes will succumb to legal challenges and will cease to be a factor in the hopes of removing drugs in sports.

The information presented in this chapter is *not* intended to disclose the specific guidelines and timetable methods for athletes to avoid the detection of anabolic steroids and testosterone abuse. Unfortunately, much of that type of information is already available to them from various sources, including the Internet. Also, information will *not* be provided to educate the athlete on how to "doctor" his or her urine with masking or disguising agents or techniques. In other words, this chapter is not a "how to" treatise on how to beat urine drug testing. Most competitive athletes already know how to accomplish that task.

Historical Highlights

A historical perspective will be employed here to examine the evolution of the urine drug testing of elite athletes for the recent abuse of these anabolic agents. Much of the science of urine drug testing for anabolic agents has been pioneered by the International Olympic Committee (IOC). Therefore, much of the focus in this discussion will be patterned after the program developed by the IOC's Medical Commission. Available methods for detection of these agents have their strengths, weaknesses, and outright blind spots.[2] For instance, only the recent abuse (within a few weeks) for anabolic steroids and (within a day or so) for testosterone abuse can be detected.

Currently, no tests exist for discovering the life-long previous abuse history of anabolic steroids. Many elite athletes can build their bodies through months or years of anabolic steroid use, stop for a month or so, and compete as if they had never used such agents. At best, the most sophisticated urine tests can only detect recent use in some athletes for some anabolic agents, some of the time. After such use is detected, the official reporting of this fact may bow to political, financial, and legal pressures.

The Development of the "Sink Method"

Current urine detection of anabolic agents relies on very expensive and sophisticated machinery coupled with a very specialized branch of laboratory analysis. But, anabolic steroid detection has not always been conducted in this manner even at the highest levels. During my work as a physician crew chief for the United States Olympic Committee's (USOC) Drug Control and Education Program from 1984 to 1988, I was educated in the earliest form of the testing for testosterone and anabolic steroids. Prior to 1983, the basic method used was inexpensive and did not rely on elaborate laboratory equipment. It was called the "sink method" for testosterone and anabolic steroid detection.[3]

Because of their chemical structures, certain drugs that may enhance athletic performance were more readily detected than anabolic steroids. Therefore, legitimate and accurate drug testing protocols had been developed for many of these substances, including central nervous system stimulants and narcotic analgesics.[4]

The International Olympic Committee was well aware of the major problem posed by testosterone and anabolic steroid abuse by Olympic athletes competing in the Olympic Games. By most accounts, this problem has existed since the 1950s, but it may have been a problem even before then. Some type of measure was deemed necessary to test for these steroids prior to the development of any accurate and reliable laboratory techniques. These test measures were needed to counteract the growing claims and concerns that hormonally manipulated athletes were winning the lion's share of medals, especially in the track and field events.

The political and financial ramifications of having "clean" athletes compete in the Olympic Games have been and still are enormous. If the money-contributing factions were to find out that the Olympic Games were nothing short of "'roid heads" competing for gold, fame, and fortune, then the financing for the "Olympic movement" would come to an abrupt halt. This would especially be the case if these wealthy sponsors found out that the general public knew this as well.

So, the IOC developed the sink method for anabolic steroid detection. The entire fate of the "Olympic movement" relied for years on the sink method to discount the growing claims that anabolic steroid abuse had become a major factor in winning Olympic medals. For the most part, the sink method succeeded in keeping the Olympic image clean for a decade or so.

The basics of this simple sink method were to collect urine from the medal winners, and pour the urine down the sink and report that none of the athletes tested positive for testosterone and anabolic steroid abuse. Basically, it was a window dressing phenomenon that was contrived to convince the public, media, and wealthy sponsors that there was no anabolic steroid problem in Olympic sports. Meanwhile, the anabolic steroid epidemic was well on its way to becoming a reality in the late 1980s among all sorts of athletes and fitness buffs in the United States.[5]

The first encounter of sink method testing for anabolic steroids and other anabolic hormones by the IOC was due to the lack of technology to test for the drugs. Later, it will be shown that the second encounter with sink methods has occurred because of the threats of litigation plus the advent of genetically engineered anabolic and growth hormones.

Technology Begins to Catch Up with Anabolic Steroid Use

The first, relatively accurate, testing of competitive athletes for the recent abuse of anabolic steroids was introduced at the 1983 Pan American Games held in Caracas, Venezuela. The results of this new type of testing for steroids found 15 positive tests for anabolic steroids after the first few days of these games.[6] As a result, dozens of American Olympic hopefuls who were scheduled to compete in the upcoming days returned home. They did not compete. The reasons they gave for withdrawing from these games were based on an assortment of excuses, injuries, and ailments. Most experts now agree that this exodus was induced by the fear that many American athletes would test positive for recent anabolic steroid abuse and forfeit their ability to compete in the 1984 Olympic Games in Los Angeles, California. The reaction to the very first use of relatively accurate drug testing for anabolic steroids was dramatic. The news about it sent a shock wave throughout the competitive athletic world, sports organizations, and the countries that sponsored these amateur athletes.

In 1983, five laboratories were accredited by the IOC to perform national and international amateur sport drug testing, including anabolic steroid testing.[7] The certification of these testing sites was based on initial results using expensive equipment that provided the ability to identify a few anabolic steroid metabolites in urine. Very little of these newly discovered scientific techniques were published in the scientific literature. Some of this information has never been published or critically reviewed by peers outside the Olympic movement. There was still a substantial amount of "eye winking" that went along with the credibility of this newly developed technique for anabolic steroid detection.

Here is how the initial laboratories became IOC certified. First, the laboratory must have purchased several hundred thousand dollars of equipment and learned certain designated detection techniques. Once the laboratory had a degree of experience with the new equipment and techniques, then the IOC sent a few urine samples (known to contain a certain anabolic steroid and or its metabolites) as "unknowns" to be evaluated. If the laboratory could detect these metabolites, then it became certified by the IOC. If the laboratory failed, then IOC officials worked to improve the laboratory's techniques until they passed.

The 1984 Los Angeles Olympic Games

The initial laboratory directors were trained in these techniques by a select group of IOC laboratory personnel dominated by German scientists.

(We now know that some of these East German medical scientists were involved with designing hormonal manipulation techniques that avoided the same techniques that they proffered to the IOC as certified detection methods.) At the heart of the whole matter was another con game. For instance, the IOC would certify a laboratory based on its ability to find provided "unknown" samples of certain anabolic steroids. Then, some of the IOC scientists would turn around and instruct athletes from their country not to use those steroids (detectible ones); and to use these (undetectable ones). In this manner, the East German scientists were able to continue their hormonal manipulation project right under the IOC's nose.

Technical limitations and international politics within these accredited laboratories accounted for the ability to detect and identify only a few of the anabolic steroids that were being abused by international athletes. This phenomenon set the stage for the international game of hide and seek for anabolic steroid abusers in the five countries that possessed the only accredited labs. These countries, including the United States, had the advantage of pretesting their athletes prior to sending them to the 1984 Olympic Games.

Other countries that did not possess IOC certified labs were faced with the possibility of sending "dirty" athletes to the games or completely withdrawing their athletes prior to the games. The Soviet Union, which had no accredited laboratory, withdrew from and boycotted the 1984 Olympic Games held in Los Angeles. The Soviets claimed that there were security reasons for their withdrawal. Others have felt that their decision was in retaliation for the American boycott that had occurred four years earlier at the 1980 Olympic Games in Moscow.

Without the Soviet athletes (who dominated the 1980 Olympic Games which the Americans boycotted) competing in the games, the Americans went on to win a record number of medals. No American athlete tested positive for anabolic steroids, although a few athletes from other countries did.

So, from the USOC leaders' standpoint, the results were a mission accomplished. The Olympic image was untarnished for the Americans, but most experts were aware that many of the American athletes were taking anabolic agents up to and during the 1984 Olympic Games. These agents included:

a) anabolic steroids, especially ones that did not have a urine detection method;
b) human growth hormone, since it did not have a urine detection method, and;
c) testosterone, since it had no urine detection test which was enforced during the games.

Because of the testosterone loophole in the detection methods, it became the anabolic steroid of choice for many competitors. This gap in the drug testing capabilities led some experts to call the 1984 Olympic games in Los Angeles the "testosterone games."

The 1988 Seoul Olympic Games

The 1988 Seoul Olympic Games were the first time since Munich in 1972 that there was no organized boycott of the Summer Olympics. Cuba and Ethiopia supported North Korea when the IOC turned down the North Koreans' demand to co-host the Games. These countries declined participation. Other than that, there were few or no major political demonstrations at these games.

Four years prior to these Games, the USOC set up a volunteer program with U.S. Olympic hopefuls for them to submit their urine for anabolic steroid testing. The athletes, who volunteered, had to declare the anabolic steroids that they were using with the agreement that no subsequent punishment would be assessed. The purpose was to set up "steroid maps" as discussed in a later section. In other words, the USOC was attempting to avoid an embarrassment at the upcoming Olympics by "cleaning-up" the athletes who were using anabolic steroids. This author was a member of the USOC's program during this time.

In 1986, I submitted a research proposal to the USOC and NCAA (National Collegiate Athletic Association) to link anabolic steroids with overly aggressive and violent behavior. I enlisted two doctorate level psychologists and drug experts from Washington State University in the study. Even though I was a member of the USOC's Drug Control Program, my study proposal was turned down. The reason that I was given was that the NCAA and USOC could not verify the anabolic steroid use of the subjects.

Nonetheless, the 1988 Olympic games went on. Ten days into the Games, Canadian Ben Johnson beat defending champion Carl Lewis in the 100-meter dash with a world record time of 9.79 seconds. Johnson's time still represents the fastest-ever time for the 100-meter dash. Johnson tested positive for the anabolic steroid, stanozolol, and the U.S. sprinter Carl Lewis was awarded the gold medal.

Florence Griffith Joyner, "Flo Jo," won four medals. She died a few years after these games. She appeared to be the epitome of health. There were some claims that anabolic steroids played a role in her death. It was doubtful that medical examiners at that time could test for anabolic steroid use.

The 1996 Atlanta Olympic Games

It will never be known how many Olympic records prior to the 1984 Olympic Games were set by athletes who used anabolic steroids. Without a doubt, there were many. Since then, the hormonal manipulation of athletes has continued and expanded with an even more sophisticated array of anabolic and growth hormones which have no current method of urine detection.[8] A detailed discussion of these anabolic hormones has been presented in Chapter 10. These include the pharmaceutical replicas of the body's own hormones (endogenous hormones) as illustrated by the following quotation from Don H. Catlin, director of the UCLA Olympic Analytical Laboratory: "Doping with endogenous hormones is the most serious issue facing sport today; when cleverly administered, these are very difficult to detect."[9]

I met Dr. Catlin in his UCLA laboratory in June of 1984, just prior to the Olympic Games in Los Angeles, through a personal introduction from Dr. Robert O. Voy, who was the chief medical officer of the United States Olympic Committee at that time. Dr. Catlin was and continues to be a major player in the USOC's and IOC's drug doping detection project. He was working on trying to close the testosterone loop-hole in order to have a urine detection method for exogenous testosterone abuse by athletes. Dr. Catlin told me that there would be no real enforcement of testosterone abuse during the upcoming Olympic Games.

This revelation proved to be a green light for American Olympic athletes. Dr. Catlin later published his rationale for using caution in reporting testosterone abuse because it would be readily attacked by litigation attorneys and lay-adjudicators who often did not understand the measurement variability of the test.[10] I began to understand the enormous array of implications embedded within the financial, political, and legal framework that had become such a major part of the Olympic movement.

During that meeting, Dr. Catlin indicated that he had begun working on a urinary detection method for growth hormone abuse by athletes. I knew that this was going to be a difficult, if not impossible, task to accomplish using urine specimens. I shared with him my belief that the only possible way to detect GH abuse by urinary detection methods was to encourage the various drug companies, who were destined to produce synthetic GH, to incorporate an isotope of carbon into the formulation of the genetically-engineered GH product.

Dr. Catlin seemed frustrated with the growth hormone issue. He stated that "GH couldn't enhance athletic performance anyway; so why should the IOC even worry about it?" He claimed that the idea that GH would be used for such purposes was just "hype."[11] Unfortunately, the lack of a detection method, coupled with the anabolic nature of human growth hormone, ushered in the 1996 Olympic Games, held in Atlanta, Georgia, that some athletes and members of the press have referred to as the "Growth Hormone Games."[12]

It seems that after each summer Olympic Games over the last half century, dozens of athletes, coaches, sports administrators, and anabolic steroid traffickers come forth with testimonies that describe the games as a carnival of experimentation with the latest and best anabolic drugs available to enhance athletic performance. The following quotes, obtained shortly after the 1996 Olympic games in Atlanta, illustrate this point.

> The testers know that the [drug] gurus are smarter than they are. They know how to get in under the radar.... And there is no official push for blood testing.... It's very difficult for sport organizations that depend on sponsorship money to have their athletes caught taking performance enhancers. The IOC fears exposing the high levels of drug use. It turns the public off. The IOC is very nervous about testing.... I've had American athletes tell me that they were doing performance-enhancing drugs and that most of them really didn't want to do the drugs, but unless you stop the drug use in sport, I *have* to do drugs. I'm not going to spend the next two years training — away from my family, missing my college education — to be an Olympian and then be cheated out of a medal by some guy from Europe or Asia who is on drugs."[13] [Dr. Robert O. Voy, M.D., former USOC director of sports medicine, former USOC chief medical officer.]

Dr. Voy resigned his position in 1989 because he felt that neither the IOC nor the USOC was committed to eliminating the abuse of illicit performance-enhancing drugs. Other expert officials have stated their beliefs, such as the director of the IOC-accredited drug-testing laboratory at UCLA.[14]

"I don't think that every athlete in Atlanta was doped ... the sophisticated athlete who wants to take drugs has switched to things we can't test for" (Don H. Catlin, M.D., director, UCLA Olympic Analytical Laboratory).

The $2.5 million drug testing effort in the 1996 Atlanta Olympic Games was ineffective even after upgrading the drug testing technology to the use of the high-resolution mass spectrometer (HRMS). During the Games the HRMS revealed what appeared to be five additional positive tests for anabolic steroids that would have been missed by the older technology. However, these tests were never reported as being positive tests by the IOC. Olympic officials, fearful of expensive lawsuits, decided that the positive test results might not stand up in court and reported them as negative because this newer technology was still relatively untested. The result of this decision was that these five athletes went on to receive their respective medals and further added to the "window dressing" atmosphere of drug testing at the Olympic Games. The lack of reporting the positive drug test results for anabolic steroids will be discussed in a later section that specifically deals with the nandrolone issue.

The 2000 Sydney Olympic Games

A great deal of silence enveloped the world of covert drug abuse surrounding the 2000 Olympic Games held in Sydney, Australia. There have been some exceptions to this silence. For example, huge quantities of performance-enhancing synthetic erythropoietin (EPO) were stolen from a hospital in Australia and diverted to the athletic black market about six weeks prior to the games. Another example involved a European track and field coach who was arrested for bringing a substantial amount of synthetic GH into Australia prior to the Games. Elite athletes from a few nations had been disqualified for the upcoming 2000 Games for positive anabolic steroid results. Some of these athletes had litigated their cases and won large sums of money.

Squabbles and whistle blowing added to the broken silence that surrounded the 2000 Games. For instance, the International Olympic Committee (IOC) president levied charges against the United States, claiming that U.S. sporting federations had not reported as many as 15 cases of positive anabolic steroid tests in time to prevent these athletes from competing at the 2000 Games. In some cases, the U.S. sports federations had as many as four positive tests for anabolic steroids in Olympic hopefuls, but did not notify the IOC.

The IOC also made some decisions that put it squarely in the mix of controversy. For example, some of the members of the Chinese 1996 women's swimming team (almost the entire team was disqualified for anabolic steroid use) were approved for competition in the 2000 Games. This decision sent the message that an athlete could build the muscularity of her body, serve a short period of disqualification, and then come back and use her hormonally-manipulated body to compete against others who may have never used performance-enhancing anabolic drugs. Reports have indicated that 27 potential women swimmers competing for spots on the Chinese Olympic team were eliminated, by the Chinese government, for anabolic steroid use that would show positive results if they won a medal at the 2000 Games. The Chinese government wanted to avoid a similar embarrassment that occurred during the 1996 summer games in Atlanta.

During the 2000 Olympic Games, several athletes lost medals due to positive test results for anabolic steroids. The final litigation results on these cases may be years away. However, it is very likely that huge monetary awards (hundreds of millions of dollars) will be awarded to athletes who contest the IOC's drug testing results. This result seems evident at this point in time. The continuing pervasiveness of the abuse of performance-enhancing drugs has spawned a splinter group of competitors and sports administrators who promote the concept of officially legalizing use of anabolic steroids and other banned substances.

The 2000 Olympic Games featured six groups of competitive athletes:

a) a dwindling group of athletes who are not using or abusing performance-enhancing drugs and hope to compete with those who are. This group has been represented by a 1995 poll of assorted U.S. Olympians and Olympic hopefuls. The poll asked: if you are offered a banned performance-enhancing substance with the guarantees that you will not be caught and that you will win, would you take the substance? Of the 198 athletes questioned, 195 answered affirmatively with only three saying no to the proposition.[15]
b) a small group of athletes who are *unknowingly* taking performance-enhancing drugs disguised as athletic supplements or vitamins provided by coaches, trainers or medical personnel. Some of these supplements contain copies of endogenous steroids such as dihydrotestosterone (DHT), dehydroepiandrosterone (DHEA), androstenolone ("Andro") and nortestosterone derivatives. "Endogenous steroids pose an increasing challenge because of their availability in 'nutritional supplements.'"[16]
c) a large and burgeoning group of athletes who abuse performance-enhancing drugs and evade the drug testing "radar" of even the most sophisticated urine testing.
d) a small group of athletes who abuse performance-enhancing drugs and get caught when they are addicted, sloppy with their abuse, ignorant of the known detection times, or some combination of these.
e) a very small group of athletes who may be sabotaged by the "spiking" of their food or drink with small quantities of a banned substance.
f) a very small group of athletes which may test positive for anabolic steroids derived from the meat eaten just days prior to competition. In some countries, including the United States, livestock destined for human consumption is legally treated with anabolic steroids that may show up as a positive test for anabolic steroids.[17–23]

It can be easily seen that drug testing for anabolic steroids and growth hormones has not been an effective measure for the prevention of the abuse of these agents at even the highest levels of competition. Even by employing the most elaborate equipment available for analysis of urine samples, all detection methods have fallen short of their intended deterrent goals. But, both drug use and methods to detect this type of drug use in athletes are evolving in very sophisticated ways.

Basic Principles of Current Anabolic Steroid Detection

Any informative presentation regarding the current and near-future methods to detect the use of anabolic agents is likely to contain some complex terminology and medical concepts. Much of this complexity is due to the technical nature of the beast.

The current methodology for the detection of anabolic steroids and testosterone metabolites in the urine of athletes employs a computerized gas chromatograph combined with high-resolution mass spectrometry. The cost of this equipment is over $500,000. In general, few hospitals and local medical laboratories can afford this equipment.

The *basic principle* for this methodology is to separate and identify these compounds based on their individual molecular weights and overall ionic charge from all of the other urinary metabolites. Recent anabolic steroid use can be identified by HRMS detection if a small fraction of its molecular structure is found unchanged in the urine. If this occurs, detection is a simple task. Some anabolic steroids can be identified by this method alone if the molecular weight of the structure doesn't coincide with another naturally occurring urine metabolite. Examples of this and other detection methods are listed in Table 11-1.

If the molecular weight of the anabolic steroid found in the urine is the same as a naturally occurring metabolite, then other detection principles are used. In this case, the first step is to identify and determine the molecular weights of as many of the urine by-product metabolites of the parent steroid as possible. The determination of the metabolite profile of an anabolic steroid has generally been performed by allowing volunteers or athletes to take the steroid and submit their urines for analysis. Often, unique steroid metabolites can be identified and later synthesized, computerized, and shared with other labs to make a reference "steroid map." This "steroid map" is actually a profile of the anabolic steroid's known urinary metabolites based on ionization and molecular weight properties.

TABLE 11-1. URINE DETECTION OF ANABOLIC AGENT METABOLITES BY GAS CHROMATOGRAPHIC–MASS SPECTROGRAPHIC TECHNIQUES

Anabolic Agent	*Detectable*	*Description of Method*
Anabolic steroids	yes	Unique peak of the steroid's molecular weight with no overlying of naturally-occurring molecules with the same molecular weight Examples: stanozolol, boldenone[24,25]
Anabolic steroids	yes	Unique molecular weight peak(s) of the steroid's degradation metabolites with no overlying of naturally-occurring molecules with the same molecular weight Example: nandrolone[26]
Anabolic steroids	yes	Both the steroid and one or more degradation molecules have detectable unique molecular weight peaks Examples: stanozolol, methandienone,[27] boldenone[28]
Anabolic steroids	no	Steroid and its metabolites have no known unique peaks which can be separated from naturally-occurring molecules with the *same* molecular weights Example: undetectable anabolic steroids
Testosterone preparations	no	Exogenous steroid and its metabolites are all identical with endogenous testosterone; further *quantitative* analyses with arbitrary ratio values using a metabolite, epitestosterone, are utilized[29]
Human growth hormones (GHs)	no	Exogenous hormone and its metabolites are all identical with endogenous GH
Growth hormone (GHRHs)	no	Exogenous hormone and its metabolites are all releasing hormones identical with endogenous GHRH
Insulin-like growth (IGF-1)	no	Exogenous hormone and its metabolites are are all factor-1 identical with endogenous IGG-1
Growth hormone–releasing proteins (GHBPs)	no	Small peptides cannot be detected by this method
Growth hormone secretagogues (GHSs)	no	Small peptides cannot be detected by this method
Luteinizing hormone–releasing hormone (LHRH)	no	Polypeptide hormones are broken down to small peptides that cannot be detected by this method
Luteinizing hormone (LH)	no	Polypeptide hormones are broken down to small peptides that cannot be detected by this method

Anabolic Agent	*Detectable*	*Description of Method*
Human chorionic gonadotrophin (hCG)	no	Polypeptide hormones are broken down to small peptides that cannot be detected by this method
Erythropoietin (EPO)	no	Exogenous hormone and its metabolites are all identical with endogenous EPO

The ability of the certified laboratories to detect the athletic abuse of anabolic steroids has continued to improve over the past two decades. Several factors have led to the improvements. First, there has been a growing body of knowledge that pertains to the metabolism of the various anabolic steroid compounds that goes into the production of the computerized "steroid maps." The major metabolites of most of the anabolic steroids are known and have been synthesized. Second, the recent development of methods for analysis by HRMS has been an important, but expensive advance. This HRMS technology has expanded the detection period of prior anabolic steroid abuse. It has provided the ability to detect these steroids for longer periods of time after the athlete discontinues them.

Urinary detection techniques have come a long way from the "sink method" days and have become very sophisticated. Currently, there are 25 accredited laboratories globally. Seventeen of the laboratories are in Europe, three in North America, three in Asia, one in Australia, and one in South Africa. There are still no accredited laboratories in South America or the Middle East. In the countries without such a laboratory, there is generally little or no reliable testing for anabolic steroids. An elite athlete from such a country may only be tested at major national or international competitions.[30] There is very little opportunity to test for anabolic steroid abuse among professional athletes, since the majority of the accredited laboratories have provided such a service for elite amateur athletes only. Typical hospital and regional laboratories are essentially void of the knowledge, the computerized "steroid maps," and the expensive equipment to provide for this type of testing nationwide. Urinary detection of anabolic steroids is expensive. A typical price range is from $200–300 per urine sample.

Although the laboratory equipment and techniques have evolved to a great degree, this level of sophistication has resulted from major legal problems when athletes choose to appeal their cases in court. The very complexities of the detection methods, along with the uncertainty of the origin of the steroid consumption, such as in contaminated meat products, have provided fodder for these legal cases. And, with the detection of exogenous testosterone abuse, the complexities have resulted in a much greater challenge. These complexities will be discussed in the next section.

Basic Principles of Testosterone Detection

The abuse of testosterone for its performance-enhancing capabilities is one of the most serious issues facing sports today. In most of the previous discussions, grouping testosterone with anabolic steroids has been done to simplify the effects that this class of drugs have on the human body. However, in this section regarding the urine detection of these steroids, testosterone abuse must be separated from the remainder of the anabolic steroids due to the nature of the testing techniques. As illustrated in Table 11-1, the available testing techniques do not provide a satisfactory method to detect exogenous hormones when they are identical to the endogenous hormones.

There is no simple test for recent testosterone abuse by athletes that is valid. Moreover, there is no valid test for its use in the more distant past. Various approaches have been considered within the practical constraint that only a single, untimed urine is available for the screening test. Other testing methods have utilized multiple urine tests, conducted over weeks or even months, to catch the athlete who abuses testosterone. The various methods that have been utilized to find a fail-safe method for the detection of recent testosterone abuse are shown in Table 11-2. No legally defendable, reliable test exists today.

Because pharmaceutical and physiological testosterones have identical structures and molecular weights, mass spectrometers cannot distinguish between the two. Their urinary metabolites are identical. Moreover, the average urine testosterone concentration is approximately 1 percent of the daily production in normal adults and only briefly increases after exogenous testosterone administration. This phenomenon makes single sample testing of urine for testosterone insufficient for the development of a simple test.

TABLE 11-2. VARIOUS URINARY TEST METHODS TO DETECT RECENT TESTOSTERONE (T) ABUSE UTILIZING GAS CHROMATOGRAPH–MASS SPECTROMETRY

Method of urine detection	*Difficulties with this method*
Identification of a unique metabolite	Pharmaceutical and physiological spectra are identical
Ratio of T to luteinizing hormone (LH)	T to LH ratios have proved unreliable on spot urine tests,[31] a valid LH reference is unavailable,[32] and false positives are a problem[33]
Ratios of T metabolites to other T metabolites	Other endogenous steroids are metabolized to identical metabolites as T[34]

Method of urine detection	*Difficulties with this method*
Ratio of T to epitestosterone (E)	T to E ratio is set arbitrarily high to avoid false positives; allows for moderate T use; false positives are still a problem[35]
T to E ratio time profile	Requires multiple tests over weeks or months[36]; cumbersome for Olympic competition; can be masked by preparations of both T and E administered together in proper amounts[37]
T carbon isotope ratio (CIR)	Based on the premise that pharmaceutical T has more radioactive carbons than natural T; on-going studies are anticipated[38,39]

In 1982 it was proposed that the urinary ratio of testosterone (T) to its 17-alpha epimer, epitestosterone (E), might prove to be a useful test for the recent exogenous use of testosterone.[40] The chemical structures of T and E vary only with the hydroxyl configuration on the C-17 carbon atom but have the same molecular weight and chemical structure otherwise. Within the body, there seems to be no conversion from T to E or vice versa.[41] If T is administered or taken by an athlete, then the urine concentration of T rises for a short period of time while E does not. In fact, the urine E concentration lowers slightly.[42] In other words, exogenous use of T raises the T/E urinary ratio by increasing the T concentration and lowering the E concentration. This phenomenon provided the basis for the original IOC detection test, namely an elevated T/E ratio.

Later that year, with very limited data on all of the factors that can influence the T/E ratio, the IOC Medical Commission adopted this detection method. The IOC defined a positive test for exogenous testosterone abuse to be a T/E ratio of >6:1 based on a single analysis. At that time this was an arbitrary threshold for reporting a positive test. Since the overall normal T/E ratio is generally accepted to be 1:1 in the urine of the majority of normal humans, this high threshold allowed for moderate testosterone abuse during the 1984 Olympic Games.

A test which reveals a T/E ratio which is *less than* 6:1 does not rule out recent testosterone use prior to the testing. In this case, the official laboratory report issued is negative, but it has been recognized that this may be describing a false-negative sample. A negative test report could be consistent with:

a) recent use of a short-acting formula of testosterone which leaves the body fast enough (within 4–6 hours) to fall below the 6:1 threshold[43];

b) recent use of testosterone and epitestosterone together as in a gel formulation, even during competition[44];
c) recent use of epitestosterone to camouflage recent or long-term testosterone use, even during competition; and,
d) no use of testosterone at all.

Due to the potential legal challenges and laboratory advancements, the IOC's definition of a positive test for recent testosterone abuse has been changed. For athletes who have T/E ratios of *greater than* 6:1, further testing is required before any conclusions are reached about reporting a positive test. These additional tests may include:

a) multiple urinary T/E ratio tests over weeks and or months to determine the T/E-time profile. Analysis of the T/E-time profile can determine abnormal variations of the T/E ratios and whether or not the T/E values remain consistently elevated above 6:1. If the initial T/E ratio is above 6:1, and subsequent testing reveals that the ratio falls and continues to remain below the 6:1 threshold, then this is usually considered a positive testosterone test for that athlete.
b) multiple blood tests for a full endocrine evaluation and a physical exam to rule out the presence of a testosterone-secreting tumor or other biochemical abnormality which is responsible for the elevated T/E ratios.

However, even with these additional tests, which are cumbersome, time consuming, and expensive, there have been some recently reported cases in athletes where the T/E ratio has remained in the 9–13:1 range despite as many as five additional urine samples collected with less than 24-hour notices. *These cases have not been reported.*

Additional tests, which are necessary, do not fit in well with the flow of competition, such as in the Olympic Games. These cases present a growing concern to the IOC, because they may be the result of sophisticated testosterone delivery systems which produce very high, yet stable T/E ratios over an extended period of time. This type of hormonal manipulation may be on the rise in athletic circles.[45]

Other types of urinary testing methods for recent testosterone abuse have been proposed. One of these proposals involves the determination of a carbon isotope ratio (CIR) of testosterone found in the urine of athletes.[46] The basis for this test is that pharmaceutically synthesized testosterone preparations contain a greater number of carbon isotopes than does naturally produced testosterone. Further studies are ongoing to evaluate and improve this detection method.[47] This test was not the definitive detection method for the 2000 Olympic Games.

Another method that has been suggested as a potential candidate for future detection of testosterone abuse involves hair sample analysis.[48–50] Hair samples are tested using the usual gas chromatograph–mass spectrometry equipment. The early results of this method are inconclusive. It is very doubtful that hair analysis methods for testosterone abuse will be adopted by the IOC.

Detection of Recombinant Anabolic and Growth-Stimulating Hormones

The athletic use of these recombinant hormones has spread globally and is an integral part of the recent past, upcoming, and probable future Olympic games. Moreover, as future medical advances provide a greater variety of recombinant anabolic and growth hormones and factors, then these new drugs will be likely used by athletes.

Currently, no accurate urine drug detection test exists for any genetically engineered copies of hormones that are replicas of its natural chemical structure. Exogenously administered recombinant hormones produce urinary metabolites that are identical to the endogenously produced hormone's metabolites.

With regards to the very small (defined by their chemical structures) neuropeptides, such as GHRPs and GHSs, these are not identical to any endogenous hormone. However, *the use of these drugs is currently impossible to detect utilizing the most modern laboratory techniques.*

New developments in enzyme-linked immunosorbent assay techniques (Norditest) have been recently suggested as rapid methods to detect exogenous GH use. However, these methods have been shown to be unable to detect elevated GH levels if the test is administrated 24 hours after GH use.[51] Using this method for other recombinant hormones that have short half-lives will suffer from the same problem. It is unlikely that any of these methods will be adopted by the IOC.

Another investigative method to detect GH preparations has explored the possibility that the recombinant versions of GH contain detectable levels of carbon isotopes. Three GH preparations were evaluated (Humatrope, Nutropin, and Protropin) and the results indicated that only Humatrope had a carbon isotope ratio that may be markedly different from endogenous GH.[52] It is unlikely that this method could evolve into a valid urine test for exogenous GH use.

Blood Testing for Anabolic Hormones

Over the years various medical scientists have recommended that blood testing be considered to detect performance-enhancing drugs. The major goal of blood testing would be to determine better methods for detecting the use of anabolic steroids, testosterone, GH, EPO, and other recombinant hormones and products. A number of studies have been conducted utilizing blood as the tested body fluid.[53–58]

Although there may be some advantages to blood testing, it is much too early in its development to comment on. If blood testing proves effective, it would probably take several years or longer to administer in a fashion that would be able to withstand the onslaught of legal challenges.

The Nandrolone Controversy

The nandrolone controversy may prove to be the demise of anabolic steroid testing in athletes. Nandrolone is an anabolic steroid that is bioactive and has been shown to enhance various aspects of athletic performance. Since the relatively accurate forms of anabolic steroid testing of athletes began, nandrolone presence (via urine metabolites) in urine samples has been the most reported result for a positive anabolic steroid test. Prior to or during the 2000 Olympic Games, several hopeful competitors were disqualified because a urine sample showed detectable levels of nandrolone metabolites. Table 11-3 shows the number of Olympic hopefuls who have been disqualified for having nandrolone metabolites in their urine.

TABLE 11-3. ATHLETES WHO HAVE BEEN DISQUALIFIED FROM OLYMPIC COMPETITION OR BEEN STRIPPED OF THEIR MEDALS DUE TO POSITIVE NANDROLONE METABOLITES IN THEIR URINE TESTS WITHIN THE PAST TWO YEARS.

Athlete	*Country*	*Olympic Event*
Linford Christe	Britain	runner; sprinter
Merlene Ottely	Jamaica	runner; sprinter
Doug Walker	Britain	runner; sprinter
Mark Richardson	Britian	swimmer
Petr Korda	Czech.	tennis player
Djamel Bouras	France	judo player
Spencer Smith	Britain	triathlete
Igor Shalimov	Russia	soccer player
Christophe Dugarry	Russia	soccer and rugby player
C.J. Hunter	United States	shot putter

Athlete	*Country*	*Olympic Event*
Unnamed	Bulgaria	weightlifters (entire team)
Unnamed	China	women swimmers (most team members)

Nandrolone metabolites are the most easily detected, yet most controversial, metabolites found in the urine of competitive athletes alleged to have used anabolic steroids. There are two major reasons for this ease in detection. First, nandrolone and its metabolites are not made by the human body. Therefore, *nandrolone metabolites (at any level of detection) indicate that there is no physiological reason for them to appear in the urine.* Second, the preparations of nandrolone that are available have long half-lives and the longest detection times of any anabolic steroid currently known. As a result (positive for anabolic steroid use) urine metabolites of nandrolone have been the most commonly reported as a positive test for recent anabolic steroid use in athletes.

Nandrolone, and its metabolites, could appear in the urine of competitive athletes by three known mechanisms:

a) ingestion of meat products (within 24 hours) that contain these metabolites has been documented by the medical science literature (see Chapter 4);
b) ingestion of dietary supplements that contain nor-testosterone products (OTC in the U.S.) that contain nandrolone-like chemicals (and test for same) that result in positive urine tests for nandrolone use; or,
c) nandrolone use.

Recent studies have shown that the most up-to-date urine testing for nandrolone use cannot completely exclude the use of OTC nandrolone-like substances.[59] These OTC products, that have preparations of nor-19-testosterone supplements (legally available), are difficult to distinguish between illegal nandrolone use and legal supplement use in the United States.

Athletes' claims that they may have eaten meat containing nandrolone metabolites may be valid. Several investigational studies have confirmed that consumed meat products may contain nandrolone metabolites. Athletes who consume (within 24 hours) these products are likely to test positive for anabolic steroids.

Legal challenges by Olympic athletes may also be valid. Those who have been disqualified via positive urine tests for nandrolone use, and litigate, are likely to be successful. The monetary awards given to these athletes will probably be lethal to all drug testing programs that test for anabolic steroid use.

For those who doubt the monetary influence in the judicial system in this matter, the current and potential monetary portfolio of a potential Olympic athlete must be considered. Recently, it has been shown that an Olympic gold medal can add significantly to the portfolio of a marketable athlete. For example, it has been widely reported that Cathy Freeman, medal winner in the 2000 Games, will have sports sponsorship contracts estimated at over $10 million over the next three years. Athletes like Freeman can afford the best legal representation that money can buy to defend them if a positive drug test is reported.

Summary: "Say It Ain't So, Joe, Say It Ain't So!"

Cheating in elite and professional sporting events was never brought to the attention of the American public in a greater manner than with the scandal that involved the Chicago White Sox in 1919. Shoeless Joe Jackson was the star of the team that has often been regarded as one of the greatest in professional baseball history. With World War I raging, Shoeless Joe became a national hero for many American youths. Several members of this team took financial payoffs to lose specific games, and ultimately, the entire World Series. The team earned the nickname of "The Black Sox." Whether or not Shoeless Joe was truly involved has never been totally resolved; he was banned anyway. History also tells us that young fans, after the conspiracy trial was over, ran after him and exclaimed, "Say it ain't so, Joe, say it ain't so!" In other words, these *young fans didn't want to think that their baseball hero was a cheater.*

The early use of drugs, or doping, as a form of cheating was first seen in prize fighting. This method of doping utilized the administration of a drug or substance to an athlete to attain a *reduction* in athletic performance. For instance, a drug, such as a strong tranquilizer, could be slipped to a prizefighter in order to affect the outcome of the match by reducing his performance. Such methods were linked to betting and financial rewards, and have cast negative shadows on professional athletics.

In some ways, the Canadian sprinter Ben Johnson became a modern-day version of Shoeless Joe. The Olympic winner of the 100-meter dash has traditionally been called "the world's fastest man," and Ben Johnson earned that title in the 1988 Olympics by using anabolic steroids. Two days after the race, his drug test indicated a positive test for anabolic steroids. Never before had the use of these steroids by an athlete been such a shock to the sporting fans. Ben Johnson was disqualified and stripped of his gold medal.

Although he won the race, he lost his medal, fame, and potential fortune. But those within the athletic drug culture have claimed that Ben Johnson actually *won* by getting caught because it further illustrated and promoted the performance-enhancing effects of anabolic steroids and other drug use in sports. This is the major dilemma that confronts sports each and every time a successful athlete tests positive for the use of anabolic steroids or other performance-enhancing drugs. Can the testing outlast the legal onslaughts? And, what outcome does it have if it does?

The new era of monstrous athletes and the drugs they use has spread rapidly to nearly all sports at all levels. Drug use has been the dirty and universal secret of sports that is not so secret anymore. The new phase of anabolic hormone use involves the use of recombinant growth hormones and other growth factors that are basically nothing short of being the biochemical "fertilizers" for suprahuman growth and development. They can distort the norms for ultimate adult height and afford suprahuman muscle mass and strength which can be converted to fame and fortune on the athletic field. But what a pity and at what ultimate cost to the users? Whatever happened to the natural athlete?[60]

The drug testing of athletes in the future will probably continue to have an uncertain role in deterring this form of cheating and human experimentation. Unless the methods of drug testing improve drastically, and quickly, then it will continue to be a "window dressing" and everyone will know it. There is a good chance that drug testing of athletes will be rendered bankrupt by legal challenges, legitimate or not.

12
The Early Search for Medical Applications of Testosterone

Introduction: "The Forgotten Sex Steroids"

Despite the fact that testosterone was the first sex steroid ever synthesized from chemical reactions over 65 years ago, it and its later derivatives (anabolic steroids) have been *the least studied and least prescribed* of the major classes of sex steroid hormones.[1] Significantly more medical attention has been paid to the corticogenic, estrogenic, and progesterogenic steroids.[2] For instance, corticosteroids have been very well studied for over 50 years and remain widely prescribed today. Likewise for estrogens, which are widely used today in hormone replacement regimens and in a variety of drug formulations for oral contraceptives. By combining these applications, it becomes apparent that estrogens are one of the most prescribed classes of drugs in modern medicine. Progesterogenic steroids are also widely utilized in oral contraceptive formulations and for use orally as a form of "morning after pill" contraception. Its injectable use and subcutaneous use are as a single-component, long-lasting form of contraception. Also, progesterone (Depo-Provera) is utilized as a form of "chemical castration" for a variety of male sexual offenders.

A significant number of medical practitioners have become so complacent with their use of terminology that the term *steroid* means only corticogenic steroid or cortisone to them. Many of them have forgotten that various steroids include corticosteroids, estrogenic steroids, vitamin D, cholesterol, progesterogenic steroids, testosterone, and anabolic steroids. Say "steroids" to many medical doctors and they immediately think corticosteroids, or cortisone. Say "steroids" to bodybuilders and they immediately think testosterone and anabolic steroids. Both groups are partially correct and partially incorrect as shown by some of the various types of steroids that are found within or utilized by the human body as illustrated in Table 12-1. The term *steroid* only refers to a specific chemical structure, and to further define the chemical structure, one must learn the various types of "steroids" and to apply the terminology appropriately. If some physicians think that "steroids" means only corticogenic steroids or cortisone, then is there any wonder that testosterone and anabolic steroids have become "the forgotten sex steroids?"

Table 12-1. Common Steroids That Function Within the Human Body

Classification	*Common Names*	*Some Pharmaceutical Drug Names*
Estrogenic steroids	Estrogens	Premarin, Estrace, Ogen
Progesterogenic steroids	Progesterones	Depo-Provera, Provera
Androgenic steroids	Androgens and anabolic steroids	Deca-Durabolin, Anavar, Testosterone, Winstrol
Corticogenic steroids	Corticosteroids	Cortisone, Prednisone
Vitamins	Vitamin D	Vitamin D
Cholesterol	Cholesterol	none

The history of the search for medical applications for testosterone and anabolic steroids has been plagued by several factors. These steroids have been on an "on again, off again" pendulum which resembles a bipolar clinical history. The continuing controversies and mistakes that have plagued the scientific advancements associated with testosterone and anabolic steroids are perhaps unparalleled in medical history.[3]

A historical summary of the search for medical applications of testosterone and anabolic steroids will be presented in this chapter. This historical approach is important for several reasons. First, no other hormone parallels the history of the early development of medical endocrinology better than that of testosterone. Second, a historical review can reveal insight into how important *timing* is for the discovery and clinical use of medications. Third, a historical review can reveal some of the pitfalls which can occur when medical politics attempts to thwart scientific inertia by the promotion of false dogma promulgated by medical authorities who wish to mold the practice of medicine and medical education the way *they* want it to be. Fourth, it uncovers some of the medical antipathy that has been associated with drugs or hormones that significantly alter sexual desire, pleasure, and performance. Depending on the social mores of the times, testosterone and anabolic steroids have been swept under the medical rug only to be removed and experimented with again and again.

The new millennium has retained a degree of enthusiasm and social pressure to revive the use of testosterone and anabolic steroids for their libido-enhancing effects. A quick glance at any magazine stand illustrates the many magazines, such as *Women's Day, Good Housekeeping, Prevention,* and *American Health*, that address the female population's interest in sexual intimacy throughout the lifespan, specifically identifying the role of testosterone and its influence on libido. Another example is the recent widespread use of Viagra for enhancement of sexual performance in both men and women, exemplifying the current American social milieu regarding sexual performance and its effects on medical ethics and clinical practice. This illustrates the powerful role of patients in exerting pressure on their physicians to review the roles of testosterone and anabolic steroids.

Finally, a historical review is important so that the reader can better understand where we are and why we are there regarding the current and future clinical uses of anabolic agents for disease conditions and longevity advancements. For instance, testosterone was labeled "medical dynamite" and "sexual TNT" by premier physicians in the mid–1930s.[4] Even the pharmaceutical industry couldn't avoid using tempting promotional phrases in the past such as "the lure of the Land of Bimini," which caused a medical uproar.[5] Certainly, there was some truth to these extravagant labels.

It seems that the search for medical applications has been revived during the mid–1990s for several serious diseases, illnesses, and conditions. It's about time that medical science got its collective head out of the sand. Testosterone has been available for clinical use for 65 years and the anabolic steroids have been clinically available for over 40 years. An elite endocrinologist may know nearly everything about the biochemical interplay of all of the human body's hormones, but if a lack of knowledge persists with a single class of sex steroid hormones (testosterone and anabolic steroids), then serious consequences are in store for patients and physicians alike. Androgens are "the forgotten steroids" in modern medicine.[6]

But wait a moment: Wasn't the abuse of anabolic steroids part of the reason that Ben Johnson ran the world's fastest time ever in the 100-meter dash in the 1988 Olympic Games? Yes, Ben Johnson ran while under the influence of anabolic steroids for which he tested positive and was later disqualified. So, the drug that helped a man run the fastest 100-meter time ever recorded, and by a good margin, is useful in a variety of disease conditions? Yes, but, to compare the huge amounts of anabolic steroids abused by bodybuilders to the small amounts prescribed for legitimate medical purposes is ludicrous. In other words, the *abuse* of anabolic steroids should not be compared to the legitimate use of anabolic steroids for medical conditions.

For most people, consuming two cups of coffee daily is safe, but how about consuming 200 cups of coffee daily? Such an intake would be lethal for many. For most people, taking two aspirin tablets daily is safe, but how about taking 200 aspirin tablets daily? This practice would be lethal for most. And to further the point of the importance of dosage, what if patients increased their prescribed insulin dosage by 100-fold? All patients would go into a coma and die! Thus, as with any drug or hormone, the dose and type of anabolic steroids used in clinical settings are important parameters. Even though strength athletes and bodybuilders take 10 to 100 times or more of the clinical doses of anabolic steroids, most do not die. However, at these dosages, many of them experience serious side effects as outlined in previous chapters. In contrast, the goal of any drug therapy is to identify and utilize the effective dose and at the same time minimize any potential adverse effects.

As the following sections will indicate, many physicians and researchers have been able to accomplish this goal for the betterment of their patients. Still, the majority of the medical profession has avoided prescribing this class of drugs entirely; practitioners have been frightened away by the so-called adverse effects which are usually only seen when the dose of anabolic steroids used is much too high and over too long a period of time. The abuse of anabolic steroids in supratherapeutic doses causes adverse effects. The appropriate use of anabolic steroids under medical supervision most often does not.

Effects of Medieval Organotherapy on Modern Medicine

Since recorded time the customs of primitive societies provided for the use of human and animal organs in treating disease conditions. This type of therapy, organotherapy, was based on observation, speculation, and a smattering of science. For instance, some medieval physicians suggested that warriors eat animal or human hearts to enhance bravery, or that rulers and philosophers ingest animal or human brains to enhance intellect. During the Dark Ages, organotherapy perhaps reached its peak, for the people of this period indulged in consuming such bodily substances as bile, blood, bones, brains, feathers, feces, animal horns, intestines, placenta, testicles, and teeth.[7]

Reviewing the theories of the ancient and medieval scientists, it seems that they may have had considerable comprehension regarding the presence and function of the body's glands even though they had no way to prove their theories. In practice organotherapy was a composite of mysticism, religion, philosophy, and customary dogma.

Modern Remnants of Organotherapy

Organotherapy still has some modern remnants. Organ extracts have been used in modern medicine to treat disease conditions in humans. For instance, until very recently, brain extracts (pituitary glands from human cadavers) were used to treat dwarf children and allow them to grow to an acceptable adult height. Today, through the development of genetic engineering techniques, scientists have learned to isolate and synthesize from the human pituitary gland unlimited amounts of synthetic human growth hormone to treat short-statured children. However, there is usually a downside to pharmaceutical advancements. In this case, the downside is the abuse of human growth hormone for athletic purposes and for forcing ultimate height gains for still immature athletes by their family members, coaches, or physicians. This form of organotherapy has been outdated by the methods that utilize the techniques of genetic engineering.

Other organotherapy remnants include the self-use and prescription use of glandular extracts that are sold in the nation's health-food stores. These glandular preparations are usually available for oral consumption and may contain extracts from plant, animal, or human adrenal glands, ovaries, pituitaries, livers, or testicles. The effectiveness of these extracts in treating disease conditions remains controversial and scientific studies are certainly needed to determine the safety and effectiveness of these over-the-counter products. Even today, the debate continues as to whether or not these types of "supplements" should be regulated as drugs by the United States Food and Drug Administration. As an historical example, the widespread use of plant-derived phytoestrogens to replace human estrogens has been shown to be ineffective in maintaining integrity of bone strength.[8] However, many women flock to the health food stores to buy these products under the mistaken belief that they are beneficial. Recent scientific reports have taken the position that these phytoestrogens have little proven benefit. So-called natural plant-derived estrogens are ineffective when orally ingested for use within the human body.

Another remnant of organotherapy that relates to athletic performance is the use of extra blood (blood doping or hypertransfusion of red blood cells) by endurance athletes such as marathon or middle-distance runners and long-distance cyclists. This practice, proven scientifically to enhance aerobic capacity in elite athletes, has been phased out due to the genius of genetic engineering techniques. Now available is synthetic human erythropoietin (EPO), which is a recombinant human hormone that can stimulate red blood cell production within the cardiovascular system to a much greater extent than normal. The use of synthetic EPO by endurance athletes remains undetectable by even the most elaborate drug-testing procedures and certainly enhances aerobic capacity and endurance of 10 percent or more. However, there have been several recent deaths associated with this practice. Theoretically, the athlete is able to take advantage of the increased hemoglobin and hematocrit during strenuous exercise because of the vascular bed dilation, but after exercise, the athlete is dehydrated and the vascular dilation returns to normal, leaving a hyperviscous blood with all the usual clotting factors. This phenomenon at rest could be a setup for a stroke or heart attack waiting to happen. Several case studies regarding this phenomenon have been reported in the literature; but, in most cases, the athletes are not alive to tell their stories. This is another area where medical science, via genetic engineering techniques, has "improved" on organotherapy.

The early roots of the discovery of many hormones began with crude, experimental organotherapy. Whether it was eating wild animal hearts for bravery, blood transfusions for endurance, or the use of testicular extracts for strength development and vitality, organotherapy has had deep roots in society and in attempts to enhance athletic performance. These brief remarks introduce organotherapy and serve to begin the tracings of the "male sex hormone" from its earliest recorded history. Moreover, they serve to build a foundation for the following chapters, which deal with anabolic steroid use in more modern times.

Early Empirical Knowledge About Testosterone

The earliest empirical knowledge regarding the male sex hormone comes from the ancient accounts of castrated animals and men and the observation of the subsequent effects this castration had on the body. But even before these observations, in about 1,400 B.C., a physician from India recommended the use of testicular extracts as a cure for impotence in men.[9] Prior to 300 B.C., the Greek philosopher Aristotle documented the effects of castration in many species of animals in his *Historis Animalium.*[10] The earliest documented correlation between testicular function and the aging process is found in the works of Aretaeus the Capadocuean in A.D. 150. In one chapter he wrote: "For it is the semen, when possessed of vitality, which makes us to be men, hot well braced in limbs, well voiced, spirited, strong to think and act. For when the semen is not possessed of its vitality, persons become shriveled, have a sharp tone of voice, lose their hair and their beard, and become effeminate, as the characteristics of eunuchs prove."[11]

It was several centuries later (about A.D. 800) that Johannes Mesue was reported to have prescribed testicular extracts as an aphrodisiac and for the treatment of pulmonary tuberculosis.[12] Centuries later in 1664, Willis published the following: "The blood poured out something — through the spermatic arteries to the genitalia — and that it received in turn certain ferments from these parts — hat is, certain particles imbued with a seminal tincture and carried back to the blood — which makes it vigorous and instills into it a new and lively virtue."[13]

The Experimental Use of Testicular Implants and Extracts

It was about a century later in 1792 that anatomist-scientist John Hunter, during the Enlightenment, attempted to approach the functioning of the testicles in a scientific experiment. He attempted to remove the testicles from cocks and transplant the testicles into the abdomens of hens and observe the subsequent changes in the hens. However, due to infection and an apparent rejection of the testicular implants, he failed to observe the expected "masculinization" of the hens.[14]

Testicular Extracts and "Rooster Science"

Another century passed before the landmark work of the German scientist A.A. Berthold was reported in 1848. In his experiment, he removed the testes of four roosters and surgically replaced one testis into the abdomen of two different capons (castrated roosters). After this surgical implantation of the testis, he allowed the experimental capons (with implanted testis) to live for six months, observed them and then killed them. He reported that "these animals remained male in regard to voice, reproduction instinct, fighting spirit, and growth of comb and wattles ... is maintained by the productive influence of the testicle."[15]

Early Human Experiments with Testicular Extracts

There was a lengthy interim following this fundamental "rooster science" of Berthold before other scientists would attempt to experiment further with the testicular substance in humans. According to the historical record of this era, Brown-Sequard, who epitomized the French scientific world, described some of the syndromes for human disease conditions that still bear his name. During his time he had been a keen-thinking physiologist, who was acutely interested in developments regarding the infancy of the science of hormones. But he was aging, and at the end of his career at age 72, he made the quantum leap from the pages of the "rooster science" to self-experimentation. He rationalized that there was much more work which he wanted to accomplish, but his health was fading quickly.

Brown-Sequard began his experiment by removing the testicles of dogs and guinea pigs. He then smashed these testicles and brewed them in a salt solution, giving rise to a sort of "testicle stew." He then began to inject himself with this crude testicular extract. With a new fire in his eyes, he lectured to the premier French physiologists stating that these testicular extracts had rejuvenated him. He claimed a remarkable return of physical strength and endurance, a rejuvenated bowel system, and enhanced mental capacity.[16]

Never before had there been such a powerful report on how to attain a new lease on life by such a prestigious scientist. Unfortunately, Brown-Sequard's reported fountain of youth lasted for only a few months, and he died shortly thereafter of apparently unrelated causes. Perhaps it might have been an infection acquired from the injections or a withdrawal phenomenon from the discontinuation of the injections. No one will ever know. Even with all of the other important discoveries that Brown-Sequard made in the medical field, he died one of the most discredited scientists in the history of medicine. Perhaps his theory was correct, but his methodology was flawed. The response of the scientific world was to break into laughter that can still be occasionally heard in some medical circles today. The very idea of testicular extracts affording such strength, endurance, and vitality! And for his perceived scientific blunder, Brown-Sequard had critics who have tried to wipe him completely off the scientific map. But what the critics of his era seemed to have forgotten was that Brown-Sequard had a unique ability to think keenly and that he had dedicated nearly 50 years of his life to science.

By jumping into human experimentation too soon, Brown-Sequard handed down a message that still has meaning today. If you are going to experiment with the secret of vitality hidden within the testicular substance, then you had better be correct. Brown-Sequard had attempted to make a new man of himself during his elderly years, and this Dr. Ponce de León imitation resulted in an act that would place the study of and search for the male sex hormone in the scientific doghouse for 35 years. For nearly four decades, the early endocrine scientists didn't forget Brown-Sequard's apparent failure. The medical world was not only disappointed but was somewhat furious.[17] No one dared to attempt to follow up on Brown-Sequard's work for fear of medical antipathy and criticism. So, until the 1920s, the prevailing medical knowledge tended to disregard the existence of a "male substance" contained within the testicles.

The unfortunate aspects of Brown-Sequard's work were the unscientific manner of his investigation and his extravagant claims of rejuvenation. With the possible exception of the search for the Fountain of Youth by Ponce de León, the search for perpetual youth was never brought so closely and prominently to the attention of the world. Perhaps the inevitable result of Brown-Sequard's work was that there was strong prejudice against a mode of therapy built not on controlled observation and experimentation, but on wishful conclusions. The susceptibility of many minds of that time to matters relating to sex and false hopes raised by extravagant claims led inevitably to a viewpoint strongly antagonistic to the acceptance of the efficacy of any testicular substances.[18] However, a history of research for the "male hormone" would be incomplete without some mention of searches for rejuvenation.

The quest for some sort of drug or elixir that affords perpetual life or a fountain-of-youth effect has been with humanity for a long time, and perhaps it has intensified with the progress of medical science. If not the male sex hormone, then perhaps some other hormone could aid longevity? The modern hormone that is perceived to delay aging or reverse some aspects of aging has been recombinant human growth hormone. One of the first scientific papers on the potential powers of human growth hormone in the anti-aging process was published in 1989,[19] but other supportive reports have since been published. However, the manner in which the media portrayed these scientific articles of human growth hormone as a possible youth restoring drug resulted in physicians nationwide being bombarded by phone calls from their patients requesting treatment to delay aging.

The Isolation and Synthesis of Testosterone

Following the fate of Brown-Sequard, it seems that research in the area of testicular extracts took a few steps backward. Then, after little attention for nearly four decades, attempts to extract the male sex hormone from animal testicles were begun.

The Isolation of Testosterone

In 1926, Professor Fred C. Koch and a young medical student, Lemuel C. McGee, flirted with being called the laughingstocks of the scientific world by reopening the search for the male sex hormone. With money donated from Squibb pharmaceuticals, these University of Chicago scientists began their search by castrating enough bulls to obtain 40 pounds of bull testicles. By utilizing some of the extraction techniques afforded them by the advances in organic chemistry, they stewed these bull testicles in benzene, alcohol, and acetone solutions. Out of the 40 pounds of bull testicles, they ended up with a mere 20mg of a fat-soluble extract that they believed contained the "male hormone substance." Since they presumed that this resulting testicular extract had male-sex-hormone capacities, they had to prove it. They couldn't just submit their bull testicle extract for evaluation in some laboratory as we would today. Of course, the chemical analytical techniques, such as infrared scanning, gas chromatographic scanning and mass-spectrophotometer scanning techniques utilized in more modern times were decades away from being discovered. So, the only proven and available techniques which were available to show that Koch's extract contained some sort of chemical manhood was to resort to the old "rooster science." They had to castrate some roosters, wait several weeks to watch the roosters' wattles and combs atrophy, and then inject the roosters with their version of a bull testicular extract and observe the results. Unfortunately, the small quantity of extract obtained from 40 pounds of bull testicles did not allow them to use hundreds, or even a dozen roosters, for the study.

Koch selected a capon with its combs and wattles mere remnants of its former proud rooster-hood for the experiment. They then divided the scanty amount of "testicular substance" which they had previously extracted from the bull testicles and began injecting this substance into the capon on a daily basis. Within two weeks, the capon's combs and wattles turned redder and brighter, like a normal rooster's.[20] Prior to publishing their results, since the topic of this experiment was so controversial, Koch sent the medical student McGee back to the laboratory to repeat the entire experiment, from the bull testicles on up. The results of the second experiment were the same. Koch and McGee must have realized that they had the information that they were looking for. This experiment became the first documented proof of the existence of a "male sex hormone" derived from the testicles. Koch and McGee became the first of the great hormone hunters.[21]

Three years after McGee had graduated from medical school, Koch and Dr. T. F. Gallagher, aided by a modest sum of research money from the Committee for Research in Problems of Sex of the National Research Council, began with 10,000 pounds of bull testicles and refined Koch's earlier extraction technique.[22] With their version of testicular extract, Gallagher and Koch, along with Dr. A. T. Keynon, performed the first documented human experiment on a human eunuch to prove the efficacy of the "male sex hormone" in humans.

The Synthesis of Testosterone

Now momentum was gathering in the scientific world to further isolate, identify, and synthesize the "male sex hormone." There was now no doubt that it existed, at least in a crude form. In the summer of 1935 organic chemists in the laboratory of the German-Jewish pharmacologist Ernst Laqueur in Amsterdam extracted a few milligrams of pure "male sex hormone," named it *testosterone*, and precisely determined its chemical structure.[23] Then, within the same year, two different scientists, Ruzicka (a Yugoslav chemist) and Butendandt (a German chemist), synthesized testosterone from cholesterol in a manner like that the human body uses.[24] Both of these research groups were later awarded Nobel prizes for the independent synthesis of testosterone. Only Ruzicka accepted the award; the Germans declined, apparently due to the influence of World War II.[25]

During this period, organic chemistry was burgeoning, and was greatly influencing the field of medicine. Drugs such as sulfa antibiotics, known as "God's powder," and drugs to fight malaria were discovered by organic chemists. But the first great hormone hunter was Dr. Fred Koch, who overcame the previous decades of medical antipathy to extract the "male sex hormone." He opened the gateway for others to isolate and synthesize it.

Prior to Koch's work, the general feeling was that there was no such thing as a "male sex hormone." Until his discovery, manhood was manhood and womanhood was womanhood with no known biochemical reason for the differences between the sexes. An obituary published in a 1948 issue of the *Journal of Clinical Endocrinology* contained the following comments regarding Dr. Koch's contributions to medical science: "His (Koch's) diversified contributions to endocrine research are well known to all. He will best be remembered, however, by his influence on the development of our understanding of testicular function ... the details of biological relations to male hormone and hormone-like substances were described."

Dr. Koch had taken the warning of the late famous or infamous Dr. Brown-Sequard, which was that when one tinkers with the testicular substance, the result better be the correct one. He turned out to be correct. But as history will indicate, it didn't keep others from tinkering with the "male sex hormone" and its analogs. Some of this later research which was done during World War II was dehumanizing. This latter research will be briefly covered in an upcoming section.

In summary, the testis was the first organ ever suspected of producing an internal secretion of hormone-like abilities. Testicles were the first glands subjected to experimentation with animals and humans. Testicular extracts were the first glandular extracts to be self-injected in an experiment. The desire to do so, with all of the rejuvenation expectations, was tempting to even one of the most hailed early medical scientists. Testosterone and other androgens were the first hormones, and perhaps the first true drugs, ever synthesized from chemical reactions. Prior to the synthesis of testosterone, all other drugs were obtained via chemical extracts from herbs, fungi and other plants. The discovery, isolation, and synthesis of testosterone ushered in the science of endocrinology as we know it today. A detailed chronological tabulation of this history, adapted from Newerla,[26] as represented in Table 12-2, is a tribute to the search for these steroids.

TABLE 12-2. A TABULATION OF THE HISTORY OF THE DISCOVERY AND ISOLATION OF THE "MALE SEX HORMONE"

Dates	*Description of Event*
1400 B.C.	The *Ayrveda* of Susruta recommended testis tissue for impotence.
460–370	Hippocrates used the word "hormone" for certain ferments.
384–322	Aristotle described the castration effects in animals and man.
A.D. 40	Matthew cited in the Bible that eunuchs were made both by God (congenital) and by man (castrated).
150	Aretaeus the Capadocuean suggested that the semen was the basis of male characteristics.
131–201	Galen of Pergamus recognized the pituitary gland and believed that it secreted a "phlegm" into the nose.
777–837	Johannes Mesue the Elder prescribed testicular extract as an aphrodisiac.
1664	Willis postulated that the blood received certain ferments from the spermatic veins that made it vigorous and lively.
1762	John Hunter transplanted the gonads of one gender into the other gender unsuccessfully.
1848	Arnold Berthold performed the first successful transplants in capons proving an endocrine function of the testes.
1850	Franz von Leydig described certain testicular cells (Leydig interstitial cells).
1889	Brown-Sequard published his famous paper on self-injection with testicular extracts and claimed self-rejuvenation.
1896	Reinke described the crystalloids of the interstitial testicular cells and postulated that these (Reinke crystalloids) secreted male substances.
1905	Starling introduced the term "hormone" for internal secretions.
1907	Tandlerand and Grosz described the muscular changes in eunuchs.
1909	Pende coined the term "endocrinology" for the science of internal secretions.
1911	Pezard discovered the capon comb and wattle growth as a potential test for male hormone determination.
1912	Steinach coined the term "puberty gland" for the testes.
1926	McGee and Koch extracted "male substance" from bull testicles.
1929	Koch and associates treated a human enuch with "testicular substance" and proved its effectiveness.
1929	Loewe and Voss extracted "androgens" from urine.
1931	Butenandt isolated "the male sex hormone" and other androgens from human urine.
1934	Ruzicka and co-workers synthesized androsterone.

Dates	*Description of Event*
1935	David and co-workers isolated crystalline "male sex hormone" from bull testicles.
1935	Ernst Laqueur isolated pure "male sex hormone," named it *testosterone*, and precisely determined its chemical structure.
1935	Ruzicka and co-workers synthesized testosterone from cholesterol.
1935	Butendandt and Hanisch synthesized testosterone from cholesterol.

It should be apparent to the reader that there was quite a historical cast of characters, who lived over the past decades and centuries, who were driven to learn about the chemical nature of manhood. Famous men, great scientists, biblical authors, and others wanted to know if there was a gland which secreted something "male" that explained the major differences observed between the human sexes. What if Aristotle or Matthew had been alive in 1935, and what if they were to read the scientific literature of that decade; well, they would have learned that the major differences between the sexes are biochemical in nature! We know of this history because of the medical literature and of its summary as presented here.

Early Clinical Experimentation with Testosterone

As soon as testosterone was discovered and synthesized it became available for clinical experimentation on patients who had a wide variety of complaints and illnesses. There was no strict approval or review process for any newly synthesized drugs at that time. The U.S. Food and Drug Administration (FDA) was in its infancy. Medical doctors thus tended to use testosterone therapy without the assistance of a clinical laboratory to measure appropriate serum amounts. No one knew what a normal level of testosterone was in the blood of men, much less in the blood of women. The early uses and scientific reporting of the uses of testosterone certainly resembled a biochemical version of shooting from the hip. Testosterone therapy had positive results in several disease conditions; but it also had some adverse effects.

Experimentation with Testosterone by Nazi Scientists

The ugliness of clinical experimentation with testosterone reared its head during World War II. In the records of this war are numerous accounts of hormonal manipulation and experimentation on human prisoners by Nazi scientists.[27] After all, a group of German research scientists pioneered the synthesis of testosterone and other hormones. They were awarded the Nobel Prize in medicine for it. Several anecdotal accounts have been published suggesting that testosterone and its analogs, anabolic steroids, were given to the Nazi Gestapo and Nazi troops to make them more muscular, sexually aggressive, and mean fighters in battle. One of the first and certainly the most famous anabolic steroid users was Adolf Hitler. From the records of Hitler's personal physician, it was reported that Hitler was given injections of the "derivatives of testosterone" for a variety of presumed mental and physical conditions.[28] Hitler may have been best described as a drug addict in the last years of his life. Hitler's personal physician reported that Hitler was prescribed injections of methamphetamines and several other drugs that are now considered to be narcotics. Who will ever know how much these psychoactive anabolic steroids, "speed" and other drugs affected Hitler's irrational judgments and dehumanizing tactics? Today, the drugs Adolf Hitler used are commonplace and are used among anabolic steroid–using strength athletes and bodybuilders who train in gyms and health clubs across America. The abnormal mental health conditions of heavy anabolic steroid users, such as mania, acute paranoid psychoses, overly aggressive and violent behavior, withdrawal depression, withdrawal suicide, and so forth, describe the documented behaviors of Adolf Hitler.

Clinical Experimentation with Testosterone

Putting ethics and morals aside, the results of experiments that were believed performed by Nazi medical scientists were never published in the international body of scientific literature and will probably be lost forever. But if we take the stairs down to the basement of any major medical library in the United States and blow the dust off of the journals of the late 1930s and early 1940s, we are able to recap many of the early (and often forgotten) experimental work with testosterone on both normal and ill men and women. In reviewing these published articles, it is important to reflect briefly on some of the differences in scientific modalities, designs, and freedoms that were in vogue during this earlier period as compared to more modern times. First, the code of ethics was certainly much more relaxed in the late 1930s, with fewer regulations on the researcher as compared to today. Second, much of the research was published in the form of case studies and with fewer numbers of subjects as compared to modern times. Third, there was often a lack of strict scientific methodology and lack of control groups in the early publications. For these reasons and others, these early publications and their findings have essentially been erased from current scientific and medical maps. Nevertheless, there was such a flurry of publications regarding the clinical uses of testosterone that a review of these papers should indicate that some of these early uses proved to be valid.

During the first five years or so pertaining to the early clinical uses of testosterone a number of other potential uses were identified. Testosterone directly influences a number of human tissues. Therefore, its effects on a broad range of medical conditions should be entertained, and that is exactly what the early medical scientists believed about testosterone's effects. The following chronological listing of these effects is summarized below in Table 12-3.

Table 12-3. The First Five Years of Testosterone's Clinical Experimentation

Dates	*Description of Event*
1936	Mocquot and Moricard found that testosterone acetate therapy was useful in treating women following surgical ovarian removal. Androgen euphoria was a frequent finding among these treated women.[29]
1936	Margiel and Zwilling reported the first treatment of the female menopause by injections and tablets of androgens.[30]
1936	Butendandt reported that some androgens induced sexual desire.[31]
1936	Robson demonstrated the suppressive effect of androgens on menstruation.[32]
1936	Leipner reported improvement in some skin conditions with androgen therapy.[33]
1936	Laqueur and coworkers reported that a decrease in androgens in older men caused an imbalance in the androgen/estrogen ratios resulting in prostatic enlargement.[34]
1936	Zuckerman and Greene showed improvements in prostatism in older men treated with testosterone proprionate.[35]
1937	Salmon successfully used testosterone proportionate for the relief of menopausal symptoms in women.[36]
1937	Zuckerman reported the antagonistic action of androgens on ovulation.[37]
1937	Koch reported that some androgens affect libido positively.[38]
1937	Kochakian reported no abrupt changes in urinary excretion of male hormones associated with aging.[39]
1937	Hamilton treated male hypogonadism with testosterone therapy[40]
1938	Hamilton and Hubert reported enhancement of suntanning of the human skin in women patients treated with androgens.[41]
1938	Barahal treated male involutional melancholia with testosterone.[42]
1938	Dix demonstrated the use of testosterone in the treatment of prostatism in older men.[43]
1938	Cary showed improvement of prostatitis in older men with testosterone propionate treatment.[44]
1939	Kurzrok and associates reported their positive findings with treating over 20 menopausal women with testosterone therapy.[45]
1939	Edwards and coworkers reported benefits with the use of androgens in the treatment of peripheral vascular disease.[46]

Dates	*Description of Event*
1939	Lafitte and Huret reported the improvement of a variety of psoriatic skin conditions with androgen therapy.[47]
1939	Reichert reported improvement in eczema with androgen therapy.[48]
1939	Bolend demonstrated the use of testosterone in prostatism.[49]
1939	Day demonstrated the use of testosterone in prostatism.[50]
1939	Hamilton reported enhanced suntanning with testosterone therapy.[51]
1939	Kurzrok and coworkers reported the use of testosterone therapy in the female menopause.[52]
1939	Mazer and Mazer prescribed testosterone for dysfunctional uterine bleeding in women.[53]
1940	Albright and coworkers prescribed testosterone as therapy for postmenopausal osteoporosis.[54]

It can be shown that in the first five years after its initial synthesis testosterone was tried in a number of clinical situations with success. Of interest is that this so-called male sex hormone was prescribed to treat the symptoms of the surgical menopause in women as early as 1936. Also of interest was the use of testosterone therapy for the treatment of women with postmenopausal osteoporosis in 1940 and the normally occurring menopause in women in 1939.

Attempts at Controlling Clinical Experiments with Testosterone

In an attempt to gain control of the American physicians' testosterone prescribing habits and clinical experimentation, the American Medical Association's Council on Pharmacy and Chemistry took a drastic legislative step. In 1939 this group declared testosterone as "not acceptable for New and Nonofficial Remedies."[55] It was obvious that testosterone therapy for a variety of disease conditions was going to have a difficult time becoming medically reputable. Boundary lines between the medical scientists who were conducting the clinical studies with testosterone and the authorities who represented the governing voice of medicine were being drawn. As illustrated in Table 12-3, medical scientists were just beginning to scratch the surface of potential uses for this powerful sex steroid. In other words, the AMA's council was making conclusions about testosterone therapy with just a paucity of published studies and not after a lengthy period of profound study. The AMA's declaration was a blatant attempt to thwart the scientific inertia regarding the study of testosterone therapy. This dogmatic declaration was based on opinion and just a smattering of science that eventually would prove damaging for further progress in the scientific arena. A retrospective look at these facts tends to render this action as almost unbelievable.

No one seemed to deny that testosterone therapy was indicated in obvious cases of testosterone deficiency, but the arguments began when this form of therapy was used for other types of ill-health conditions. The fact that clinical scientists were prescribing the "male sex hormone" to women patients, which had been shown to enhance a woman's libido, certainly influenced the formation of this misdirected policy. It must be remembered that the United States Food and Drug Administration, established in 1931,[56] was still in its infancy. This was the year in which the 19th Amendment of the Constitution was passed by Congress ending the national prohibition on ethanol. Perhaps some remnants of Prohibition carried over to the medical legislators of this period. New drugs were quickly added to the medical practice that outpaced their clinical laboratory evaluations. As a result, testosterone had only been clinically available for approximately four years prior to this official political attempt to sweep it under the medical rug forever. This result, brought about by the AMA's council, had a major impact on the direction of testosterone research, and later, anabolic steroid research.

During the mid–1930s, the widespread use of sulfa drugs as anti-microbial agents precipitated concerns by physicians and legislators regarding drug safety. Overzealous use of sulfa drugs was linked to infant deaths. This phenomenon prompted Congress to pass the 1938 Food, Drug, and Cosmetic Act, which required the safety of a particular drug to be documented to the FDA in the form of a new drug application (NDA). Prescription drugs had to now carry a label—"Caution: To be used only by or on the proper prescription of a physician." However, much confusion still existed as to which drugs were intended to be prescription medications.[57] In other words, clinical availability and the early search for clinical uses of testosterone arrived on the medical scene at the same time that Congress was passing new drug laws, and the pharmaceutical companies weren't sure which drugs that they produced were going to be controlled by physicians' prescriptions. From 1938 to 1962, the FDA was bombarded with approximately 13,000 new drug application submissions, and about 70 percent of them were allowed to become effective or essentially approved for clinical use.[58]

In spite of these legislative attempts, the early clinical experimentation with testosterone therapy continued, albeit at a slower pace. There were some medical pioneers who continued to publish their findings in the medical literature.

American Public Abuses Testosterone

Regardless of what the medical establishment and national legislators were trying to do with testosterone therapy, for society, nature would take its usual pathway. Society wanted to try drugs that could enhance libido, treat depression, relieve menopause symptoms, and so forth. Once the word about testosterone was publicly known, a variety of hucksters began selling various supplements that were claimed to contain sex steroids, including testosterone. This phenomenon became so widespread nationally that the FDA had to establish a special unit to evaluate these products by setting up assay laboratory techniques.[59] The FDA was also involved with prosecuting a number of manufacturers and distributors of these sex hormone supplements in three ways. They took legal actions against:

1) a number of preparations found to be deficient in their labeled potency;
2) a number of adulterated and or misbranded aqueous preparations; and,
3) several products of this type based on representations made for them by the manufacturers and distributors.[60]

Summary: Clinical Uphill Battle for Testosterone

In this chapter, a history of the discovery and synthesis of testosterone has been presented. As soon as it was made clinically available, clinical experiments started with testosterone therapy. Testosterone proved to be a powerful drug with abuse potentials. The pharmaceutical industry had synthesized its first powerful hormone and it was counting heavily on testosterone's clinical successes.

Testosterone's role in medicine proved difficult to define even though it could prove beneficial as therapy in a wide array of disease conditions. Political factors entered into testosterone's early clinical history. Extravagant claims were made about testosterone's effects on libido and longevity. The American public abused testosterone and that influenced both lawmakers and physicians alike.

It has been shown that the search for the clinical uses of testosterone was not likely to receive a balanced approach. The scientific tools and methods to evaluate testosterone's clinical abilities were unsophisticated. And, the mores of the times were not accepting of a sex steroid that played such a prominent role in the sexual desire of both men and women. The net result of these historical events combined to make the search for clinical uses of testosterone an uphill battle.

13

Current and Future Medical Uses of Anabolic Steroids

Introduction: Anabolic Steroids Can Build a Brighter Future

After the early clinical experimentation with testosterone concluded, medical uses, for the most part, were relegated to the back of the drug closet. The lack of sophisticated research tools to evaluate testosterone's potential clinical roles slowed progress.

Some clinical physicians and medical scientists continued to search for appropriate medical uses of testosterone, and later, the anabolic steroids. The pharmaceutical companies that manufactured these sex steroids felt confident that these drugs would eventually find solid places in medical formularies. This can be evidenced by the fact that by 1963, the pharmaceutical industry had received FDA approval for over a dozen anabolic steroid compounds to go with a previously approved number of testosterone preparations.[1]

It can be illustrated that the clinical uses of testosterone and anabolic steroids have had potential in a wide range of categories as listed in Table 13-1.

In this chapter some of these clinical uses will simply be listed and referenced with literature citations. Other medical uses will be covered in some detail with an historical perspective.

Table 13-1. Categories of the Clinical Uses of Testosterone and Anabolic Steroids

- Bone Metabolism Conditions
  - Corticosteroid-Induced Osteoporosis
  - Postmenopausal Osteoporosis
  - Osteoporosis in Elderly Men
- Testosterone-Deficiency Conditions
  - Male Climacteric, Male Involutional Melancholia, and Male "Andropause"
  - Hypogonadism in Males
  - Female Climacteric and Female Menopause
- Cardiovascular Conditions
  - Angina Pectoris, Hypertension, and Coronary Artery Disease
  - Raynaud's Syndrome and Cryofibrinogenemia
- Microgravity and Prolonged Space Travel
- Rehabilitation Conditions
- Chronic Anemia and Related Conditions
- Benign Prostatic Hypertrophy
- Sarcopenia
- AIDS
- Miscellaneous Conditions

Several factors have been influential in the renewed interest in anabolic steroids for the treatment of disease conditions. First, the tools and methods used by modern medical science have evolved greatly since the early period of clinical experimentation with testosterone and anabolic steroids. Methods have been developed that prove the anabolic potentials of these steroids. New tools have been used to study the mechanisms of actions. These advances have caused a new excitement over the use of anabolic steroids to treat a wide variety of diseases and disabling conditions.

Second, the turnabout by medical science has also been fueled, in part, by obvious observations that these drugs were not mere placebos for muscle and strength enhancement. Some thanks can be given to the athletic community for this obvious contribution.

A third factor has been the effects that the aging population of America has had on medicine. If Americans are going to live longer, then why not strive to be in better shape as they age? The use of anabolic agents for conditions associated with aging is a rapidly expanding concept among today's physicians.

The fourth factor of influencing has advanced in the areas of physical medicine and rehabilitation. A major role in this expanding area of medicine deals with helping patients with disabling diseases and injuries return to an independent and productive lifestyle. Anabolic steroids and other anabolic agents have expanding roles in achieving these goals for both physicians and patients.

A fifth factor that has influenced the medical uses of anabolic steroids has been the financial aspect. Compared to the genetically engineered anabolic and growth-stimulating hormones and agents, anabolic steroids are a real bargain. Efforts that focus on cost containment have determined that anabolic steroids are often the best choice as anabolic agents.

A sixth factor has dealt with the traditional physicians' resistance to prescribe anabolic agents for their patients who need them. Progress is being made in this area. The ongoing clinical investigations with anabolic steroids and other anabolic agents are beginning to define solid uses for these medications. With these improved clinical studies, the resistance to prescribe these anabolic agents in clinical medicine will begin to subside.

All of these factors combine to form an exciting new area of anabolic agent use in modern medicine. The horizon for many patients can be a brighter one. Let us look then, at the diseases, aging conditions, and injury conditions in which anabolic steroid therapy has established a role, and where these roles are likely to be in the near future.

Corticosteroid-Induced (CST-Induced) Osteoporosis

Osteoporosis is a condition that is mistakenly thought to be confined to that of postmenopausal osteoporosis in women (to be covered in the next section) or senile osteoporosis in men. However the most common drug-induced cause of osteoporosis is the result of prolonged corticosteroid therapy for other medical conditions.[2,3] Corticosteroid-induced (CST-induced) osteoporosis has been recognized for nearly 60 years as a major risk factor for contributing to bone fractures with little or no associated trauma. It is the most common form of iatrogenic (caused by physicians) osteoporosis, and for this reason this topic will be presented first in this chapter.

In younger people, prolonged corticosteroid therapy is the most common cause of osteoporosis.[4] Although the true incidence of CST-induced osteoporosis varies, as many as 90 percent of patients treated with prolonged corticosteroid therapy develop osteoporosis.[5] Patients with rheumatoid and other inflammatory arthritis combined with patients with chronic asthma account for nearly half of all patients who are treated with prolonged corticosteroid therapy.[6] Although most physicians are aware of this condition, recent studies have indicated that fewer than 50 percent of patients on prolonged corticosteroid treatment receive the aggressive therapies required to prevent and reverse bone mineral density losses.[7,8]

Prolonged corticosteroid therapy accelerates the rate of bone mineral density (BMD) loss by several specific mechanisms as illustrated in Table 13-2. The greatest rate of BMD loss is within the first 6 to 12 months of therapy.[9] It is not unusual for patients to lose as much as 20 percent of their bone mass within the first year of corticosteroid therapy.[10]

There are a number of other factors or underlying conditions that may further increase BMD losses and fracture risks of CST-induced osteoporosis, such as smoking, excessive ethanol intake, menopause, perimenopause, relative immobilization, chronic obstructive pulmonary disease, inflammatory bowel disease, absolute or relative hypogonadism in men, autoimmune diseases, rheumatoid arthritis, organ transplantation, cancer chemotherapy regimens, neuroleptic medications, thyroid medications, and low calcium intake.[11,12] A listing of the currently known aggravating factors that can accelerate the risk for CST-induced osteoporosis is contained in Table 13-3.

Table 13-2. Specific Mechanisms for Corticosteroid-Induced Osteoporosis

Abnormal Mechanism	*Mechanisms*
Reduction in bone formation	Reduced osteoblast stimulation due to a relative reduction in serum testosterone levels (via adrenal suppression).
	Reduced osteoblast stimulation due to direct competitive (with androgens) osteoblast receptor binding; corticosteroid binding inhibits, and androgen binding stimulates.
	Reduced osteoblast stimulation from CST-induced decrease in serum insulin-like growth factor-1 (IGF-1).
	Reduced osteoblast stimulation from blunted levels of luteinizing hormone (LH) levels which reduces serum androgen levels.
Increased bone resorption	Increased osteoclast activity caused by a reduction of serum estrogens (in women) due to blunted LH levels. Estrogens inhibit the osteoclast.
	Increased osteoclast activity probably due to corticosteroid binding to osteoclast receptors (competitive with estrogens).
	Secondary hyperparathyroidism which stimulates the osteoclasts to increase bone resorption.

Abnormal Mechanism	*Mechanisms*
Alterations in calcium metabolism	Reduction of calcium absorption from the intestines.
	Increased loss of calcium in the urine due to renal tubular reduction in calcium reabsorption.
Alterations in bone architecture	Disproportionate loss of trabecular bone mass resulting in much greater fracture risks.

TABLE 13-3. ADDITIONAL RISK FACTORS FOR CORTICOSTEROID-INDUCED OSTEOPOROSIS

Corticosteroid-related factors
  Dosage — the higher the dose the greater the risk
  Duration — the longer the duration of treatment the greater the risk
General osteoporosis risk factors
  Ethanol consumption
  Sedentary lifestyle
  Cigarette smoking
  Prolonged period of relative immobilization
  Underlying disease conditions (e.g., rheumatoid arthritis, Crohn's disease, hyperthyroidism, multiple sclerosis, scleroderma)
  Underlying medical conditions (e.g., perimenopause, menopause, hypogonadism)
  Low peak bone mineral density
  Genetic factors
Dietary factors
  Low calcium intake
  Low boron intake
  Low vitamin D intake
Medication factors
  Thyroid medications
  Anticonvulsant and neuroleptic medications
  Immunosuppressive drugs
  Diuretics (loop diuretics)
  Gonadotrophin releasing–hormone (GnRH) agonists or antagonists
  Antiandrogens
  Progesterone implants or progesterone injections for birth control

MECHANISMS FOR CST-INDUCED OSTEOPOROSIS

Prolonged corticosteroid therapy causes accelerated osteoporosis through several interacting mechanisms that affect both local and systemic factors. These individual mechanisms cause a net result: decreased bone formation, increased bone resorption, increased urinary calcium excretion, and detrimental changes to bone architecture.

Decreased Bone Formation. Corticosteroids tend to interact competitively with androgens in the osteoblasts (bone forming cells). When androgens bind to osteoblast receptors the osteoblast is stimulated to form new bone. However, when corticosteroids bind to osteoblast receptors, the osteoblast is suppressed and bone formation is reduced. In other words, corticosteroids act directly on osteoblasts by activating some genes while suppressing others.[13] Corticosteroids also act indirectly by decreasing the levels of insulin-like growth factor-1 (IGF-1) by either suppressing its synthesis or by modifying IGF-1 binding proteins.[14] These steroids also reduce testosterone and other androgen levels by three mechanisms: first, they blunt the luteinizing hormone response to luteinizing hormone–releasing hormone that normally stimulates the testicular or ovarian production of androgens. Second, they suppress secretion of testosterone, dehydroepiandrosterone (DHEA), and androstenedione from the adrenal glands, which has more of an effect in women. Third, corticosteroids cause an increase in steroid hormone–binding globulin (SHBG) that binds more strongly to the reduced supply of circulating androgens.

Increased Bone Resorption. Corticosteroids increase bone resorption by three possible known mechanisms. First, they bind to the osteoclasts (bone dissolving cells) and compete with estrogens for those binding sites. Estrogen binding to the osteoclast tends to partially inhibit the osteoclast and ultimately slow down bone resorption. On the other hand, when corticosteroids bind to the osteoclast receptor, the osteoclast accelerates its resorption of bone. Second, corticosteroids can induce a secondary hyperparathyoidism that further stimulates the osteoclast and bone resorption is increased.[15,16] Third, corticosteroid therapy may induce an increase in SHBG that binds more strongly to already reduced circulating estrogens.

Changes in Calcium Balance. Treatment with corticosteroids can cause a serum calcium imbalance by two mechanisms. First, these drugs decrease the calcium and phosphate absorption from the small intestine, which reduces the efficiency of the absorbed calcium from the diet or from supplementation.[17] Second, corticosteroids affect the kidney by increasing the excretion of calcium by decreasing renal reabsorption of calcium.[18] These two effects combine to stimulate the parathyroid gland to secrete parathyroid hormone (PTH) that, in turn, stimulates the osteoclast to resorb more bone and release more calcium into the bloodstream, which increases urinary calcium excretion. About 30 percent of patients treated with prolonged corticosteroid therapy develop this form of hypercalcuria.[19]

Alterations in Bone Architecture. Studies of bone biopsies from patients treated with prolonged corticosteroid therapy reveal changes in the bones' normal microscopic structure. The bone mineral density and mass losses are greater in the trabecular bone regions when compared to other types of osteoporosis.[20] This means that for any measured decrease in bone mineral density, there is a greater risk for fracture than in other forms of osteoporosis.

With all of the aforementioned mechanisms, it is readily apparent that CST-induced osteoporosis is the most dangerous and "brittle" type of osteoporosis. The first symptom that a patient may have is typically a non-traumatic vertebral or rib fracture. The usual fractures (unlike with postmenopausal osteoporosis where lumbar spine fractures are more common) with CST-induced osteoporosis are more common in the thoracic spine, ribs, distal forearm, and femur.[21,22]

Pharmacological Treatment of CST-Induced Osteoporosis

The best prevention of and drug treatment of CST-induced osteoporosis has been known for decades; however, most physicians have not prescribed the best medicinal therapy. Testosterone therapy in women and men was used empirically for several decades. For postmenopausal women and for women who have undergone surgical menopause, an androgen/estrogen combination proved effective for decades. Some of the early studies on the sex steroid therapy for osteoporosis did not distinguish between the various types or causes; patients with various types of osteoporosis were grouped together. Unfortunately, during this period objective methods to evaluate the effectiveness of any therapy on the osteoporotic process were crude compared to more recent times. As the anabolic steroids became available for clinical use in the late 1950s, they were shown to be an effective treatment for preventing and reversing the catabolic bone effects brought on by prolonged and concurrent corticosteroid therapy in patients with rheumatoid arthritis in both men and women.[23] Using the available technology of the times (nitrogen, calcium, and phosphorus balances), this study showed convincingly that the catabolic effects induced by corticosteroids were reversed by anabolic steroid treatment.

A chronological listing of some of the major events and publications regarding the pendulum-type history of anabolic steroid therapy for CST-induced osteoporosis is shown in Table 13-4.

Table 13-4. A Chronological Listing of Events Influencing Anabolic Steroid Therapy for CST-Induced Osteoporosis

1959	Mortensen and coworkers publish their findings indicating anabolic steroid therapy reverses the catabolic actions of corticosteroids in CST-induced osteoporosis in patients with rheumatoid arthritis.[24]

1959 Ciba Laboratories published its package insert for the anabolic steroid, Dianabol (methandrostenolone), for an osteoporosis indication.[25]

1962 Parsons and Sommers's textbook *Gynecology* stated that in menopausal women the estrogen-androgen combination improves physical, mental, and emotional status.[26]

1962 Williams's *Textbook of Endocrinology* stated that, for women, "Endocrine therapy consists of administration of estrogen or estrogen plus androgen."[27]

1963 Cecil-Loeb's *Textbook of Medicine* recommended that for CST-induced osteoporosis, androgens or androgen-estrogen combination "is the therapy of choice."[28]

1965 Winthrop Laboratories published its package insert for the anabolic steroid, Winstrol (stanozolol), with indication for CST-induced osteoporosis.[29]

1970 Goodman and Gilman's textbook *The Pharmacological Basis of Therapeutics* stated that "The current consensus seems to be that androgens and their various anabolic steroids are useful in the treatment of osteoporosis. In women, estrogen given concurrently with small doses of androgen to minimize virilization."[30]

1971 Krusen's textbook *Physical Medicine and Rehabilitation* stated that for osteoporosis, "Although several medical approaches to treatment are recommended, the most unanimously endorsed, as well as the most definitive, is the use of anabolic steroids."[31]

1971 Winthrop Laboratories published its revised package insert for the anabolic steroid, Winstrol (stanozolol), with FDA classifying it as "probably" effective in osteoporosis.[32]

1980 Ciba Pharmaceuticals published its revised package insert for the anabolic steroid, Dianabol (methandrostenolone), with FDA classifying it as "probably effective in osteoporosis."[33]

1984 FDA removed the osteoporosis indication from the package inserts from all brands of anabolic steroids.

1984 Woodard, in a letter to the editor (*New Engl. J. Med.*), strongly condemned the FDA's decision: "The recent decision of the FDA to withdraw approval for the use of anabolic steroids in treating osteoporosis appears counterproductive and unjustified by the available research."[34]

1990 First DEXA (dual-energy x-ray absorptiometers) became clinically available to provide the first definitive, diagnostic, and long-term scanning for osteoporosis.

This chronological listing has been provided in detail to enable discussion of several points. First, from this listing, there can be no doubt that from the late 1950s through the early 1980s anabolic steroids should have played a predominant role in treating and reversing CST-induced osteoporosis. Many of the major medical textbooks discussed of the time from a variety of medical disciplines indicated so. And, the FDA, through approved package insert, indicated so as well. Second, this listing points to strong evidence as to why America currently has millions of patients with osteoporosis who have not been provided the proper medications for its treatment. Third, this listing provides further proof of the "on again, off again" clinical history of testosterone and the anabolic steroids. Fourth, this listing points to strong evidence that medical politics again attempted to thwart medical scientific research when the FDA removed the osteoporosis indication from the package inserts and *Physicians' Desk Reference* (PDR) for all of the anabolic steroids in the early 1980s. Not one single study ever showed that this class of steroids did not treat osteoporosis, yet the FDA mysteriously dropped the indication! The effect of this action was to effectively wipe anabolic steroids off the medical science map. This inexcusable error happened nearly a decade *before* the definitive osteoporosis scanner was available for scientific and clinical use! Whatever happened to preventive medicine and the patients and appropriate patient care?

The question remains as to why the FDA removed the osteoporosis indication from the package inserts and PDR. Was it because the FDA staff knew something that the rest of world's scientists didn't? I, for one, find such a proposition *impossible* to believe. Was the FDA's decision truly a mystery or were there precipitating factors which took place to instigate the move? Yes, there were, and they are listed in Table 13-5.

TABLE 13-5. PRECIPITATING INFLUENCES FOR THE FDA ACTION TO ERASE THE OSTEOPOROSIS INDICATION FOR ANABOLIC STEROIDS

Dates	*Event or Publication*
1976	The American College of Sports Medicine published its official position on the athletic use/abuse of anabolic steroids claiming that they were mere placebos when used to enhance athletic performance.[35]
1976	The FDA approved the italicized statement in the PDR, "*Warning: anabolic steroids do not enhance athletic performance.*"[36]
1977	Harrison's *Principles of Internal Medicine* stated that "Anabolic-androgenic steroids are defined biologically as substances that stimulate masculinization (in women) … clinical hirsutism (facial hair) … ammenorrhea (lack of menstrual periods), atrophy of the breasts and uterus, enlargement of the clitoris, deepening of the voice, acne, increased muscle mass, increased heterosexual drive, and receding hairline … with testosterone preparations and anabolic steroids there is no advantage to their use in women in view of their masculinizing properties. There is also no proved advantage to combinations of estrogens and androgens."[37]
Early 1980s	FDA was given a mandate to "clean up" the medical indications for a variety of drugs contained in the PDR.
Early 1980s	Congress passed the generic drug law which resulted in a burgeoning anabolic steroid black market for muscle-building and the anabolic steroid epidemic. It also removed the financial incentives for the pharmaceutical industry to reapply for the osteoporosis indication.

Swayed by the prevalence of such blatantly incorrect medical dogma and the passing of new national drug policies, it is not surprising that osteoporosis, including CST-induced osteoporosis, has reached an epidemic level in the United States.

The pharmaceutical industry had its hands tied when it lost both patent protection and the osteoporosis indication for anabolic steroids at about the same time. There was no incentive for the industry to reapply for the osteoporosis indication and provide the hundreds of millions of dollars required to regain the indication. Even if an individual pharmaceutical company did attempt to regain the indication, there would be dozens of upstart generic drug companies, which do not contribute to the money required for new applications, and which would end up reaping most of the profits. Instead, the pharmaceutical industry shifted its research and development efforts to finding newly discovered drugs that might be useful in treating osteoporosis. That shift of efforts was where the potential financial rewards were likely to be found.

Practicing physicians were frowned upon if they continued to utilize anabolic steroids for treating and reversing osteoporosis. If they prescribed these steroids, then they were doing so in an "off label" manner and opened themselves up for medical malpractice if significant adverse effects were to arise. Physicians were also frightened away from prescribing anabolic steroids by the overblown claims of adverse effects of such therapy, especially in women, which had become entrenched in many of the major medical textbooks. Since it became taught that anabolic steroid therapy had no role for women patients, most physicians decided that it was safer (for themselves) to accept what they were taught and to avoid prescribing anabolic steroids. For some physicians, just a mere mention of prescribing anabolic steroids, especially for women patients, became a source of profound antipathy.

The single major event that started the pendulum back in the appropriate direction was the invention and availability of the DEXA (dual-energy x-ray absorptiometer) for the scientific and clinical testing for osteoporosis. This scanner provided an objective measure for testing and retesting patients for bone mineral density. It became the "gold standard" for osteoporosis detection and for the long-term follow-up in patients to determine which treatments actually worked. This machine has prompted a flurry of drugs to be tested on patients with osteoporosis and "anabolic steroids have recently made a comeback."[38] This comeback has primarily occurred in the international medical science community. In the United States, medical scientists have been slow to recover from the mounds of previous promotion of incorrect and misguided information and mistaken FDA policies. The comeback regarding the research and use of anabolic steroids for treating and reversing CST-induced osteoporosis will be chronologically listed in Table 13-6.

Table 13-6. Chronological Listing of the "Comeback" Use of Anabolic Steroids for the Treatment of CST-Induced Osteoporosis

Dates	*Events or Publications*
1991 & 1993	Adami and coworkers reported increases in bone mineral density (BMD) in patients treated with corticosteroid (CST)-induced osteoporosis.[39,40]
1993	Adachi and coworkers recommended that "anabolic steroids be considered in patients with CST-induced osteoporosis when fractures occur or ongoing bone loss is evident."[41]
1994	Renier and coworkers reported long-term studies with anabolic steroid treatment of osteoporosis caused by corticosteroid excess.[42]
1995	Geusens reported significant increases in BMD, diminished vertebral pain and increased mobility of the spine of women patients treated with anabolic steroids for CST-induced osteoporosis.[43]
1996	Reid and associates showed that testosterone therapy reverses the deleterious effects of corticosteroids on bone and muscle in men.[44]
1996	Picado and Luengo recommended the use of anabolic steroids for men patients with CST-induced osteoporosis and women patients who are postmenopausal with CST-induced osteoporosis.[45]
1999	Zaqqa and Jackson recommended the evaluation of gonadal sex steroid deficiency and treatment with the appropriate sex steroids in patients with CST-induced osteoporosis. Other anabolic regimens may include growth hormone and IGF-1.[46]

The concept of physicians prescribing anabolic agents with the intent to build up and restore body tissues, including bone tissues, has been around for decades. This concept has continued to be met with an inordinate amount of resistance by the medical profession itself. Even when medical research has indicated that various medications may be anabolic in nature to the body, physicians in the United States have been slow to accept them. With this in mind, the scientific mechanisms known regarding the hows and whys of anabolic steroid use to reverse the catabolic effects of CST-induced osteoporosis are listed in Table 13-7.

Table 13-7. Mechanisms of Anabolic Steroids on Preventing and Reversing CST-Induced Osteoporosis

Causes direct stimulation of the osteoblasts
Forms normal bone according to histomorphologic studies
Treats androgen deficiency
Reverses catabolic actions induced by corticosteroid therapy
Improves mental depression often caused by corticosteroid tapering

Direct osteoblast stimulation (caused by anabolic therapy) has been shown by measuring serum markers that measure osteoblast activities, such as osteocalcin.[47] Study results have shown increased osteoblast activity in patients with osteoporosis as indicated by elevated osteocalcin associated with anabolic steroid therapy,[48–50] and in normal healthy volunteers treated with anabolic steroids.[51]

Recent studies have shown that the anabolic steroid-induced osteoblast is prolonged and restorative. The beneficial effects of anabolic steroids (Winstrol) when used as a treatment for osteoporosis include a direct stimulation of the osteoblasts, and this stimulation may continue after the therapy is discontinued.[52] Anabolic steroid therapy with nandrolone decanoate has also been shown to return osteocalcin levels back to the normal range in CST-induced osteoporosis.[53] These measures of direct osteoblast stimulation have been shown by *in vitro* studies with human osteoblast-like cells[54] and with serial bone biopsy (before and after treatment) confirmation with osteoporotic men and women patients treated with anabolic steroids (Winstrol).[55] In this latter study, histological examination bone tissue showed:

a) active-appearing osteoblasts within the trabecular bone tissue;
b) increased trabecular bone turnover and increased trabecular bone mass; and,
c) increased endocortical turnover and increased cortical and endocortical bone masses.

These site-specific and differential effects of anabolic steroids have important implications in long-term use in the management of osteoporosis. This increase in trabecular bone tissue turnover and increased trabecular mass may prove useful in CST-induced osteoporosis, especially when used with exercise or therapeutic physical therapy to improve the trabecular bone mass in patients who have lost significant trabecular bone integrity.[56]

A recent study indicates that anabolic steroids may have another mechanism relating to osteoblast stimulation. This study has linked circulating insulin-like growth factor components to sex steroid levels in middle-aged and elderly men and women.[57] These growth factors also tend to stimulate bone osteoblasts. It has also been shown that anabolic steroid treatment increases insulin-like growth factor-1 (IGF-1) levels.[58] IGF-1 receptors have been found in bone tissues and stimulation of them enhances the genetic machinery for bone formation. Further studies are needed in this area to delineate the anabolic steroid influence on these growth factors.

Summary

This extensive discussion of CST-induced osteoporosis clearly indicates that anabolic steroid therapy has a predominant therapeutic role in CST-induced osteoporosis. Other pharmaceutical agents have been and continue to be used in patients with little success, especially on *increasing* BMD and normal bone mass in patients who already have sustained significant BMD and bone mass losses due to corticosteroid therapy. Continued clinical use and scientific studies could be united to form a definitive multi-site project to further investigate this form of therapy for CST-induced osteoporosis. Until then, anabolic steroid therapy should be considered for not only prevention, but for treatment of CST-induced osteoporosis on a case-by-case method. Due to the continued post-treatment stimulation of the osteoblasts, one should consider a cyclical regimen, especially for women patients, to fully minimize virilization potentials and impact on serum lipids. In my clinical studies, prescribing 2 to 4 mg of Winstrol (stanozolol) daily for 10 to 14 days consecutively each month to CST-induced osteoporosis women patients has reversed BMD loses.

For men, my practice has been to prescribe 10 mg Winstrol daily for three weeks each month after the men have been screened with a rectal (prostate) exam and a normal serum prostate specific antigen (PSA) test. Baseline DEXA scans should be obtained and repeated every six months or so to evaluate the efficacy of the anabolic steroid therapy.

Anabolic steroid therapy appears also to help reduce the mental depression that can often accompany the tapering-off phases of prolonged corticosteroid therapy. In this manner these steroids may treat some of the effects of long-term corticosteroid dependence.

Postmenopausal Osteoporosis

Introduction

Osteoporosis may be defined as a reduction in bone mass per unit volume of bone such that bone fractures may occur as a result of minimal or no trauma. The reduction in bone mass is mostly the loss of calcium and associated matrix structure, which results in the loss of structural integrity and strength of bones. Simply put, osteoporosis means porous and brittle bones.

Osteoporosis is perhaps the most common chronic disease among American white women today, and is the most common metabolic disease in the

Western World. The most common type of osteoporosis is the postmenopausal type. Osteoporosis is *not* a normal aging process. Postmenopausal osteoporosis begins when a normal aging process occurs, namely the diminished production of sex steroid hormones during the years leading up to (perimenopause) and more abruptly during and after the menopause. These sex steroids play major roles in maintaining the normal bone cell equilibrium as presented in the previous section on CST-induced osteoporosis. The appropriate sex steroid replacement therapy may prevent, reverse, and perhaps cure postmenopausal osteoporosis through these steroids' effects on the various types of bone cells involved in the normal bone equilibrium processes. Other hormones and minerals are involved with this equilibrium process, but the major factors involved are the sex steroids. Therefore, the keys to understanding postmenopausal osteoporosis process are linked to understanding the basic sex steroid biochemistry as it relates to the bone cells.

Basic Sex Steroid Biochemistry of the Perimenopausal and Postmenopausal Woman

The glands that produce the sex steroids in women are the ovaries and the adrenal glands. The ovaries make three classes of sex steroids, namely androgenic, estrogenic, and progesterogenic steroids. Estrogens and progesterones are synthesized from cholesterol within the oocytes (eggs) in the ovaries. Testosterone and other anabolic steroids are synthesized within the thecal cells outside of the oocytes in the stromal tissue. The adrenal glands produce androgenic steroids. It has been demonstrated that approximately 85 percent of circulating testosterone and other anabolic-androgenic steroids come from the ovaries, with remaining, smaller percentages secreted by the adrenal glands in normal premenopausal women.[59,60] In normal ovulating women, the amount of testosterone and other anabolic steroids fluctuates throughout the phases of the menstrual cycle. During the middle third of the menstrual cycle a small, but significant, serum elevation of testosterone and other anabolic steroids occurs.[61] This elevation in the serum androgen levels is due to ovarian androgen secretion by the ovarian thecal cells as stimulated by an elevated luteinizing hormone (LH) release from the pituitary gland. During the other phases of the menstrual cycle the serum level of androgens is lower. This elevation of serum androgens during the middle third of the menstrual cycle is enough to stimulate the osteoblast to begin the bone formation cycle. It also plays a role in procreation; the elevated testosterone increases a woman's libido around the same time the oocyte is ovulated and ready for fertilization.

About a decade or so before menopause proper (known as the perimenopause), a woman's ovaries may begin to produce less and less of the sex steroids. Previously normal menstrual cycles may become irregular as ovarian function declines. The class of sex steroids that diminished earliest is probably the androgens. This has caused some authors recently to refer to the perimenopausal years as "andropause." The decline in total circulating androgens results from ovarian failure and the age-related decline in adrenal androgen and preandrogen production. This relative androgen deficiency of women may manifest itself as impaired sexual function, lessened well-being, loss of energy and losses in bone mineral density (BMD).[62–64] Since the absolute decline in circulating androgen levels generally begins in the decade prior to menopause proper, it is not surprising that many women experience the aforementioned symptoms and conditions in the perimenopausal years.[65,66] This phenomenon differs from the sudden drop in estrogen levels that occurs late in the menopausal transition.[67] In other words, the symptoms and BMD loss due to "andropause" during the perimenopausal years develop insidiously, in contrast to the more abrupt onset of symptoms of estrogen deficiency. Thus it can be shown that the roots of postmenopausal osteoporosis occur during the perimenopausal years and that the early osteoporosis condition that begins in the perimenopausal years is due decreasing androgen levels. Thus, the term "andropause."

After a year or so without menstrual cycles, a woman is officially labeled as postmenopausal. All of the oocytes within the ovaries have been ovulated and as a result there is little or no estrogen or progesterone being produced by the ovaries. The ovarian production of all three classes of sex steroids has greatly diminished, and they will remain diminished for the remainder of the woman's life unless they are therapeutically replaced by hormone replacement therapy (HRT). In the typical postmenopausal state the ovaries tend to become fibrotic and a poor source of sex steroids; in such women, the adrenal gland becomes the main androgen source.[68] However, the adrenal gland cannot produce enough androgens to make up the difference when "andropause" followed by ovarian involutions occurs. Many women can expect to live over half of their adult lives suffering from the symptoms of "andropause" and ovarian involution. So to treat many of the physical and mental symptoms associated with diminished sex steroid production, including postmenopausal osteoporosis, it makes sense that therapy utilizing the proper sex steroid hormone replacement, or HRT, would be beneficial. It seems so simple to prevent and reverse the BMD losses of postmenopausal osteoporosis, doesn't it? Simply replace the types of sex steroids, in the proper doses, that the ovaries used to make when they were functioning. This concept is why I believe that mimicking ovarian function through the proper HRT is the answer for postmenopausal osteoporosis.

Additional Historical Perspectives

If this simple conceptual method of treating and reversing postmenopausal osteoporosis is true, then why isn't it the standard of care in the United States today? Much of the answer to this question has been presented in the previous section on CST-induced osteoporosis and will not be repeated here. However, some additional historical highlights may further enlighten the reader and, therefore, seem appropriate to present.

Shortly before and during World War II, biology and biochemistry began to change the face of medical practice forever. Actually, the biochemical aspects of science were far ahead of the medical profession in general. A profusion of drugs were chemically synthesized and quickly brought onto the medical scene. All sorts of new diseases were being described by the medical profession, mostly based on observation and physical examination. There was little or no clinical laboratory support to back up many clinical diagnoses. Many drugs were used on patients before their effects were fully known. So-called medical authorities began, often arbitrarily, to place all of these new drugs in various classes and to give these classes names based on what they knew about the drugs' effects at that time.

Mistakes were made, and errors in nomenclature were not uncommon. For example, testosterone was called the "male sex steroid hormone." Most physicians even today refer to testosterone and other androgens in this misleading manner, even though it is now known that these steroids are common to both genders. Likewise, estrogens were called the "female sex steroid hormones" and are still known as such though they too are normal steroids produced by both sexes. With these nomenclature mistakes, medical science soon ignited the flame of controversy with sex steroid therapy. It appeared that the early researchers wanted medical physiology to categorize the sex steroids as gender specific. But no matter how much they wanted the sex steroids to be gender specific, it just wasn't that way.

By the early 1940s physicians began to become polarized in their views of testosterone and other androgen therapies in women. This became evident from the opposing viewpoints expressed in articles and letters published in medical journals. For instance, the pioneer of sex steroid replacement that mimicked the ovarian function in women patients was Robert B. Greenblatt, who was an expert in endocrinology, gynecology and obstetrics. He wrote in 1942:

> In a recent letter to the Editor which sharply condemns the use of androgens in the practice in gynecology ... one point which is fundamental and with which none will take issue is that the excessive use of any pharmacological agent, hormonal or otherwise, is harmful. The voices that have been raised against the use of androgens in the female arise from the concept that

> gonadal hormones should be sex specific.... Pharmacologically effective doses of testosterone propionate, which are far below the virilizing level, have been employed in several hundred cases in our group.[69]

Dr. Greenblatt knew that there was no such thing as the gender specific nature of sex steroids, but this quotation clearly showed that some prominent physicians were already committed to the idea that so-called male sex steroids should only be used in men and that the so-called female sex steroids only in females. He knew that all classes of sex steroids were common in both men and women. Other physicians during the early 1940s echoed Dr. Greenblatt's work and statements. Dr. Melvyn Berlind, in 1941, published an article that contained the following quote: "The use of androgenic hormones for the relief of varied functional gynecologic disorders, including menopause, has now been thoroughly accepted."[70]

A year later, Dr. Goldman wrote in an article that "One should be careful in condemning the general use of a valuable drug, like testosterone, just because some practitioners abuse it.... [One] should condemn the improper use of any new drug by such practitioners, but not the drug itself."[71]

Early battle lines were drawn over the use of testosterone and other androgen therapy for postmenopausal osteoporosis in women. But it was much too early to be drawing such battle lines, for research was in its earliest phase. The conflict quickly became political and dogmatic in nature. The testosterone pendulum was swinging back and forth. Physicians were choosing sides. Apparently, some physicians were abusing androgen therapy in some of their patients by utilizing much higher doses than others had. Granted, there was some guesswork involved, for strict guidelines had not been established early. In some women patients, adverse effects such as deepening of the voice, acne, and some facial hair were common complaints when higher doses were administered.

Perhaps the major point of political, social, and moral contention dealt with the effect of androgens on sexual drive and pleasure in women, especially when the doses were too large. Physicians of this period began to feel more and more uneasy about prescribing any drug that increased the sex drive and orgasmic response in their women patients. One must remember that at that time the woman's orgasmic response was very poorly understood and was essentially a taboo subject in both medically and socially speaking. Perhaps the final nail in the coffin of testosterone therapy for osteoporosis was driven by the hammer of medical politicians. The "nail" was a major article published in 1943, which proved that testosterone had a major libido-enhancing effect on women.[72] This study showed definitively that testosterone therapy had a triple effect on the psychosexual mechanism of women as demonstrated by:

a) heightened susceptibility to psychosexual stimulation;
b) increased sensitivity of the external genitalia, particularly the clitoris; and,
c) intensified sexual gratification as demonstrated by an increased number and depth of orgasms.

This publication was the ammunition necessary to echo the earlier claims by medical politicians that testosterone *was* "sexual TNT" and "medical dynamite." This influence took effect by the late 1940s and early 1950s so that testosterone and the forthcoming anabolic steroids were largely abandoned by the medical community, even though they were known to play a predominant role in bone metabolism and in the treatment of postmenopausal osteoporosis. It is highly doubtful that aging Baby Boomers *would* consider this aspect of an androgen component to their hormonal replacement regimens for the prevention and reversal of postmenopausal osteoporosis as problematic!

The androgen pendulum swung so far to the extreme in the 1960s through 1990s that androgens *did* become the "forgotten sex steroids" for the most part. Textbook authors denied, for instance, that testosterone levels in men decreased in the last few decades of life. They dissembled about the effects of androgens on athletic performance and muscle building. And, they grossly misrepresented the effects of androgens regarding the menopause completely. It was as if medical science had to go through the entire post–Brown-Sequard period of 35 years all over again. In effect, the medical profession in the United States stuck its collective head into the sand for several decades. This can best be exemplified by the following statement quoted from the most widely circulated medical textbook of its times:

> Mild depression is not uncommon in menopausal women, its frequency tending to be inversely proportional to the patient's understanding of menopausal physiology. A "menopause syndrome" in a psychiatric sense appears to be nonexistent. Women with anxiety neurosis, hysteria, phobic states, hypochondriasis, or obsessive-compulsive neurological illness during the menopause are generally found to have had the illness earlier in life. Psychological problems related to the menopause per se are common in the 40–55 year old group and related to the "empty nest" syndrome; responsibility for the care of adolescent children and aging parents; ungratified sexuality; fears of obesity, cancer, and loss of sexual attractiveness; and the fear of having to ultimately depend on children or charity.[73]

This account prove that Dr. Harrison heard the complaints of perimenopausal and postmenopausal women. Yet, he ignored the fact that many middle-aged men have all of the same feelings. Actually, Dr. Harrison used the above paragraph to summarize some of the mental and physical conditions associated with "andropause" and the menopause. Yet, he ignored the role that diminished sex steroids play. Instead, he would have better labeled the women with these complaints as "psych" cases. In fact, if an individual woman knew enough about the perimenopause and menopause, she could just "will away" these conditions, including postmenopausal osteoporosis, couldn't she? Dr. Harrison was exposed to the mounds of scientific evidence that linked postmenopausal osteoporosis and other conditions of the perimenopausal and menopausal states with sex steroid deficiency, but he ignored the evidence. It appears that he would much rather mimic a woman's complaints than mimic her younger ovarian function. Somehow, I don't think that this sort of attitude and bedside manner will be tolerated by aging women of the Baby Boomers generation.

A persistent and contrasting view of the biochemistry of sex steroids in women was presented by an American pioneer who studied the effects of combined estrogen-androgen therapy in women for over 50 years, Dr. Robert Greenblatt. In 1987, in one of his last publications prior to his death, and while still fighting the pressures of the medical establishment, he stated:

> Androgens are psychotropic drugs, participating in both physiologic and psychological components of sexual behavior. They modulate the neurohumors of the brain and influence affective behavior. Androgens in nonvirilizing doses complement estrogens, are synergistic rather than contraphysiologic, and may be employed effectively by most women administered alone or in combination with an estrogen. The menopausal woman who has failed to experience the benefits of estrogen replacement should be offered a trial of estrogen-androgen combination. Androgens are helpful in many gynecologic and nongynecologic disorders. Their use has not been exploited fully.[74]

Recent Research with Androgens and Postmenopausal Osteoporosis

The single event that took anabolic steroid therapy off the shelf was the invention and clinical availability of the DEXA osteoporosis scanner in the early 1990s. It has proven to be the definitive test for determining BMD both for the diagnosis of postmenopausal osteoporosis and for the repeat scans necessary to determine the effectiveness of pharmacological therapies used in attempts to treat and reverse the postmenopausal osteoporosis condition. A chronological tabulation of the significant events that highlight the "comeback" of "the forgotten sex steroids" in the treatment of postmenopausal osteoporosis is contained in Table 13-8. A detailed history of the use of anabolic steroids in the treatment of postmenopausal osteoporosis can be found in my recent book *Osteoporosis: Medical Blunders and Treatment Strategies*.[75]

Table 13-8. Recent Advancements with the Utilization of Anabolic Steroids in Postmenopausal Osteoporosis

Dates	*Events or Publications*
1990	The first DEXA machines became available for scientific and clinical use.
1992	Taylor and Alanis showed that adding an androgen (Winstrol) to the standard estrogen therapy can reverse BMD losses in athletically fit women who underwent surgical menopause and presented with osteoporosis despite estrogen therapy.[76]
1992	Szucs and coworkers reported the positive effects of using a calcitonin-anabolic steroid combination for the treatment of postmenopausal osteoporosis. "Intermittent administration of low-dose calcitonin, especially together with an anabolic steroid, seems to be a safe and effective therapy in established osteoporosis."[77]
1993	Hassager and Christiansen reported that "anabolic steroid therapy can increase BMD a few percentages a year in postmenopausal women with established osteoporosis" over and above estrogen therapy alone.[78]
1993	Need and coworkers reported that BMD gains with androgen therapy is on the order of 3 percent per annum, with the maximal gains seen within the first few months of therapy in patients with established osteoporosis.[79]
1993	Passeri and coworkers reported their double-blind, placebo-controlled study conducted with 46 postmenopausal women to evaluate the anabolic steroid, nandrolone, on the effects of BMD in women with established post-menopausal osteoporosis. "Nandrolone exerts positive effects on vertebral BMD and bone pain." Calcitonin and hemoglobin increased, HDL only slightly decreased. Two of 46 women withdrew from the study due to mild hirsutism and hoarseness. BMD increased by 2.9 percent (treatment group) and decreased by 2.3 percent (control group) over 18 months.[80]
1994	Taylor and coworkers published a study on estrogen (Estrace)-androgen (Winstrol) therapy for postmenopausal osteoporotic women who had failed conventional therapies. BMD increases were very significant at both six months and one year of therapy.[81]
1994	Lyritis and coworkers published a report that concluded that "nandrolone decanoate (anabolic steroid) has a beneficial effect in clinical symptoms, bone mineral density and biochemical parameters in postmenopausal women with established osteoporotic vertebral fractures."[82] In this 1-year study none of the 88 women dropped out due to adverse effects.
1994	Erdtsieck and coworkers reported on a 4-year study that included 33 post-menopausal osteoporotic women. One group was treated with estrogen + progesterone (E+P) therapy. The other group was treated with estrogen + progesterone + nandrolone (E +P+ AS) therapy. Bone mass showed a

statistically significant difference in the E+P+AS group over 3 years and the year after treatment. Addition of an anabolic steroid increased BMD over and above estrogen and progesterone therapy. No women dropped out of the study due to adverse effects.[83]

1995 Watts and coworkers showed that an oral estrogen-androgen therapy was superior to oral estrogen alone. Combined estrogen-androgen therapy resulted in a statistically significant increase in BMD in women with the surgical menopause over a two-year period compared to estrogen alone. The conclusions were that "Oral estrogen-androgen increased vertebral BMD compared with pre-treatment values and relieved somatic symptoms. Safety indices, including lipoprotein levels, indicated that the combination was well tolerated over the 2 years of treatment."[84]

1996 Adachi published a review article that recommended the use of anabolic steroids to stimulate bone formation for osteoporotic postmenopausal women.[85]

1997 Flicker and coworkers published their findings on 123 osteoporotic women undergoing a two-year randomized 2 × 2 factorial design to evaluate the effect of calcitonin and anabolic steroid, nandrolone, therapy. Intranasal calcitonin had deleterious effects on trabecular BMD at the lumbar spine and total BMD at the proximal femur. Nandrolone treatment had positive effects on BMD at the lumbar spine and proximal femur. Significant antagonism between calcitonin and nandrolone may exist when used together.[86]

1997 Phillips and Bauman published a paper summarizing all post-marketing safety surveillance data collected between 1989 and 1996 for Solvay Pharmaceutical's version of oral estrogen-androgen combination. More than 1 million woman-years of exposure occurred. The findings indicate that this combination when used as directed is safe. Marginal adverse effects can be managed by appropriate patient selection and monitoring.[87]

1999 Barrett-Connor and associates reported that estrogen-androgen therapy was statistically better than estrogen alone for increasing BMD losses and menopausal symptoms over in a two-year double-blind study.[88]

Summary

Anabolic steroid therapy has a major role in the prevention and treatment of postmenopausal osteoporosis. Use of anabolic steroid treatment should result in a dramatic impact on the osteoporosis epidemic.

Recent official estimates have indicated a dramatic rise in the number of annual osteoporotic hip fractures in the United States despite the other therapies brought about by conventional wisdom. A woman's risk of an osteoporosis-related hip fracture is greater than her *combined* risk of developing breast, uterine, and ovarian cancer. One out of two women, following menopause, will sustain this type of hip fracture! And, the ultimate death rate six months after a woman sustains this type of hip fracture is *greater* than the ultimate death rate six months after a woman has a myocardial infarction (heart attack).

Perhaps postmenopausal osteoporosis is not "glitzy" enough to receive the media attention that it deserves. It directly affects more than 25 million Americans. Gail Sheehy, author of a 1994 book entitled *Menopause*, states that the condition of osteoporosis "has not been worthy of recognition" and "represents another political medical scandal regarding women's health issues." Anabolic steroid therapy is a major answer for the osteoporosis predicament. Soon, one hopes that large multi-site studies will be undertaken to prove the role of anabolic steroid therapy in treating, reversing, and perhaps, curing postmenopausal osteoporosis. Without anabolic steroid therapy, the financial costs to the American taxpayer will be over $30 billion annually.

Osteoporosis in Elderly Men

Osteoporosis in elderly men is a significant medical condition. The estimated incidence suggests that it afflicts men about five times less that does postmenopausal osteoporosis in women. These estimates indicate that there are five to ten million older men with "senile osteoporosis" currently in America. Hip, pelvic, and vertebral fractures in osteoporotic men have become more commonplace. As the male lifespan continues to increase, so will the osteoporosis rate. For instance, I recently was involved in the rehabilitation of two elderly, active men who had slipped and fallen to the ground from a standing position sustaining crush fractures to the pelvis. The morbidity, the length of rehabilitation, and the amount of money required to attempt to repair this type of condition is enormous.

Prior to his fall, one 89-year-old man, who appeared much younger than his stated age, was an active golfer who routinely shot his age when he played. Following surgery and prolonged rehabilitation, it became doubtful that he would ever play again. Before his fall he was completely independent and lived alone. Upon his discharge from the rehabilitation unit, he was to live in an assisted living facility and ambulate by wheel chair. What a major change in lifestyle! It could have been prevented.

Several of the studies presented in the last two sections have had men as subjects. The mechanisms by which the osteoblasts are stimulated by androgen therapy have also been previously covered in detail in the previous sections. As a recap, androgen therapy in men with osteoporosis stimulates osteoblasts to form new and normal bone. Physicians in the 1940s and 1950s empirically treated men whom they suspected to have osteoporosis with androgen therapy. It was postulated that the serum testosterone levels in men began to decline at about age 50. Therefore, replacement therapy with testosterone or anabolic steroids was indicated.

Eventually, laboratory values were developed for the "normal" range of testosterone levels of men living in the United States. These laboratory tests concluded that the "normal" range of testosterone could vary four-fold and still be considered normal. With this standard, in order to be below normal, a man would have to be almost completely testosterone deficient. For example, a man when he was younger could have as much as four times the testosterone level which he would have 40 or 50 years later, but his latter level would be considered normal. In the mid–1970s the prevailing medical belief was that testosterone production *did not* decline in aging men. This belief can be demonstrated by the following quotation from Dr. Harrison's 1977 edition of the *Principles of Internal Medicine*:

> Since this disorder (involutional melancholia and osteoporosis) occurs in conjunction with either the menopause or the male climacteric, endocrine depletion has been thought to play a role in its genesis. However, since there is no specific accompanying endrocrinologic abnormality, and since its course has never been influenced by hormone replacement, such does not seem to be the case.[89]

It is difficult to estimate the resulting and prolonged effects that such statements have on the practice of medicine. Harrison's *Principles of Internal Medicine* has been and continues to be the most used textbook for the education of the nation's medical students and physicians.

Today, it is common knowledge that testosterone levels in aging men do decline just as they did over 50 years ago. And, even though testosterone became clinically available in 1935, modern medicine finds itself in the same therapeutic dilemma as it was decades ago in dealing with androgen replacement therapy for elderly men with osteoporosis.

A recent study published by researchers from East Tennessee State University has reopened the concept of prescribing anabolic steroids in elderly men with osteoporosis.[90] More studies are sure to follow. Perhaps large, multi-site studies should be conducted to reevaluate the use of androgens for treating and reversing osteoporosis in elderly men. Until then, I feel that testosterone or anabolic steroid therapy should be viewed as an appropriate therapy in treating osteoporosis in men.

My clinical experience shows that one of the best treatments utilizes a cyclical Winstrol (stanozolol) regimen of 10 mg daily for 2–3 weeks each month. In this manner, the osteoblasts are stimulated to continue through their bone forming cycles even in the days after therapy. This cyclical regimen also minimizes any perturbations in serum lipids and minimizes any hepatic tolerance issues. When male patients are treated with this regimen, BMD increases without unwanted adverse effects in lipids, hepatic function, or testicular atrophy. Rectal prostate exams and PSA tests are recommended prior to Winstrol therapy.

Male Climacteric, Male Involutional Melancholia, and Male "Andropause"

The early description of "andropause" in aging men has been described for centuries. Shortly after the discovery, isolation, and synthesis of testosterone it became an accepted treatment to combat this aging condition. In the late 1930s and through the 1940s, testosterone therapy was the treatment of choice for male climacteric and involutional melancholia. A chronological listing of the early publications citing the use of testosterone therapy in men with "andropause" is shown in Table 13-9.

TABLE 13-9. EARLY STUDIES USING TESTOSTERONE THERAPY FOR THE MALE CLIMACTERIC AND MALE "ANDROPAUSE"

Dates	*Event or Publication*
1939	Turner reported that testosterone therapy "brought about considerable relief of the subjective and sexual diminution associated with senescence and benign prostatic hypertrophy in aging men."[91]
1941	Thomas and Hill reported on two cases of testosterone therapy in aging men with the male climacteric. "Both cases showed remarkable improvement"[92]
1942	Goldman and Markham reported on seven cases of the male climacteric treated with testosterone therapy to alleviate the symptoms.[93]
1942	Samuels and coworkers published their report on the use of testosterone therapy for increasing muscular strength and work capacity in normal healthy male medical students.[94]
1942	Davidoff and Goodstone reported a 65 percent clinical response to testosterone therapy for 20 men with severe involutional melancholia.[95]
1942	Danziger and Blank reported on five aged men institutionalized with involutional melancholia treated with testosterone therapy. Two men improved enough to be released and one other improved sufficiently enough to be paroled. Two others improved to a lesser degree.[96]
1943	Robie reported on testosterone therapy used for the male climacteric. "Remarkable personality alterations may occur in deficiency states that respond to gonadal substitution therapy."[97]
1943	Werner published his study of 37 aging men with symptoms of the male climacteric treated with testosterone. "Testosterone is effective in relieving these symptoms in the male."[98]

A considerable amount of knowledge was accumulating by the early 1940s regarding the effects of aging due to reduction in testosterone levels in men. This is best illustrated by a review article published in 1940 in which the major points about the role of testosterone deficiency in the aging male are summarized below.

a) Chemically the androgens and estrogens are intimately related to cholesterol from which they are prepared synthetically.... Both are hormones which are found in both men and women.... The normal predominance of the respective hormone in each sex determines the orientations in both the physiological and psychological spheres.
b) The production of testosterone in males follows a parabolic curve with its ascent started between the ages of 10 and 14, and continued gradually up to the age of 22 or 25. It then remains almost at the same level for 5 to 10 years, and then starts a gradual decline, almost insensible at first, at the ages of 32 to 35. This decline will be rapidly accentuated between 40 and 50, and at the age of 55 to 60, in most men, the activity of the Leydig cells (testosterone producing cells) is about the same as that before puberty.
c) The number of Leydig cells is known to decrease in the interstitial tissue along with the passing of years, and in old age there is a reversal to a state of that of early childhood, with the Leydig cells reduced to a minimum in the senile atrophied testicles.
d) The prostate, on the contrary, usually starts a process of fibrous hypertrophy at about 40, in some cases slowly, in others rapidly, reaching a large size and interfering with the free elimination of urine under the influence of increased impulses of the gonadotrophic pituitary hormone.
e) Proved effects of testosterone propionate therapy in men past 40 are: (1) definite improvement of the usually depressed and melancholic psychics with marked improvement in concentration and memory and ability to perform mental work. (2) rapid established euphoria and renewed ambition with apparent increase in "pep" and general bodily vigor. (3) reduction of prostatism and nocturia. (4) in climacteric men whose testes have not suffered too extensive degeneration, sexual powers and libido can be restored in a moderate degree, bringing in many cases peace and renewed marital happiness to them. (5) because of the advances of the last half century of medical progress, his span of life is being prolonged far beyond his fifties, and we can also make those added years happier and more comfortable, creating with this addition of our armamentarium, a new weapon of incalculable possibilities.[99]

A historical review, as shown by the various quotations contained in the preceding sections, indicates that by the mid–1970s, a relative testosterone deficiency *did not* exist in elderly men who had symptoms of the male version of "andropause." Over many years hundreds of thousands of men went through this phase of life as the medical profession stood by supporting the medical dogma that was taught to them. Statements such as "he's just going through a mid-life crisis" had become a commonplace attempt to explain away the declining levels of testosterone in aging men. The medical establishment went through a lengthy period of denial regarding these declining levels in normal aging men.

Textbooks of this period begrudgingly contained a paragraph or two regarding involutional melancholia and "andropause" symptoms in aging men, but the authors of such textbooks tended to greatly minimize the hormonal cause of such a condition. During the 1970s it was as if these authors really didn't believe the results and conclusions of the earlier studies. In other words, there was no biochemical explanation of the male climacteric and so there was no sex steroid replacement for it.

As aging Baby Boomers had a greater impact on the direction of medical research, conditions like the male "andropause" began to receive a flurry of renewed concern. The use of testosterone replacement for the male "andropause" was considered to be brand new. In the 1990s the pharmaceutical industry found ways around the patent laws by offering different methods of testosterone replacement utilizing a new transdermal testosterone patch first offered in 1996[100] and by developing testosterone gel preparations offered to the public via prescription in 2000.[101] The sexual performance in aging men was back in the public's view in a major way. Pressures have been mounting on physicians to prescribe these new testosterone preparations for sexual enhancement much as they had nearly 60 years previously.

Paralleling these events was the change in attitude exemplified by the medical science community. "Andropause" was discussed as if it were a newly discovered condition. It was described as an ill-defined collection of symptoms that is seen in aging men, typically past 50 years of age, who may have low androgen levels.[102] Many of these "new" findings regarding this condition echoed the findings from the medical scientists who published their findings over a half-century earlier.

Over the decades the male menopause or "andropause" has been debated as a concept originating from fact or fiction.[103] Most men, according to recent research, do experience a gradual loss of testicular function and testosterone production as they age.[104] Cross-sectional and longitudinal studies have confirmed the results of the older studies that serum total testosterone, as well as free testosterone levels, begin to decline at about the age of 50 years.[105,106] In addition, the binding of testosterone to sex hormone binding globulin (SHBG) increases with aging thus reducing the serum-free (which is bioavailable) testosterone to even lower levels.[107] Although this decrease in testosterone levels is seen in otherwise healthy elderly men,[108] a gradual decline in testosterone is also seen in patients with concomitant illness.[109] Andropause may be associated with decreased testosterone levels along with decreased levels of growth hormone and other anabolic hormones and factors.[110]

The decline in gonadal (testes) function leads to a lower testosterone level and may present with symptoms such as erectile dysfunction (ED), generalized weakness, mood and memory changes and a loss of BMD. The aging man is known to lose muscle mass particularly after the age of 40 years. The typical man loses about 20 pounds of muscle, 20 percent of bone mass and nearly two inches of height between the ages of 40 and 70 years.[111] And, in the years beyond 70, these physiological losses continue.

A very recent study reported the findings that define the perceived male "andropause."[112] In this study 89 percent of aging men admitted that they had symptoms that they believed were synonymous with the andropause. These self-reported symptoms included ED, muscle weakness, osteoporosis, mood swings, depression, and memory losses. Testosterone replacement has been recommended for elderly men who do not possess contraindications to such therapy.

In summary, the treatment of "andropause" with testosterone or anabolic steroids in men is making a major comeback. Unfortunately, little attention is paid to research done prior to the 1970s and it is feared that the earliest work and medical opinions may be lost forever. I believe that the medical scientists during the 1930s and 1940s were correct in many ways. They were the medical experts of their times long before medical politics came into play.

There exists more than one way to treat the symptoms and conditions associated with the male "andropause." Since the male "andropause" is brought about by a testosterone deficiency, then simply replacing this deficiency with testosterone tends to alleviate many of the symptoms, complaints, and conditions. However, it is not uncommon to find an aging man, with the typical "andropause," being treated with numerous medications. Each of the medications is targeted for a single symptom or condition as shown in Table 13-10 below. Wouldn't it be simpler and more cost effective just to replace what was lost?

Table 13-10. Various Treatment Options for the Male Andropause

Symptom or Condition	*Modern-Day Medication*	*Androgen Therapy Alleviation*
mental depression	Prozac, Zoloft, Paxil, Elavil	yes
muscle mass loss	growth hormone, IGF-1	yes
libido loss	testosterone, anabolic steroids	yes
erectile dysfunction	Viagra	yes
osteoporosis	Fosamax, calcitonin	yes
memory losses	ginseng and other herbs	yes
slowed reflexes	CNS stimulants	yes
reduced immune system function	interferon	yes

Symptom or Condition	*Modern-Day Medication*	*Androgen Therapy Alleviation*
benign prostate enlargement	Flomax, Proscar, saw palmetto	yes
reduced energy level	B-12, CNS stimulants	yes
low-grade anemia	Epogen (EPO)	yes
reduced cardiac output	Accupril, Vasotec, Zestril	yes
reduced pulmonary function	corticosteroids, beta-agonists	yes
mildly elevated serum cholesterol	Mevacor, Lipitor	yes

In short, as men age testosterone levels decrease. Replacement of testosterone or other anabolic steroids is paramount in treating the associated complaints and conditions brought on by this biochemical condition. No other modern-day therapy alleviates the medley of conditions brought about by this hormone deficiency and at such a relatively low expense. As men age into the 80s and beyond, this form of therapy will prove to be effective both physiologically and financially. Treating each individual symptom or condition can be ultra expensive and complicated with potential adverse effects and multiple drug interactions. It makes sense to replace androgens for androgen deficiency as first line therapy. If some of the symptoms or complaints continue to persist, then other more specific medications could be added to androgen replacement therapy as needed. This regimen is cost-effective and can reduce the overall medication burden of many elderly male patients.

Male Hypogonadism

One of the obvious therapies utilizing testosterone would be in those men who lacked or had a relative lack of the normal production of testosterone. As covered in the previous section, the male "andropause" could be considered a form of hypogonadism. In primary male hypogonadism there is either a lack of normal testosterone production or an insensitivity of receptors within the testicles or the various target organs that manifests itself by sexual organ underdevelopment and a delay in the normal maturation processes. Many of these causes are genetic in nature. Some of the causes of primary hypogonadism in males are contained in Table 13-11. Primary hypogonadism in the male can also be caused by a lack of testicles or a loss of testicles. Secondary male hypogonadism can result from a variety of systemic illnesses or brain trauma.

The first case report in the scientific literature using testosterone for the treatment of sexual underdevelopment of a 27-year-old white male medical student was published in 1937.[113] Several other early reports were published in the early 1940s.[114–118] Over the next 50 years, the use of testosterone therapy in the treatment of male hypogonadism and delayed puberty has been refined. This use of testosterone and anabolic steroids has remained the primary treatment in modern medicine. Men who are afflicted with this condition are often taught to self-inject long-acting testosterone preparations. However, this prescribed use can be abused as indicated in a case report of a 21-year-old man who suffered a stroke by overzealous (greater than five times the prescribed dose) self-injection of testosterone.[119]

TABLE 13-11. SOME CAUSES OF PRIMARY MALE HYPOGONADISM

Prepubertal Chromosomal Abnormalities
- Klinefelter's syndrome
- Reifenstein's syndrome
- Male Turner's syndrome

Prepubertal Non-Chromosomal Abnormalities
- Sertoli-cell-only syndrome
- Anorchia including undescended testis at birth

Postpubertal Chromosomal Abnormalities
- Cystic fibrosis
- Laurence-Moon-Biedl syndrome
- Myotonic dystrophies

Postpubertal Non-Chromosomal Abnormalities
- Orchitis or infections involving the testes
- Irradiation or trauma to the testes
- Testicular neoplasms
- Surgical castration

Heavy, prolonged anabolic steroid abuse

Leydig-cell failure (male andropause)

Secondary hypogonadism in men is caused by conditions associated with hypothalamic or pituitary disorders. Androgen therapy may be indicated for these conditions. Table 13-12 includes some of the causes of secondary male hypogonadism. Some of these causes of secondary male hypogonadism will be covered in some detail in the upcoming sections of this chapter.

TABLE 13-12. SOME CAUSES OF SECONDARY HYPOGONADISM IN MALES

Prepubertal Genetic Abnormalities
- Isolated gonadotrophin deficiency
- Kallman's syndrome
- Froehlich's syndrome

Postpubertal Acquired Conditions
- Severe systemic infections
- Severe medical illnesses including myocardial infarction
- Post-surgical conditions
- Closed brain injury
- Chronic respiratory insufficiency
- Pituitary neoplasms
- Hypothalamic neoplasms
- Pituitary infections
- Prolonged immobilization
- Microgravity (space travel) conditions
- Heavy, prolonged anabolic steroid abuse
- Chronic alcoholism

Female Climacteric and Female Menopause

When a particular gland ceases to function, either completely or partially, it makes sense to replace the hormone or hormones the gland produced previously. It is just a matter of common sense to do so. As previously discussed, the functioning human ovaries make three classes of sex steroids: testosterone and anabolic-androgenic steroids (androgens), estrogenic steroids, and progesterogenic steroids. When the ovaries are removed surgically as with a total hysterectomy or when the ovaries cease to produce sex steroids in adequate quantities as in natural menopause, it makes sense to utilize a hormonal replacement regime that includes some combination of these classes of ovarian sex steroids. As with the male climacteric or male "andropause" there are a variety of symptoms and conditions that occur with ovarian involution. However, the female menopause generally has a more abrupt onset than that seen in aging men. Some of the more common symptoms and conditions which are associated with the surgical or natural menopause in women are hot flashes, mental depression, mood swings, headaches, loss of energy, osteoporosis, loss of libido, loss of orgasmic response, increased risk for coronary heart disease, increased serum cholesterol levels, body fat gain, and a general loss of the sense of well-being.

Estrogen has traditionally been the primary choice for sex steroid replacement in women. A progesterogenic steroid, in recent years, has been added to protect against uterine cancer. For women who still possess an intact uterus, adding a daily low-dose progesterone can prevent menses in most cases. Many women, however, continue to experience symptoms and conditions with estrogen monotherapy or with combination estrogen-progesterone therapy. This fact is not surprising since testosterone and other anabolic-androgenic steroids have such a powerful effect on the mental and physical well being of women. Thus, the addition of a small amount of testosterone or other androgen, with estrogen monotherapy or estrogen-progesterone combination therapy, can produce major beneficial effects on postmenopausal women. These regimens can be tailored to closely mimic the normal ovaries' production of the sex steroids.

Low-dose testosterone or anabolic steroid therapy should be considered in addition to the other sex steroid regimens for a variety of symptoms or complaints. These indications are listed in Table 13-13.

Table 13-13. Symptoms and Conditions Indicating Addition of an Androgen as Part of an HRT Regimen in the Female Climacteric

Continued hot flashes with estrogen therapy
Return or worsening of migraine headaches
Reduced libido
Loss of sexual orgasmic response
Decreased energy level or chronic fatigue
Family history of postmenopausal osteoporosis
Significant history of corticosteroid use
Current regular or prolonged use of corticosteroids
Concomitant diagnosis of osteoporosis
Concomitant diagnosis of anemia
Mental depression
Memory losses
Concomitant diagnosis of various diseases (e.g., rheumatoid arthritis, AIDS, systemic lupus, multiple sclerosis, chronic obstructive pulmonary disease, scleroderma, nephrotic syndrome)
Thyroid hormone replacement therapy
As a routine component for HRT therapy

The question as to whether an androgen component should be added to "traditional" hormone replacement therapy (HRT) to treat the female climacteric has been a non-debatable issue for some physicians. The results obtained from decades of previous promotion of HRT that mimics ovarian function have been impressive. However, some readers may require further convincing evidence that supports this concept. Without providing an "instant replay" of the clinical history which has been provided in the previous sections covering CST-induced osteoporosis and postmenopausal osteoporosis, it seems prudent to cover some of the appropriate science which addresses the literature regarding the medley of menopausal issues and the role that androgen replacement plays in alleviating these symptoms and conditions. Since osteoporosis is one of the most common conditions occurring with the female climacteric, it can be easily shown that there is considerable overlap in the science that addresses the issues of sex steroid therapy for the menopause and therapies for postmenopausal osteoporosis. With this in mind, a historical perspective regarding the role of androgen therapy for the female menopause will be provided.

The concept of replacing the sex steroids that mimic ovarian function was pioneered in the late 1930s and early 1940s by Dr. Robert Greenblatt of the Medical College of Georgia. He promoted and prescribed HRT consisting of estrogen-androgen combinations for the female menopause. Additional publications during the 1950s addressed further the advantages of estrogen-androgen combinations over that of estrogen monotherapy alone.[120–123] These studies recognized the superiority of estrogen-androgen combinations in alleviating the symptoms and conditions associated with the female climacteric.

In 1962, in their textbook on gynecology, Parsons and Sommers stated, "Symptoms based on physical, mental and emotional depletion tend to improve under the combined estrogen and androgen therapy.... Testosterone is a potent anabolic stimulant, as well as having a protein-sparing effect. The patient therefore feels better. Androgens also tend to increase libido."[124]

During the 1970s and early 1980s hormone replacement therapy in general fell from grace with the medical profession. The attitudes and quotations taken from a major medical textbook have been presented in previous sections. However, by the mid–1980s, the use of estrogen-androgen combinations for the treatment of the female menopause was revived by a number of scientific publications.[125–131] These studies again showed the superior effects of estrogen-androgen combinations.

By the mid–1990s the concept of mimicking ovarian function by estrogen-androgen combination therapy was gathering significant attention. In May 1995 a scientific symposium was held on the topic of the "Emerging Role of Androgens in Menopausal Treatment" in San Francisco, California. Lectures were given by specialists from across the country. Some of the salient points that were made are listed below.

(1) Women who use combination sex steroid therapy (estrogen-androgen) in menopause lead better lives, as judged by most quality-of-life measures, and live longer as well. This type of sex steroid replacement therapy should be provided for all women who desire it, and should be continued indefinitely. Many women can expect to live nearly half of their lifespan suffering from the sequelae of ovarian involution. Menopause should be considered as a continuum rather than a passage.
(2) Androgens may be used to improve the quality of life without detracting from the cardiovascular benefits of estrogenic monotherapy alone.

Androgens have a growing role in menopausal therapy when combined with estrogenic steroids, and they appear to be both safe and beneficial.

(3) Treatment with combined estrogenic and androgenic steroids can increase bone mineral density more than estrogenic steroids alone. Addition of an androgenic steroid to the replacement therapy has a positive effect on osteoblast activity, which is not seen with estrogenic steroids.

(4) By correlating perceived distress from menopausal symptoms with sexual drive, the physician can offer treatment and improve the potential for the patient's adherence to therapy for the other aspects of menopause, by utilizing combined estrogenic and androgenic steroids. Estrogen-androgen therapy improves energy level and mood in menopausal women. Testosterone and anabolic-androgenic steroids are responsible for the sexual drive in women, and sexual drive has been shown to increase adherence to therapy in some women after estrogen-androgen therapy.

(5) Progesterogenic steroids can be added to the hormonal treatment regimen to help reduce the small risk of uterine cancer.

In 1997, at the 15th World Congress of Gynecology and Obstetrics meeting in Copenhagen, Denmark, a daylong symposium entitled "The Emerging Role of Estrogen-Androgen Therapy in the Care of the Postmenopausal Patient" was presented. The important points of this symposium were:

(1) Adding small amounts of androgen to estrogen replacement therapy can restore failing libido, resolve persistent hot flashes and restore decreased bone mineral density, all consequences of menopause that can affect the quality of life of postmenopausal women.

(2) Androgen, for some women, is the "missing hormone" of hormone replacement therapy. Estrogen-androgen combination therapy can be a significantly better option for some women than estrogen alone.

(3) The notion that menopause is a one- or two-year "event" is an outdated way of looking at what is really a spectrum of symptoms over a decade or longer period of time. Androgen production in women decreases gradually over the years leading up to menopause and for decades later. As a result, symptoms due to androgen depletion are expected as the menopausal transition begins and will continue to persist beyond menopause.

(4) Postmenopausal women who received combined estrogen-androgen therapy showed an improvement in sexual desire, fantasy, frequency of intercourse and a decrease in painful sexual intercourse when compared with

women receiving estrogen therapy alone. Estrogen-androgen therapy is superior to estrogen therapy in reducing hot flashes, insomnia, and vaginal dryness.

(5) There is a growing body of research in HRT indicating that "one-size-doesn't-fit-all." Sex steroid replacement therapy should be tailored to each individual according to her postmenopausal symptoms and conditions.

The conclusions of these symposia have been echoed by recent articles focusing on the role of androgens in maintaining the health and emotional well being of postmenopausal women.[132,133] Additional benefits of adding an androgen to estrogen therapy may be two-fold:

a) the estrogen dose may be minimized to afford the maximal response when a low-dose androgen is added. Estrogens and androgens work synergistically to reduce hot flashes and other vasomotor symptoms by returning the luteinizing hormone levels to normal levels;
b) the addition of an androgen may *reduce* the risk of breast cancer when combined with the minimally effective estrogen dose. In fact, in women with a history of breast cancer, androgens are valid alternatives for treating postmenopausal symptoms and conditions such as hot flashes, decreased libido, and osteoporosis.[134]

In summary, treating the symptoms and conditions of the female menopause is best performed by mimicking the normal ovarian production of the sex steroids. Optimizing the three classes of sex steroids produced by the ovaries, in an individualized, tailored fashion, is expected to become the standard of care for this condition. In Europe, a single steroid which possesses both estrogenic and androgenic components has been used for years. Although this steroid, tibolone, has never been approved for use in the United States, the literature shows responses similar to estrogen-androgen combination therapy in treating the postmenopausal symptoms and conditions, such as osteoporosis.[135–151] An extensive literature review indicates the concept of estrogen-androgen therapy, or as shown by the European studies indicating that a single steroid which may have combined estrogen-androgen activity, is not only here to stay, but is correct from a biochemical standpoint.

In order to fully minimize the potential adverse effects of both aspects of estrogen-androgen replacement therapy, it is important to use the lowest possible dose and the correct type of each component. Common complaints of estrogenic steroid replacement include breast tenderness, fluid retention, headaches, increased blood pressure, threat of blood clots, body fat gains, and concerns about breast cancer. These adverse effects can be minimized or avoided completely by both the appropriate selection of the estrogen component and in the proper dose. Likewise, common complaints, such as hirsutism, voice tone deepening, facial acne, and virilization can be minimized or completely avoided by the appropriate selection of the androgen component in the proper dose and schedule. Therefore, close medical monitoring individualized for both subjective complaints and results from objective measures is indicated.

My personal experience has been to start with the following regimens and alter them as necessary:

(1) for women without a uterus, the estrogen-androgen therapy of Estrace 0.5 mg daily and Winstrol (stanozolol) 2–4 mg daily for each day 1–10 each month.
(2) for women with a uterus, the estrogen-progesterone-androgen therapy of Estrace 0.5 mg daily, Provera 2.5 mg daily and Winstrol (stanozolol) 2–4 mg daily for each day 1–10 each month.[152–153]

Winstrol is used due to its unique characteristics as an anabolic steroid. First, it has one of the highest anabolic-to-androgenic (therapeutic index) ratios of all of the androgens. This high therapeutic index significantly reduces any virilization potentials. Second, because of its biochemical structure, Winstrol is not aromatized to estrogens that further reduce any adverse effect potentials due to the excess of estrogens. Third, Winstrol has been shown to directly stimulate osteoblast activity and produce an increased normal bone mineral density in both trabecular and cortical bone. Fourth, Winstrol possesses a fibrinolytic action that may reduce the potential of abnormal blood clots that can be an adverse effect of estrogen therapy. Finally, Winstrol prescribed in small doses for 10 days each month mimics the 10-day testosterone elevation produced by the normally functioning ovaries as stimulated by the pituitary's spike in luteinizing hormone (LH) release. This 10-day schedule tends to minimize any changes in serum lipids and lipoproteins and does not seem to induce liver tolerance so that the same low dose can be repeated on a monthly basis.

The time is right for multi-site large research studies to determine the best androgen and androgen dose schedule for menopausal women. But it is safe to say that an androgen component to the HRT for postmenopausal women is both beneficial and safe when prescribed correctly.

Angina Pectoris, Hypertension, and Coronary Artery Disease

One of the more interesting areas in which testosterone therapy has been considered to be beneficial was discovered by medical scientists who were searching for clinical applications for androgens. It was noted that testosterone treatment reduced the complaints of angina pectoris (chest pain), hypertension, and coronary heart disease. The reduction in angina pain and other cardiovascular conditions was uncovered when early scientists prescribed testosterone for the treatment for the male climacteric.

The earliest report on the topic of testosterone therapy and vascular disease was published in 1939 by a group of clinicians working with Dr. J.B. Hamilton.[154] A year later, three clinical professors of medicine from Ohio State University College of Medicine published their results of a study of 23 patients with coronary artery disease in which 22 of 23 showed clinical improvement with sex steroid therapy (testosterone, estrogen, or a combination of these).[155]

Perhaps the greatest proponent of testosterone therapy for relieving the pain of angina pectoris was Maurice A. Lesser, M.D., professor of preventive medicine at Boston University School of Medicine and Massachusetts Memorial Hospitals. In 1942 Dr. Lesser published his results on the use of 25 mg of testosterone propionate injected twice or thrice weekly in 24 patients with angina pectoris. "Favorable results were obtained in all cases (20 men and 4 women) in that the frequency, severity and duration of attacks of angina pectoris were diminished, and these patients have been able to increase their physical activities to a considerable degree without precipitating attacks.... The beneficial effects of this treatment persisted between two and twelve months after treatment was discontinued."[156]

Dr. Lesser believed testosterone might prove to be a valuable drug in the treatment of angina pectoris and that its use warranted further study. Also in 1942, a private physician in Boston published the results of his study on seven patients who experienced relief from angina pectoris and hypertension using testosterone therapy.[157] Then in 1943, Lesser published further results utilizing testosterone therapy in patients with angina pectoris.[158] The most definitive results utilizing testosterone therapy in 100 patients were published in 1946.[159] Ninety-one of the 100 patients (92 men and 8 women) with angina pectoris showed moderate (40 patients) to marked improvement (51 patients).

Similar findings with testosterone therapy for angina pectoris and mild hypertension were found by several other groups.[160–166] Another convincing study during this period was conducted by Waldman who showed that seven of eight patients with positive electrocardiograms during exercise stress testing responded favorably to treatment with testosterone propionate.[167] Waldman postulated that the mechanism of testosterone's action was through increasing the phosphorus and creatine content of the heart muscle, providing an increase in contractility of the heart muscle. This improved efficiency of contractility was proposed to reduce the strain of the heart and reduce or eliminate chest pain.

It is a mystery as to why testosterone therapy to reduce the symptoms of angina pectoris is prescribed by only a small number of cardiologists today. Interestingly, many of today's younger cardiologists have never heard of this use of testosterone to relieve the symptoms of angina pectoris when it was the "drug of choice" for this condition in the 1940s. It is also certain from these early studies, that testosterone and anabolic steroids have positive effects on the cardiovascular system, such as enhancing cardiac output and cardiac contractility. The fact that angina pectoris in men and women tends to occur when testosterone levels are reduced during the climacteric stages also provides a clue as to its mechanism of action.

Androgen receptors are located in the hearts and lungs of both men and women.[168–169] Androgen binding to these tissue receptors may play a role in optimum functioning. One study showed that the quantity of androgen concentrations in heart and lung tissues reduces in a statistically significant manner with age, and more so in aging women than in aging men.[170] Moreover, androgen concentrations are higher in cardiac muscle and lung tissues than in striated muscle, which is surprising. Hence, it is possible that the age-associated decrease in androgen concentrations in cardiac muscle and pulmonary tissues may have a major influence on the decreased functioning of these organs.

There has been a recently revived interest in the effect of sex hormones on cardiovascular risk factors and as a therapeutic modality in both men and women. It has been shown that the serum testosterone decreases in men and women as they age. Otherwise healthy men with low testosterone levels can have *increased* cardiovascular risk factors, including high fasting and two-hour post-prandial plasma glucose, elevated triglycerides, total cholesterol, low-density lipoprotein (LDL) cholesterol, and apo A-1 lipoprotein. Returning these men to the mid-normal range of testosterone levels, with testosterone therapy, has been shown to:

a) reduce total cholesterol levels;
b) reduce LDL cholesterol levels;
c) have antianginal effects;
d) increase high-density lipoprotein (HDL) cholesterol levels;
e) augment the fibrinolytic system and antithrombin III activity; and,
f) reduce mildly elevated systolic blood pressures.[171]

Another heart-related use of androgens has recently been identified. Anabolic steroids have been used to enhance the muscular strength of the latissimus dorsi muscle for greater contraction ability when this muscle is harvested for use in cardiomyoplasty for patients with near end-stage congestive heart failure. Anabolic steroid administration makes the latissimus dorsi muscle stronger and therefore more useful for cardiomyoplasty.[172]

In summary, returning serum androgens to a mid-normal range in aging men and women has multiple and dramatic effects on their health and well-being. Future studies are necessary to fully evaluate the use of testosterone and anabolic steroids as therapeutic cardiovascular agents. There appears to be a significant potential for these steroids, especially in patients undergoing cardiac rehabilitation and for men and women with reduced cardiac outputs.

Raynaud's Syndrome and Cryofibrinogenemia

In Raynaud's syndrome (RS), episodes of circulatory arrest occur in the digits of the hands and sometimes the feet. These episodes occur most often in response to cold or emotional stress. Nicotine, caffeine, and other types of stimulants, and anti-depressive medications can exacerbate RS.

In traditional cases, the fingers develop a tri-color response in that the proximal aspects of the fingers take on a cyanotic gray pallor, the middle aspects are a blanched white, and the distal aspects of the digits are red or pink in color. Initially, there is a loss of or reduction in sensation, followed by a period of increased sensitivity and pain in the fingers. In many ways, this occlusive digital artery disease mimics the vasospastic conditions often seen with migraine headaches. Simply put, an easy way to understand this condition is to consider it as a migraine syndrome of the fingers. In severe cases, patients frequently are at risk for developing ischemic fingertip ulceration and are at a greater risk of frostbite in cold climates.

Raynaud's syndrome may be a harbinger of other diseases and conditions, or it can be a condition that stands alone (idiopathic RS). Although RS can be associated with numerous underlying conditions, it is most commonly seen in vascular conditions with or without an immune system disorder as shown in Table 13-14.

TABLE 13-14. VARIOUS CLASSIFICATIONS OF RAYNAUD'S SYNDROME

Idiopathic Raynaud's syndrome
RS associated with immunologic disorders
  Scleroderma
  Dermatomyositis
  Systemic lupus erythematosus
  Rheumatoid arthritis
  Mixed connective tissue diseases
  Cryoglobulinemia
RS associated without immunologic disorders
  Thromboangiitis obliterans
  Arteriosclerosis
RS associated with miscellaneous causes
  Occupational vibration or direct arterial trauma
  Drug or medication-induced

There have been a number of medications used for the treatment and clinical management of RS. However, for severe RS, the anabolic steroid Winstrol (stanozolol) has been used with significant results.[173] Prior to the FDA's "cleaning up" of the indications for various drugs in the early 1980s, Winstrol was approved by the FDA for use in irretractable Raynaud's syndrome.[174] Winstrol therapy reduces plasma fibrinogen levels and thus has been of important value in the treatment of patients with severe RS. More recent studies have reconfirmed the value of Winstrol for its fibrinolysis,[175] and relief and healing of cutaneous ulcers caused by cryofibrinogenemia associated with severe RS.[176,177] Therefore, the use of the anabolic steroid Winstrol has a specific indication in patients who have severe sequelae associated with Raynaud's syndrome. This indication should not have been thrown away by the FDA in the early 1980s. Winstrol therapy may also be of benefit in alleviating or reducing many symptoms associated with the underlying immunologic diseases and RS, such as muscle wasting, immunologic compromise, osteoporosis, mental depression, loss of libido, and reduced general well-being.

Microgravity and Prolonged Space Travel

This section regarding the use of anabolic steroids and other anabolic and growth-stimulating hormones as therapy may seem misplaced to many readers. However, as will be shown, anabolic steroid therapy has important implications in this area. During prolonged space travel certain biochemical and hormonal changes occur that may be best treated with anabolic steroids and other anabolic and growth-stimulating agents. The knowledge gained in this area will likely be useful in conditions resulting from prolonged immobilization of patients who are bedridden for lengthy periods of time.

Dramatic changes occur within the human body within the first 2 weeks of microgravity exposure that is experienced in space travel. These major changes include alterations in the sex steroid receptors throughout the body,[178] significant losses in skeletal and cardiac muscle mass, bone mineral density losses, and major reductions of serum testosterone, human growth hormone, and erythropoietin.[179,180] A summary of these biochemical, cardiac, and skeletal muscle mass changes concomitant within the first two weeks of space travel seen in Russian and U.S. space travelers is contained in Table 13-15.

Table 13-15. Summary of the Biochemical, Hormonal, and Physical Abnormalities During the First Two Weeks of Space Travel

Biochemical and Hormonal Changes

Major reduction in serum testosterone levels
Major increase in serum corticosteroid levels
Significant reduction in human growth hormone (GH) production
Significant increases in serum parathyroid hormone (PTH) levels
Major reduction in serum erythropoietin (EPO) levels
Major increases in serum epinephrine and norepinephrine levels
Increased serum anti-diuretic hormone (ADH) levels
Elevated serum calcitonin levels
Unknown effects on insulin-like growth factor-1 (IGF-1) but postulated decreased levels

Cardiovascular Changes

Marked reduction in plasma volume levels
Marked reduction in cardiac output at rest and during exercise
Marked reduction in red blood cell hemoglobin concentration
Marked reduction in total red blood cell production and total blood volume
Significant elevations in resting heart rate
Marked reduction in carotid baroreceptor reflexes
Marked increase in the cephalic fluid shift which increases blood pressure in the brain
Marked reduction in blood flow to the lower extremities

Musculoskeletal Changes

Marked reduction in skeletal muscle mass and strength
Rapid onset of BMD losses and accelerated osteoporosis of bone
Extreme and rapid onset of lower body neuromuscular weakness
Marked reduction in fast-twitch and slow-twitch muscle fiber diameters
Marked reduction in skeletal muscle oxidative capacity
Marked reduction in eccentric contractile force of skeletal muscles
Marked decrease in protein synthesis
Enhanced catabolic effects on skeletal muscles

Worrisome changes take place with the immune system, primarily in the T-lymphocyte cells, causing a decreased number of several T-cell lines and overall a reduced T-cell responsiveness to viral invasion and protection against potential autoimmune conditions.[181] The basic alterations in the immune system that take place within the first two weeks of space travel are contained in Table 13-16.

TABLE 13-16. IMMUNOLOGICAL DISRUPTIONS MEASURED DURING SPACE TRAVEL WITHIN THE FIRST TWO WEEKS

Immune System Parameter	*Changes from Pre-Flight Baselines*
B-cell lymphocytes	little or no consistent changes
Serum immunoglobulin levels	little or no consistent changes
T-cell lymphocytes	
Total counts	decreased
T-inducer cells	decreased
T-cytotoxic cells	decreased
T-killer cells	decreased
T-helper cells	little or no consistent changes
T-suppressor cells	decreased
T-cell activity (overall)	significantly decreased

The biochemical, hormonal, and physical abnormalities seen in the first two weeks of space travel are further magnified by space travel of a month or longer. The basic human physiological responses to prolonged space travel are listed in Table 13-17. Many of these changes are devastating and *irreversible* according to current medical knowledge. However, promising results suggest the use of anabolic steroids and other growth-stimulating hormones may prevent and reverse the physiological effects caused by microgravity conditions.

TABLE 13-17. PHYSIOLOGIC EFFECTS OF PROLONGED MICROGRAVITY CONDITIONS ON THE HUMAN BODY (ONE MONTH AND LONGER)

Loss of BMD of 25% or greater, but increased BMD of the skull
Loss of neuromuscular strength of up to 50% or more
Marked loss of all aerobic muscle enzymes with reduced aerobic capacity up to 50%
Marked loss of muscle capillary density and mitochondrial density in muscle tissues
Marked loss of red blood cell mass of 20% or more
Greatly blunted or absent carotid baroreceptor reflexes
Marked loss in eccentric muscle contraction abilities
Dramatic losses (over 25%) in maximum aerobic capacity
Dramatic losses (over 25%) in hemoglobin concentrations

Dramatic losses (30% or greater) in cardiac muscle mass
Extreme atrophy in the lower extremities
Marked atrophy in the slow-twitch muscle cell fibers
Dramatic reductions (50% or more) in serum testosterone, GH, and EPO levels
Gross impairments in the neuromuscular coordination of the lower extremities
Extreme inability to overcome these maladies on return to Earth

In the early days of space travel astronauts circled the globe, returned to earth, and after quickly acknowledging the public interest, they disappeared for medical evaluations for a few weeks. Their return to life on earth seemed rather routine and occurred in a relatively short period of time.

The public now accepts the likelihood of prolonged space travel and the eventual habitation of other planets. We have been made aware of the problems, disasters, and near disasters involving the engineering aspects of prolonged space travel, but what about the inability of human physiology to adapt to such extreme environmental conditions? It has been shown that losses of up to 30 percent in muscle mass, cardiac output and mass, and bone mineral density (BMD) occur from prolonged exposure to microgravity conditions as experienced in prolonged space travel.

Recently, two space travel expeditions took place, one with a postmenopausal woman and the other involving an elderly politician. These astronauts added another important variable to be considered in examining the body's response to microgravity, that of aging. As we have already discussed, aging results in decreasing levels of various hormones that affect multiple body systems. Both of these astronauts were put through extensive training and were deemed to be healthy and ready to travel in space. You may remember that upon their return, they both were unsteady as they attempted to walk and stand without assistance. What man or woman, let alone a postmenopausal woman and elderly man, could stand to lose 30 percent of his or her muscle mass, cardiac output and mass, and BMD and not exhibit adverse effects? What can be learned from their experience and what remedies are available to counteract the compounded adverse effects of aging and prolonged exposure to microgravity?

A number of measures to counteract the marked biochemical and physiological alterations brought on by space travel have been considered and utilized. For humans, most of these countermeasures center on exercise while in space. However, in spite of all the elaborate exercise equipment tested by astronauts while in space, the results of using exercise alone to counteract the adverse effects of prolonged exposure to microgravity have been less than promising.[182,183] But, in non-human space travelers, the biochemical replacement of anabolic steroids, human growth hormone, and erythropoietin have been shown to *reverse* these adverse effects. The future of prolonged space travel may depend on human research utilizing testosterone, anabolic steroids, human growth hormone, insulin-like growth factor-1, erythropoietin and others to reverse the adverse effects of prolonged space travel. This point is supported by the following quotation:

> There needs to be applied research utilizing animal and human models in conjunction with modern molecular probes coupled with novel physical activity, hormonal and pharmacological experimental treatments. This work is important because the transformations having an impact on muscle during weightlessness are often similar to those transformations occurring with chronic inactivity and aging on Earth. A major challenge facing society will be to maintain the functional integrity of an ever aging population with an inherent proneness to injury and incapacitation.[184]

Although information regarding the ability of anabolic steroids to reverse many of the adverse biochemical and physiological effects caused by prolonged space travel is interesting, only a small number of people become astronauts. So what benefits can the rest of us gain? Current on-going research indicates that some of the symptoms and conditions resulting from prolonged space travel are similar to those experienced by patients who are bedridden and immobile for prolonged periods of time. These exciting research principles may offer promising results for patients immobilized from fractures, strokes, brain injuries, and other debilitating conditions.

While doing research for this book, as well as observing results in patients with hormonal changes, it occurred to me that there may be hypothalamic receptors which are activated or repressed in reduced gravity conditions. There are three distinct conditions in human life in which these "gravity" receptors may cause very similar hormonal adjustments as shown in Table 13-18. In effect, these receptors detect low gravity conditions acting on the human body and adjust hormonal levels accordingly.

Table 13-18. Human Conditions Suggesting Hypothalamic Receptors for Low Gravity

Human Condition	*Hormonal Response from the Hypothalamic Gravity Receptor*
fetal stage (in utero)	low testosterone level low growth hormone (GH) level low erythropoietin (EPO) level
microgravity conditions	low testosterone level low GH level low EPO level
prolonged immobilization and aged condition	low testosterone level low GH level low EPO level

In the fetal stage the amniotic fluid that bathes us blunts the effects of gravity. We all have fetal testosterone and growth hormone receptors, and if stimulated by a hypothalamic response, then we would undergo a significant calcification of the developing skeletal system that would make it impossible for vaginal delivery. Fetal skulls would also calcify and make molding of the head impossible. This molding is important to temporarily allow for the skull to adapt through the vaginal cavity. Conditions of low gravity probably blunt the feedback messages to the hypothalamus causing it to reduce the production of stimulating hormones, thereby keeping testosterone levels low. If there weren't such a mechanism, then babies with a more mature and more calcified skeleton would develop and be impossible to deliver, causing mortality and morbidity to the mother.

We know that during fetal development growth hormone secretion by the fetus is kept very low, unless the mother is diabetic. Huge babies cannot be delivered vaginally. Growth hormone production and release is under the regulatory control of the hypothalamus.

Fetal blood supply production is very limited. The blood circulation is from the mother's expanded blood volume with fetal EPO levels low or nonexistent. Any hemoglobin that is made by the fetus is of a different structure than that of the mother.

After birth and exposure to gravity, the gravity receptors are now free of the blunted feedback influences. Normal growth and development phases begin to take place. But, the "gravity" receptors are still intact in the hypothalamus and will respond to changes of relative or absolute microgravity. These hypothalamic "gravity" receptors may recognize conditions similar to those in utero and respond, causing a reduction in the production of serum androgens, growth hormone, and EPO. The body responds with a rapid and major loss of muscle mass and BMD, as well as anemia. To reverse these conditions, replacement of these anabolic hormones seems to be not only prudent, but medically necessary. Thus it seems that the concept of hypothalamic "gravity" receptors may account for the hormonal responses seen in utero, during space travel, and during periods of immobilization.

Rehabilitative Conditions

There are many chronic disease states, post-surgical conditions, and post-injury conditions that place the human body into a catabolic state of breaking down its own tissues. Results from the 1940s have shown that anabolic agents counteract these catabolic effects and hasten the rebuilding processes in a number of these conditions.[185–198] The results published in these early studies suggested the possible therapeutic value of using androgens to promote protein anabolism in conditions of debilitation, inadequate dietary intake, and other disorders.[199]

One of those other disorders in which the use of androgens was prescribed was in the treatment of premature infants of both genders. One study concluded that 7 of the 15 infants would have probably died had it not been for use of testosterone treatment, and all premature infants had their progress enhanced by the androgen treatment.[200] A year later, a study was conducted on 74 male and female premature infants (birth weight under 2,000 grams) at the Los Angeles County General Hospital. The infants were divided into three groups: a control group, a group which received 5 mg methyl testosterone daily, and a group treated with 4 mg testosterone propionate daily while in the hospital and followed for several months after treatment. The study's findings were:

a) a distinct and statistically significant shortening in the time required to regain birth weight and in the time to gain a body weight of 2,500 grams;
b) a significant decrease in the length of hospital stays;
c) a significant difference noted in four sets of twins; in each instance the sibling on testosterone therapy (the smaller of the premature twins) increased somatic development over its control sibling; and,
d) a significant finding that no adverse effects were noted in either of the two testosterone treated groups.

In the late 1950s several studies were published which indicated favorable results when anabolic steroids were given to debilitated underweight patients,[202–204] patients with congestive heart failure,[205] and in post-surgical patients.[206–209] In 1960, a summary of the results of anabolic steroid therapy for surgical patients concluded:

a) that the clearest indication for use of anabolic steroids in surgical patients was in those surgical problems related to osteoporosis;
b) that anabolic steroid therapy should be considered in patients who are in a profound catabolic state;
c) that in diseases associated with excess production or administration of catabolic agents, the use of anabolic steroids was logical, harmless, and in many instances indicated;
d) that there was evidence that convalescence following average surgical procedures may be shortened by the use of anabolic steroids;
e) that anabolic steroids have been used extensively without troublesome side effects; and,
f) that anabolic steroid therapy should be considered not as a substitute for sensible nutritional management, but as a useful adjunct to it.[210]

The conclusion drawn from early studies using anabolic steroid therapy for debilitating conditions, surgical patients, and other conditions clearly showed beneficial results. At the very least, further studies were indicated. However, during the 1960s through mid–1980s androgen therapy was rarely utilized in the United States.

Advances in technology, especially in the area of analyzing the body's protein metabolism in response to catabolic conditions, has ushered in another attempt to show the beneficial effects of anabolic steroids for treating various debilitating and muscle wasting conditions.[211–214] A 1981 study of patients with debilitating conditions placed on total parenteral nutrition (TPN) showed that there was a 13 percent increase in protein balance in patients who received low-dose anabolic steroid therapy as compared with those who received only TPN over a five-week period of treatment.[215] Another study reported that there was a dose response curve which could be used to predict the effects of anabolic steroids on the increases in lean body mass.[216] In 1987, the National Institute of Health (NIH) announced a large research effort planned by the Arthritis Institute to evaluate the short- and long-term benefits of anabolic steroids use in the treatment of neuromuscular and connective tissue conditions.[217,218] This resulted in a flurry of research in the areas of muscle wasting conditions, traumatic conditions, debilitating disease conditions, and other catabolic disease conditions as listed in Table 13-19.

Table 13-19. Rehabilitative Conditions Showing Improvement with Anabolic Steroid Therapy

Disease or Condition	*Published Results with Anabolic Steroid Therapy*
Chronic Obstructive Pulmonary Disease (COPD)	Enhanced respiratory muscle function without adverse effects noted (1995).[219–222]
Wasting conditions in patients with Tetraplegia	Enhanced pulmonary function and nutritional status (1999).[223] Enhancement of metabolic changes and musculoskeletal wasting (2000).[224]
Congestive heart failure (CHF)	Antianginal, fibrinogenic and muscle strengthening effects (1999).[225]
Alcoholic hepatitis	Reduced muscle wasting (1993).[226]
Pressure sores in bed ridden patients	Enhanced closure of bed sores (1995)[227] and (1998).[228]
Cutaneuous lesions	Faster healing of ulcers in diabetes mellitus (1993).[229]
Patients on TPN	Use with TPN resulted in a more rapid correction of the malnourished catabolic states(1993).[230]
Skeletal dysplasia	Increased height in children with this condition (1993).[231]

Disease or Condition	*Published Results with Anabolic Steroid Therapy*
Acute muscle injury	Enhanced speed of recovery in severe muscle contusions (1999).[232]
Duchenne muscular dystrophy	Beneficial effects on functional abilities (1997)[233] and (1999).[234]
Major burns	Enhanced recovery over dietary protein alone (1997-2000).[235-239]
Cancer therapy	Significant improvements in appetite and food intake with 600 cancer patients (1992).[240]
Musculoskeletal	Significant improvements in functional independence rehabilitation measure (FIM) of older men and muscular strength (2000).[241]
Osteomyelitis in the elderly	Improved healing of bone and joint infections (2000).[242]

In summary, the use of anabolic steroids and other anabolic agents in the field of rehabilitative medicine has only begun to recognize the potential beneficial effects, especially in conditions with muscle and bone loss. It is hoped that larger, multi-center clinical trials will be conducted over the next 10 years. It is likely that the use of anabolic steroids will become a significant component in the therapy of patients afflicted with a variety of debilitating conditions. The medical specialty of physical medicine and rehabilitation, including cardiopulmonary rehabilitation, will likely be a leader in research and patient care that utilizes anabolic steroid therapy.

Chronic Anemias and Related Conditions

Testosterone and anabolic steroids have been used to treat chronic anemia and related conditions of bone marrow suppression or failure since the 1940s. These steroids stimulate several lines of stem cell development within the bone marrow. They also increase the production of erythropoietin. They may also play a direct role in the development and maturation of stem cells that ultimately become red blood cells, white blood cells, and platelets. Androgens also increase the quantity of hemoglobin contained within mature red blood cells. As a result, adult men normally have a 10 to 15 percent higher hemoglobin concentration than adult women. Clinical anemias and related condition that have benefited from anabolic steroid therapy include myleofibrosis with myeloid metaplasia,[243-246] chronic lymphocytic leukemia,[247] hemolytic anemias including sickle cell anemia,[248-250] anemia associated with chronic renal failure,[251-254] aplastic anemias,[255-259] and other chronic refractory anemias.[260-266]

Over the past few years, many physicians have used genetically engineered synthetic erythropoietin (EPO) to treat a variety of anemias. In pure red blood cell anemias, EPO is the specific stimulator of stem cells destined to become mature red blood cells. Synthetic EPO is very expensive and effective in pure red cell anemias. In the variety of cases that involve more than one line of stem cell maladies, other specific stimulating factors have been used along with synthetic EPO, such as genetically engineered synthetic granulocyte stimulating factor. This combination of new synthetic recombinant hormones and factors is extremely expensive. A recent prospective study compared the use of androgen therapy alone versus the use of synthetic EPO alone in the treatment of male and female patients with renal failure associated anemia and undergoing hemodialysis. This study concluded that androgen therapy produced results similar to those achieved by the use of recombinant human EPO but at a much lower cost.[267] Thus, androgen therapy may still have a role in chronic anemia and related disorders, especially in the anemias with multiple stem cell line involvement.

Benign Prostatic Hypertrophy

Enlargement of the prostate gland is a common condition in aging men. What causes it? Current medical theories postulate that benign prostate enlargement (BPH) is caused by testosterone or other androgens that make the prostate gland grow and enlarge, resulting in problems with urination. The male urethra passes through the center of the prostate gland. When this gland enlarges, it often encroaches on the lumen of the urethra and partially obstructs urine flow from the urinary bladder. If testosterone causes BPH, then why does it occur in aging men when testosterone levels are low? This explanation of the cause of BPH seems not to make sense based on what is known about the effect of testosterone in normal male organ growth and development. If testosterone causes BPH, then all young men would have enlarged prostates since testosterone levels are much higher in them compared to aging men.

Looking at results from early studies we learn that testosterone therapy *reduces* BPH and prostatism. Several early researches published papers to that end in the late 1930s and 1940s. All of these early medical scientists associated BPH with a *decrease* in serum androgens. That is because youthful androgen levels *do not* cause prostate enlargement. Instead, it seems more reasonable to look at elevated luteinizing hormone (LH) levels. As serum androgen levels decrease in aging men, LH release by the brain increases in an attempt to *raise* serum testosterone levels back to previously normal and youthful levels. Years of elevated LH secretion may be the more likely cause of BPH. Therefore, testosterone administration which returns the testosterone level (and LH level) back to the mid-normal ranges tends to reduce the size of the prostate and reduce the symptoms of BPH just as the early medical scientists knew. As a note of caution, when there is androgen abuse as in supratherapeutic doses for an extended time as often seen with bodybuilders, BPH may result. The potential mechanism of this type of BPH is currently unknown and warrants further investigational studies.[268]

Sarcopenia

Advancing adult age is associated with profound changes in body composition, the principle component of which is a decrease in skeletal muscle mass. This age-related loss in skeletal muscle has been referred to as sarcopenia.[269] Prevalence rates of sarcopenia have been shown to be 13–24 percent in persons less than 70 years of age to over 50 percent in persons over 80 years of age.[270] Sarcopenia seems to be an intrinsic age-related condition[271] that results in an overall muscle strength and mass decline of 30–50 percent between the ages of 30 and 80 years of age.[272] A more rigorous definition for sarcopenia has been defined as muscle mass more than two standard deviations below the gender-specific young-normal mean as determined by total body scan using dual-energy X-ray absorptiometry (DEXA).[273]

At the present time, there is only limited understanding of the public health significance of sarcopenia. The well-recognized functional consequences of sarcopenia include gait and balance problems and increased risk for fall. Ultimately, these impairments can lead to the loss of functional independence.[274]

The hormonal systems that show decreasing production during normal aging that play the key roles in sarcopenia are androgens (andropause) and the hormones of the growth axis (somatopause).[275,276] The significantly decreased levels of these anabolic hormones decrease the capacity for protein synthesis in the elderly.[277,278] Diminished anabolic hormone levels contribute the mechanisms that cause sarcopenia.[279]

In 1995, the National Institute on Aging convened a "Workshop on Sarcopenia" to address several important issues. The research recommendations from the workshop underscored the need for more dialogue among the different fields (e.g., endocrinology, exercise physiology, bone biology). It has been suggested that this lack of coordination of the various fields has presented major obstacles to the formation of therapies to prevent or reverse sarcopenia in the elderly.[280]

Strength training has been shown to be one of the therapies that help patients with sarcopenia. Progressive resistance training in the elderly can have a positive influence on whole body energy expenditure, muscle growth, and functional abilities.[281] Strength training can produce substantial increases in strength and muscle size, even in the oldest old, if these people are willing and able to undergo a progressive program.[282] It has been stated that no segment of the population can benefit more from exercise training than the elderly.[283]

Anabolic agents have been proposed to treat sarcopenia.[284] These anabolic agents include anabolic steroids, GH, IGF-1, and other agents that have anabolic influences on the growth axis.[285–295] These anabolic hormones and factors could be used alone or in combination, with or without concomitant strength training. Anabolic steroid therapy deserves special attention in the clinical arena as an intervention against muscle and bone losses in sarcopenia.[296] Anabolic steroid therapy, either alone, or in a growth-axis stimulator, is likely to prove to be the best and most cost-effective anabolic agent for treating sarcopenia.

Clinical trials utilizing anabolic interventions for sarcopenia are ongoing. The results from the initial reports have been encouraging. The effects of anabolic hormone replacement on body composition and functional capacity are only beginning to be studied.[297] The results of these studies are likely to revolutionize the practice of geriatric medicine in the near future.

Acquired Immunodeficiency Syndrome (AIDS)

The use of anabolic steroid therapy in patients with human immunodeficiency virus (HIV)–associated wasting has had dramatic impacts on patients with AIDS. Halting the progression of HIV-associated wasting, with anabolic steroids and other anabolic hormones, has been associated with improved survival, enhanced physical and social functioning, and enriched quality of life.[298]

Anabolic steroids and other anabolic hormones (GH and IGF-1) have been used, with and without weight training, to treat the wasting associated with AIDS. Clinical studies have shown:

1) substantial increases in muscle mass and strength[299–303]
2) improved immune function in some patients[304,305]
3) no interference with antiviral medications[306]
4) restored libido, energy level, and alleviated depressed mood[307]

Anabolic agents, anabolic steroids, and GH-axis stimulators, have been included in the multidisciplinary team approach for effective management of AIDS wasting. Optimal maintenance of lean body mass and reversal of wasting involves a combination of appropriate antiretroviral use, opportunistic infection prophylaxis, optimal nutrition, exercise, body composition monitoring, anabolic agents, mental health support, economic aid, and legal assistance.[308]

Miscellaneous Conditions

Testosterone and anabolic steroids have been used with success in a variety of medical conditions. These conditions are listed below to illustrate just some of the potential uses for anabolic steroid therapy. They include:

a) the treatment of enuresis (bed-wetting) in children of both sexes[309]
b) the treatment as a male contraceptive method[310]
c) the treatment of dysfunctional uterine bleeding in women[311]
d) the treatment of premenstrual syndrome (PMS) in women[312]
e) the adjunct treatment of diabetes mellitus for glycemic and lipid control[313]
f) the treatment of hypogonadotrophic hypogonadism caused by critical illness[314]
g) the stimulation of collagen synthesis for wound healing[315,316]
h) the treatment of hereditary angioedema and lipodermatosclerosis[317,318]
i) the treatment of vitiligo[319]
j) the use as a body fat reducing agent in older men[320]
k) the use as a body fat reducing agent in postmenopausal women[321]
l) the treatment of constitutional delay of growth and puberty[322] and,
m) the treatment of breast cancer[323–328]

From the listing above it can be shown that medical scientists have been investigating the use of testosterone and anabolic steroids in patients with a wide variety of symptoms or complaints. Much more objective research is needed to fully discover the potential power of these steroids in clinical practice. *No other class of drugs has ever had such an expansive range of therapeutic potentials.* Medical scientists are reviewing some of the older clinical uses and investigating new ones.

Summary: The Line Between Use and Abuse

An anti-aging revolution is insidiously woven into the minds of the American public. Never before has the average lifespan of humans been so long. The Human Genome Project has already mapped our genetic code. Some of the various biochemical building blocks which are being found have anabolic effects on the human body. Science is discovering that many of them are under the influence and regulation of testosterone and anabolic steroids. This is especially true in the human brain, where androgens act as direct neurotransmitters themselves and also act to influence other neurotransmitters. These actions combine to have powerful effects on human thought processes, behaviors, and actions.

The line between the use and abuse of such powerful agents as testosterone and anabolic steroids has provided for major medical debates for nearly two generations. No other drug or hormone has survived the medical blacklisting that testosterone and anabolic steroids have. No other drugs continue to make comeback after comeback.

Testosterone and anabolic steroids could easily be considered to be the most powerful class of drugs in the 21st century. The challenge in medicine is to sort out the powerful beneficial effects that these steroids have in treating human disease conditions. It is hoped that medical science will quickly avail itself of technology advances in laboratory techniques to definitively discover not only the range of positive effects of anabolic steroids, but the appropriate dosage and administration schedules to eliminate adverse side effects.

There are several clinical conditions that affect many Americans that can be treated successfully with anabolic steroid therapy. Anabolic steroids and other anabolic agents have been shown to have great potential to enhance the quality of life of patients with a number of disabling conditions directly intertwined with aging and longevity. Medicine must define these anabolic agents as properly used in these conditions. It must not get too bogged down in the history and abuse potentials of anabolic agents. Adequate training of physicians and changes in our present approach in caring for these patients may be the greatest obstacles to overcome if full application of anabolic agents is to be realized.[329]

14

Muscle Building and Ergogenic Supplements

Introduction: Breaking the Four-Minute Mile Broke the Ergogenic Barrier

Many chemicals possess bioactive properties within the biochemical machine, the human body. Medical science continues to discover more chemicals with bioactive properties each year. These chemicals are classified according to their specific or overall physiological effects on the body or according to their chemical structures. They are then labeled as drugs, supplements, food or food products, vitamins, or plant extracts. In this chapter, *ergogenic* drugs, chemicals that enhance athletic performance, especially through anabolic and growth stimulating properties, will be discussed.

Until recently, physicians and medical scientists steadfastly held to the "official" policy that no chemical was an ergogenic aid, especially one that would build muscle mass and strength. The prevailing belief, at least in the United States, was that the human body could not be chemically altered to enhance athletic performance. In other words, the trained human body was as good as there was and that was that.

May 6, 1954, became a great day in the English history of sports. On that day, Roger Bannister, a medical student, broke the four-minute mile. This was a record that many felt was impossible. At that time, it became England's most impressive athletic achievement and was hailed throughout the world.[1]

Sir Roger Bannister demonstrated that the prevailing theory about ergogenic chemicals was incorrect. However, it was not until 30 years later that he admitted that amphetamine use helped him break the four-minute mile barrier. Due in part to this disclosure, medical science began to wonder if other chemicals possessed ergogenic properties. Studies conducted showed that carbohydrate loading, anabolic steroids, and caffeine do enhance athletic performance but by different mechanisms. As a result, medical science put aside the old "barriers" regarding ergogenic chemicals. Instead of claiming that chemicals can't enhance athletic performance, medical science began to critically evaluate the ergogenic potential of many chemicals.

Muscle Building Supplements

It has been shown that several over-the-counter supplements enhance muscle mass and strength, over and above weight training alone. Other supplements have been shown to have anabolic actions on the growth axis in various combinations or as a single supplement. Investigational studies have shown that the following supplements build muscle mass over and above weight training effects:

a) creatine[2–8]
b) beta-hydroxy-beta-methylbutyrate (HMB)[9–11]
c) anabolic saponins[12,13] and,
d) amino acid combination of L-arginine and L-ornithine[14]

Creatine

What is Creatine? Creatine is an amino acid that is predominately found in the skeletal muscle of animals and humans. Creatine in human skeletal muscle cells comes from two primary sources. One comes from the consumption of skeletal muscle tissue in meat. The other source is through synthesis within the body. Human skeletal muscle cells *do not* synthesize creatine. Creatine is synthesized in the kidneys, liver, and pancreas from the amino acids glycine, arginine, and methionine. The body is able to synthesize both glycine and arginine from other amino acids. Methionine, however, is an essential amino acid that must be consumed from dietary sources. Diets that are low in methionine, such as strict vegetarian types, can result in low methionine intake and reduced creatine content within human skeletal muscles.

Creatine, either synthesized or consumed, is carried to the skeletal muscle cells through the circulatory system. The skeletal muscle cells have a limited capacity to store creatine. It readily diffuses in and out of skeletal muscle cells with excessive creatine converted to *creatinine,* a degradation product that is excreted in the urine. Creatinine cannot be directly converted back to creatine. In healthy people, the urinary excretion of creatinine is relatively constant (1 to 2 grams/day).

It has long been taught that the capacity of skeletal muscle cells to store creatine was fairly fixed. In fact, based on this theory, clinical medicine uses a diagnostic test, called the creatine tolerance test, to look for certain muscle diseases. In a creatine tolerance test, 3 grams or more of creatine are administered until the muscles become saturated with creatine, and unable to store additional amounts. The excess creatine excreted in the urine as creatinine is then measured. In people with muscle disease or reduced muscle mass, the creatine storage capacity is reduced within muscle cells, and elevated urine creatinine is seen when smaller amounts of creatine are administered.

It had been taught that the storage capacity for creatine is very limited and can only be significantly *reduced,* not increased. Therefore, additional dietary creatine would simply be degraded to creatinine and wind up in the urine. No wonder, when physicians were asked about creatine as an ergogenic aid to build muscle, they replied, "it makes for expensive urine."

The Key Biochemical Adaptations

Exercise physiology teaches that exercise produces a myriad of biochemical changes in the human body. Traditionally, very little of these adaptive biochemical changes is taught during the medical education process. A basic knowledge of these biochemical changes or adaptations is *the key* to understanding how creatine enhances athletic performance, muscle mass, and neuromuscular strength.

Exercise is biochemical training for the biochemical machine, the human body. Exercise produces certain specific biochemical reactions within the body. Different types of exercise result in different, specific biochemical adaptations. For instance, the biochemical adaptations that occur from progressive strength training regimes are somewhat different from those that occur when training for a marathon.

To understand how creatine supplements enhance athletic performance, we must first know how creatine functions in the human biochemical machine. Then, we must determine how creatine works differently in trained athletes than in sedentary people and why trained athletes can store more creatine than sedentary people. The final step is to understand how the additional stored creatine works with the biochemical adaptations brought about by physical training.

Creatine (Cr) is a precursor for the energy reservoir, creatine phosphate (CrP), in skeletal muscle cells as shown in Figure 14-1. Creatine phosphate is stored temporarily in the muscle cells and provides a rapid source of energy (high-energy phosphate bond) to resupply phosphate to adenosine triphosphate (ATP) that is lost when ATP responds to instant energy requirements. To supply this energy, ATP transfers its power through high-energy phosphate bond hydrolysis becoming adenosine diphosphate (ADP). These high-energy phosphate bonds are the *energy currency* with the skeletal muscle cells. ATP is formed again when ADP takes a high-energy phosphate bond from CrP.

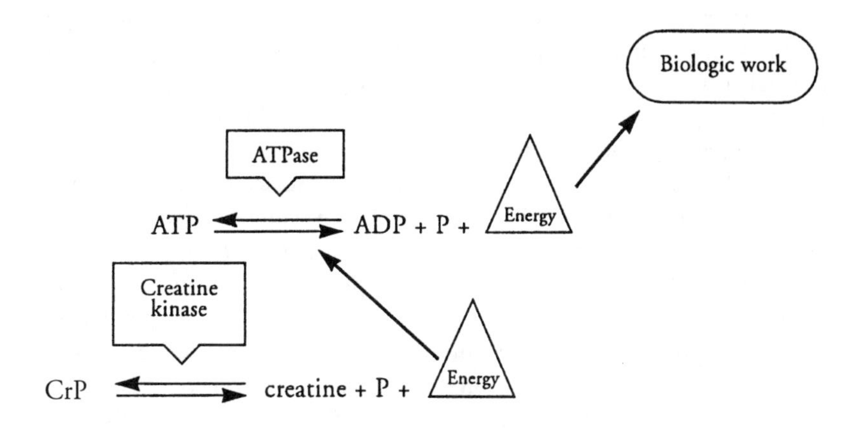

Figure 14-1. Instant energy transfer within the skeletal muscle cell.

Physical training causes skeletal muscle cells to increase their creatine storage through an enzymatic process that supplies power for both instant and maximum energy expenditure. This enzyme involved is creatine kinase. It increases its concentration within the muscle cell in response to repetitive and regular explosive power demands. *The major cellular change that occurs with instant, explosive, and repetitive power demands is an elevated level of creatine kinase.* This elevation of creatine kinase is produced by genetic machinery that is stimulated by physical training regimens such as strength training, interval training, and sprinting.

Creatine is in biochemical equilibrium with CrP. If CrP concentrations are reduced by instant energy demands, then Cr, through enhanced creatine kinase concentrations, is converted to form a greater concentration of CrP for the next round of instant power demands. In the trained skeletal muscle cell, there is an increased level of creatine kinase enzymes, therefore, when creatine is available through supplementation, the storage of CrP is enhanced above that seen in sedentary people. Thus, the more CrP available to the muscle cell, the greater the biochemical power delivered instantly and longer. *Creatine supplements enhance athletic ability by increasing the capacity to deliver additional instant biochemical energy and power.* When training intensities are reduced or discontinued, the cellular concentrations of creatine kinase tend to return to their previously "untrained" levels. In this manner, the skeletal muscle cells lose their enhanced capacity to deliver additional instant biochemical energy and power.

Creatine Loading and Use Guidelines

A review of investigational studies shows that creatine loading, ingestion of creatine monohydrate at a rate of 20 grams/day for 5–6 days, increases the total creatine concentration of skeletal muscle by about 6 percent.[15] Creatine loading has been shown to increase both Cr and CrP in skeletal muscles. About 30 percent of the total additional creatine is in its phosphorylated form, CrP. This is believed to aid athletic performance by providing more short term energy and increasing the rate of CrP resynthesis during rest intervals.[16] Increasing the creatine intake above 20–30 grams/day does not further increase the loading effect. There appears to be an endocrine-like homeostatic feedback mechanism that limits the quantity of creatine that can be incorporated into skeletal muscle cells.[17] This mechanism is probably a function of the concentration of creatine kinase in these cells.

After creatine loading, it has been shown that the creatine levels can be maintained, with strength training, with a low-dose creatine intake of 5 grams/day. When creatine supplementation is discontinued (after creatine loading and daily maintenance), creatine levels return to normal within four weeks.[18] Weight gain with creatine loading occurs for a few days due to water intake that is required to load creatine into the skeletal muscles.

Prevalence of Creatine Use

A recent study conducted at a major university indicated that 48 percent of men and four percent of women in all athletic programs use creatine. A substantial number of adolescents begin taking creatine supplements in high school.[19] Creatine has become a best-selling over-the-counter muscle-building supplement worldwide.[20] Studies show that creatine works so well, some have suggested that it should be reclassified as a drug.[21]

Ergogenic Effects of Creatine Use Are Proven

A review of the literature has convinced sports medicine physicians that creatine is an ergogenic aid. As we have seen at a biochemical level, creatine provides additional biochemical energy. This additional energy enhances athletic performance in two major ways:

1) Creatine provides an energetic boost to the skeletal muscle cells' immediate energy transfer system.[22] Creatine use provides for a little extra cellular energy for the quick starts that are necessary in so many sports. Creatine supplementation has also been shown, with electromyographic (EMG) studies, to delay the onset of neuromuscular fatigue.[23] It also shortens the recharge period between repetitive quick starts, direction changes, or explosive power demands by enhancing ATP resynthesis.[24] Creatine loading prior to competition or training has been shown to directly enhance athletic performance skills in NCAA division IA football players,[25] elite swimmers during interval training,[26,27] competitive soccer players,[28] well-trained students performing repetitive sprint exercises,[29] elite athletes performing high-intensity bouts of ergometer training,[30] and elite ice-hockey players.[31]
2) Creatine is associated with enhanced strength and muscle mass in strength-training programs.[32] It is believed creatine use enables athletes to increase their workout quality and quantity, which, in turn, sends a stronger stimulus to the skeletal muscle cell's genetic machinery.

Adverse Effects Associated with Creatine Use

There is little or no evidence that creatine supplementation is associated with physical side effects other than weight gain or mild fluid retention.[33] It was once thought that creatine use caused kidney damage, but studies now indicate that neither short-term, medium-term, nor long-term oral creatine supplement use causes detrimental effects to the kidneys of healthy people.[34] At this time, there have been few, if any, significant physical health risks associated with the ergogenic use of creatine.

A word of caution is warranted. While there is no evidence to suggest that creatine, in and of itself, has addictive or mental health risks, there are some concerns that creatine use by adolescents could lead to anabolic steroids and or anabolic hormone use. In other words, "If I can get this big on creatine, how much bigger might I get if I add anabolic steroids?" Since anabolic steroids and creatine work by different mechanisms, their use is likely to produce additive or synergistic results. Creatine will probably not replace anabolic steroids. It may become a mainstay supplement for anabolic steroid users.

HMB

Beta-hydroxy beta-methylbutyrate (HMB) is a metabolite of the essential amino acid leucine. It is one of the latest dietary supplements promoted to enhance gains in muscle mass and strength when taken in conjunction with strength training. Similar to an effect seen with anabolic steroids, HMB has been reported to increase strength and lean body mass by acting as an anti-catabolic agent. HMB minimizes protein breakdown and damage to muscle cells that may occur with intense athletic training. The exact mechanism of action for HMB on muscle mass enhancement is unknown. There have been some claims that HMB causes a heightened GH release, but there have been no studies to substantiate that HMB causes a GH release.

A review of the available, but preliminary, literature shows some support for the claims made regarding HMB supplementation in young, previously untrained people.[35] HMB supplementation during resistance training has been reported to increase fat-free body mass in both athletic and nonathletic people.[36]

A review study concluded that HMB is safe when taken as an ergogenic aid and persons taking HMB showed an increase in objective measures of health and perception of well-being.[37] HMB has also been shown to increase the body mass of feedlot steers.[38] However, a recent study reported that HMB use does not elevate testosterone levels.[39] Further studies are needed to substantiate or refute claims that HMB is an ergogenic aid for muscle building.

Anabolic Saponins

Herbal medicine (or alternative medicine) has been a part of European and Soviet medicine for quite some time. Recently, in the United States, the use of herbal medicine has gained credibility. Two products that have greatly increased interest among American physicians are St. John's wort and kava kava. Both are psychoactive herbal supplements. St. John's wort is an herb effective in treating mild depression and kava kava is used as a mild, but potent, tranquilizer.[40]

Throughout the world are reports of the effectiveness of many herbal medicines. However, obtaining scientific articles from many of the countries that study the effects of these herbs is a difficult task. In other countries, scientists are naming and classifying herbal medicines so quickly that it is hard to keep up.

Various plants produce ginseng products. Some of them produce steroid compounds called saponins. Saponins are bioactive steroids that have been extracted from exotic plants. They differ structurally from human steroids in that they have a cyclical six-member carbon ring attached to the D ring of the testosterone molecule. They also have various small ester and alkyl groups attached to this additional ring. Some reports have referred to these plant steroids as the "perfect" natural steroids.

A review of the literature strongly suggests that some of these saponins have endocrine-like functions. For example, Korean red ginseng has been shown to have positive effects on menopausal women,[41] and Panax ginseng has been shown to increase male fertility.[42]

Recently, two studies have been published that show that anabolic saponins enhance athletic performance, muscle mass, and strength. The mechanisms of actions of anabolic saponins appear to be similar to anabolic steroids. The available, preliminary published reports have shown that these saponins enhance muscle mass, strength, and work output. If these results from these studies are confirmed, the use of herbal saponins will probably prove to be another nightmare for international athletic competition and drug detection.

Oral Amino Acid Preparations

The use of oral amino acids as ergogenic aids has been around for over 20 years. Whether or not oral amino acid supplements enhance athletic performance has not been completely answered. The results from studies (notwithstanding the design flaws) investigating oral amino acid supplementation and enhanced athletic performance are mixed, but overall indicate no improvement.[43–46] However, some studies do show ergogenic properties and results.[47–49]

Oral amino acid supplements probably do not enhance GH release in and of themselves. However, they do play a role in GH release. It is conceivable that oral amino acids have an input into the multifactored nature of GH release, but, when they are taken as the sole GH-releasing agent, the results are mixed.

It has been shown that *oral* arginine supplementation augments GH release when combined with the most potent GH-releaser.[50] This fact is an important piece of the growth axis puzzle and has renewed medical interest in oral amino acid therapy when combined with other anabolic factors (e.g. GH, GH-releasing hormones, and GH secretagogues) for the management of patients with catabolic disease states.[51]

Over-the-Counter Anabolic Hormones and GH-Releasers

The "win at all costs" attitude is becoming increasingly common in youth sports.[52] Young athletes are often looking for methods to improve sports performance and avoid injury. Chemical aids and supplements with ergogenic properties are currently used by many adolescent athletes.[53] The availability of hormones and supplements that release GH is particularly worrisome. One product that facilitates the release of GH is gamma-hydroxy-butyrate (GHB). It was first available over-the-counter, but due to deaths and serious injuries, it has recently been reclassified as a controlled substance. Unfortunately, the GHB black market is a growing business.

Other chemicals, not classified as supplements and obtained as over-the-counter drugs or from chemical supply houses, are becoming a problem among adolescent athletes. Among these are chemicals such as nitrous oxide and human insulin that have been shown to be potent GH-releasers.

Some chemicals, through their abilities to induce a powerful growth hormone release, are potentially strong ergogenic aids (see below). However, they are not the only known GH-releasing agents. Several prescription drugs augment GH release. Other over-the-counter hormones and supplements have the potential to enhance growth and athletic performance through a direct stimulation of the growth axis. To date, there have been no studies that have evaluated the effects of these chemicals on athletic performance. Over-the-counter hormones and supplements that have ergogenic and growth-stimulating potentials include:

a) dehydroepiandrosterone (DHEA), dihydrotestosterone (DHT), and nortestosterone supplements. The discussion of these anabolic steroids is in Chapter 4.
b) melatonin and melatonin analogs.[54–56] Melatonin plays a role in the regulation of GH secretion. It apparently has its own receptor in the pituitary gland. Studies with over-the-counter doses of oral melatonin have been shown to be powerful GH releasers in normal people. Melatonin use has also been shown to magnify the GHRH effects on GH release.
c) gamma hydroxybutyrate (GHB).[57–79] The chemical GHB is one of the most powerful stimulators of GH secretion known. Oral administration of GHB stimulates GH release in supranormal amounts. It stimulates GH release even when most of the known growth axis inhibitors are present. GHB has been widely used by bodybuilders and athletes since the late 1970s. The clinical uses of GHB include alcohol detoxification and treatment and opiod addiction withdrawal treatment.

The use of clinical doses of GHB causes a potent GH release and is associated with few adverse effects. However, GHB has proven to be a drug of abuse. Addiction to GHB has been reported. In recent years, GHB has become a party drug and its use has led to date rape and deaths. Dozens of deaths, comas, and near deaths have been reported in bodybuilders and partygoers consuming excessive GHB or GHB mixed with ethanol.

In 1999, GHB was added to the Federal Controlled Substance Act of 1970. However, black market supplies of GHB are omnipresent, especially at "Raves" and other adolescent gatherings. GHB is a very dangerous chemical when it is mixed with ethanol.

In garage labs, GHB is easily made from readily available chemicals. For this reason, it is expected to be a worldwide abuse problem for years to come.

Even though GHB is a potent GH stimulator, no studies have been conducted to determine its effectiveness as a muscle builder through growth axis stimulation. Drug tests for its use are difficult to conduct and interpret.

d) nitric oxide (NO) and nitric oxide donors.[80–89] Nitric oxide (NO) exerts widespread and fundamental physiological effects. Endurance athletes were the first to experiment with nitric oxide. Numerous investigational studies have indicated that NO causes a testosterone and growth hormone release. NO donors, such as Viagra, have been shown to mimic many of the effects of NO. Since NO is used by a wide variety of pulmonary patients to enhance breathing performance, the abuse of inhaled NO is expected to increase. NO acts as a powerful neurotransmitter and mimics several neurohormones.
e) human insulin.[90,91] Human insulin has been used by bodybuilders for over a decade to enhance GH release. Insulin use causes GH release, but several reported and unreported cases of insulin-induced coma and death have occurred in insulin-using athletes. Some athletes have the hormone glucagon handy for reversing insulin-induced hypoglycemia.

Discussion: Athletic "Shade Tree" Endocrinologists

Anyone who has known a competitive bodybuilder knows someone who will try anything that is supposed to release testosterone or GH. Information from the scientific and medical journals about GH-releasing agents spreads quickly in the weight training community. In recent years, Internet sites have contributed to this effect. The Internet has also increased the availability of GH-releasers for sale.

For some athletes, "winning at all costs" has translated to experimenting with anabolic agents regardless of the financial or physical cost. The presence of over-the-counter anabolic agents and the easy availability of anabolic agents on the Internet seem to further fuel this phenomenon. The competitive bodybuilder becomes a "shade tree" endocrinologist who will try anything and everything to gain a competitive edge.

Although some experimenters have died, and many are incarcerated for violent behavior and criminal possession, the experimentation continues.

15
Heroes and Hulks Hooked on Hormones

In this chapter several examples of the consequences of anabolic steroid abuse will be presented. It is hoped that one or more of these examples will clearly illustrate the consequences that result from the abuse of these drugs. There are many more stories about the users of anabolic steroids than are presented here. These examples are just a few.

Barry Minkow: The Wall Street Swindler

This is a true story of a young anabolic steroid–using hulk who swindled Wall Street, at least for a while.[1] This 1990 best-selling story illustrated that the altered personalities and body images induced by anabolic steroid abuse are not just confined to the athletic world. This true story is also an illustration of the pervasiveness of anabolic steroid abuse in society and its impact on others.

At the age of 14, Minkow began lifting weights. Shortly after his weight lifting commenced he began taking anabolic steroids to increase his gains, becoming an adolescent "hulk." In college, he was considered a "heavy" anabolic steroid user. His heavy steroid use produced feelings of being invincible. He became more and more aggressive and appeared to be in a continual state of euphoria. He graduated from college and began his career on Wall Street. His success as a stockbroker quickly earned him the title "Wonder Boy of Wall Street." His business empire grew, with Minkow using his "steroid charisma" to swindle sophisticated bankers, accountants, lawyers, and Wall Street giants. Many people lost large amounts of money while Minkow's earnings skyrocketed.

Minkow's success largely depended on his anabolic steroid addiction. This addiction, which produced feelings of aggression, euphoria, and invincibility, with the heightened energy level that these drugs induced, became the driving force for more and more success. But, eventually, his steroid-altered judgment got him into trouble. He was indicted on charges of fraudulent and criminal behavior. His scheme unraveled and he was convicted of numerous felonies. Minkow is now serving time in a federal prison on a lengthy sentence.

Eric Elofson: The Case of Adolescent Suicide

This is a true story of an 18-year-old boy whose life ended tragically; he was found hanging from a tree in his parents' front yard.[2] To prepare for his senior year of high school football, Eric began using anabolic steroids. He became heavily involved with bodybuilding, gaining 30 pounds of muscle over a short time.

Soon after Eric began taking anabolic steroids, his body became covered with hives and blemishes. He had frequent nosebleeds and complained of symptoms of heartburn or gastric reflux. Headaches were common and he began to have insomnia and nightmares. During the day his mental state alternated between sluggishness and hyperactivity.

Eric exhibited many episodes of abnormal aggressiveness during the year before his death. He exhibited several bouts of "road rage" when he beat up other drivers. Several times Eric became enraged at his family members over inconsequential events. He threatened them with violence. There was no way to predict what would set him off. He once pounded dents into the hood of the family car. After these episodes of violence, he was not able to explain his rage to himself or others. He would explain to his friends and parents that he felt confused and angry with himself for "acting so stupid."

Eric's large increase in muscle mass (his muscles were well developed and defined) led his parents to suspect anabolic steroid use. While they were aware of the muscle enhancing and physical side effects they were unaware of the mental effects, especially the mental effects that occur upon withdrawal from heavy anabolic steroid use. They persuaded Eric to stop using steroids.

Throughout his last few months, Eric could not make decisions and acted more confused and frustrated. He alternated between rational and irrational thoughts. His friends (he had many) gradually quit calling. The day before his suicide, Eric spent time at the mall with his friends, later bringing friends home to spend the night. Everything seemed to be fine. Early the next morning, Eric was seen walking down the street in a confused state.

He hanged himself from a tree in the front yard. Eric ended his life without a note or clue that would have informed others about his overwhelming depression.

His parents published Eric's story to alert others about the psychological dangers of anabolic steroid abuse. Only in retrospect did Eric's parents recognize the mental effects of anabolic steroid abuse. The Eric they knew was an amazing kid who never took any other drugs or drank more than an occasional beer. Very few of his friends knew of the confusion, deep depression, and hopelessness that Eric was struggling with from his anabolic steroid withdrawal. His parents have hoped that their publication would help prevent someone else's tragedy.

Peter Lear's "Goldengirl"

There comes a point in many adolescent athletes' lives when height becomes a limiting factor in athletic performance and thus, future athletic career opportunities. Those of us who have been involved with athletics as children and adolescents can easily relate to just how important a few inches of greater height can be. In many sports, additional height can mean the difference between stardom and mediocrity, translating into financial fortunes for a select few.

For a young athlete, the question of whether or not to use athletic-enhancing drugs is strongly influenced by peer and adult pressure. For most children, these pressures will translate into taking the anabolic and growth-stimulating hormones or not playing. What choice is really left to the young athlete?

Sports sponsorship is one of the most powerful influences in modern American society. Everyone knows that sports sponsorship can be very lucrative. We are constantly inundated with stories of the enormous amounts of money that can be made.

In 1977, Peter Lear depicted some of the moral questions confronting modern society and athletics in his Doubleday novel, *Goldengirl*. His book portrayed the complicated moral questions involved in using anabolic steroids and human growth hormone to produce "giants" that will succeed on the athletic field.[3] Lear's powerful novel was made into a movie staring Susan Anton as the anabolic and growth-stimulating hormone–produced Olympic champion. Lear showed us the dark side of life humans *using* other humans to gain money and power. He portrayed the misguided genius of a medical scientist, the compulsiveness of a coach who had fallen short of his own Olympic dreams, the greed of a pharmacist, the ego of a wealthy sports sponsor, and the genetic potential of an athletic young girl, all of whom combined to create a monstrous victim called Goldengirl. These adults "programmed" Goldengirl to win three Olympic gold medals at the 1980 Moscow Olympic summer games.

According to the story, Goldengirl does not know that she is actually the product of anabolic and growth hormonal manipulation until she develops a severe case of diabetes from the repeated growth hormone injections. Nor did she know that her own father was the scientist behind the experiment. Lear depicted the scientist as a person driven by his desire to publish his theories on human growth and development. He wanted to make the potential properties and abuse of anabolic steroids and human growth hormone a "truth, secure for the rest of time." He did so by using his own daughter as the subject in his experiment.

The adverse effects of the anabolic hormones drastically altered Goldengirl's normal feminine facial appearance and physique. In order to be accepted as a woman athlete by the American public, Goldengirl had to undergo multiple plastic surgery procedures. We also saw Goldengirl in psychotherapy with a sports psychologist, to help her deal with acceptance of her body and her grossly underdeveloped social self. While the scientist proves his theory on human growth and development via "selective gigantism" techniques, he goes beyond his ability to rationalize the effects on his daughter. After he is forced to disclose to his daughter, Goldengirl, his role in the experiment, she rejects and curses him. Unable to cope with this turn of events, the medical scientist becomes irrational and commits suicide.

Lear's book points out the moral and ethical issues involved in hormonal manipulation. The greed-driven manipulation of unknowing individuals produces disastrous results.

The recent exposé of the East Germans' sponsorship of hormonal manipulation experiments on children and other athletes bears a striking resemblance to the story of *Goldengirl.* The testimonies of the former East German athletes in the aftermath of the experimentation are frightening and serve to illustrate the misuse and abuse of such powerful anabolic agents.

The "Blond Beach Boy"

This is a true story about a fitness guru who died in the spring of 2000. To many he was a local hero, helping others to achieve the "fit" lifestyle. "Blond Beach Boy" (BBB) grew up in Virginia Beach and played college football as a tight end for a southern California university. After college, he moved to Florida and bought a health club.

BBB was 6'2" and weighed over 250 pounds. He was a classic muscular hulk, in the muscle world mainstream. BBB was a 20-year anabolic steroid user and a black market dealer. He had used nearly every muscle-building drug or supplement that came along. He was the first athletic user of growth hormone that I ever met. On the walls of his health club were pictures of him with many of the "greats" in the bodybuilding and professional wrestling worlds. It was not unusual for these "greats" to come in and talk with BBB when they were in town.

Following a minor surgical procedure, BBB was found dead in a closet in his house. The police investigation ruled out foul play and the autopsy results revealed that BBB had died from a drug overdose of prescription pain medication. The death of this 46-year-old epitome of health and fitness shocked many in the area's muscle factories.

"The Knee, Always the Knee"

On two occasions in the early 1980s, Howard Cosell interviewed me for his controversial ABC sports television program entitled *Sports Beat*. The focus of our discussions, both on and off videotape, was anabolic steroid use in college and professional athletics. After each of the videotaped interviews, Mr. Cosell called me from New York and told me the he couldn't air my interviews because it was decided that telling the truth about anabolic steroid use would hurt sports sponsorship advertising income for ABC.

A few years later, after the anabolic steroid epidemic was spreading rapidly among high school students, ABC videotaped an interview with me again. This time, small segments of my interview aired on their television program *20/20*. ABC personnel told me that they had kept the old *Sports Beat* tapes. They also told me that they were going to televise an anabolic steroids program on *20/20* about anabolic steroid use in high schools. They explained that they could now do so without having a negative impact on sports sponsorship and their advertising budget.

This true story illustrates the conflict of interest that is inherent with the media coverage of the anabolic steroid issue in sports. An occasional news story appears in the televised media on this topic. However, this limited coverage is not in proportion to the huge problem of anabolic steroid abuse in America.

16
Questions and Answers

In this chapter, some of the questions that I have been asked over the past 20 years about anabolic steroids, growth hormone (GH), supplements, health risks, and so forth will be answered. These questions have come from a variety of situations, including my lectures, graduate school teaching, medical practice, and from athletes, coaches, trainers, and parents.

QUESTION 1: *I was wondering about college athletes taking anabolic steroids. Don't they test for them?*

ANSWER: Most people think that college athletes are routinely tested for anabolic steroid use. There is some testing conducted, but it is much less than most people may believe. A 1994 study by researchers at Johns Hopkins University surveyed the drug testing policies for college athletes.[1] Of the 288 athletic directors surveyed, 245 responded to their inquiries. Only 29 percent of the athletic directors said that they performed some drug testing on student athletes. Of those colleges that drug tested, only 56 percent of them did any anabolic steroid testing. Therefore, in 1994, only 11 percent of college programs tested for anabolic steroid use in their athletes.

QUESTION 2: *Aren't prescription anabolic steroids sold over-the-counter in some countries?*

ANSWER: Yes, that is one of the reasons that some athletes go to other countries to "train." Because anabolic steroids are sold over-the-counter in Mexico, many athletes and anabolic steroid dealers in the Southwest drive across the American-Mexican border and buy large quantities of anabolic steroids and other drugs. In some of the border cities in Mexico, the number of pharmacies is far out of proportion to the population needs. The NAFTA agreement has allowed the Mexican anabolic steroid black market trade to flourish. If you go to one of those cities, you'll find pharmacies all over the place. It is difficult to find a health club there. Guess where all of the anabolic steroids these pharmacies sell go?

QUESTION 3: *My mother is in her 70s and hard of hearing. I read somewhere that anabolic steroids could help hearing. Is that true?*

ANSWER: A recent study indicates (in a double-blind, placebo-controlled study of 24 postmenopausal women) that anabolic steroid therapy with tibolone improves auditory function via brainstem auditory neural pathways.[2] The authors concluded that this therapy might offer new strategies in treating hearing loss in the aged.

QUESTION 4: *I have chosen my senior project for my college paper on anabolic steroids and sports. We are required to complete an extensive literature search on the topic we chose. I know a little about anabolic steroid use by athletes. But, when I reviewed some of the older literature when researchers provided anabolic steroids to athletes to see if they worked or not, I noticed something seemed wrong with a study from England. I can't believe that they gave 100 mg/day of Dianabol for six weeks to the athletes and found that it had no more effects on muscle mass and strength than a placebo. I know enough to know that the prescribed dose for patients is 5 mg/day. Shouldn't this large dose have shown some results?*

ANSWER: This is an interesting study. It is a study that reveals one of the quirks of research that sometimes happens. I believe the study that you have referred to was conducted by Dr. Hervey's group.[3] In 1984, I met one of the graduate students who worked with Dr. Hervey on this study. I was on the United States Powerlifting Sports Medicine Committee at the time. I supervised the medical care and drug testing procedures at the Women's World Powerlifting Championships in Santa Monica, California. This graduate student, who had become an anabolic steroid dealer and guru, was there with several of his women powerlifters from Alabama. He wanted to talk anabolic steroids "shop" and we did.

As it turns out, he stole some, if not all, of the Dianabol from the study and sold it to his gym buddies. The reason that the "Dianabol" was no better than a placebo was because it was a placebo. All of the athletes in the study were given placebos.

The following week I had the opportunity to meet and talk with Dr. Hervey about his study. We were both speakers during the daylong symposium on drugs in sports at the 1984 Annual Meeting of the American College of Sports Medicine in San Diego. I explained to Dr. Hervey what had happened to his study.

During your literature search you should find Dr. Hervey's second study. In the second study the real Dianabol was provided and the results were different.

QUESTION 5: *Can strength training reverse the condition called sarcopenia that is so common in our elderly population?*

ANSWER: An intense, progressive weight-training program can attenuate physical frailty. The problem with this generality is that it starts with the statistics. Only about 7 percent of Americans over the age of 55 participate in physical fitness activities once weekly. Even in young people, physically active participation once weekly is not enough to have much of an impact on health.

Over 95 percent of older Americans don't engage in physical fitness activities even once weekly! They never have done so and the overwhelming majority of them won't participate even with a physician's prescription and encouragement. For example, older Americans who have had a heart attack and are involved in a prescribed rehabilitative exercise program rarely break a sweat.

Investigational studies in older Americans show that a regular strength-training program can have beneficial impacts on sarcopenia. The problem is, that once the senior citizens leave the investigational structure, most of them revert to their old ways. And, by the time a senior citizen is told by a physician that he needs to get involved in a regular, structured, and progressive exercise program, the patient's hormonal milieu is incapable of responding to it in a significant manner. The hormones that work should be replaced. A good place to start is prescribing anabolic steroids and growth hormone.

The saddest part of this situation is the bad example that 95 percent of older Americans are setting. Younger people peer at older Americans (aged 70 years) and think to themselves that they never want to be 70 years old. The truth is that the example that older Americans are setting is the product of laziness.

Often older Americans can't and won't exercise to the levels that it takes to benefit their own health. There is that 5 percent of older Americans who will. That is the same 5 percent that doesn't chew up the health care budget for the preventable conditions that are solved by adequate exercise programs.

QUESTION 6: *I am taking DHEA as a supplement. I have an employment physical and a drug screen in two weeks. Do they have a drug test for DHEA?*

ANSWER: A recent article has indicated that DHEA use can be detected but it is difficult. It has been shown to elevate the testosterone/epitestosterone ratio.[4] It is possible that DHEA use would show a positive test for testosterone use even though you are not taking testosterone. It will be interesting to see what happens with these over-the-counter anabolic steroids at the 2000 summer Olympic Games and beyond. In general, no employment drug screens test for anabolic steroid use.

QUESTION 7: *My husband has been taking anabolic steroids and has had major mood swings with bouts of anger and depression. I persuaded him to get some therapy. I went with him to the psychologist's office and sat in therapy with him. It didn't seem that the psychologist knew anything about the mental health effects of anabolic steroids. Is that common?*

ANSWER: Psychologists have been slow to recognize and link anabolic steroid use with mental health effects. Psychologists have neglected prevention programs for anabolic steroid abuse, in part because of a lack of knowledge about these drugs.[5] Bouts of anger and depression can be caused by anabolic steroid abuse.[6,7] Several studies have found evidence that there are changes, perhaps long-lasting ones, to the serotonin receptors that could account for this pattern.[8,9,10] Fluoxetine (Prozac) treatment has been helpful in treating the serotonin receptor-induced depression-anger chemical imbalance link. Some cases are due to a common neurochemical etiology.

QUESTION 8: *My workout partner injects insulin at night about four hours after we lift weights. I've noticed that he has a nose spray with a label that says glucagon on it. What is this nasal spray for?*

ANSWER: Some bodybuilders inject insulin to obtain a growth hormone release. It works, but it can be a dangerous way to elevate growth hormone levels. Injected insulin in normal people can cause severe hypoglycemia (low blood sugar), coma, and death. The nose spray that contains glucagon that can reverse the effects of insulin in a rapid manner. Glucagon nasal spray is clinically used by insulin-dependent diabetics who have the tendency to suffer occasionally from severe hypoglycemia.[11]

QUESTION 9: *I am a bodybuilder who used pituitary extracts of growth hormone before the synthetic version of growth hormone was available. I have read that I have a risk for Creutzfeld-Jacob disease. What I read said that it was some sort of a brain disease. Can you tell me about it?*

ANSWER: Creutzfeldt-Jakob disease is similar to "mad cow" disease. It is believed to be caused by a virus that affects the brain slowly and progressively. Use of extracted growth hormone has been associated with this disease. Your risk of having this disease is real but low.[12] There is no test for it. Only time will tell.

QUESTION 10: *My workout partner and I take anabolic steroids. When he does cocaine at parties he gets violent. Is it the cocaine or the steroids?*

ANSWER: It is generally accepted that anabolic steroids and stimulants don't mix. There have been no scientific studies that have directly evaluated this drug combination in humans. An animal study supports the concept that cocaine and anabolic steroids interact to produce additive effects on aggression.[13]

QUESTION 11: *I am a football player who works out. I read where clonidine is good for increasing my growth hormone. Is that true?*

ANSWER: There are several prescription drugs that can cause a release of growth hormone. Clonidine, which is used for hypertension and narcotic withdrawal, can release growth hormone and elevate normal growth hormone levels. Other prescription drugs that release growth hormone include propranolol and a few others. Clonidine can cause drowsiness and mental confusion.

QUESTION 12: *A few years ago I played college football and ruptured my Achilles tendon. I was on anabolic steroids at the time. Do anabolic steroids do something to the muscle tendons?*

ANSWER: Probably not. A recent study investigated the ultrastructure of ruptured tendons and found no differences between anabolic steroid users and non-users.[14] However, anabolic steroid use can make the muscle so strong, that under maximal contraction, the muscle tendon can tear away from the bone. The muscles can eventually become stronger than their attachments. This may explain why complete muscle tears seem more common in some sports.

QUESTION 13: *Since anabolic steroids can cause violent and criminal behavior, why aren't felons tested for anabolic steroids?*

ANSWER: Testing felons for anabolic steroids abuse sounds like a sound idea. A paper published in 1994 has shown that experts in Australia have considered testing violent offenders.[15] Testing costs would be prohibitive at this time ($200–300) per test. Of course, as the demand for anabolic steroid testing increased, it is possible that enough state laboratories would purchase the expensive equipment necessary. The equipment costs for confirmation testing are about $500,000. It is possible that rapid immunosorbent disks could serve as a screening test. I was a research consultant for a firm in California that was working on this project. I am not sure what the status is today. If the costs drop considerably, depending on the politics of the matter, then anabolic steroid testing may be a good idea. It is a felony to possess them without a prescription in the United States.

QUESTION 14: *I am a 23-year-old woman who has developed a moderate case of facial acne that I can't seem to get rid of. My dermatologist has prescribed a topical medication for me to use. My husband is a bodybuilder who uses anabolic steroids. Is there any connection? I know anabolic steroid use can cause acne.*

ANSWER: I have been asked this question many times. The answer is yes. There could be a connection. I have seen this condition in some of my women patients. I think that this phenomenon has become a mild problem that most physicians don't consider. It has been shown that the seminal fluid contains a significant level of testosterone.[16] Men who take anabolic steroids probably have higher levels in their seminal fluid. And, if they are having some damaged sperm cells because of the anabolic steroid use or other reasons, this study has indicated that this can cause a statistically significant elevation of seminal testosterone levels. Testosterone from seminal fluid can be absorbed via the vaginal or oral mucosa. Oftentimes, it doesn't take much additional androgen for women to break out.

Another possible mechanism to transfer anabolic steroids from your husband to you is through the skin. Anabolic steroid use can cause a man to excrete bioactive residues in his sweat and skin oil. An old study showed that some anabolic steroids can penetrate skin surfaces.[17] This study also suggested that the low level of overall penetration of the skin by the steroid is capable of being metabolized by bacteria, such as the bacteria involved with acne. Testosterone is also found in human saliva.

QUESTION 15: *My wife and I just got back from our missionary trip to one of the rural areas of Africa. Rickets is a major medical problem there. I have read that anabolic steroids are good for bones. Would they help rickets?*

ANSWER: As you know rickets is not a problem in the United States anymore. There are no human studies using anabolic steroids to treat rickets. One study addresses anabolic steroid use in rats. The study results showed that anabolic steroids plus vitamin D were superior to vitamin D alone for treating rickets in rats.[18]

QUESTION 16: *I see my father aging. He is in his 70s. We play golf together, but in the last two or three years, he doesn't seem to want to play. He seems shorter than he used to be. He just had a complete physical exam and lots of blood work. I was worried that he may have prostate cancer so I made sure that he has a PSA test. It was normal. He seems depressed to me. I talked with his doctor about all of this and he said that there was not much that he could do. I recently read a magazine article about andropause in men. Do you think that my dad may have it?*

ANSWER: I know where you are coming from. Watching our parents grow older is difficult. It sounds like he does have andropause. There are several important hormones that diminish significantly and contribute to aging. These include androgens, growth hormone, thyroid hormone, and melatonin. Replacing these hormones seems prudent. You have identified a major problem: physician resistance to hormonal replacement in the elderly. A recent study has shown that this is a significant problem. Many physicians just don't feel comfortable with replacing growth hormone and androgens because they never have. There are over 100 medical journal articles that recommend growth hormone and or androgen replacement, but most physicians resist. I believe in hormonal replacement in men, but many physicians do not and it doesn't matter what the literature on the subject shows. I suggest that you physician shop, if your dad is willing to do so. There are some areas of the country where there are clinics that focus on this issue and are not afraid of prescribing these medications.

QUESTION 17: *Are people getting taller?*

ANSWER: Yes. Many of us have recognized that people are growing taller. A recent study has addressed this issue. Since the 19th century there have been clearly documented trends for increasing adult height. The current rates are estimated in Europe to be 10–30 mm/decade.[19] I believe that the trends in America are much higher. Experts from other countries believe that Americans grow taller because of the anabolic hormone residues in the meat.

QUESTION 18: *Have anabolic steroids ever been used to treat depression?*

ANSWER: Testosterone was prescribed to treat depression in men and women in the 1940s. A survey of the medical literature during that period indicates that the treatment was highly successful in older people. There is a sporadic article or two that appears in the literature every decade or so. In 1984, a study was published on anabolic steroid therapy in depressed young men.[20] The results were mixed. Anabolic steroid therapy for depression seems to work much better in older patients. Unfortunately, mental health professionals don't even consider this form of therapy in older depressed patients. I hope that this changes.

QUESTION 19: *I am a bodybuilder. I bought some growth hormone last week that is bovine growth hormone. Will it work on me?*

ANSWER: It has been taught that distinct mammalian species have their own growth hormone. Also, I was taught that human growth hormone works on every species below humans, but the converse is not true. After seeing all of the concept changes that pertain to the growth axis, I am not sure anymore. Several local bodybuilders claim that bovine growth hormone is better than human growth hormone for muscle development. There have been no studies published on the effects of bovine growth hormone on humans.

QUESTION 20: *Are there any mental effects of growth hormone?*

ANSWER: During the past few years, there has been increasing interest in functions that growth hormone may play in the central nervous system. There are receptors in the central nervous system for growth hormone. The studies that deal with growth hormone replacement in older people consistently report an improved sense of well-being. I wouldn't be surprised if growth hormone replacement had a positive impact on dementia.

QUESTION 21: *I have been working "shifts" for over 20 years. I've always had problems sleeping during the day. I seem to be aging faster than other men my age. What is the connection between shift work and aging?*

ANSWER: Both daytime sleep and night work are associated with disturbed endocrine functions[21] that could help explain your question. Since growth hormone secretion is a function of quality sleep and aging, it seems likely that many shift workers will age faster than others their age who work days.

QUESTION 22: *I am a 42-year-old woman who has asthma. I have been on cortisone shots and pills for several years. Can growth hormone reverse the changes that I have now? I have lost muscle and I have osteoporosis.*

ANSWER: Growth hormone is one of the hormones that can help counteract the catabolic effects of cortisone therapy.[22] Anabolic steroid therapy is better.

QUESTION 23: *I am a 30-year-old woman who runs 40 miles per week. I have noticed over the past two years that my periods are irregular. I have read where osteoporosis can occur when a woman's menstrual periods stop. Mine haven't. Do I need to worry about having a higher risk for osteoporosis now that my periods are irregular?*

ANSWER: Menstrual dysfunction severity has a linearly associated decline in bone mineral density.[23] You have a higher risk for osteoporosis and stress fractures.

QUESTION 24: *My son was diagnosed with growth hormone deficiency. He is seven years old and is now taking growth hormone shots. Do you think that he will grow to a normal height?*

ANSWER: There is only limited data addressing the issue of final adult height following treatment with recombinant human growth hormone. A recent study has shown that final adult height is greater with growth hormone therapy than it would be otherwise.[24]

Afterword

It is hoped that this book has contributed to the understanding of the two faces of anabolic steroids. These two faces stem from the powerful anabolic effects that these steroids have on the human body. Both faces present serious issues that will impact many Americans. The future impact that anabolic steroids will have on society will depend on how they are used.

Controlling the dark side of anabolic steroid use will largely depend on stiffer regulation policies, improved educational efforts, and substantial legal enforcement. The most important factor in curbing anabolic steroid abuse may be through federal actions that reclassify anabolic steroids as Schedule II narcotics under the Federal Controlled Substance Act of 1970. I fully endorse this federal action.

Encouraging the bright side of anabolic steroids for expanded medical uses will largely depend on medical politics and physicians' attitudes. Anabolic steroid therapy should become a part of an overall plan to assist patients with disabling conditions and diseases resulting in muscle loss, bone loss, and overall decrease in physical health. As research continues to show positive results in many areas, anabolic steroids will become a staple in the area of rehabilitation medicine.

This book has examined the mechanisms and results of anabolic drugs and hormones. These anabolic agents that stimulate the growth axis are rapidly pushing back the boundaries of traditional medicine. The array of potential clinical uses and non-medical abuses of these products are staggering. At the present time, the abuse of these anabolic agents is ahead of medical science just like it has been with anabolic steroids. Anabolic agents, the fruits of genetic engineering, are best studied in controlled medical settings rather than in "clinical trials" conducted by competitive athletes and athletic youths.

Congress must work quickly to reconsider and act on the proposals to make all genetically engineered anabolic and growth-stimulating hormones and drugs controlled substances under federal law. Medical science must respond by accelerating its pace of studies in clinical trials to evaluate the potential of these products for the numerous people who are, and will be, in need of them. I fully endorse both actions. We simply cannot just stand by and let the unregulated hormonal manipulation of children, athletes, and bodybuilders continue. Nor should we deny access to anabolic agents to those people with debilitating disease conditions who could greatly benefit from their use. We must act now to increase the bright face of anabolic agents and decrease or eliminate the dark side.

Appendix 1: Author's Statement Before Congress, 1987

Statement of the Author, April 8, 1987, to the Subcommittee on Health and the Environment of the Committee on Energy and Commerce, U.S. House of Representatives 100th Congress, First Session, in *Hearings on Medical Devices and Drub Issues.*

STATEMENT OF WILLIAM N. TAYLOR

Mr. Taylor. Mr. Chairman, I am William Taylor, M.D., student health physician at Washington State University. I am also media spokesperson for the American College of Sports Medicine on their recent position paper for human growth hormone use and abuse in athletics.

Recently, the AMA did need to consider reclassifying human growth hormone as a Class 2 substance. Although they have not totally acted, some statements from a recent document that is entitled "Drug Abuse in Athletes: Anabolic Steroids and Human Growth Hormone." Report of the Council on Scientific Affairs, Resolution 57 and A-86, 1986.

Human growth hormone has a clear-cut application in growth hormone deficiency and other legitimate investigational uses, and also has great potential for misuse.

Another statement from this paper goes to the following: Increased availability; i.e., unlimited quantities of human growth hormone for other legitimate uses presumably would increase accessibility for illicit use.

My work with human growth hormone was really a serendipitous start. In 1981, I was studying the effects of anabolic steroids on self-using athletes, the black market, and other parameters dealing with this subject. In 1981 I discovered human growth hormone, the extracted version, being used and abused by athletes in a Florida health club. Vials with accompanying package literature were witnessed by me. The athletes wanted to know exactly what the package literature meant.

Athletes claimed a non-medical source for the drug. By the spring of 1982, I attempted to define the diversion of this particular product. At that time I was taught that the only way that you could get human growth hormone was through hospitalization, provocative studies for a slow growing child to see whether there was a growth hormone deficiency or not, X-ray studies, and entire hospital course and records sent with a prescription, written prescription to either the National Pituitary Program or two private companies.

From that point, the boards of those companies would decide whether or not there was an actual need; then the hormone would be shipped to either the pharmacy or a physician that was administering the growth hormone for a child.

So that is a very, very strict measure, and I wondered why growth hormone was being black marketed. There seemed to be no way. That was a very strict control measure.

I attempted to find out what the diversion was like. I sent bogus prescriptions as a medical intern for human growth hormone to the National Hormone and Pituitary Association and two private companies which supplied the growth hormone. Boxes of the growth hormone came on a monthly basis from the private companies. I destroyed the growth hormone and refused further shipments. These shipments came directly to my home, and I was only a first year medical resident, not even a licensed physician.

Spring of 1982, I witnessed selling of human growth hormone transactions among athletes and black market suppliers including mail order forms. I witnessed athletes self-using human growth hormone along with anabolic steroids by illegal diversion.

In May of 1982, I reported the use of human growth hormone at the American College of Sports Medicine at its national convention in Minneapolis.

In June of 1982, I wrote about human growth hormone abuse in athletics in my book, "Anabolic Steroids and the Athlete," and a complete chapter was on this subject.

In 1983, I began to receive letters, phone calls, visits from athletes including olympic and professional athletes who were self-using human growth hormone obtained from the black market. They sought advice on how to use it. They also requested prescriptions for human growth hormone.

Also in 1983 I began receiving letters and phone calls and visits from parents requesting the following: (A) For me to prescribe growth hormone to their adolescents for the purpose of increasing height and athletic potential. (B) For advice on how much black market growth hormone to give their children. They had already obtained a supply of growth hormone, and they wanted to make their son or daughter a blue chipper in athletics.

I received and witnessed human growth hormone listed on black market mail order forms, directed at young athletes. I have written about human growth hormone and its abuse, and methods for control of the hormone in over a hundred medical, non-medical, and lay publications.

Spring of 1984, I attended private meetings and heard testimony from an olympic coach who claimed: "From 30 to 50 percent of all U.S. olympic athletes, both men and women, are using growth hormone because they think it works and because it is not detectable. I am also concerned about their health."

In May of 1984, I presented a paper at the American College of Sports

Medicine on the abuse of growth hormone by athletes, the black market sources, and recommendation to reclassify it as a controlled substance.

In May of 1985, again more media: The NBC nightly news; Steroid Abuse and Growth Hormone Abuse.

In June of 1985, I wrote my second book, "Hormonal Manipulation," which clearly outlined the abuse potential and the use of human growth hormone by athletes. This book discussed the black market network, suggests for reclassification of human growth hormone as a Schedule II drug under the Federal Controlled Substance Act.

April 1986 I presented a paper at the University of Texas entitled, "The Case Against Human Growth Hormone Administration in Normal Children" in a day-long meeting sponsored by the University of Texas discussing abuse potential of growth hormones by athletes and adolescent athletes.

Leading pediatric endocrinologists and sports medicine physicians presented papers, and in the debate about how to control, this particular subject arose.

June 1986, I presented testimony to the AMA House of Delegates Reference Committee E to support the proposal to reclassify human growth hormone in a Class II of the Federal Substance Control Act.

October 1986, 2 years after the growth hormone is removed from the market because of slow virus disease, I presented testimony as an expert witness for the FDA against a black market steroid dealer in Florida. A significant supply, over 100 vials of Cres Cormon, the extracted version of growth hormone, was seized by police and was part of the court record.

This black market for steroids and growth hormone is part of a $100 million annual black market that is estimated by Federal agents.

In March of 1987, I witnessed black market source for synthetic Protropin, and use of such by an athlete. This particular vial looked to be the true Protropin, with the lot number etched off of the vial. The athlete claimed that the lot number would be traced back and that he would be in major trouble if the lot number on this particular vial was recorded.

Anecdotal claims by athletes today are prevalent about the synthetic Protropin on the black market.

I think, in summary, it is better to study all of the ramifications of growth hormone in a controlled setting versus self-use and social experimentation, which is what is the case with steroids.

It is difficult for anyone to fully access the steroid charisma that is afflicting our youth, and the emphasis on body image that is afflicting our youth. I support with all my efforts, courage and heart the proposal to place human growth hormone into the Class II substance. I do not see any other mechanism that I feel that will work at this time. Thank you.

[The prepared statement of Dr. Taylor follows:]

Statement of William N. Taylor

Introduction

Human growth hormone has a clear therapeutic application in growth hormone deficiency and other legitimate investigational uses, and also has great potential for misuse. (1) the agent has wide abuse potential, particularly if pharmacologic benefits are shown to result from use in normal athletes (1-10) and in adolescents wishing for additional height gains for athletic or other purposes. (2-10)

Diversion of human growth hormone to the well-developed athletic black market is significant, (2-11), even though relatively strict format existed for its distribution. This format included the following:

(a) proof of need by clinical documentation to include provocative diagnostic studies during hospitalization, radiographic studies and clinical evaluation for children with growth hormone deficiency;

(b) a written prescription accompanying the clinical proof of need provided in (a) above.

Methods to control general prescription drugs with "wide abuse potential" by allowing for pharmaceutical companies to restrict their distribution in some manner have failed to date. When widespread abuse or abuse potential for a general prescription drug has been identified, appropriate control mechanisms have usually included reclassifying the drug within the Federal Control Substance Act. Amphetamines and tranquilizers, once general prescription drugs, are now controlled substances due to widespread abuse and abuse potentials. (11)

Currently, the particulars of the diagnosis and treatment of growth hormone deficiency and relative growth hormone deficiency are points of debate among pediatric endocrinologists. And, years of investigational research are required to fully define the effectiveness and safety of human growth hormone in other illnesses. Specifically controlling the distribution of human growth hormone for legitimate uses and further investigational work would not be hampered by reclassifying it as controlled substance. It is the best method for preventing abuse by medical and nonmedical individuals.

It is my recommendation, supported by my testimony (summary to follow), that human growth hormone (all types) be reclassified in Class II of the Federal Controlled Substance Act.

Current AMA recommendations are being developed from the following recommendations for regulatory actions for synthetic anabolic-androgenic steroids and human growth hormone. (1) The AMA should continue to endorse current activities of the FDA, FBI, and DOJ directed toward curbing illegal distribution of these drugs. If these efforts are ineffective, the AMA should undertake a study of alternate methods of monitoring and limiting distribution. (1)

The use of HGH in normal children is an ethical problem of far-reaching proportions. (1) Increased availability (unlimited quantities) of HGH for other legitimate uses presumably would increase accessibility for illicit use. (1)

Testimony Overview

1981—I discovered growth hormone (extracted) use/abuse by athletes in a Florida health club; vials with accompanying package literature were witnessed. Athletes claimed a nonmedical source for the drug.

Spring 1982—I attempted to define the diversion of HGH. I sent bogus prescriptions for HGH to the National Hormone and Pituitary program (NHPP) and to private companies (Serono and Pharmacia) supplying the hormone. Boxes of HGH came on monthly schedules from both private companies. I destroyed the growth hormone and refused further shipments. These shipments came directly to me at home. I was a first-year medical resident.

Spring 1982 — I witnessed HGH selling transactions among athletes and black market suppliers, including mail orders. I witnessed athletes self-using HGH and with anabolic steroids obtained by illegal diversion.

May 1982 — I reported HGH use by athletes from black market sources at the American College of Sports Medicine annual meeting in Minneapolis, MN.

June 1982 — I wrote about the abuse of HGH by athletes and by adolescents striving for athletic success in a chapter in my first book *Anabolic Steroids and the Athlete.*

1983 — I received letters, phone calls and visits from athletes, including Olympic and professional athletes, who were self-using HGH obtained from the black market. They usually sought advice on how to use it. Some requested prescriptions for HGH.

I received letters, phone calls and visits from *parents* requesting:

(a) for me to prescribe HGH to their adolescents for the purpose of increased height and athletic potential;

(b) advice on how much black market HGH (they had obtained a supply) to give their adolescent athletic children.

I received and witnessed HGH listed on black market mail-order materials directed at young athletes.

I have written about HGH abuse and methods for control of the hormone in over 100 medical, nonmedical and lay publications and newspapers.

Spring 1984 — I attended private meetings and heard testimony from an olympic coach who claimed, "from 30–50 percent of my 1984 Olympic athletes (men and women) are using HGH because they think it works and is not detectable — I am concerned about their health."

May 1984 — I presented a paper to the American College of Sports Medicine on growth hormone use and abuse by athletes, black market sources and recommendations to reclassify it as a controlled substance.

May 1985 — I appeared on *NBC Nightly News* and reported abuse of HGH among athletes using anabolic steroids.

June 1985 — I wrote my second book on anabolic and growth hormone abuse entitled *Hormonal Manipulation: A New Era of Monstrous Athletes.* The book discussed HGH abuse, the black market network for the hormone and suggests reclassifying HGH as a Class II drug in the Federal Controlled Substance Act.

April 1986 — I presented a paper entitled: "The case against HGH administration to normal children" at a day-long meeting sponsored by the University of Texas discussing the abuse potential of HGH by athletes and adolescent athletes. Leading pediatric endocrinologists and sports medicine physicians presented papers. *The McNeil-Lehrer Report* televised portions of the meeting. A debate about reclassifying HGH as a controlled substance arose.

June 1986 — I presented testimony to the AMA House of Delegates Reference Committee E to support the proposal to reclassify HGH into Class II of the Federal Controlled Substance Act.

October 1986 — I presented testimony as an expert witness for the FDA against a black market anabolic hormone dealer in Florida. A significant supply of HGH was seized by police. (11)

March 1987 — I have witnessed a black market source for synthetic HGH (Protropin®) and use by an athlete. Anecdotal claims by athletes are prevalent.

References

1. Moxley, JH: Drug Abuse in Athletes: Anabolic Steroids and Human Growth Hormone. AMA, Report of the Council on Scientific Affairs, Resolution 57, A-86, 1986.

2. Taylor, WN: Anabolic Steroids and the Athlete. Jefferson, NC, McFarland, 1982.

3. Taylor, WN: Hormonal Manipulation: A New Era of Monstrous Athletes. Jefferson, NC, McFarland, 1985.

4. Taylor, WN: Are anabolic steroids for the long distance runner? Letter. Ann Sport Med 1984; 2(1):51–52.

5. Taylor, WN: Effects and actions of human growth hormone. Presented at a symposium on drugs in sports, American College of Sports Medicine annual meeting, San Diego, May 24, 1984.

6. Taylor, WN and AB Black: Pervasive anabolic steroid use among health club athletes. Ann Sports Med, to be published.

7. Taylor, WN: Growth hormone: preventing athletic abuse. Technology Rev 1985; 88(7):14–15.

8. Taylor, WN: Human growth hormone: a controlled substance, proposal. Testimony to AMA House of Delegates Reference Committee E, Chicago, IL, June 16, 1986.

9. Taylor, WN: Synthetic HGH should be classified as a controlled substance to prevent abuse. Genetic Eng News 1986; 6(4):4.

10. Taylor, WN: Super athletes made to order? Psychology Today 1985; 19(5):62–66.

11. Taylor, WN: Synthetic anabolic-androgenic steroids: A plea for controlled substance status. Physician Sportsmed 1987, May, in press.

Appendix 2: AMA Statement, 1987

Statement of the American Medical Association, April 22, 1987, to the Subcommittee on Health and the Environment of the Committee on Energy and Commerce, U.S. House of Representatives, 100th Congress, 1st Session, in *Hearings on Medical Devices and Drug Issues.*

The American Medical Association takes this opportunity to comment on the issue of whether human growth hormone (HGH) should be scheduled under schedule II of the Controlled Substances Act.

Comments

Recent advances in biomedical research now permit the synthesis of human growth hormone by recombinant DNA technology. This advance has permitted the production of a growth hormone that is free from viral contamination and, at the same time, is identical in its physiological activity to the naturally occurring hormone. The enhanced capacity to "manufacture" human growth hormone assures access to the definitive treatment for growth hormone deficiency for all children who need this important drug. However, in addition to this proven therapeutic benefit, it has been stated that HGH may be misused or abused by athletes and others in order to attempt to increase their size and strength.

The AMA opposes legislation that would schedule HGH under the Controlled Substances Act. The proper route for scheduling a drug is through the well-developed regulatory process — not by legislation. We also believe that scheduling HGH administratively under schedule II would be inappropriate. HGH does not meet the criteria for scheduling under schedule II of the Controlled Substances Act in that it does not "lead to severe psychological or physical dependence" [emphasis added], as required by Section 202(b)(1)(C) of the Act (21 U.S.C. 812(b)(1)(C). In addition, the Controlled Substances Act, heretofore, has included only those drugs whose abuse potential proceeds directly from their psychoactive or psychotropic effects. The inclusion of an "atypical" compound such as HGH is a major change in policy that demands in-depth study. Finally, we are concerned that inclusion of HGH in schedule II could serve to restrict the availability of the drug for those children who truly need it and could impede important research.

Regulatory Mechanism for Drug Scheduling

The appropriate avenue for scheduling a drug is through the well-established administrative process. The Controlled Substances Act authorizes the Attorney General, through the Drug Enforcement Administration (DEA), to initiate proceedings to schedule or reschedule drug or to remove controls on a drug. Before action can be taken, the Attorney General must request a "scientific and medical evaluation" of the drug from the Secretary of Health and Human Services through the Food and Drug Administration (FDA). The FDA also makes a recommendation as whether the drug should be controlled (and if so under what schedule) or removed from the schedules. If the DEA concludes that the information provided by the FDA constitutes substantial evidence that a drug has potential for abuse, it must initiate proceedings to schedule it. If, however, the FDA recommends that a drug not be controlled, the DEA is not allowed to control it. Finally, if the data provided by FDA constitutes substantial evidence that a drug should be removed entirely from the schedules, proceedings for removal of the drug must be initiated by DEA.

This regulatory mechanism, which relies heavily on the expertise of the FDA and DEA, has proven to be highly satisfactory in reviewing and evaluating drugs. No convincing reasons exist to forego this process set up by Congress in favor of direct legislative rescheduling. The legislative process would inappropriately preempt a well-developed program designed to deal specifically with the scientific, medical and regulatory issues.

Scheduling of HGH is Inappropriate

The factors that the FDA must consider in making its recommendation concerning whether a substance should be controlled include:

1) the drug's actual or relative potential for abuse;
2) its history and current pattern of abuse;
3) the scope, duration and significance of abuse; and
4) the risk, if any, to the public health.

We do not believe that these criteria have been met.

While the AMA recognizes that HGH has a limited potential for abuse, little or no data exist that substantiate or define a history, pattern, scope, duration or significance of abuse. Nor is there reliable evidence to indicate that HGH poses any significant risk to the public health. Finally, data to substantiate a relative abuse potential similar to other schedule II drugs — such as cocaine — is lacking. Thus, we believe that if the FDA were to conduct a rigorous "scientific and medical evaluation" of HGH, it would conclude that the drug should not be controlled under scedule II at this time.

We question whether it is appropriate to regulate, under the Controlled Substances Act, substances for which the basis for abuse potential is not psychoactivity. At present, all compounds included under the Controlled Substances Act derive their reinforcing properties, abuse potential, and capacity for producing psychological and/or physical dependence directly from the effects on the central nervous system. Human growth hormone, however, is released from the anterior pituitary, outside the central nervous system, and its most direct effects are on physiological systems other than the central nervous system. Indeed, the claimed potential for abuse is unrelated to any psychoactive or psychotropic effect.

Human growth hormone represents the second major medical product produced by recombinant DNA technology. This technology proffers many great advances for medicine. Many of its products will be endogenous hormones that serve to replace or correct deficiencies extant in specific patient populations. This capacity to produce biological products identical to modulators of all types of human functions is raising important scientific, clinical, ethical and legal issues. It is important for appropriate resolution of such issues that credible scientific and clinical evidence constitute the basis for the decisions that address such issues — not anecdotal reports and vague concerns.

We are also concerned that the rigid production and distribution controls for Schedule II drugs could serve to impede the availability of HGH for those children who truly need the drug. We believe strongly that the benefit of enhanced availability of HGH to those with serious medical problems far outweighs any risk posed to the public health by anecdotal reports of "abuse" of the drug.

Finally, wider therapeutic applications of HGH are now being studied. Inclusion of HGH under the controls of the Controlled Substances Act, particularly under Schedule II, could restrict valuable research.

Conclusion

The AMA opposes legislation that would schedule HGH under the Controlled Substances Act. The proper avenue for scheduling a drug is through the well-established regulatory process, not by legislation. In addition, scheduling HGH under Schedule II would, at this time, be inappropriate. HGH does not meet the criteria for scheduling under Schedule II of the Controlled Substances Act. Moreover, the Controlled Substances Act, heretofore, has included only those drugs considered psychoactive or psychotropic. The inclusion of an "atypical" compound such as HGH is a major change in policy that demands in-depth study. We are also concerned that rigid quotas for Schedule II drugs could impede the availability of HGH for those children who truly need the drug. Finally, we are concerned that inclusion of HGH under the Controlled Substances Act, particularly under Schedule II, could serve to curtail important research on the drug.

Appendix 3: Report of the Council on Scientific Affairs, 1987

Report of the Council on Scientific Affairs on Drug Abuse in Athletes: Anabolic Steroids and Human Growth Hormone. Included in *Medical Devices and Drug Issues*, hearings before the Subcommittee on Health and the Environment of the Committee on Energy and Commerce, U.S. House of Representatives, 100th Congress, First Session, April 8, 21, and May 4, 1987.

REPORT OF THE COUNCIL ON SCIENTIFIC AFFAIRS

Report: B
(I-86)

Subject: Drug Abuse in Athletes: Anabolic Steroids and Human Growth Hormone (Resolution 57, A-86)

Presented by: John H. Moxley, III, M.D., Chairman

Referred to: Reference Committee E (R. Robert Tyson, M.D., Chairman)

This report, the first in a three-part series on drug abuse by athletes, responds to adopted Resolution 4 (A-84) and to Resolution 57 (A-86), "Human Growth Hormone," which was referred to the Board of Trustees for action. Subsequent reports will cover other classes of abused drugs.

Introduction

The problem of misuse of anabolic hormones (both steroids and growth hormone) is complex and can be considered from different perspectives:

(1) Psychological:
  (a) the importance of winning;
  (b) Placebo effect of drugs.

(2) Pharmacologic:
  (a) the possibility that these hormones may provide a real physiologic advantage for the athlete;
  (b) The adverse effects of such misuse.

(3) Ethical:
  (a) The concept of violation of fair play;
  (b) Implicit coercion to use drugs in order to be competitive;
  (c) The concept of hormonal manipulation, particularly in children, to alter body size andbuild in a manner perceived to be beneficial forathletics or other life endeavors.[1]

General solutions to the problem range from prevention (eg, regulatory action limiting production and/or distribution of drugs) through symptomatic treatment (eg, drug testing of competitors) to cure (eg, motivation of the individual to reject drugs). The personal decision to reject or discontinue drug use is based on the individual's values and reasons for considering drug use. Hence, an ethical argument based on the concept of fair play may be ineffective in an individual who is motivated to win at any physical cost.

Anabolic steroids and growth hormone will be discussed separately. The following questions will be considered for each:

(1) Does the drug provide real or perceived benefit for the athlete?
(2) What are the adverse effects of the drug in this setting?
(3) Who promotes, distributes, and uses the drug?
(4) Is abuse of the drug a significant problem?

Anabolic Steroids

Anabolic steroids are synthetic androgens that have greater anabolic relative to androgenic activity than testosterone, but in large quantities, these drugs have strong androgenic effects. In general, they are not as useful and effective as earlier thought, but do have legitimate uses in several conditions (eg, certain anemias, hereditary angioedema, breast cancer, and possibly osteoporosis).

Anabolic steroids have been used by athletes for more than two decades in the belief that they increase body mass, muscle tissue, and strength. More recently, testosterone has been used because it is more difficult to detect in drug screening programs than anabolic steroids. Although studies of these agents have not shown uniformly increased muscular strength, certain benefits to athletic performance seem probable: increased body weight, partly due to fluid retention, may include increase in lean muscle mass. in a continuing program of intensive exercise coupled with a high protein diet, increased muscular strength may be realized in some individuals. In contrast, aerobic capacity is probably not increased beyond that due to aerobic training.[2,3] Increased aggressiveness is also reported among anabolic steroid users, but the degree to which this influences the intensity of training is unknown.[4] It should be noted that small, difficult-to-measure increments in muscular performance of psychological benefit may constitute the difference between winning and losing, particularly at a professional or world-class level. Therefore, these changes may be perceived to be critical to an athlete.

There are clear adverse effects associated with use of androgenic steroids. The doses and patterns of administration utilized by athletes often differ markedly from those used therapeutically. Athletes have been reported to take steroids cyclically for one to several months followed by a drug-free period up to a year. Doses may be far greater than those considered to be therapeutic, and drugs are sometimes "stacked" (several agents taken simultaneously).[5] Exogenous androgens affect the reproductive system of healthy males: gonadotropin and testosterone secretion are suppressed and oligospermia and temporary infertility may occur. Gynecomastia is common.[6] Agents that are 17-alkylated compounds (eg, oxandrolone, methandrosteneolone) are associated with liver pathology, including abnormal liver function tests, cholestasis, peliosis hepatis, hepatic adenomas, and hepatocellular carcinoma.[7] Although hepatic effects have been described and documented most often in patients treated for disease, one case of hepatocellular carcinoma has been reported in an athlete who had taken several anabolic steroids to increase skeletal muscle mass.[8] Anabolic steroid ingestion by athletes is also associated with an athergonic blood lipid profile (eg, elevated low-density lipoprotein cholesterol and decreased high-density lipoprotein cholesterol).[9] Increased irritability and aggressiveness may occur.

In women, androgenic hormones produce masculinizing effects (eg, hirsutism, deepened voice, oily skin, acne, male pattern balding, menstrual irregularities, increased libido). In children, these drugs may accelerate pubertal changes and limit eventual adult height by causing premature skeletal maturation and closure of the epiphyses.

Steroids apparently are used at all levels of athletic activity. Although the prevalence is difficult to assess accurately, such use is believed to be widespread.[10] Steroid abuse is particularly common among athletes in strength sports (eg, weight lifters, body builders, shot putters, and discus and javelin throwers). Use among weight-trained women athletes has been reported. Anabolic steroids have a more significant effect on female muscular development than on males. In one study, the women reported typical masculinizing side effects, which they considered an acceptable price for the anabolic benefits.[11] A particular concern is that the wide availability of these agents is likely to make them accessible to adolescents and children, as well as adults.[12]

Anabolic steroids are easily obtained on the black market through gymnasiums or mail order sources. In a survey of 250 weight lifters, almost half admitted using steroids at some time. Although most steroids were obtained illegally, some athletes claimed that they had been given a prescription for the drugs.[13]

In 1985, the Food and Drug Administration (FDA), Federal Bureau of Investigation (FBI), and Department of Justice (DOJ) began a nationwide criminal investigation of black market distribution of anabolic steroids and other drugs purported to enhance athletic performance. Manufacturers and distributors were advised of their responsibility to ensure distribution only to authorized customers and were requested to monitor and report unusual order activity (eg, large or frequent orders, orders by pharmacies for veterinary products). Indictments have been obtained as a result of this effort.

Growth Hormone

Human growth hormone (hGH) or somatotropin is a polypeptide hormone secreted by the anterior pituitary gland. GH has widespread metabolic effects, including stimulation of cellular amino acid uptake and protein synthesis, stimulation of lipolysis, and inhibition of glucose utilization in tissue, which tends to increase blood glucose levels. Growth hormone is necessary to achieve normal genetic growth potential. Severe deficiency in childhood results in dwarfism. Human GH is necessary to treat this condition, because GH from other species is ineffective.

Human pituitary-extracted GH was available from the National Hormone and Pituitary Program and commercial sources until 1985. After the appearance of several cases of Creutzfeldt-Jakob disease believed to have been caused by contaminated pituitary extracts, distribution of the product was halted voluntarily for an indefinite period. Following withdrawal of the pituitary products, a recombinant DNA-derived GH product was approved for marketing in the United States. It is identical to endogenous hGH except for the addition of methionine on the N-terminus of the molecule. This preparation is available commercially.

The results of hypersecretion of hGH are of particular interest in the context of this report. Uncontrolled hypersecretion in childhood results in gigantism, and in adulthood, acromegaly. The latter condition is associated with glucose intolerance, heart disease, impotence, and bony overgrowth (eg, protuding forehead and jaw, enlarged hands and feet).

Adverse effects of hGH use by athletes have not been documented but can be predicted on the basis of known effects of endogenous hypersecretion (vide supra). Whether limited exogenous administration may produce beneficial or deleterious effects in healthy athletes is unknown. The effect of hGH administration to normal children is unknown, but might be expected to produce a permanent increase in build and stature. Beyond the physiologic considerations, use in normal children is an ethical problem of far-reaching proportions.[1]

In contrast to the problem of anabolic steroid abuse, hGH abuse, to the extent that it exists, is a relatively new phenomenon. Reports of its use in athletes are anecdotal[15]; they suggest that hGH is currently favored because of anticipated body growth and increased strength potential and also because it is undetectable in current drug testing procedures. Use is probably limited by the great expense of the product.

The source of illicit supply is questionable. One physician reportedly obtained supplies of pituitary-extracted hGH simply by mailing prescriptions to companies supplying the product.[16] This account is inconsistent with the companies' stated distribution policies, which required screening of requests and documentation of need. Bogus hGH preparations, animal GH preparations, and foreign products should also be considered as potential illicit sources. To knowledge, there have been no reports verifying that the GH products bought by athletes are in fact hGH.

Since withdrawal of pituitary-extracted hGH from the U.S. market in 1985, the only U.S. source of hGH is the recombinant DNA product. Although the technology to mass-produce hGH is available, the manufacturer states that it limits production and follows rigorous screening and post marketing surveillance procedures to verify legitimate use in GH-deficient patients.

In summary, the status of growth hormone abuse is undetermined, but the agent has wide abuse potential, particularly if pharmacologic benefits are shown to result from use in normal athletes. Human GH also may have additional legitimate therapeutic applications for other growth disorders, fractures, burns, and other conditions. Research in these areas has been hampered by the limited supplies of hormone available, but is expected to be undertaken in the future now that it is possible to produce unlimited quantities of the hormone. Increased availability of hGH for other legitimate uses presumably would increase accessibility for illicit use.

Conclusions

Abuse of anabolic products by athletes differ in the two types of drugs discussed. Anabolic steroids have therapeutic benefits for certain conditions and proven abuse potential among athletes. The abuse of hGH is a recent phenomenon of undetermined extent. Human GH has a clear therapeutic application in growth hormone deficiency and other legitimate investigational uses, and also has great potential for misuse.

This report responds directly to concerns regarding the abuse of anabolic steroids; future reports will deal with other classes of abused drugs. The report also addresses the issue of the abuse of human growth hormone, which was raised in referred Resolution 57 (A-86). Recommendations for AMA action will be developed after completion of all reports on drug abuse in athletes. The following possibilities will be considered in developing the recommendations:

1. Regulatory Action (for anabolic steroids and growth hormone):

   The AMA should continue to endorse current activities of the FDA, FBI, and DOJ directed toward curbing illegal distribution of these drugs. If these efforts are ineffective, the AMA should undertake a study of alternate methods of monitoring and limiting distribution.

2. Education action (for drugs with abuse potential):

   The AMA should endorse educational activities at various levels including sports group administrators, coaches, parents, and athletes. Activities suggested for consideration are:

   a) Preparation and distribution of educational pamphlets on drug abuse in athletes emphasizing the adverse effects and limited benefits of such use.

   b) Development of a nationwide network of physicians who would be available to give presentations on this topic to interested community groups.

   c) Preparation of a videotape(s) on drug abuse in athletes for distribution and use by schools, sports programs, parent groups, and community organizations.

   d) Judicious use of the news media and editorials and articles in AMA publications to publicize the AMA's interest and availability to work on this problem.

The Council on Scientific Affairs recommends the adoption of this report in lieu of Resolution 57 (A-86).

REFERENCES

1. Benjamin M. et al: Short children, anxious parents: Is growth hormone the answer? Hastings Center Rep 1984;14:5–9.

2. Haupt HA: Anabolic steroids: A review of the literature. Amer J Sports Med 1984; 12:469–484.

3. American College of Sports Medicine Position Stand on the Use of Anabolic-Androgenic Steroids in Sports. Amer J Sports Med 1984;12:13–18.

4. Mellion MB: Anabolic steroids in athletes. AFP 1984;30:113–119.

5. Tatro DS: Use of steroids by athletes. Drug Newsletter 1985;4:33–34.

6. Limbird TJ: Anabolic steroids in the training and treatment of athletes. Comp Ther 1985;11:25–30.

7. Ryan AJ: Anabolic steroids are fool's gold. Federation Proceedings 1981;40:2682–2688.

8. Overly WL, et al: Androgens and hepatocellular carcinoma in an athlete. Annals Intern Med 1984;100:158–159 (letter).

9. Webb OL, et al: Severe depression of high-density lipoprotein cholesterol levels in weight lifters and body builders by self-administered exogenous testosterone and anabolic-androgenic steroids. Metabolism 1984;33:971–975.

10. Johnson WD: Steroids: A problem of huge dimensions, (special report) Sports Illustrated; 1985;62:38(12).

11. Strauss RH, et al: Anabolic steroid use and perceived effects in ten weight-trained women athletes. JAMA 1985;253:2871–2873.

12. Dyment PG: Drugs and the adolescent athlete. Pediatric Annals 1984;13:602–604.

13. Frankle MA, et al: Use of androgenic anabolic steroids by athletes. JAMA 1984;252:482 (letter).

14. Underwood LE: Report of Conference on uses and Possible Abuses of Biosynthetic Human Growth Hormone. N Engl J Med 1984;311:606–608.

15. Taylor WN: Hormonal Manipulation. McFarland, Jefferson, North Carolina, 1985.

16. Taylor, WN: Growth hormone: Preventing its abuse in sports. Technology Review 1985;88:14(3).

Appendix 4: The Steroid Trafficking Act of 1990

Report of the Committee on the Judiciary, U.S. Senate, 101st Congress, 2d Session. (Preceded here by a letter to the author from Judiciary Committee Chairman Joseph R. Biden, Jr.)

JOSEPH R. BIDEN, JR., DELAWARE, CHAIRMAN

EDWARD M. KENNEDY, MASSACHUSETTS
HOWARD M. METZENBAUM, OHIO
DENNIS DeCONCINI, ARIZONA
PATRICK J. LEAHY, VERMONT
HOWELL HEFLIN, ALABAMA
PAUL SIMON, ILLINOIS
HERBERT KOHL, WISCONSIN

STROM THURMOND, SOUTH CAROLINA
ORRIN G. HATCH, UTAH
ALAN K. SIMPSON, WYOMING
CHARLES E. GRASSLEY, IOWA
ARLEN SPECTER, PENNSYLVANIA
GORDON J. HUMPHREY, NEW HAMPSHIRE

RONALD A. KLAIN, CHIEF COUNSEL
DIANA HUFFMAN, STAFF DIRECTOR
JEFFREY J. PECK, GENERAL COUNSEL
TERRY L. WOOTEN, MINORITY CHIEF COUNSEL
AND STAFF DIRECTOR

United States Senate

COMMITTEE ON THE JUDICIARY
WASHINGTON, DC 20510-6275

September 28, 1990

Dr. William Taylor
1125 Tall Pine Trail
Gulf Breeze, Florida 32561

Dear Dr. Taylor:

The illegal use of anabolic steroids is a major drug abuse problem in this country. A recent report by the Department of Health and Human Services confirms the results of the Judiciary Committee's two-year investigation into steroid trafficking and abuse. Steroids are dangerous drugs that threaten the physical and mental health of hundreds of thousands of young people.

With your help, I have called attention to this problem through a series of hearings on steroid abuse in amateur and professional sports. As a result of these hearings, I introduced S.1829, the Steroid Trafficking Act of 1989. This legislation would attack the steroid problem by adding steroids to schedule II of the Controlled Substances Act. This change would boost the penalties for steroid trafficking, impose tight production controls on pharmaceutical companies and incorporate steroid prevention and treatment programs in our national drug abuse strategy.

The reason that I am writing to you is that the full Senate will take action on S.1829 in the near future. Although the bill enjoys broad support, it is important that leaders in the amateur and professional sports industry, coaches, athletes and others take a strong stand against the use of performance-enhancing drugs.

I have enclosed a copy of the report that summarizes the findings of the Judiciary Committee's investigation along with a transcript from the steroid hearings.

I hope I can count on your support as this bill overcomes the final hurdle to becoming law. If you have any questions or need additional information, please do not hesitate to contact me.

Sincerely,

Joe Biden

Joseph R. Biden, Jr.
Chairman

Enclosures

Calendar No. 787

101ST CONGRESS 2d Session	SENATE	REPORT 101-433

THE STEROID TRAFFICKING ACT OF 1990

AUGUST 30, 1990.—Ordered to be printed
Filed under authority of the order of the Senate of August 2 (legislative day, July 10), 1989

MR. BIDEN, from the Committee on the Judiciary, submitted the following

REPORT

[To accompany S. 1829]

The Committee on the Judiciary, to which was referred the bill (S. 1829), having considered the same, reports the bill, as amended, and recommends that the bill do pass.

CONTENTS

I. PURPOSE

The purpose of the proposed legislation is to amend the Controlled Substances Act to further restrict the use of steroids. By designating anabolic steroids as a schedule II controlled substance, the bill would crack down on illegal steroid use in four ways:

**Not included in this appendix*

(1) it would increase steroid trafficking penalties to match the penalties for selling cocaine and other dangerous drugs;

(2) it would impose tight record-keeping and production control regulations to prevent the diversion of legally produced steroids into the illicit market;

(3) it would give the Drug Enforcement Administration the authority and responsibility to investigate violations involving the illegal production, distribution, or possession with intent to distribute steroids; and

(4) the bill would require U.S. demand reduction agencies to incorporate steroids in all federally supported drug abuse prevention, education, and treatment programs.

This legislation would also amend the Food, Drug, and Cosmetic Act to restrict the illegal distribution of human growth hormone which is chemically distinct from steroids.

II. Legislative History

Senators Biden, Simon, and Levin introduced S. 1829, the Steroid Trafficking Act of 1989, on November 1, 1989. This legislation was the result of a year-long investigation by the committee into the problem of steroid abuse in America. S. 1829 builds on the provisions authored by Senator Biden in the Anti-Drug Abuse Act of 1988, which made the illegal sale of steroids a felony, punishable by 3 years imprisonment.

Despite enactment of the steroids provisions in the 1988 drug bill, illegal steroids trafficking remains a major drug problem in the United States. In one blatant example, Mexican firm, United Pharmaceuticals of Mexico, mailed a solicitation to U.S. citizens giving them directions to a hotel across the border where they could go to buy steroids. The company urged its customers to "tell your friends that here in Mexico there is no prescription necessary to obtain steroids." To crack down on steroid trafficking through the mails, Senator Biden introduced S. 466 on February 28, 1989. S. 466 makes the distribution of steroids through the mail a criminal offense. By adding steroids to schedule II of the Controlled Substances Act, S. 1829 would incorporate the prohibition on steroids shipments through the U.S. mail as proposed in S. 466.

The committee held 2 full days of hearings on the problem of steroid abuse, focusing on the problem of steroid abuse in amateur and professional sports. Chairman Biden convened the first hearing at the University of Delaware, in Newark, DE, on April 3, 1989. The hearing featured testimony from world-class athletes Evelyn Ashford, Diane Williams, and Pat Connolly, Ashford's coach and a former U.S. Olympian. According to two-time Olympic gold medalist Evelyn Ashford, approximately 5 percent of the female medalists in the 1988 summer games used steroids. Her desire to be No. 1 led Diane Williams, former U.S. national championship and winner of the bronze medal in the 1983 world championship in the 100 meters, to use steroids from 1981 to 1984. Now steroid-free, Diane Williams' testimony included stories of physical and mental anguish associated with her steroid abuse.

Testimony from a panel of sports medicine experts reinforced the evidence of steroid use among amateur and professional athletes and warned the committee about the adverse physical and psychological effects linked to steroid use. Dr. Charles Yesalis, a professor at Pennsylvania State University and a leading expert on the prevalence and consequences of steroid abuse, testified about the behaviors, attitudes, and perceptions — consistent with psychological dependence — exhibited by a significant percentage of high school athletes who use steroids. The committee also heard testimony regarding the strong connection between steroid abuse and psychiatric disorders from Dr. David Katz, recognized as one of the leading medical experts on the psychological effects of steroid use. Dr. Katz warned in his testimony that individuals should pay special attention to the phenomenon of steroid use and psychotic episodes, depression, and mania.

Other witnesses at the hearing included: Dr. Edward Langston, American Medical Association; Pat Croce, conditioning trainer for the Philadelphia 76ers and the Philadelphia Flyers; Mike Quick, captain and all-pro receiver with the Philadelphia Eagles; Otho Davis, head trainer for the Philadelphia Eagles and executive director of the National Athletic Trainers Association; and Dorothy Baker, Delaware representative to the Executive Board of State Chairmen of the U.S. Olympic Committee.

The second hearing on steroids, held on May 9, 1989, in Washington, DC, featured testimony from representatives of professional and college football. Recognized as a sport plagued by alarming levels of steroid use, football has always favored those players that are bigger, bulkier, and more aggressive than their opponents. According to Bill Fralic, three-time all-pro offensive lineman and National Football League player representative for the Atlanta Falcons, the pressure to gain that competitive edge begins in high school and is the start of a vicious cycle.

Pete Rozelle, outgoing commissioner of the NFL, testified on the NFL's effort to combat steroid abuse among its players. College football coaches also told of their efforts to prevent steroid use among their players. Bo Schembechler, head football coach and athletic director at the University of Michigan, spoke of his support for random, unscheduled testing, while Joe Paterno, head football coach at Penn State University, admitted that "we are now finding ourselves with a disease that is spreading." The hearing also featured testimony from: Jay Moyer, NFL executive vice president; Chuck Noll, head coach, Pittsburgh Steelers; Joe Purzycki, head coach, James Madison University; Harold Raymond, head coach, University of Delaware; and Marty Schottenheimer, head coach, Kansas City Chiefs.

III. Discussion

Anabolic steroids are synthetic derivatives of the male sex hormone testosterone. Technically referred to as androgenic-anabolic steroid, steroids occur naturally in the human body and are essential in the normal physiological processes of men and women. Androgens are hormones responsible for the development of male sex characteristics, including the growth of facial hair and the deepening of the voice. The term "anabolic" refers to the constructive or building process of tissue. For the purposes of this report, the term "steroid" shall refer to androgenic-anabolic steroid.

Although androgenic-anabolic steroids have been approved for the treatment of numerous medical conditions, including hypoganadism, certain anemias, breast cancer and angioedema, they remain the least prescribed and the least studied of the steroid hormones.[1]

A. STEROIDS: A HALF-MILLION HIGH SCHOOL USERS

Steroid abuse has become a major drug abuse problem in America. As many as 1 million Americans or more have used or are currently using steroids for nonmedical purposes, primarily to increase athletic performance and improve physical appearance.[2]

Most disturbing, however, is the widespread steroid abuse among high school students and other young people. Steroid abuse by male high school seniors is nearly as widespread as the use of "crack" cocaine. The most complete study of this subject found that the number of male high school seniors who had used steroids within the previous 30 days was 75 percent of the number of male seniors who had used crack within the last month.[3] Another nationwide study of 12th grade male students found that 6.6 percent had used steroids.[4]

Taken together, these studies suggest that up to 500,000 male high school students use, or have used, steroids. Worse still, more than one-third of the users began using steroids at the age of 15 or younger; two-thirds had started by the age of 16. And the phenomenon is not limited to any one part of the country. Recent reports from Michigan, Texas, and Arkansas have all found that 5 to 11 percent of high school males admit to having used steroids.5 These four studies also concluded that 1 to 2 percent of high school girls reported steroid use.

The severity of the steroid abuse problem among young people is compounded by the extremely high percentage of "hard-core" steroid users. Approximately 40 percent of steroid users can be considered "hard-core" users.[6] More than 90 percent of the anabolic steroid users who began at age 15 or younger are repeat-steroid users. "Stacking"—or the simultaneous use of different steroids—is a popular and dangerous pattern of steroid use among teenagers. 44 percent of the high school student users take more than one steroid at a time, and almost two out of five have used both oral and injectable steroids.[7]

B. PHYSICAL EFFECTS OF STEROIDS

Teens take steroids because they "work."[8] As medical experts now concede, steroids are effective in promoting muscle growth, although early denials of this fact,[9] unfortunately, have discredited subsequent warnings issued by medical experts about the serious physical and psychological consequences of steroid use. This has been a deadly mistake.

The abuse of steroids has been associated with serious physical disorders. Steroids have been linked to fatal liver and kidney failure.[10] An increased risk of cardio-vascular disorders is also associated with steroid use due to the drug's effect on the balance of high density and low density lipoprotein (HDL/LDL), which result in increased cholesterol levels and high blood pressure.[11]

Changes in sexual characteristics and reproductive function are common in both female and male athletes who take steroids.[12] Common in female athletes who take steroids are menstrual irregularities, shrinkage of the breasts, increased facial hair, male-pattern baldness, deepening of the voice, and clitoral enlargement.[13]

The last four effects in women tend to be irreversible.

In men, steroids reduce the production of luteinizing hormone and follical-stimulating hormone by the pituitary. This can lead to lower levels of circulating testosterone, testicular atrophy, oligospermia (low sperm count), and infertility.[14]

Prolonged steroid use may be particularly harmful to young people. Premature fusion of the long bones from steroids use can result in stunted growth in adolescents and preadolescents.

In sum, the evidence is clear: steroids are dangerous drugs that can permanently disfigure young users — and, in some cases, can take young lives.

C. STEROIDS AND AGGRESSION: A DEADLY MIX

In our society, which is filled with images of beauty, flawlessness, and excellence, steroids hold the promise of perfection. The promise is shattered, however, when individuals are faced with the brutal reality of steroid abuse: steroids not only cause physical damage but can cause severe psychological disorders. Attempting to strengthen the body, a steroid user can destroy his mind.

The psychological effects associated with steroid abuse include increased aggression, violent episodes, paranoia, depression, and hallucinations.[15] Despite the drastic and sometimes immediate psychological effects of steroid abuse reported by athletes, very few of these side-effects have been adequately researched.

Countless steroid users, however, provide anecdotal accounts of "roid rages" — the increased aggression and irritability associated with steroid use.[16] Numerous accounts of increased aggression and violence by steroid users have been reported:

> Glenn Woolstrum, a former deputy sheriff in Clackamas County, Oregon, was obsessed with weight lifting. Woolstrum took three steroids at the same time: anavar, testosterone, and dianabol. Although Woolstrum was known by many to be a pleasant, gentle man, overnight his personality became aggressive and violent. When Woolstrum asked a store owner if he could use her phone, the owner replied, "I should charge all you cops using this phone. You come in here all the time." The next day, angered by the store owner's remark, Woolstrum went back to the store, ordered her into his car at gunpoint and shot her. Today, Leslie Myers, the owner of the store, is paralyzed for life.[17]
>
> At age 13, Mike Keys began weight lifting to build his slender frame. By age 17, Mike Keys stood 5'9", weighed 193 pounds, and injected himself daily with testosterone obtained from the local gym. Never satisfied with the results, Mike continued to take steroids, despite pleas from his family to stop. His grades began to slip, he threw temper tantrums, and his mood swings worsened. According to his parents, on the morning of December 16, 1988, Mike was fine, even cheerful. That evening Blaine Keys discovered his son's body lying next to his weight-lifting equipment — dead from suicide.[18]

At Harvard Medical School, Dr. Harrison G. Pope, Jr., an associate professor of psychiatry, and Dr. David L. Katz, a psychiatrist, conducted one of the leading scientific studies on mental disorders associated with steroid use.[19] Of the 41 bodybuilders and football players studied, approximately one-third suffered mild to severe forms of mental disturbances. All 39 men and 2 women used steroids, usually obtained from the black market. The researchers concluded that "major psychiatric symptoms may be a common adverse effect of these drugs."[20]

More than 10 percent of Pope's and Katz' subjects experienced psychotic symptoms, and approximately 25 percent of the athletes experienced manic symptoms, including an inflated self-esteem, recklessness, and a feeling of invincibility. Dan, an obsessed steroid user who went from 140 pounds to 270 pounds in 3 years, borrowed $1,500 from the bank to support his steroid habit. Convinced he was immortal, he drove a car at 40 mph into a tree, while a friend videotaped him. Since giving up steroids, Dan's destructive urges have disappeared.

Dr. William Taylor, in his study of the psychological alterations associated with anabolic steroid use, argues that the psychological damage continues even after steroid use has stopped. According to Taylor:

> There is no doubt that the use of anabolic steroids, even in low doses, potentiates certain psychological behavior in men. And with men athletes who are using moderate and larger doses of anabolic steroids, total personality changes may take place, both while on the anabolics and after the anabolics are stopped.[21]

And a yet-to-be-released study — the only controlled study of personality disorders among steroid users ever conducted — will demonstrate that steroid users, like alcoholics, have an increased risk of developing personality disorders.[22] Steroid users experience frequent episodes of depression, anxiety, and hostility during cycles of steroid use.

D. STEROIDS ARE ADDICTIVE

The leading study of the addictive nature of steroid dependence cites the following four symptoms: (1) loss of control; (2) continued use despite adverse consequences; (3) tolerance; and (4) withdrawal.[23] Almost every leading expert in the field agrees: steroids are addictive.

In one case a 24-year-old noncompetitive weight lifter sought professional help for his dependence on anabolic steroids.[24] After a year of anabolic steroid use, the patient suffered from severe mood swings and temper outbursts. Two weeks before he was admitted to a hospital emergency room, the man separated from his wife of 5 years. The night before his admission, he had thoughts of suicide. When he attempted to stop taking anabolic steroids, he became depressed and weak; his craving for the "high" he felt when he took the drug was unbearable. After 5 days at the hospital, the man signed out against medical advice.

The perception by the user of anabolic steroids that the drug enables them to become stronger and bulkier is a key element of anabolic steroid dependence. And part of the difficulty in quitting the steroids habit is that the users think they look better and perform better when they take the drug.[25] According to leading experts, the overreliance on the body for self-worth is an element that differentiates anabolic steroid abusers from other drug abusers.[26]

Prominent surveys of male high school seniors who took steroids reveal similar perceptions. More than 50 percent of the users surveyed believed their strength to be above average. Only 27.8 percent of the nonusers felt their strength to be greater than average. Similarly, almost 40 percent of the users felt themselves to be in "excellent" health, compared to 24.1 percent of the nonusers.[27]

Several medical researchers warn that the current trend of anabolic steroid dependence is particularly troubling in adolescent athletes.[28] Adolescents are especially vulnerable to adverse effects because of their developing nervous and skeletal systems. Therefore, the psychological side effects may be intensified in the adolescent because he or she may not have the psychological maturity to cope with the mood changes associated with anabolic steroids.[29] At least one author has suggested that adolescent males may prove to be especially vulnerable to addiction, because its use is associated with low self-esteem, a characteristic common in adolescents.[30]

One study found a shocking attitude among adolescent habitual steroid users[31] who began taking anabolic steroids at a young age: when these users were asked if they would stop using anabolic steroids if it was "proven beyond a doubt" that they would lead to permanent sterility, liver cancer, and a heart attack, approximately 40 to 50 percent responded that they would "definitely" continue to take anabolic steroids despite the health risks.

The reported use of anabolic steroids suggests that there may be a psychological and physical basis for anabolic steroid dependence. Although physical dependence has been hyphothesized, few documented cases exist. One theory of physical dependence states that withdrawal symptoms are a response to lower levels of testosterone in the body after anabolic steroid use has stopped.[32] Another theory suggests that anabolic steroids increase opioids, or pleasure producing stimulants, that originate within the brain.

Psychological addiction to steroids includes the desire by some to become bigger and stronger. When an athlete watches his body size and strength decrease during withdrawal, his confidence and self-esteem decrease. Psychological addiction to anabolic steroids can be so severe that suicidal depression can occur during withdrawal. Experts warn that "close professional monitoring is required" during this period to avoid what they perceive to be "life-threatening" withdrawal symptoms.[33]

E. THE FAILURE OF CURRENT EFFORTS TO FIGHT STEROID ABUSE

Current enforcement efforts to control the misuse of steroids are clearly inadequate. Last year, the General Accounting Office conducted a year-long investigation into the steroid problem in America pursuant to the steroid provisions authored by Senator Biden in the 1988 Anti-Drug Abuse Act. Among the major findings in the GAO report is that the illegal steroids trade is a $300 million to $400 million a year industry.

Based on seizures of illicit drugs and other information, the Justice Department believes that the supply of black-market steroids is divided evenly between three sources: clandestine U.S. laboratories; imports smuggled into the United States from foreign countries; and diversions from legitimate U.S. steroid manufacturers.

The U.S. Food and Drug Administration is currently charged with the responsibility for enforcing steroids control laws. However, according to the FDA, only 38 full-time personnel were devoted to steroids enforcement efforts in 1988. In addition, FDA personnel have neither the expertise nor the authority to conduct the complex and time-consuming investigations that are necessary to attack the increasingly sophisticated illegal steroid trade. For example, FDA investigators are not authorized to carry firearms, execute search warrants, or conduct undercover investigations.

The current regulatory scheme is also inadequate to control the diversion of legally produced steroids produced or sold in the United States.

> The FDA does not require manufacturers to submit information on the amount of steroids produced or sold in the United States.
>
> The FDA does not collect information on the amount of steroids legally prescribed by physicians.
>
> The FDA has no estimate of whether steroid production is increasing or decreasing, whether prescriptions have increased or decreased, nor the amount of diversion occurring in the steroid industry.

This is why S. 1829 is desperately needed legislation. Adding anabolic steroids to schedule II of the Controlled Substances Act would impose tight record-keeping and production controls on steroids. Steroids manufacturers and distributors will be required to comply with production and distribution regulations established by the Attorney General. For example, producers will be required to store steroids in secure facilities. Moreover, distributors will be required to keep detailed records on steroids shipments and make those records available to Drug Enforcement Administration investigators.

S. 1829 will also address the problem of clandestine steroids production and illegal steroids smuggling. By adding steroids to the list of schedule II controlled substances, the Steroid Trafficking Act of 1990 will give the Nation's lead drug-fighting agency — the Drug Enforcement Administration — the jurisdiction to investigate steroids-related offenses. Although DEA is already pressed in its fight against other illegal drug trafficking, DEA is better positioned to commit the resources and expertise necessary to mount an aggressive national crackdown on steroid trafficking than are the handful of steroids personnel at the FDA.

In addition, adding steroids to schedule II will significantly increase the penalties for steroid offenses. Under current law, steroid dealers at most face up to 3 years imprisonment, regardless of the quantity involved. Under S. 1829, steroid pushers would face up to 20 years imprisonment and fines of up to $1 million. Similar penalties would apply to illegal steroids smuggling, under the Controlled Substances Import and Export Act (21 U.S.C. 961).

IV. Vote of the Committee

On March 8, 1990, the Committee on the Judiciary by unanimous consent approved an amendment in the nature of a substitute by Senators Biden and Thurmond to S. 1829, and ordered the bill, the Steroid Trafficking Act of 1990, as amended, favorably reported.

V. Text of S. 1829, as Reported

[101st Cong. 1st sess.]

A BILL To amend the Controlled Substances Act to further restrict the use of steroids and human growth hormones

Be it enacted by the Senate and House of Representatives of the United States of America in Congress assembled,

SECTION I. SHORT TITLE.

This Act may be cited as the "Steroid Trafficking Act of 1990."

TITLE I — ANABOLIC STEROIDS

SEC. 101. STEROIDS LISTED AS CONTROLLED SUBSTANCES.

(a) Adding Steroids to Schedule II of the Controlled Substances Act. — Subdivision (b) of schedule II of section 202(c) of the Controlled Substances Act (21 U.S.C. 812(c)) is amended by inserting at the end thereof the following:

"(22) Anabolic Steroids."

(b) Definition. — Section 102 of the Controlled Substances Act (21 U.S.C. 802) is amended by adding at the end thereof the following:

"(41) The term 'anabolic steroids' means—

"(A) any drug that is chemically and pharmacologically related to the male hormone testosterone and that promotes or purports to promote muscle growth, including any amount of the following chemical designations and their salts, esters, and isomers:

"(i) boldenone,
"(ii) chlorotestosterone,
"(iii) clostebol,
"(iv) dehydrochlormethyltestosterone,
"(v) dihydrotestosterone,
"(vi) drostanolone,
"(vii) ethylestrenol,
"(viii) floxymesterone,
"(ix) formabulone,
"(x) meserolone,
"(xi) methandienone,
"(xii) methandranone,
"(xiii) methandriol,
"(xiv) methandrostenolone,
"(xv) methenolone
"(xvi) methyltestosterone,
"(xvii) mibolerne,
"(xviii) nandrolone,
"(xix) norethandrolone,
"(xx)oxandrolone,
"(xxi) oxymesterone,
"(xxii) oxymetholone,
"(xxiii) stanolone,
"(xxiv) stanozolol,
"(xxv) testolactone,
"(xxvi) testosterone,
"(xxvii) trenbolone, and

"(B) any substance which is purported, represented or labeled as being or containing any amount of any drug described in subparapraph (A), or any substance labeled as being or containing any such drug.

As used in schedule II, such term shall not include an anabolic steroid which is expressly intended for administration through implants to cattle or other nonhuman species and which has been approved by the Secretary of Health and Human Services for such administration, except that if any person prescribes, dispenses, or distributes such steroid for human use, such person shall be considered to have prescribed, dispensed, distributed a steroid in schedule II of this Act."

(c) EFFECT OF SCHEDULING ON PRESCRIPTIONS—Any prescription for anabolic steroids subject to refill on or after the date of enactment of the amendments made by this section may be refilled without restriction under section 309(a) of the Controlled Substances Act (21 U.S.C. 829(a)).

(d) EFFECTIVE DATE—This section and the amendments made by this section shall take effect 90 days after the date of enactment of this Act.

SEC. 102. REGULATIONS BY ATTORNEY GENERAL.

(a) Abuse Potential — the Attorney General, upon the recommendation of the Secretary of Health and Human Services, shall, by regulation, exempt any compound, mixture, or preparation containing a substance in paragraph (41) of section 102 of the Controlled Substances Act (as added by section 101 of this Act) from the application of all or any part of the Controlled Substances Act if, because of its concentration, preparation, mixture or delivery system, it has no significant potential for abuse, and, at a minimum, shall exempt estrogens, progestins and corticosteroids.

(b) Drugs for Treatment of Rare Diseases — If the Attorney General finds that a drug listed in paragraph (41) of section 102 of the Controlled Substances Act (as added by section 101 of this Act) is —

(1) approved by the Food and Drug Administration as an accepted treatment for a rare disease or condition, as defined in section 526 of the Federal Food, Drug and Cosmetic Act (21 U.S.C. 360bb); and

(2) does not have a significant potential for abuse, the Attorney General may exempt such drug from any production regulations otherwise issued under the Controlled Substances Act as may be necessary to ensure adequate supplies of such drug for medical purposes.

(c) DATE OF ISSUANCE OF REGULATIONS. — The Attorney General shall issue regulations implementing this section not later than 45 days after the date of enactment of this Act, except that the regulations required under subsection 102(a) shall be issued not later than 180 days after the date of enactment of this Act.

TITLE II — HUMAN GROWTH HORMONE

SEC. 201. AMENDMENT TO THE FOOD, DRUG AND COSMETIC ACT.

Section 303 of the Federal Food, Drug and Cosmetic Act (21 U.S.C. 333) is amended by inserting a new subsection (e) as follows:

"(e)(1) Except as provided in paragraph (2), whoever knowingly distributes, or possesses with intent to distribute, human growth hormone for any use in humans other than the treatment of a disease or other recognized medical condition pursuant to the order of a physician is guilty of an offense punishable by not more than 5 years in prison, such fines as are authorized by title 18, United States Code, or both.

"(2) Whoever commits any offense set forth in paragraph (1) and such offense involves an individual under 18 years of age is punishable by not more than 10 years imprisonment, such fines as are authorized by title 18, United States Code, or both.

"(3) Any conviction for a violation of paragraphs (1) and (2) of this subsection shall be considered a felony violation of the Controlled Substances Act for the purposes of forfeiture under section 413 of such Act.

"(4) As used in this subsection the term 'human growth hormone' means —

"(A) somatrem, somatropin, and any of their analogs; and

"(B) any substance which is purported, represented or labeled as being or containing any amount of any drug described in clause (A)(i), or any substance labeled as being or containing any such drug; and

"(5) The Drug Enforcement Administration is authorized to investigate offenses punishable by this subsection."

SEC 202. CONVICTION OF SECTION 303(e) OF THE FEDERAL FOOD, DRUG, AND COSMETIC ACT.

Section 2401 of the Anti-Drug Abuse Act of 1988 (Public Law 100–690; 102 Stat. 4181) is repealed.

VI. Section-by-Section Analysis

Section 1 sets forth the short title of the bill as the "Steroid Trafficking Act of 1990."

TITLE I—ANABOLIC STEROIDS

Section 101(a) adds anabolic steroids to schedule II of the Controlled Substances Act (21 U.S.C. 812(c)), the same schedule under which cocaine and opium are controlled. The Controlled Substances Acts sets forth specific criteria to determine under what schedule a specific substance should be controlled. The criteria for placing a substance under schedule II include:

(a) The drug or other substance has a high potential for abuse.

(b) The drug or other substance has a currently accepted medical use in treatment in the United States or a currently accepted medical use with severe restrictions.

(c) Abuse of the drug or other substance may lead to severe psychological and physical dependence.

The committee believes that steroids satisfy each of the criteria for control under schedule II. First, steroids have a high potential for abuse. An estimated 1 million Americans use anabolic steroids for nonmedical reasons; 500,000 of these users are high school children. Second, steroids are indicated for the treatment of certain medical conditions, including specific forms of anemia and reproductive disorders. The committee notes, however, that with the development of new drugs and given the harmful side effects associated with steroids therapy, steroids are the primary or favored pharmacological treatment for a decreasing number of medical disorders. Finally, steroid abuse may lead to severe psychological and physical dependence. As noted in the discussion section, numerous medical and public health experts have found that steroids can lead to severe psychological addiction. For example, Dr. Charles Yesalis, a leading steroids expert at Penn State University, found that 40 percent of the male high school students who use steroids were "hard-core" users. A limited number of studies have also linked steroids abuse to physical dependence. The committee concludes that the abuse potential of steroids is similar to that of cocaine hydrochloride and other so-called hard drugs, and that steroids should be regulated under the safeguards and controls of schedule II substances.

Section 101(b) creates new subsection (41) of section 102 of the Controlled Substances Act (21 U.S.C. 802), which provides a new definition for "anabolic steroids." To be classified as an anabolic steroid, and drug must be both chemically and pharmacologically related to the male hormone testosterone, and the drug must promote or purport to promote muscle growth. Section 101(b) contains a list of 27 chemicals that are to be considered anabolic steroids under the Controlled Substances Act. The list, however, is not exclusive. Any drug that meets the general definition is paragraph (A) of the new subsection (41), except human growth hormone and subject to the exemptions specified in section 102 of the bill, shall be considered an anabolic steroid. Paragraph (B) of the new subsection (41) expressly provides that counterfeit drugs that are purported, represented or labeled as containing any amount of a drug described in paragraph (A) shall be considered anabolic steroids. However, the term anabolic steroid does not include anabolic steroids that are expressly intended for use in animals and approved for such purposes by the Secretary of Health and Human Services, unless the drug is distributed for human use. In these circumstances, the drug would be considered an anabolic steroid under schedule II.

Section 101(c) sets forth an exemption under section 309(a) of the Controlled Substances Act for prescriptions subject to refill on or after the date of enactment of section 101 of the bill.

Section 101(d) provides that the effective date of section 101 shall be 90 days after the date of enactment. The committee believes that this period provides sufficient time for Federal agencies to implement their responsibilities under this act and for private industry to come into compliance with the requirements of this act.

Section 102(a) requires the Attorney General to issue regulations that exempt any compound, mixture or preparation containing a substance in the new paragraph (41) from the application of the Controlled Substances Act if, because of its concentration, preparation, mixture or delivery system, it has no significant potential for abuse. The Attorney general shall base such exemptions on the recommendation of the Secretary of Health and Human Services. At a minimum, section 102(a) authorizes and directs the Attorney General to issue regulations that exempt estrogens, progenstins and corticosteroids from the application of the Controlled Substances Act. These substances shall not be considered anabolic steroids under the new paragraph (41) of section 102 of the Controlled Substances Act. The committee recognizes that many compounds, mixtures and preparations that contain steroids have no abuse potential, such as oral contraceptives. Although these substances shall not be controlled under the Controlled Substances Act, they will continue to be regulated under the provisions of the Federal Food, Drug and Cosmetic Act.

Section 102(b) authorizes the Attorney General to exempt any substance under the new paragraph (41) and any production regulations otherwise issued under the Controlled Substances Act as may be necessary to ensure adequate supplies of such drug for medical purposes. The Attorney General, however, may only exempt substances that meet the following criteria: (1) the substance must be accepted treatment for a rare disease or condition; and (2) the substance must have no significant potential for abuse. The committee is concerned that the significant costs associated with the production controls imposed on schedule II drugs may make the production of steroids related-drugs for rare diseases excessively expensive to patients or lead pharmaceutical firms to stop production entirely. Section 102(b) is intended to balance the need to ensure adequate medical supplies of such drugs with the need to prevent the abuse of anabolic steroids, particularly among young people.

Section 102(c) provides that the regulations required under section 102(a) shall be issued not later than 180 days after the date of enactment. The regulations required under subsection (b) shall be issued not later than 45 days after the date of enactment.

TITLE II—HUMAN GROWTH HORMONE

Section 201 amends the Federal Food, Drug and Cosmetic Act (21 U.S.C. 333) to create a felony offense for trafficking in human growth hormone (HGH). Given the separate regime established under title II to control illegal HGH distribution,

HGH shall not be considered an anabolic steroid under title I. Specifically, section 201 creates a new subsection 303(e) of the Food, Drug and Cosmetic Act to make it a felony punishable by up to 5 years imprisonment for knowingly distributing, or possessing with intent to distribute, HGH for any use in humans other than the treatment of a disease or other recognized medical condition pursuant to the order of a physician. Paragraph (2) of the new subsection 333(e) of the Food, Drug and Cosmetic Act doubles the penalty for illegally distributing HGH to any person under the age of 18.

The new paragraph (3) authorizes Federal law enforcement agencies to seize and forfeit the proceeds and instrumentalities of illegal HGH distribution in the same manner and under the same procedures as authorized under section 413 of the Controlled Substances Act.

The new paragraph (4) sets forth the definition of "human growth hormone." HGH is defined as somatrem, somatropin and any analog of these substances. The definition also includes any substance that is purported, represented or labeled as being or containing any amount of HGH.

The new paragraph (5) authorizes the Drug Enforcement Administration to investigate violations involving the illegal distribution or possession of HGH and to pursue forfeiture actions under paragraph (3). Given the close link between illegal sales of anabolic steroids and HGH, this provision is needed to ensure that DEA has full authority to investigate and arrest persons for illegal distribution or possession of HGH.

Section 202 repeals section 2401 of the Anti-Drug Abuse Act. This subsection is no longer necessary, given the new and tighter restrictions and penalties contained in titles I and II of this bill.

VII. Cost Estimate

U.S. Congress,
Congressional Budget Office,
Washington, DC, March 20, 1990.

Hon. Joseph R. Biden, Jr.
Chairman, Committee on the Judiciary,
U.S. Senate, Washington, DC.

Dear Mr. Chairman: The Congressional Budget Office has reviewed S. 1829, the Steroid Trafficking Act of 1990, as ordered reported by the Senate Committee on the Judiciary, March 8, 1990.

CEO estimates that S. 1829, if enacted, would increase costs to the federal government by roughly $250,000 annually, assuming appropriation of the necessary funds. This estimate is based on information provided by the Drug Enforcement Administration (DEA) and the Food and Drug Administration (FDA). S. 1829 would amend the Controlled Substances Act to define certain anabolic steroids as controlled substances. This bill would also modify the criminal penalties for illegally distributing human growth hormone.

Under this bill, the DEA would have primary responsibility for regulating these substances; the FDA has this responsibility under current law. CBO expects that the DEA would need roughly $250,000 annually to issue regulations required by the bill and maintain records in accordance with its regulatory responsibilities under the

Controlled Substances Act. If the DEA were also to undertake an active investigatory and enforcement role, costs would be higher. There would be no significant offsetting change in costs to the FDA, because that agency spends little for this purpose.

Enactment of this bill would not affect the budgets of state or local governments.

If you wish further details on this estimate, we will be pleased to provide them. The CBO staff contact is Michael Sieverts, who can be reached at 226-2860.

Sincerely,

ROBERT F. HALE
(For Robert D. Reischauer).

VIII. REGULATORY IMPACT STATEMENT

In compliance with subsection (b) of paragraph 11 of rule XXVI of the Standing Rules of the Senate, the committee finds that the bill would have a limited regulatory impact.

Manufacturers, producers and distributors of steroids will be required to meet the record-keeping and production control requirements for schedule II controlled substances. These requirements include: registering with the Drug Enforcement Administration; storing and producing steroids in secure facilities; acquiring a production or distribution quota from DEA; and compiling and maintaining records of shipments of steroids. Since DEA already has promulgated regulations concerning the manufacture, production and distribution of schedule II controlled substances, only minor modifications or additions should be required to cover the addition of steroids to schedule II.

The bill requires the Attorney General to issue two specific sets of regulations. Section 102(a) of the bill requires the Attorney General to promulgate regulations to exempt any compound, mixture, or preparation containing a steroid if, because of its concentration, preparation, mixture or delivery system, it has no significant potential for abuse. Section 102(b) requires the Attorney General to issue regulations that exempt certain drugs in the new paragraph (41) of section 102 of the Controlled Substances Act from any production regulations as may be necessary to ensure adequate supplies of the drug for medical purposes. According to the Congressional Budget Office, the cost of issuing the regulations necessary and required under the bill is approximately $250,000.00.

IX. CHANGES IN EXISTING LAW

In compliance with paragraph 12 of rule XXVI of the Standing Rules of the Senate, changes in existing law made by S. 1829, as reported, are shown as follows (existing law proposed to be omitted is enclosed in black brackets; new matter is printed in italic, existing law in which no change is proposed is shown in roman):

UNITED STATES CODE
TITLE 21—FOOD AND DRUGS

* * * * * * *

CHAPTER 9—FEDERAL FOOD, DRUG, AND COSMETIC ACT

* * * * * * *

§333. Penalties.

* * * * * * *

(d) EXCEPTIONS INVOLVING MISBRANDED FOOD.—No person shall be subject to the penalties of subsection (a) of this section for a violation of section 331 of this title involving misbranded food if the violation exists solely because the food is misbranded under section 343(a)(2) of this title because of its advertising, and no person shall be subject to the penalties of subsection (b) of this section for such a violation unless the violation is committed with the intent to defraud or mislead.

(e) ANABOLIC STEROIDS.—[(1) Except as provided in paragraph (2), any person who distributes or possesses with the intent to distribute any anabolic steroid for any use in humans other than the treatment of disease pursuant to the order of a physician shall be imprisoned for not more than three years or fined under title 18, United States Code, or both.]

[(2) Any person who distributes or possesses with the intent to distribute to an individual under 18 years of age, any anabolic steroid for any use in humans other than the treatment of disease pursuant to the order of a physician shall be imprisoned for not more than six years or fined under title 18, United States Code, or both.] *(1) Except as provided in paragraph (2), whoever knowingly distributes, or possesses with intent to distribute, human growth hormone for any use in humans other than the treatment of a disease or other recognized medical condition pursuant to the order of a physician is guilty of an offense punishable by not more than 5 years in prison, such fines as are authorized by title 18, United States Code, or both.*

(2) Whoever commits any offense set forth in paragraph (1) and such offense involves an individual under 18 years of age is punishable by not more than 10 years imprisonment, such fines as are authorized by title 18, United States Code, or both.

(3) Any conviction for a violation of paragraphs (1) and (2) of this subsection shall be considered a felony violation of the Controlled Substances Act for the purposes of forfeiture under section 413 of such Act.

(4) As used in this subsection the term "human growth hormone" means—

(A) somatrem, somatropin, and any of their analogs; and

(B) any substance which is purported, represented or labeled as being or containing any amount of any drug described in clause (A)(i), or any substance labeled as being or containing any such drug; and

(5) The Drug Enforcement Administration is authorized to investigate offenses punishable by this subsection.

* * * * * * *

CHAPTER 13 — DRUG ABUSE PREVENTION AND CONTROL

* * * * * * *

§802. Definitions.

* * * * * * *

(40)The term "chemical mixture" means a combination of two or more chemical substances, at least one of which is not a listed precursor chemical or a listed essential chemical, except that such term does not include any combination of a listed precursor chemical or a listed essential chemical with another chemical that is present solely as an impurity.

(41) The term "anabolic steroids" means —

(A) any drug that is chemically and pharmacologically related to the male hormone testosterone and that promotes or purports to promote muscle growth, including any amount of the following chemical designations and their salts, esters, and isomers:

(i) boldenone,
(ii) chlorotestosterone,
(iii) clostebol,
(iv) dehydrochlormethyltestosterone,
(v) dihydrotestosterone,
(vi) drostanolone,
(vii) ethylestrenol,
(viii) fluoxymesterone,
(ix) formobulone,
(x) mesterolone,
(xi) methandienone,
(xii) methandranone,
(xiii) methandriol,
(xiv) methandrostenolone,
(xv) methenolone,
(xvi) methyltestosterone,
(xvii) mibolerone,
(xviii) nandrolone,
(xix) norethandrolone,
(xx) oxandrolone,
(xxi) oxymesterone,
(xxii) oxymetholone,
(xxiii) stanolone,
(xxiv) stanozolol,
(xxv) testolactone,
(xxvi) testosterone,
(xxvii) trenbolone, and

(B) any substance which is purported, represented or labeled as being or containing any amount of any drug described in subparagraph (A), or any substance labeled as being or containing any such drug.

As schedule in schedule II, such term shall not include an anabolic steroid which is expressly intended for administration through implants to cattle or other nonhuman species and which has been approved by the Secretary of Health and Human Services for such administration, except that if any person prescribes, dispenses, or distributes such steroid for human use, such person shall be considered to have prescribed, dispensed, or distributed a steroid in Schedule II of this Act.

* * * * * * *

§812. Schedules of controlled substances.

* * * * * * *

Schedule II

(a) Unless specifically excepted or unless listed in another schedule, any of the following substances whether produced directly or indirectly by extraction from substances of vegetable origin, or independently by means of chemical synthesis, or by a combination of extraction and chemical synthesis:

(1) Opium and opiate; and any salt, compound, derivative, or preparation or opium or opiate.

(2) Any salt, compound, derivative, or preparation thereof which is chemically equivalent or identical with any of the substances referred to in clause (1), except that these substances shall not include the isoquinoline alkaloids of opium.

(3) Opium poppy and poppy straw.

(4) Coca leaves and any salt, compound, derivative, or preparation of coca leaves, and any salt, compound, derivative, or preparation thereof which is chemically equivalent or identical with any of these substances, except that the substances shall not include decocanized coca leaves or extraction of coca leaves, which extractions do not contain cocaine or ecgonine.

(b) Unless specifically excepted or unless listed in another schedule, any of the following opiates, including their isomers, esters, ethers, salts, and salts of isomers, esters and ethers, whenever the existence of such isomers, esters, ethers, and salts is possible within the specific chemical designation:

(1) Alphaprodine.
(2) Anileridine.
(3) Bezitramide.
(4) Dihydrocodeine.
(5) Diphenoxylate.
(6) Fentanyl.
(7) Isomethadone.
(8) Levomethorphan.
(9) Levorphanol.
(10) Metazocine.
(11) Methadone.
(12) Methadone-Intermediate, 4-cyano-2-dimethylamino-4, 4-diphenyl butane.
(13) Moramide-Intermediate, 2-methyl-3-morpholino-1, 1-diphynyl-propane-carboxylic acid.

(14) Pethidine.
(15) Pethidine-Intermediate-A, 4-cyano-1-methyl-4-phenylpiperidene.
(16) Pethidine-Intermediate-B, ethyl-4-phenylpiperidine-4-carboxylate.
(17) Pethidine-Intermediate-C, 1-methyl-4-phenylpiperidene 4-carboxylic acid.
(18) Phenazocine.
(19) Piminodine.
(20) Racemethorphan.
(21) Racemorphan.
(22) anabolic steroids.

* * * * * * *

ANTI-DRUG ABUSE ACT OF 1989
(Public Law 100-690)

* * * * * * *

TITLE I — COORDINATION OF NATIONAL DRUG POLICY

* * * * * * *

Subtitle E — Provisions Relating to Certain Drugs

[SEC. 2401. FORFEITURE AND ILLEGAL TRAFFICKING IN STEROIDS.]

[Any conviction for a violation of section 303(e) of the Federal Food, Drug, and Cosmetic Act (21 U.S.C. 333(e)), or any other provision of that Act, involving an anabolic steroid or a human growth hormone shall be considered, for purposes of section 413 of the Controlled Substances Act (21 U.S.C. 853), a conviction for a violation of title II of the Comprehensive Drug Abuse Prevention and Control Act of 1970, if such violation of the Federal Food, Drug, and Cosmetic Act is punishable by imprisonment for more than one year.]

* * * * * * *

REFERENCES

1. William N. Taylor, *Hormonal Manipulation: A New Era of Monstrous Athletes* (Jefferson, North Carolina: McFarland, 1985), p. 10.

2. William N. Taylor, "Synthetic Anabolic-Androgenic Steroids: A Plea for Controlled Substance Status," *The Physician and Sportsmedicine* 15:5 (1987): 140–150; and L.N. Burkett and M.T. Falduto, "Steroid Use by Athletes in a Metropolitan Area," *The Physician and Sportsmedicine* 12 (1984): 69–74.

3. National Institute on Drug Abuse, "Monitoring the Future Study," 1989.

4. William E. Buckley, et al., "Estimated Prevalence of Anabolic Steroid Use Among High School Seniors." *Journal of the American Medical Association* 260 (December 1988):3441.

5. M. Johnson, et al., "Anabolic Steroid Use in Adolescent Males," *Pediatrics* (in press); and R. Windsor and D. Dimutru, "Anabolic Steroid Use in Adolescents: Survey": *Medical Science Sports Exercise* (in press); and M. Newman, "Michigan Consortium of Schools Student Surveys," Minnesota: Hazelden Research Services, 1986, as cited in Charles E. Yesalis, J.E. Wright and J.A. Lombardo, "Anabolic-Androgenic Steroids: A Synthesis of Existing Data and Recommendations for Future Research," *Clinical Sports Medicine* 1 (1989): 109–134.

6. Buckley, p. 3443. For purposes of this report, a "hard-core" user is someone who cycles five or more times, with each cycle lasting 6 to 12 weeks.
7. Ibid.
8. Charles E. Yesalis, J.E. Wright, and J.A. Lombardo, "Anabolic-Androgenic Steroids: A Synthesis of Existing Data and Recommendations for Future Research," *Clinical Sports Medicine* 1 (1989): pp. 109–134.
9. L.A. Golding, J.E. Freydinger and S.S. Fishel, "Weight, Size and Strength—Unchanged with Steroids," *The Physician and Sportsmedicine* 2 (1974): 39-43.
10. Gary I. Wadler and Brian Hainline, *Drugs and the Athlete: Contemporary Exercise and Sports Medicine* (Philadelphia: F.A. Davis Co., 1989), p. 65, and John R. Bierly, M.D. "Use of Anabolic Steroids by Athletes: Do the Risks Outweigh the Benefits?" *Postgraduate Medicine* 82 (September 1, 1987): 72.
11. Bierly, p. 74.
12. Robert E. Windsor and Daniel Dumitru, "Anabolic Steroid Use by Athletes: How Serious Are the Health Hazards?" *Postgraduate Medicine* 84 (September 15, 1988): 49, and William P. Morgan, ed., "Ergogenic Aids and Muscular Performance" (New York: Academic Press, 1982), p. 381, and Terry Todd, "The Steroid Predicament," *Sports Illustrated* 59 (August 1, 1983): p. 71.
13. Bierly, p. 74.
14. Bierly, p. 72.
15. Todd, p. 71, and Jodie Slothower, "Mean Mental Muscles: The Psychological Price of Steroids," *Health*, January 1988, p. 20, and Taylor, "Steroid Use Among Health Club Athletes," p. 158; Bierly, p. 71; Strauss, "Side Effects of Anabolic Steroids in Weight-Trained Men," p. 93; Taylor, *Hormonal Manipulation*, p. 16; Wadler, p. 66; Windsor, p. 47; and Betsy Carpenter, "A Game of Cat and Mouse: There's a New Olympic Event Pitting Athletes Against Drug Busters," *U.S. News & World Report*, October 10, 1988, p. 38.
16. W.J. Annitto and W.A. Layman, "Anabolic Steroids and Acute Schizophrenic Episode," *Journal of Clinical Psychiatry* 41 (1980): 143; and Montgomery Brower and Carol Azizian, "Steroids Build Mike Keys Up; Then They Tore Him Down," *People*, March 20, 1989; pp. 107–108.
17. *Sixty Minutes*, CBS News, "Beefing Up The Force," November 5, 1989.
18. Brower and Azizian, p. 108.
19. Harrison G. Pope, Jr., and David L. Katz, "Affective and Psychotic Symptoms Associated with Anabolic Steroid Use," *The American Journal of Psychiatry* 145 (4)(1988): 487–90.
20. Terrence Monmaney with Kate Robbins, "The Insanity of Steroid Abuse: The Drug Can Give Athletes Major Mental Problems," *Newsweek*, May 23, 1988, p. 75, quoted in Harrison G. Pope, Jr., and David L. Katz, "Affective and Psychotic Symptoms Associated with Anabolic Steroid Use," *The American Journal of Psychiatry* 145 (4)(1988): 487.
21. Taylor, *Hormonal Manipulation*, p. 16.
22. W.R. Yates, P.J. Perry, and K.H. Andersen "Illicit Anabolic Steroid Use: A Controlled Personality Study," *Acta Psychiatrica Scand* 1990 (in press).
23. Kirk J. Brower, M.D., "Rehabilitation for Anabolic-Androgenic Steroid Dependence," based on a paper presented at the National Consensus Meeting on Anabolic/Androgenic Steroids, in press, pp. 4–5.
24. Brower, et al., "Anabolic-Androgenic Steroid Dependence," p 31.
25. Ibid.
26. Brower, "Rehabilitation," p. 2.
27. Buckley, p. 3443.
28. Wayne V. Moore, Ph.D., M.D., "Anabolic Steroid Use in Adolescence," *Journal of the American Medical Association* 260 (December 16, 1988): 3486; Windsor and Dimutru, p. 48; and Brower, et al., "Anabolic-Androgenic Steroid Dependence," p. 31.
29. Brower, et al., "Rehabilitation," p. 32.
30. Wayne V. Moore, p. 3486.
31. Charles E. Yesalis, et al., "Anabolic Steroid Use: Indications of Habituation Among Adolescents," *Journal of Drug Education* 19(2) (1989): 103–116.
32. Brower, "Rehabilitation," p. 9.
33. Ibid., p. 10.

Notes

Introduction

1. Kusserow, R.P. *Adolescent Steroid Use*. Department of Health and Human Services, Office of Inspector General, United States Government Printing Office, Washington, D.C., February 1991, p.5.

2. Lamberts, S.W., A.W. van der Beld, and A.J. van der Lely. The endocrinology of aging. *Science* 1997;278(5337):419–424.

3. Roubenoff, R. Sarcopenia: A major modifiable cause of frailty in the elderly. *J. Nutr. Health Aging* 2000;4(3):140–142.

4. Hermann, M., and P. Berger. Hormone replacement in the aging male? *Exp. Gerontol.* 1999;34(8):923–933.

5. Tenover, J.S. Androgen replacement therapy to reverse and/or prevent age-related sarcopenia in men. *Baillieres Clin. Endocrinol. Metab.* 1998;12(3):419–425.

6. Bakhshi, V., M. Elliott, A. Gentili, et al. Testosterone improves rehabilitation outcomes in ill older men. *J. Am. Geriatr. Soc.* 2000;48(5):550–3.

7. Tenover, J.S. Effects of testosterone supplementation in the aging male. *J. Clin. Endocrinol. Metab.* 1992;75(4):1092–1098.

8. Synder, P.J., H. Peachey, P. Hannoush, et al. Effect of testosterone treatment on body composition and muscle strength in men over 65 years of age. *J. Clin. Endocrinol. Metab.* 1999;84(8):2647–2653.

9. Lund, B.C., K.A. Bever-Stille, and P.J. Perry. Testosterone and andropause: The feasibility of testosterone replacement therapy in elderly men. *Pharmacotherapy* 1999; 19(8):951–956.

10. Tenover, J.L. Male hormone replacement therapy including "andropause." *Endocrinol. Metab. Clin. North Am.* 1998;27(4):969–987.

11. Casaburi, R. Rationale for anabolic therapy to facilitate rehabilitation in chronic obstructive pulmonary disease. *Baillieres Clin. Endocrinol. Metab.* 1998;12(3): 407–418.

12. Morley, J.E., and H.M. Perry. Androgen deficiency in aging men. *Med. Clin. North Am.* 1999;83(5):1279–1289.

13. Castelo-Branco, C., J.J. Vicente, F. Figueras, et al. Comparative effects of estrogens plus androgens and tibolone on bone, lipid pattern and sexuality in postmenopausal women. *Maturitas* 2000;34(2):161–168.

14. Reid, I.R., D.J. Wattie, M.C. Evans, et al. Testosterone therapy in glucocorticoid-treated men. *Arch. Intern. Med.* 1996;156(11):1173–1177.

15. Saloman, F., R.C. Cuneo, R. Hesp, et al. The effects of treatment with recombinant

human growth hormone on body composition and metabolism in adults with growth hormone deficiency. *N. Engl. J. Med.* 1989;321(26):1797–1803.

16. Jiang, Z., G. He, X. Wang, et al. [The effect of nutrition support and recombinant growth hormone on body composition and muscle function in postoperative patients]. *Chung Kuo I. Hsueh. Ko Hsueh Yuan Hsueh Pao* 1994;16(6):443–447.

17. Bhasin, S., T.W. Storer, N. Asbel-Sethi, et al. Effects of testosterone replacement with a nongenital transdermal system, Androderm, in human immunodeficiency virus-infected men with low testosterone levels. *J. Clin. Endocrinol. Metab.* 1998;83(9): 3155–3162.

18. Schambelan, M., K. Mulligan, C. Grunfeld, et al. Recombinant human growth hormone in patients with HIV-associated wasting. *Ann. Intern. Med.* 1996;125(11): 873–882.

19. Taaffe, D.R., L. Pruitt, J. Reim, et al. Effect of recombinant human growth hormone on the muscle strength response to resistance exercise in elderly men. *J. Clin. Endocrinol. Metab.* 1994;79(5):1361–1366.

20. Strawford, A., T. Barbieri, M. Van Loan, et al. Resistance exercise and supraphysiologic androgen therapy in eugonadal men with HIV-related weight loss: A randomized controlled trial. *JAMA* 1999;281(14):1282–1290.

21. Grinspoon, S., C. Corcoran, H. Askari, et al. Effects of androgen administration in men with the AIDS wasting syndrome: A randomized, double-blind, placebo-controlled trial. *Ann. Intern. Med.* 1998;129(1):18–26.

22. Bhasin, S., T.W. Storer, M. Javanbakht, et al. Testosterone replacement and resistance exercise in HIV-infected men with weight loss and low testosterone levels. *JAMA* 2000;283(6):763–770.

23. Sattler, F.R., S.V. Jaque, E.T. Schroder, et al. Effects of pharmacological doses of nandrolone decanoate and progressive resistance training in immunodeficient patients infected with human immunodeficiency virus. *J. Clin. Endocrinol. Metab.* 1999;84(4): 1268–1276.

24. Giorgi, A., R.P. Weatherby, and P.W. Murphy. Muscular strength, body composition and health responses to the use of testosterone enanthate: A double blind study. *J. Sci. Med. Sport* 1999;2(4):341–355.

25. Taylor, W.N. *Hormonal Manipulation: A New Era of Monstrous Athletes.* Jefferson, N.C.: McFarland & Company, 1985, p.126.

26. "Steroid Abuse," *USA Today*, August 31, 1988, p.D-1.

27. Editorial, *The Kansas City Star*, August 30, 1988, p. A-1.

28. Cannon, A. Steroid-using police cause brutality fears. *The Miami Herald.* May 27, 1987, p.A1.

29. "Popping steroids and pumping lead." *Time*, December 4, 1989, p.4.

30. Kusserow, R.P. *Adolescent Steroid Use.* Department of Health and Human Services, Office of Inspector General, United States Government Printing Office, Washington, D.C., February 1991, p.4.

31. "Steroids Crackdown." *USA Today*, November 30, 1990, p.A-1.

32. "Banned Substance." *USA Today*, November 2, 1989, p.A-1.

33. Taylor, W.N. *Hormonal Manipulation: A New Era of Monstrous Athletes.* Jefferson, NC.: McFarland & Company, 1985, p.ix.

Chapter 1

1. Ruzicka, L., A. Wettstein, and H. Kaegi. Sexualhoromone VIII Darstellung von Testosteron unter Anwedung gemischster ester. *Helv. Chim. Acta* 1935;18:1478.

2. Butenandt, A. and G. Hanisch. Uber Testosteron, Umwandlund des Dehydroandrosterons in Androstendiol und Testosterone; Ein Weg zur Darstellun des Testosterons aus Cholesterin. *Ztschr. F. Physiol Chem.* 1935;237:89.

3. Taylor, W.N. *Macho Medicine: A History of the Anabolic Steroid Epidemic.* Jefferson, N.C.: McFarland & Company, 1991.

4. Curtis, J.M. and E. Witt. Activities of the Food and Drug Administration in the field of sex hormones. *J. Clin. Endocrin.* 1941;1:363–365.

5. Goldman, B. *Death in the Locker Room.* South Bend, Ind.: Icarus Press, 1985.

6. Longcope, C. Adrenal and gonadal androgen secretion in normal females. *J. Clin. Endocrinol. Metab.* 1986;15:213.

7. Judd, H.L., and S.S. Yen. Serum androstenedione and testosterone levels during the menstrual cycle. *J. Clin. Endocrinol. Metab.* 1973;36:475–481.

8. Salmon, U.J., and S.H. Geist. Effect of androgens upon libido in women. *J. Clin. Endocrinol. Metab.* 1943;3:235–238.

9. Taylor, W.N. *Anabolic Steroids and the Athlete.* Jefferson, N.C.: McFarland and Company, 1982.

10. Taylor, *Macho Medicine.*

Chapter 2

1. Korenchevsky, V., and M. Dennison. The assay of fat soluble androsteronediol. *Biochem. J.* 1935;26:2122–2130.

2. _____, and S.L. Simpson. The effects of water soluble preparation of androsterone and androsterone-diol on castrated rats. *Biochem. J.* 1935;29:2131–2142.

3. Kochakian, C. D. The comparative efficacy of various androgens as determined by the rat assay method. *Endocrinology* 1938;22:181–192.

4. _____. The rate of aborption and effects of testosterone propionate pellets on mice. *Endocrinology* 1941;28:181–192.

5. _____. A comparison of the dose with the androgenic activities of various steroids. *Am. J. Physiol.* 1944;142:315–325.

6. _____. The effect of dose and nutritive state on the renotrophic and androgenic activities of various steroids. *Am. J. Physiol.* 1946;145:549–556.

7. _____. Renotrophic-androgenic and somatotropic properties of further steroids. *Am. J. Physiol.* 1949;258:51–56.

8. Chang, C.T., and H. Liu. The anabolic and androgenic activities of 17-alpha methyltestoterone and related steroids in castrated rats and mice. *Biochem. Sect. Chem. Abst.* 1965;62(3):15.

9. Baldratti, G., and G. Arcari. The anabolizing effect of 4-hydroxy-17-alpha methyltestosterone. *Panminerva Med.* 1962;4:137–139.

10. Serizawa, J. Studies on the effect of adrenal on the bioassay of androgen. *Endocrin. Jap.* 1962;7:61–75.

11. Kochakian, C.D., C. Tillotson, and J. Austin. A comparison of the effect of inanition, castration and testosterone on the muscles of the male guinea pig. *Endocrinology* 1957;60:144–152.

12. Hershberger, L.G., E.G. Shipley, and R.K. Meyer. Myotrophic activity of 19-nortestosterone and other steroids determined by modified levator ani muscle method. *Proc. Soc. Exp. Biol. Med.* 1953;83:175–180.

13. Edgren, R.A., H. Smith, and G.A. Hughes. Biological effects of synthetic gonanes. *Rec. Prog. Hormone Res.* 1966;22:305–341.

14. Dorfman, R.I., and R.A. Kinel. Relative potency of various steroids in an anabolic-androgenic assay using the castrated rat. *Endocrinology* 1963;72:259–266.

15. Vida, J.A. *Androgens and Anabolic Agents* New York: Academic Press, 1969.

16. Steinetz, B.G., T. Butler, T. Giannina, et al. The role of growth hormone in the anabolic action of menthandrostenolone. *Endocrinology* 1972;90:1396-1398.

17. Overbeek, G.A., A. Delver, and J. deVisser. Pharmacological comparisons of anabolic steroids. *Acta Endocrin.* 1962;39:7-11.

18. Stafford, R.O., B.J. Bowman, and K.J. Olsen. Influence of 19-nortestosterone cyclopentylproprionate on urinary nitrogen of castrated male rats. *Proc. Soc. Exp. Biol. Med.* 1954;86:322-329.

19. Arnold, A.A., A.L. Beyer, and G.O. Potts. Androstanazole, a new orally active steroid. *Proc. Soc. Exp. Biol. Med.* 1959;102:184-187.

20. Potts, G.O., A.A. Arnold, and A.L. Beyer. Comparative myotrophic and nitrogen retaining effects of several steroids. *Endocrinology* 1960;67:849-854.

21 Beyer, A.L., G.O. Potts, and A. Arnold. Influence of molecular unsaturation on hormonal activity pattern of certain heterocyclic steroids. *Endocrinology* 1961;68:987-995.

22. Arnold, A. Evaulation of the protein anabolic properties of certain orally active agents based on nitrogen balance studies in rats. *Endocrinology* 1963;72:408-417.

23. Arnold, A., G.O. Potts, and A. L. Beyer. The ratio of anabolic to androgenic activity of 7, 17-dimethyltestosterone, oxymesterone, mestanolone, and fluoromesterone. *J. Endocrinol.* 1963;28:87-92.

24. Arnold, A. and G.O. Potts. Oral anabolic-androgenic evaluations of four anabolic steroids. *Acta Endocrinol.* 1966;52:489–496.

25. Saunders, F.J. and V.A. Drill. Nitrogen retaining properties of 17-ethyl-19-nortestosterone. *Metabolism* 1958;7:315–321.

26. Lennon, H.D. and F.J. Saunders. Anabolic activity of 2-oxa-17-alpha-methyldihydrotestosterone (Oxandrolone). *Steroids* 1964;4:689–697.

27. Ruggieri, P., R. Matscher, R. Gondolfi, et al. A new steroid with protein anabolic activity: dimethazine. *Arch. Sci. Biol.* 1963;47:1–19.

28. Sala, G., G. Baldratti, and R. Ronchi. Influence of 4-chlorotestosterone, 4-chloro-19-nortestosterone and testosterone on the nitrogen balance in rats. *Folio Endocr. Pisa.* 1957;10:729–735.

29. Aschkenasy, A., G. Bouard, and C. Neveu. Protein anabolic effect and acute and chronic toxicities of 17-ethyl-19-nortestosterone. *Therapie* 1959;14:332–349.

30. Tomarelli, R.M. and F.W. Bernhart. Oral anabolic activity of 13-beta-17-alpha-diethyl-17-beta-hydroxy-4-gonene-3-one (Norbolethone) in a nitrogen balance assay. *Steroids* 1964;4:451–456.

31. Stucki, J.C., A.D. Forbes, J.I. Nothem, et al. An assay for anabolic steroid employing metabolic balance in the monkey. The anabolic activity of fluoroxymesterone and its 11-keto analog. *Endocrinology* 1960;66:585–596.

32. Lyster, S.C. and G.W. Duncan. Anabolic, androgenic and myotrophic activities of derivatives of 7-alpha-methyl-19-nortestosterone. *Acta Endocrinol.* 1963;43:399–411.

33. Albanese, A.A., E.J. Lorenze, and L.A. Orto. Nutritional and metabolic effects of some newer steroids. I. Oxandrolone and triamcinolone. *N.Y. St. J. Med.* 1962;63:1607–1613.

34. Albanese, A.A. Newer methodology in the clinical investigation of anabolic steroids. *J. New Drugs* 1965;5:208–224.

35. Alabanese, A.A., E.J. Lorenze, L.A. Orto, et al. Nutritional and metabolic effects of some newer steroids. III. Stanozolol. *N.Y. St. J. Med.* 1964;64:864–873.

36. Liddle, G.W. and A.H. Burke. Anabolic steroids in clinical medicine. *Helv. Med. Acta* 1960;27:504–513.

37. Fox, M., A.S. Minot, and G.W. Liddle. Oxandrolone: a potent anabolic steroid of novel chemical configuration. *J. Clin. Endocrinol. Metab.* 1962;22:921–924.

38. Metcalf, W. and H.C. Greene. A quantitative expression for nitrogen retention with anabolic steroids. I. Norethandrolone. *Metabolism* 1963;12:899–909.

39. Metcalf, W. and J. Brioch. A rapid reproducible and sensitive levator ani test for anabolic activity. *Proc. Soc. Exp. Biol. Med.* 1961;107:744–748.

40. Metcalf, W., J. Roach, and A. Ohin. A quantitative expression for nitrogen retention with anabolic steroids. III. Nortestosterone dipropionate. *Metabolism* 1964;13:539–546.

41. Metcalf, W., E.L. Dargan, C. Suwanraks, et al. A quantitative expression for nitrogen retention for anabolic steroids. II. Norethandrolone propionate comparison with testosterone propionate. *Metabolism* 1963;12:910–923.

42. Foss, G.L. The oral application of methyl testosterone and its simplification of androgen therapy. *Br. Med. J.* 1939;1:11–12.

43. Foss, G.L. A comparison of the relative efficacy of methyltestosterone by the gastric and oral transmucosal routes. *J. Endocrinol.* 1956;13:269–273.

44. Alkalay, d., L. Khemani, W.E. Wagner, et al. Sublingual and oral administration of methyltestosterone. A comparison of drug bioavailability. *J. Clin. Pharmacol.* 1973;13:142–151.

45. Segaloff, A., R.B. Gabbard, B.T. Carriere, et al. The metabolism of 17-alpha-methyltestosterone. *Steroids* 1965;1(suppl):149–158.

46. Mosbach, E.H., S. Shefer, and L.L. Abell. Identification of the fecal metabolites of 17-alpha-methyltestosterone in the dog. *J. Lipid Res.* 1968;9:93–97.

47. Alkalay, D., L. Khemani, and M.F. Bartlett. Spectrophotofluorometric determination of methyltestosterone in plasma or serum. *J. Pharm. Sci.* 1972;61:1746–1749.

48. James, K.C., P.J. Nicholls, and M. Roberts. Biological half-lives of radioactive testosterone and some of its esters after injection into the rat. *J. Pharm. Pharmacol.* 1969;21:24–27.

49. Honrath, W.L., A. Wolff, and A. Meli. The influence of the amount of solvent (sesame oil) on the degree and duration of action of subcutaneously administered testosterone and its proprionate. *Steroids* 1963;2:425–428.

50. Caminos-Torres, R., L. Ma, and P.J. Snyder. Testosterone-induced inhibition of the LH and FSH responses to gonadotropin-releasing hormone occurs slowly. *J. Clin. Endocrinol. Metab.* 1977;44:1142.

51. Junkmann, K. Long-acting steroids in reproduction. *Recent Prog. Horm. Res.* 1957;13:389–419.

52. Hirschhauser, C., C.R.N. Hopkinson, G. Sturm, et al. Testosterone undecanoate: A new orally active androgen. *Acta Endocrinol.* 1975;80:179–187.

53. Coert, A., J. Greelen, J. de Visser, et al. The pharmacology and metabolism of testosterone undecanoate (TU), a new orally active androgen. *Acta Endocrinol.* 1975;79:789–800

54. Nieschlag, E., J. Mauss, A. Coert, et al. Plasma androgen levels in men after oral administration of testosterone or testosterone undecanoate. *Acta Endocrinol.* 1975;79:366–374.

55. Rogozkin, V. and B. Feldkoren. The effect of retabolil and training on activity of RNA polymerase in skeletal muscle. *Med. Sci. Sports* 1979;11(4):345–347.

56. Liao, S., T. Liang, S. Fang, et al. Steroid structure and androgenic activity. Specificity involved in the receptor binding and nuclear retention of various androgens. *J. Biol. Chem.* 1973;248:6154–6157.

57. Price, V.H. Testosterone metabolism in the skin. *Arch. Dermatol.* 1975;111:1496–1502.

58. Wilson, J.D. and J.E. Griffin. The use and misuse of androgens. *Metabolism* 1980;29(12):1278–1295.

59. Wilson, J.D. and J.D. Walker. The conversion of testosterone to 5-alpha-androstan-17-beta-ol-3-one (dihydrotestosterone) by skin slices of man. *J. Clin. Invest.* 1969;48:371–379.

60. Lee, I.R., L.C. Greed, J.D. Wetherall, et al. Comparative measurements of plasma binding capacity and concentration of human sex hormone binding globulin. *Clin. Chim. Acta* 1984;137:131–139.

61. Belgorosky, A. and M.A. Rivarola. Dynamics of SHBG response to testosterone. Implications upon the immediate biological effect of sex hormones. *J. Steroid Biochem.* 1983;18:783–787.

62. Jones, T.M., V.S. Fang, R.L. Landau, et al. The effect of fluoxymesterone administration on testicular function. *J. Clin. Endocrinol. Metab.* 1977;44:121–129.

63. Holma, P. and H. Adlercreutz. Effect of an anbolic steroid (metandienon) on plasma LH, FSH, and testosterone on the response to intravenous administration of LRH. *Acta Endocrinol.* 1976;83:856–864.

64. Vigersky, R.A., R.B. Easley, and D.L. Loriaux. Effect of fluoxymesterone on the pituitary-gonadal axis. The role of testosterone-estradiol-binding globulin. *J. Clin. Endocrinol. Metab.* 1976;43:1–9.

65. Repcekova, D. and L. Mikulaj. Plasma testosterone response to HCG in normal men without and after administration of anabolic drug. *Endokrinologie* 1977;69:115–118.

66. Martin, L.G., M.S. Grossman, T.B. Connor, et al. Effect of androgen on growth hormone secretion and growth in boys with short stature. *Acta Endocrinol.* 1979;91:201–212.

67. Hopwood, N.J., R.P. Kelch, W.B. Zipf, et al. The effect of synthetic androgens on the hypothalamic-pituitary-gonadal axis in boys with constitutionally delayed growth. *J. Pediatr.* 1979;94:657–662.

68. Moore, D.C., D.S. Tattoni, G.A. Limbeck, et al. Studies of anabolic steroids. V. Effect of prolonged oxandrolone administration on growth in children and adolescents with uncomplicated short stature. *Pediatrics* 1976;58:412–422.

69. Wright, J.E. *Anabolic Steroids and Sports.* Natick, M.A.: Sports Science Consultants, 1978.

70. Taylor, W.N. *Macho Medicine: A History of the Anabolic Steroid Epidemic.* Jefferson, N.C.: McFarland & Company, Inc., Publishers, 1991.

71. Goodman, L.S. and A. Gilman. *The Pharmacological Basis of Therapeutics.* Toronto and London: W.B. Saunders Company, p.1570, 1970.

72. Wilson, J.D., and J.E. Griffin. The use and misuses of androgens. *Metabolism* 1980; 29(12): 1289.

Chapter 4

1. Van der Vies, J. Pharmacokinetics of anabolic steroids. *Wien Med. Wochenschr.* 1993;143(14–15):366–368.

2. Minto, C.F., C. Howe, S. Wishart, et al. Pharmacokinetics and pharmacodynamics of nandrolone esters in oil vehicle: Effects of ester, injection site and injection volume. *Pharmacol. Exp. Therapuetics* 1997;281(1):93–102.

3. Behre, H.M., F. Oberenning, and E. Nieschlag. Comparative pharmakinetics of androgen preparations: Application of computer analysis and simulation. *In Testosterone: Action in Deficiency Substitution*, ed. by E. Nieschlag and H. M. Behre, pp. 115–135, Springer-Verlag, Berlin, 1990.

4. Tanaka, T., H. Kobayashi, K. Okamura, et al. Intramuscular absorption of drugs from oily solutions in the rat. *Chem. Pharm. Bull.* 1974;22:1275–1284.

5. Fujioka, M., Y. Shinohara, S. Baba, et al. Pharmacokinetic properties of testosterone propionate in normal men. *J. Clin. Endocrinol. Metab.* 1986;63:1361–1364.

6. Schulte-Breebuhl, M. and E. Nieschlag. Comparison of testosterone, dihydrotestosterone, luteinizing hormone, and follicle-stimulating hormone in serum after injection of testosterone enanthate or testosterone cypionate. *Fertil. Steril.* 1980;33: 201–203.

7. Cockshott, W.P., G.T. Thompson, L.J. Howlett, et al. Intramuscular or intralipomatous injections? *N. Engl. J. Med.* 1982;307:356–358.

8. Modderman, E.S., M. Merkus, F.W.H.M. Zuidema, et al. Sex differences in the absorption of dapsone after intramuscular injection. *Int. J. Leprosy* 1983;41:359–365.

9. Bederka, J., A. Takemori, A.E. Miller, et al. Absorption rates of various substances administered intramuscularly. *Eur. J. Pharmacol.* 1971;15:132–136.

10. Evans, E.F., J.D. Proctor, M. Fratkin, et al. Blood flow in muscle groups and drug absorption. *Clin. Pharmacol. Ther.* 1975;17:44–47.

11. Minto, et al. Pharmacokinetics and pharmacodynamics of nandrolone esters in oil vehicle: Effects of ester, injection site and injection volume. *Pharmacol. Exp. Therapuetics* 1997;281(1):93–102.

12. Al-Hindawi, M.K., K.C. James, and P.J. Nicholls. Influence of solvent on the availability of testosterone propionate from oily, intramuscular injections in the rat. *J. Pharm. Pharmacol.* 1986;39:90–95.

13. Minto, et al. Pharmacokinetics and pharmacodynamics of nandrolone esters in oil vehicle: Effects of ester, injection site and injection volume. *Pharmacol. Exp. Therapuetics* 1997;281(1):93–102.

14. Rich, J.D., B.P. Dickinson, T.P. Flannigan, et al. Abscess related to anabolic-androgenic steroid injection. *Med. Sci. Sports Exerc.* 1999;31(2):207–209.

15. Midgley, J.S., N. Heather, D. Best, et al. Risk behaviour for HIV and hepatitis infection among anabolic-androgenic steroid users. *AIDS Care* 2000;12(2):163–170.

16. Bolding, G., L. Sherr, M. Maguire, et al. HIV risk behaviours among gay men who use anabolic steroids. *Addiction* 1999;94(12):1829–1835.

17. Elford, J., G. Bolding, M. Maguire, et al. Do gay men discuss HIV risk reduction with their GP? *AIDS Care* 2000;12(3):287–290.

18. Greenblatt, D.J., and J. Kock-Weser. Intramuscular injection of drugs. *N. Engl. J. Med.* 1976;542–546.

19. Williams, R.O., T.L. Rogers, and J. Liu. Study of solubility of steroids in hydrofluoroalkane propellants. *Drug. Dev. Ind. Pharm.* 1999;25(12):1227–1234.

20. Catlin, D.H., C.K. Hatton, and S.H. Starcevic. Issues in detecting abuse of xenobiotic anabolic steroids and testosterone by analysis of athletes' urine. *Clin. Chem.* 1997;43(7):1280–1288.

21. Salehian, B., C. Wang, G. Alexander, et al. Pharmacokinetics, bioefficacy, and safety of sublingual testosterone cyclodextrin in hypogonadal men: Comparison to testosterone enanthate — a clinical research center study. *J. Clin. Endocrinol. Metab.* 1995;90 (12):3567–3575.

22. Maibach, H.I., and R.J. Feldmann. The effect of DMSO on percutaneous penetration of hydrocortisone and testosterone in man. *Ann. N.Y. Acad. Sci.* 1967;141 (1):423–427.

23. Holden, H.E., R.E. Stoll, and K.T. Blanchard. Oxymetholone: II. Evaulation in the Tg-AC transgenic mouse model detection of carcinogens. *Toxicol. Pathol.* 1999;27(5):507–512.

24. Melvin, W.S., L.G. Boros, P. Muscarella, et al. Dehydroepiandrosterone-sulfate inhibits pancreatic carcinoma cell proliferation in vitro and in vivo. *Surgery* 1997;121(4):392–397.

25. Schmidt, W.N., and B.S. Katzenellenbogen. Androgen-uterine interactions: An assessment of androgen interaction with testosterone- and estrogen-receptor systems and stimulation of uterine growth and progesterone receptor synthesis. *Mol. Cell. Endocrinol.* 1979;15(2):91–108.

26. Kumon, Y., S.C. Kim, P. Tompkins, et al. Neuroprotective effect of postischemic administration of progesterone in spontaneously hypertensive rats with focal cerebral ischemia. *J. Neurosurg.* 2000;92(5):848–852.

27. Thomas, A.J., R.P. Nockels, H.Q. Pan, et al. Progesterone is neuroprotective after acute experimental spinal cord trauma in rats. *Spine* 1999;24(20):2134–2138.

28. Kim, N., M. El-Khalili, M.M. Henary, et al. Percutaneous penetration enhancement activity of aromatic S,S-dimethyliminosulfuranes. *Int. J. Pharm.* 1999;187(2): 219–229.

29. Pirborsky, J., K. Takayama, T. Nagai, et al. Combination effect of penetration enhancers and propylene glycol on in vitro transdermal absorption of insulin. *Drug Des. Deliv.* 1987;2(2):91–97.

30. Asbill, C.S., and B.B. Michniak. Percutaneous penetration enhancers: Local versus transdermal activity. *Pharm. Sci. Technol. Today* 2000;3(1):36–41.

31. Mora, M.P., C. Tourne-Peteilh, M. Charveron, et al. Optimisation of plant sterols incorporarion in human keratinocyte plasma membrane and modulation of membrane fluidity. *Chem. Phys. Lipids* 1999;101(2):255–265.

32. Almekinders, L.C. Anti-inflammatory treatment of muscular injuries in sport: An update of recent studies. *Sports Med.* 1999;28(6):282–288.

33. Beiner, J.M., P. Jokl, J. Cholewicki, et al. The effect of anabolic steroids and corticosteroids on healing of muscle contusion injury. *Am. J. Sports Med.* 1999;27(1):2–9.

34. Taylor, W.N.: personal observations from powerlifters.

35. Ritsch, M., and F. Musshoff. [Dangers and risks of black market anabolic steroid abuse in sports — gas chromatography-mass spectrometry analyses]. *Sportvrletz Sportschaden* 2000;14(1):1–11.

36. Musshoff, F., T. Daldrup, and M. Ritsch. [Anabolic steroids on the German black market]. *Arch. Kriminol.* 1999;(5–6):152–158.

37. Creatine and Andro: Muscle-builders or health-breakers? *Harvard Health Watch* 2000;4(6):6–8.

38. Yesalis, C.E. Medical, legal, and societal implications of androstenedione use. *JAMA* 1999;281(21):2043–2044.

39. Kachhi, P.N., and S.O. Henderson. Priapism after androstenedione intake for athletic performance enhancement. *Ann. Emerg. Med.* 2000;35(4):391–393.

40. Curtis, J.M., and E. Witt. Activities of the Food and Drug Administration in the field of sex hormones. *J. Clin. Endocrinol.* 1941;1:363–365.

41. The Steroid Trafficking Act of 1990, United States Senate, 101st Congress, submitted from the Committee on the Judiciary, United States Government Printing Office, Washington , D.C.

42. Foundation asks FDA to ban andro sales. *Pensacola News Journal.* March 21, 2000, p. A-1.

43. Baseball: Sport ponders andro ban. *The Tampa Tribune.* October 30, 1998, p. Sports-4.

44. In brief. *The Tampa Tribune.* August 28, 1998, p. Sports-3.

45. Uralets, V.P., and P.A. Gillette. Over-the-counter delta5 anabolic steroids 5-androsten-3,17-dione; 5-androsten-3beta, 17-beta-diol; dehydroepiandrosterone; and 19-nor-5-androsten-3,17-dione: Excretion studies in men. *J. Anal. Toxicol.* 2000;24 (3):188–193.

46. King, D.S., R.L. Sharp, M.D. Vucovich, et al. Effect of oral androstenedione on serum testosterone and adaptations to resistance training in young men: A randomized controlled trial. *JAMA* 1999;281(21):2020–2028.

47. Wallace, M.B., J. Lim, A. Cutler, et al. Effects of dehydroepiandrosterone vs. androstenedione supplementation in men. *Med. Sci. Sports Exerc.* 1999;31(12):1788–1792.

48. Rasmussen, B.B., E. Volpi, D.C. Gore, et al. Androstenedione does not stimulate muscle protein anabolism in young healthy men. *J. Clin. Endocrinol. Metab.* 2000; 85(1):55–59.

49. Earnest, C.P., M.A. Olson, C.E. Broeder, et al. In vivo 4-androstene-3,17-dione and 4-androstene-3 beta,17-beta-diol supplementation in young men. *Eur. J. Appl. Physiol.* 2000;81(3):229–232.

50. Leder, B.Z., C. Longcope, D.H. Catlin, et al. Oral androstenedione administration and serum testosterone concentrations in young men. *JAMA* 283(6):779–782.

51. Ballantyne, C.S., S.M. Phillips, J.R. MacDonald, et al. The acute effects of androstenedione supplementation in healthy young males. *Can. J. Appl. Physiol.* 2000; 25(1):68–78.

52. Barnhart, K.T., E. Freeman, J.A. Grisso, et al. The effect of dehydroepiandrosterone supplementation to symptomatic perimenopausal women on serum endocrine profiles, lipid parameters, and health-related quality of life. *J. Clin. Endocrinol. Metab.* 1999;84(11):3896–3902.

53. Wolf, O.T., O. Neumann, D.H. Hellhammer, et al. Effects of a two-week physiological dehydroepiandrosterone substitution on cognitive performance and well-being in healthy elderly women and men. *J. Clin. Endocrinol. Metab.* 1997;82(7):2363–2367.

54. Labrie, F., A. Belanger, V. Luu-The, et al. DHEA and the intracrine formation of androgens and estrogens in peripheral target tissues: Its role during aging. *Steroids* 1998;63(5–6):322–328.

55. Harper, A.J., J.E. Buster, and P.R. Casson. Changes in adrenocortical function with aging and therapeutic implications. *Semin. Reprod. Endocrinol.* 1999;17(4): 327–338.

56. Baulieu, E.E., G. Thomas, S. Legrain, et al. Dehydroepiandrosterone (DHEA), DHEA sulfate, and aging: Contribution of the DHEAge Study to a sociobiomedical issue. *Proc. Natl. Acad. Sci. U.S.A.* 2000;97(8):4279–4284.

57. Shomali, M.E. The use of anti-aging hormones. Melatonin, growth hormone, testosterone, and dehydroepiandrosterone: Consumer enthusiasm for unproven therapies. *Maryland Med. J.* 1997;46(4):181–186.

58. Flynn, M.A., D. Weaver-Osterholtz, K.L. Sharpe-Timms, et al. Dehydroepiandrosterone replacement in aging humans. *J. Clin. Endocrinol. Metab.* 1999;84 (5):1527–1533.

59. Schmidt, M., M. Kreutz, G. Loffler, et al. Conversion of dehydroepiandrosterone to downstream steroid hormones in macrophages. *J. Endocrinol.* 2000;164 (2):161–169.

60. Van Vollenhoven, R.F., J.L. Park, M.C. Genovese, et al. A double-blind, placebo-controlled, clinical trial of dehydroepiandrosterone in severe systemic lupus erythematosus. *Lupus* 1999;8(3):181–187.

61. Gebre-Medhin, G., E.S. Husebye, H. Mallmin, et al. Oral dehydroepiandosterone (DHEA) replacement therapy in women with Addison's disease. *Clin. Endocrinol.* (Oxf.) 2000;52(6):775–780.

62. Magri, F., F. Terenzi, T. Ricciardi, et al. Association between changes in adrenal secretion and cerebral morphometric correlates in normal aging and senile dementia. *Dement. Geriatr. Cogn. Discord.* 2000;11(2):90–99.

63. Hillen, T., A. Lun, F.M. Reichies, et al. DHEA-S plasma levels and incidence of Alzheimer's disease. *Biol. Psychiatry* 2000;47(2):161–163.

64. Zwain, I.H., and S.S. Yen. Dehydroepiandrosterone: Biosynthesis and metabolism in the brain. *Endocrinology* 1999;149(2):880–887.

65. Wolf, et al. Effects of a two-week physiological dehydroepiandrosterone substitution on cognitive performance and well-being in healthy elderly women and men. *J. Clin. Endocrinol. Metab.* 1997;82(7):2363–2367.

66. Rabkin, J.G., S.J. Ferrando, G.J. Wagner, et al. DHEA treatment for HIV+ patients: Effects on mood, androgenic and anabolic parameters. *Psychoneuroendocrinology* 2000;25(1):53–68.

67. Schifitto, G., M.P. McDermott, T. Evans, et al. Autonomic performance and dehydroepiandrosterone sulfate levels in HIV-1 infected individuals: A relationship to TH1 and TH2 cytokine profile. *Arch. Neurol.* 2000;57(7):1027–1032.

68. Barbaccia, M.L., S. Lello, T. Sidiropoulou, et al. Plama 5alpha-androstane-3alpha, 17betadiol, an endogenous steroid that positively modulates GABA(A) receptor function, and anxiety: A study in menopausal women. *Psychoneuroendocrinology* 2000;25(7):659–675.

69. Stomati, M., S. Rubino, A. Spinetti, et al. Endocrine, neuroendocrine and behavioral effects of oral dehydroepiandrosterone sulfate supplementation in postmenopausal women. *Gynecol. Endocrinol.* 1999;13(1):15–25.

70. Casson, P.R., N. Santoro, K. Elkind-Hirsh, et al. Postmenopausal dehydroepiandrosterone administration increases free insulin-like growth factor-1 and decreases high-density lipoprotein: A six month trial. *Fertil. Steril.* 1998;70(1):107–110.

71. Rubino, S., M. Stomati, C. Bersi, et al. Neuroendocrine effect of a short-term treatment with DHEA in postmenopausal women. *Maturitas* 1998;28(3):251–257.

72. Baulieu, et al. Dehydroepiandrosterone (DHEA), DHEA sulfate, and aging: Contribution of the DHEAge Study to a sociobiomedical issue. *Proc. Natl. Acad. Sci. U.S.A.* 2000;97(8):4279–4284.

73. Lapchak, P.A., D.F. Chapman, S.Y. Nunez, et al. Dehydroepiandrosterone sulfate is neuroprotective in a reversible spinal cord ischemia model: Possible involvement of GABA (A) receptors. *Stroke* 2000;31(8):1953–1957.

74. Moriyama, Y., H. Yasue, M. Yoshimura, et al. The plasma levels of dehydroepiandrosterone sulfate are decreased in patients with chronic heart failure in proportion to the severity. *J. Clin. Endocrinol. Metab.* 2000;85(5):1834–1840.

75. Haden, S.T., J. Glowacki, S. Hurwitz, et al. Effects of age on serum dehydroepiandrosterone sulfate, IGF-1, and IL-6 levels in women. *Calcif. Tissue Int.* 2000;66 (6):414–418.

76. Labrie, et al. DHEA and the intracrine formation of androgens and estrogens in peripheral target tissues: Its role during aging. *Steroids* 1998;63(5–6):322–328.

77. Harper, et al. Changes in adrenocortical function with aging and therapeutic implications. *Semin. Reprod. Endocrinol.* 1999;17(4):327–338.

78. Morales, A.J., J.J. Nolan, J.C. Nelson, et al. Effects of replacement dose of dehydroepiandrosterone in men and women of advancing age. *J. Clin. Endocrinol. Metab.* 1994;78(6):1360–1367.

79. Morales, A.J., R.H. Haubrich, J.Y. Hwang, et al. The effect of six months treatment with a 100 mg daily dose of dehydroepiandrosterone (DHEA) on circulating sex steroids, body composition and muscle strength in age-advanced men and women. *Clin. Endocrinol.* (Oxf.) 1998;49(4):421–432.

80. Abbais, A., E.H. Duthie, L. Sheldahl, et al. Association of dehydroepiandrosterone sulfate, body composition, and physical fitness in independent community-dwelling older men and women. *J. Am. Geriatr. Soc.* 1998;46(3):263–273.

81. Reiter, W.J., and A. Pycha. Placebo-controlled dehydroepiandrosterone substitution in elderly men. *Gynakol. Geburtshilfliche Rundsch.* 1999;39(4):208–209.

82. Reiter, W.J., A. Pycha, G. Schatzl, et al. Dehydroepiandrosterone in the treatment of erectile dysfunction: A prospective, double-blind, randomized, placebo-controlled study. *Urology* 1999;53(3):590–594.

83. Schifitto, et al. Autonomic performance and dehydroepiandrosterone sulfate levels in HIV-1 infected individuals: A relationship to TH1 and TH2 cytokine profile. *Arch. Neurol.* 2000;57(7):1027–1032.

84. Barnhart, et al. The effect of dehydroepiandrosterone supplementation to symptomatic perimenopausal women on serum endocrine profiles, lipid parameters, and health-related quality of life. *J. Clin. Endocrinol. Metab.* 1999;84(11):3896–3902.

85. Labrie, et al. DHEA and the intracrine formation of androgens and estrogens in peripheral target tissues: Its role during aging. *Steroids* 1998;63(5–6):322–328.

86. Harper, et al. Changes in adrenocortical function with aging and therapeutic implications. *Semin. Reprod. Endocrinol.* 1999;17(4):327–338.

87. Samber, J.A., T.J. Tatum, M.I. Wray, et al. Implant program effects on performance and carcass quality of steer calves finshed for 212 days. *J. Anim. Sci.* 1996;74 (7):1470–1476.

88. Taylor, W.N.: personal observations and testimonies obtained from health club athletes.

89. Macleod, A.D. Sports psychiatry. *Aust. N.Z.H. Psychiatry* 1998;32(6):860–866.

90. Blue, J.G., and J.A. Lombardo. Steroids and steroid-like compounds. *Clin. Sports Med.* 18(3):667–689.

91. Mader, T.L. Feedlot medicine and management. Implants. *Vet. Clin. North Am. Food Anim. Pract.* 1998;14(2):279–290.

92. Leibetseder, J. [The effect of anabolic steroids in the feed of chickens under oral administration]. *Z. Tierphysiol. Tieremahr. Futtermittlkd.* 1966;21(3):131–136.

93. Johnson, B.J., P.T. Anderson, J.C. Meiske, et al. Effect of combined trenbolone acetate and estradiol implants on feedlot performance, carcass characteristics, and carcass composition of feedlot steers. *J. Anim. Sci.* 1996;74(2):363–371.

94. Gerkin, C.L., J.D. Tatum, J.B. Morgan, et al. Use of genetically identical (clone)

steers to determine the effects of estrogenic and androgenic implants on beef quality and palatability characteristics. *J. Anim.Sci.* 1995;73(11):3317–3324.

95. Johnson, B.J., M.R. Hathaway, P.T. Anderson, et al. Stimulation of circulating insulin-like growth factor 1 (IGF-1) and insulin-like growth factor binding proteins (IGFBP) due to administration of a combined trenbolone acetate and estradiol implant in feedlot cattle. *J. Anim. Sci.* 1996;74(2):372–379.

96. Johnson, B.J., N. Halstead, M.E. White, et al. Activation state of muscle satellite cells isolated from steers implanted with a combined trenbolone acetate and estradiol implant. *J. Anim. Sci.* 1998;76(11):2779–2786.

97. Mader. Feedlot medicine and management. Implants. *Vet. Clin. North Am. Food Anim. Pract.* 1998;14(2):279–290.

98. Cranwell, C.D., J.A. Unruh, J.R. Brethour, et al. Influence of steroid implants and concentrate feeding on performance and carcass composition of cull beef cows. *J. Anim. Sci.* 1996;74(8):1770–1776.

99. _____. Influence of steroid implants and concentrate feeding on carcass and longissimus muscle sensory and collagen characteristics of cull beef cows. *J. Anim. Sci.* 1996;74(8):1777–1783.

100. Duckett, S.K., D.G. Wagner, F.N. Owens, et al. Effect of anabolic implants on beef intramuscular lipid content. *J. Anim. Sci.* 1999;77(5):1100–1104.

101. Saenz de Rodriguez, C.A., and M.A. Toro-Sola. Anabolic steroids in meat and rema premature telarche. *Lancet* 1982;(8284):1300.

102. Taylor, W.N. *Hormonal Manipulation: A New Era of Monstrous Athletes*, Jefferson, NC: McFarland & Company, 1985.

103. Fara, G.M., G. Del Corvo, S. Bernuzzi, et al. Epidemic of breast enlargement in an Italian school. *Lancet* 1979;2(8137):295–297.

104. Simontacchi, C., L. Marinelli, G. Gabai, et al. Accuracy in naturally occurring anabolic steroid assays in cattle and first approach to quality control in Italy. *Analyst* 1999;124(3):307–312.

105. Arneth, W. [Hormones in animal production — a health risk for the consumer]? *Z. Gesamte. Inn. Med.*1992;47(2):45–47.

106. Ibid.

107. Ibid.

108. Daeseleire, E., R. Vandeputte, and C.V. Peteghem. Validation of multi-residue methods for the detection of anabolic steroids by GC-MS in muscle tissues and urine samples from cattle. *Analyst* 1998;123(12):2595–2598.

109. Kendall, D. Implant ban may hurt U.S. meat sales. *Mobile Press Register*, October 24, 1987, p.2A.

110. Schilt, R., M.J. Groot, P.L. Berende, et al. Pour on application of growth promoters in veal calves: Analytic and histological results. *Analyst* 1998;123(12):2665–2670.

111. Stolker, A.A., P.W. Zoontjes, and L.A. Ginkel. The use of supercritical fluid extraction for the determination of steroids in animal tissues. *Analyst* 1998;123(12): 2671–2676.

112. Stolker, A.A., L.A. van Ginkel, R.W. Stephany, et al. Supercritical fluid extraction of methyltestosterone, nortestosterone and testosterone at low ppb levels from fortified bovine urine. *J. Chromatog. B. Biomed. Sci.* 1999;726(1–2):121–131.

113. Sterk, S., H. Herbold, M. Blokland, et al. Nortestosterone: Endogenous in urine of goats, sheep and mares? *Analyst* 1998;123(12):2633–2636.

114. Hooijerink, D., R. Schilt, R. Hoogenboom, et al. Identification of metabolites of the anabolic steroid methandienone formed by bovine hepatocytes in vitro. *Analyst* 1998;123(12):2637–2641.

115. Van Puybroeck, M., M.E. Kuilman, R.F. Maas, et al. Identification of some important metabolites of boldenone in urine and feces of cattle by gas chromatography-mass spectrometry. *Analyst* 1998;123(12):2681–2686.

116. Van Puymbroeck, M., M.E. Kuilmann, R.F. Maas, et al. In vitro liver models are important tools to monitor the abuse of anabolic steroids in cattle. *Analyst* 1998;123(12):2453–2456.

117. Daeseleire, E., R. Vandeputte, and C.V. Peteghem. Validation of multi-residue methods for the detection of anabolic steroids by GC-MS in muscle tissues and urine samples from cattle. *Analyst* 1998;123(12):2595–2598.

118. De Brabander, H.F., K. De Wasch, L.A. van Ginkel, et al. Multi-laboratory study of the analysis and kinetics of stanozolol and its metabolites in treated calves. *Analyst* 1998;123(12):2599–2604.

119. Dubois, M., X. Taillieu, Y. Colemonts, et al. GC-MS determination of anabolic steroids after multi-immunoaffinity purification. *Analyst* 1998;123(12):2611–2616.

120. Van Puymbroeck, M., M.E. Kuilman, R.F. Maas, et al. 17-alpha-ethyl-5beta-estrane-3alpha, 17beta-diol, a biological marker for the abuse of norethandrolone and ethyestrenol in slaughter cattle. *J. Chromatogr. B. Biomed. Sci. Appl.* 1999;728(2):217–232.

121. Hamoir, T., D. Courtheyn, H. De Brabander, et al. Comparison of purification procedures for the isolation and detection of anabolic residues in faeces using gas chromatography-mass spectrometry. *Analyst* 1998;123(12):2621–2624.

122. Leyssens, L., M. Van Puymbroeck, and J. Raus. Interference of Helix pomatia extracts on the determination of methandriol in veterinary residue control analysis. *Analyst* 1998;123(12):2643–2644.

123. Maume, D., B. Le Bizec, P. Marchand, et al. N-methyl-N-alkylsilytrifluoroacetamide-12 as a new derivatization reagent for anabolic steroid control. *Analyst* 1998;123(12):2645–2648.

124. Ferchaud, V., B. Le Bizec, F. Monteau, et al. Determination of the exogenous character of testosterone in bovine urine by gas chromatography-combustion-isotope ratio mass spectrometry. *Analyst* 1998;123(12):2617–2620.

125. Le Bizec, B., I Gaudin, F. Monteau, et al. Consequence of boar edible tissue consumption on urinary profiles of nandrolone metabolites. I. Mass spectrometric detection and quantification of 19-norandrosterone and 19-noreticholanolone in human urine. *Rapid Commun. Mass Spectrom.* 2000;14(12):1058–1065.

126. Sauer, M.J., T.P. Samuels, L.G. Howells, et al. Residues and metabolism of 19-nortestosterone laurate in steers. *Analyst* 1998;123(12):2653–2660.

127. Samuels, T.P., A. Nedderman, M.A. Seymour, et al. Study of the metabolism of testosterone, nandrolone and estradiol in cattle. *Analyst* 1998;123(12):2401–2404.

128. Mason, P.M., S.E. Hall, I. Gilmour, et al. *Analyst* 1998;123(12):2405–2408.

129. Coldham, N.G., G. Biancotto, C. Montesissa, et al. Utility of isolated hepatocytes and radio-HPLC-MSn for the analysis of the metabolic fate of 19-nortestosterone laurate in cattle. *Analyst* 1998;123(12):2589–2594.

130. Walshe, M., M. O'Keeffe, B. Le Bizec, et al. Studies on the determination of chlorotestosterone and its metabolites in bovine urine. *Analyst* 1998;123(12):2687–2691.

131. Illera, J.C., G. Silvan, A. Blass, et al. The effect of clenbuterol on adrenal function in rats. *Analyst* 1998;123(12):2521–2521.

132. McEvoy, J.D., C.E. McVeigh, and W.J. McCaughey. Residues of nortestosterone esters at injection sites. Part 1. Oral bioavailability. *Analyst* 123(12):2475–2478.

133. McEvoy, J.D., W.J. McCaughey, J. Cooper, et al. Nortestosterone is not a naturally occurring compound in male cattle. *Vet. Q.* 1999;21(1):8–15.

134. McEvoy, J.D., C.E. McVeigh, W.J. McCaughey, et al. Comparison of the effects of injections of nortestosterone phenylpropionate at single and multiple sites in cattle on the detection of its residues in plasma, urine and bile. *Vet. Rec.* 1999; 144(2): 42–47.

135. Simontacchi, et al. Accuracy in naturally occurring anabolic steroid assays in cattle and first approach to quality control in Italy. *Analyst* 1999;124(3):307–312.

136. Draisci, R., L. Palleschi, E. Ferretti, et al. Quantitation of anabolic hormones and their metabolites in bovine serum and urine by liquid chromatography-tandem mass spectrometry. *J. Chromatogr.* 2000;870(1–2):511–522.

137. Yoshioka, N., Y. Akiyama, and N. Takeda. Determination of alpha- and beta-trenbolone in bovine muscle and liver by liquid chromatography with fluorescence detection. *J. Chromatogr. B. Biomed. Sci. Appl.* 2000;739(2):363–367.

138. Maghuin-Rogister, G., P. Gaspar, M. Vandenbroeck, et al. Anabolics: The situation in Belgium. *Ann. Rech. Vet.* 1991;22(3):305–309.

139. Bouffault, J.C. Effect of the EEC regulation (ban) on meat world trade. *Ann. Rech. Vet.* 1991;22(3):321–325.

140. Rico, A.G. [Anabolics and French legislation: history and the present]. *Ann. Rech. Vet.* 1991;22(3):311–315.

141. Lone, K.P. Natural sex steroids and their xenobiotic analogs in animal production: Growth, carcass quality, pharmacokinetics, metabolism, mode of action, residues, methods, and epidemiology. *Crit. Rev. Food Sci. Nutr.* 1997;37(2):93–209.

142. Debruyckere, G., R. de Sagher, and C. Van Peteghem. Clostebol-positive urine after consumption of contaminated meat. *Clin. Chem.* 1992;38:1869–1873.

143. Debruyckere, G., and C.H. Peteghem. Influence of the consumption of meat contaminated with anabolic steroids on doping tests. *Anal. Chim. Acta* 1993;275:49–56.

144. Kicman, A.T., D.A. Cowan, L. Myhre, et al. Effect on sports drug tests of ingesting meat from steroid (methenolone)-treated livestock. *Clin. Chem.* 1994;40: 2084–2087.

145. Le Bizec, B., I. Gaudin, F. Monteau, et al. Consequence of boar edible tissue consumption on urinary profiles of nandrolone metabolites. I. Mass spectrometric detection and quantification of 19-norandrosterone and 19-noretiocholanolone in human urine. *Rapid Commun. Mass Spectrom.* 2000;14(12):1058–1065.

146. Snow, D.H., C.D. Munro, and M.A. Nimmo. Effects of nandrolone phenylpropionate in the horse: (1) resting animal. *Equine Vet. J.* 1982;14(3):219–223.

147. _____. Effects of nandrolone phenypropionate in the horse: (2) general effects in animals undergoing training. *Equine Vet. J.* 1982;14(3):224–228.

148. Nimmo, M.A., D.H. Snow, and C.D. Munro. Effects of nandrolone phenylpropionate in the horse: (3) skeletal muscle composition in the exercising animal. *Equine Vet. J.* 1982; 14(3):229–233.

149. Hyyppa, S., U. Karvonen, L.A. Rasanen, et al. Androgen receptors and skeletal muscle composition in trotters treated nandrolone laureate. *Zentralbl. Verterinarmed. A.* 1997;44(8):481–491.

150. Snow, D.H. Anabolic steroids. *Vet. Clin. North Am. Equine Pract.* 1993;93: 563–576.

151. Hoechst, A.R. Endocrine manipulation — toxicological frontiers. *J. Reprod. Fertil. Suppl.* 1992;45:193–201.

152. Moss, M.S. Survey of positive results from racecourse antidoping samples received at Racecourse Security Services' Laboratories. *Equine Vet. J.* 1984;16(1):39–42.

153. Ungemach, F.R. [Doping control in race horses]. *Tierarztl. Prax.* 1985;13(1): 35–53.

154. Sterk, S., H. Herbold, M. Blokland, et al. Nortestosterone: Endogenous in urine of goats, sheep and mares? *Analyst* 1998;123(2633–2636.

155. Hamoir, T., D. Courtheyn, H. De Brabander, et al. Comparision of purification procedures for isolation and detection of anabolic residues in faeces using gas chromoatography-mass spectrometry. *Analyst* 1998;123(12):2621–2624.

156. Uehara, N., and A. Momose. [Doping test for racehorses in Japan]. *Yakugaku Zasshi* 1997;117(10–12):922–935.

157. Williams, T.M., A.J. Kind, and D.W. Hill. In vitro biotransformation of anabolic steroids in canines. *J. Vet. Pharmacol. Therapeutics* 1999;23(2):57–66.

158. Allee, W.C., N.C. Collias, and C.Z. Lutherman. Modification of the social order in flocks of hens by injection of testosterone propionate. *Physiol. Zool.* 1939;12: 412–440.

159. Simon, N.G., R.E. Whalen, and M.P. Tate. Induction of male-typical aggression by androgens but not by estrogens in adult female mice. *Hormones Behav.* 1985;19: 204–212.

160. Stellis, H.D., G.L. Brammer, M.J. Raleigh, et al. Serum testosterone, male domiance, and aggression in captive groups of vervet monkeys. *Hormones Behav.* 1985;19: 154–163.

161. Buoissou, M.F., and V. Gaudioso. Effect of early androgen treatment on subsequent social behavior in heifers. *Hormones Behav.* 1982;16:132–146.

162. Kurischko, A., and M. Oettel. Androgen dependent fighting behavior in male mice. *Endokrinologie* 1977;70:1–5.

163. Bouissou, M.G. Androgens, aggressive behavior and social relationships in higher mammals. *Hormones Behav.* 1983;18:43–61.

164. Zumpe, D., and R.P. Michael. Effects of testosterone on the behavior of male Cynomolgus monkeys (Macaca Fascicularis). *Hormones Behav.* 1985;19:165–177.

Chapter 5

1. O'Shea, J.P., and W. Winkler. Biochemical and physical effects of anabolic steroids in competitive swimmers and weight lifters. *Nutr. Rpts. Inter.* 1970;2:351–362.

2. O'Shea, J.P. The effects of anabolic steroid on dynamic strength levels of weight lifters. *Nutr.Rpts. Inter.* 1971;4:363–370.

3. Bowers, R.W., and J.P. Reardon. Effects of methandrostenolone (Dianabol) on strength development and aerobic capacity. *Med. Sci. Sports* 1972; 4:54–56.

4. Ward, P. The effect of an anabolic steroid on strength and lean body mass. *Med. Sci. Sports* 1973;5:277–282.

5. Stamford, B.A., and R. Moffatt. Anabolic steroid: Effectiveness as an ergogenic aid to experienced weight trainers. *J. Sports Med. Phys. Fitness* 1974;14:191–197.

6. O'Shea, J.P. Biochemical evaluation of effects of stanozolol on adrenal, liver and muscle function. *Nutr. Rpts. Inter.* 1974;10:381–388.

7. Freed, D.L.J., and A.J. Banks. A double-blind crossover trial of methandienone (Dianabol, Ciba) in moderate dosage on highly trained experienced athletes. *Brit. J. Sports Med.* 1975;9:78–81.

8. Alen, M., H. Hakkinen, and P.V. Komi. Changes in neuromuscular performance and muscle fiber characteristics of elite power athletes self-administering androgenic and anabolic steroids. *Acta Physiol. Scand.* 1984;122(4):535–544.

9. Kuipers, H., F.M. Peeze Binkhorst, F. Hartgens, et al. Muscle ultrastructure after strength training with placebo or anabolic steroid. *Can. J. Appl. Physiol.* 1993;18 (2):189–196.

10. Giorgi, A., R.P. Weatherby, and P.W. Murphy. Muscular strength, body composition and health responses to the use of testosterone enanthate: A double blind study. *J. Sci. Med. Sport* 1999;2(4):341–355.

11. Kadi, F. Adaptation of human skeletal muscle to training and anabolic steroids. *Acta Physiol. Scand.* (Suppl.) 2000;646:1–52.

12. Hartgens, F., H. Kuipers, and J.A. Wijnen, et al. Body composition, cardiovascular risk factors and liver function in long-term androgenic-anabolic steroids using bodybuilders three months after drug withdrawal. *Int. J. Sports Med.* 1996;17(6):429–433.

13. Kadi, F., A. Eriksson, S. Holmer, et al. Effects of anabolic steroids on the muscle cells of strength-trained athletes. *Med. Sci. Sports Exerc.* 1999;31(11):1528–1534.

14. Kadi, F., P. Bonnerud, A. Eriksson, et al. The expression of androgen receptors in human neck muscles and limb muscles: Effects of training and self-experimentation of androgenic-anabolic steroids. *Histochem. Cell. Biol.* 2000;113(1):25–29.

15. Roy, R.R., S.R. Monke, D.L. Allen, et al. Modulation of myonuclear number in functionally overloaded and exercised rat plantaris fibers. *J. Appl. Physiol.* 1999;87 (2):634–642.

16. Wilson, D.L., C. Fearon, and A.C. Parrott. Multiple drug use and dietary restraint in a Mr. Universe competitor: Psychobiological effects. *Percept. Mot. Skills* 1999;88(2):579–580.

17. Sundaram, K., and N. Kumar. 7alpha-methyl-19-nortestosterone (MENT): The optimal androgen for male contraception and replacement therapy. *Int. J. Androl.* 2000;23(Suppl. 2):13–15.

18. Sundaram, K., N. Kumar, C. Monder, et al. Different patterns of metabolism determine the relative anabolic activity of 19-norandrogens. *J. Steroid Biochem. Mol. Biol.* 1995;53(5–6):253–257.

19. Kumar, N., A. Crozat, F. Li, et al. 7alpha-methyl-19-nortestosterone, a synthetic androgen with high potency: Structure-activity comparisons with other androgens. *J. Steroid Biochem. Mol. Biol.* 1999;71(5–6):213–222.

20. Anderson, R.A., C.W. Martin, A.W. Kung, et al. 7Alpha-methyl-19-nortestosterone maintains sexual behavior and mood in hypogonadal men. *J. Clin. Endocrinol. Metab.* 1999;84(10):3556–3562.

21. Pinero, V., X. Casabiell, R. Peino, et al. Dihydrotestoterone, stanozolol, androstenedione and dehydroepiandrosterone sulphate inhibit leptin secretion in female but not male samples of omental adipose tissue in vitro: Lack of effect of testosterone. *J. Endocrinol.* 1999;160(3):425–432.

22. Smith, J.L., L.L. Wilson, and D.L. Swanson. Implant sequence effects in intact male Holstein veal calves: Live and slaughter traits. *J. Anim. Sci.* 1999;77(12):3125–3132.

23. Samber, J.A., J.D. Tatum, M.I. Wray, et al. Implant program effects on performance and carcass quality of steer calves finished for 212 days. *J. Anim. Sci.* 1996; 74(7):1470–1476.

24. Mader, T.L. Feedlot medicine and management. Implants. *Vet. Clin. North Am. Food. Anim. Pract.*1998;14(2):279–290.

25. Cranwell, C.D., J.A. Unruh, J.R. Brethour, et al. Influence of steroid implants and concentrate feeding on performance and carcass composition in cull beef steers. *J. Anim. Sci.* 1996;74(8):1770–1776.

26. Johnson, B.J., N. Halstead, M.E. White, et al. Activation state of muscle cell satellite cells isolated from steers implanted with a combined trenbolone acetate and estradiol implant. *J. Anim. Sci.* 1998;76(11):2779–2786.

Chapter 6

1. Harries, M. Is an athlete born or made? *Trans. Med. Soc. Lond.* 1998:114:59–64.

2. Taylor, W.N. *Hormonal Manipulation: A New Era of Monstrous Athletes.* Jefferson, N.C.: McFarland & Company, 1985.

3. Horber, F.F. [Anabolics and sports]. *Schweiz. Med. Wochenschr.* 1990; 120(11): 383.

4. Holden, S.C., R.D. Calvo, and J.C. Sterling. Anabolic steroids in athletics. *Tex. Med.* 1990;86(3):32.

5. Celotti, F., and P. Negri Cesi. Anabolic steroids: A review of their effects on the muscles, of their possible mechanisms of action and their use in athletics. *J. Steroid Biochem. Mol. Med.* 1992;43(5):469.

6. *Physician's Desk Reference.* Montvale, N.J.: Medical Economics Company, Inc., 52nd Edition, p. 2526, 1998.

7. Taylor, W.N. Are anabolic steroids for the long distance runner? Letter, *Ann. Sports Med.* 1984;2(1):51–52.

8. Besa, E.C., D. Gorshein, and F.H. Gardner. Androgens and human blood volume changes: Comparison in normal and anemic states. *Arch. Intern. Med.* 1974;133 (3):418–425.

9. Tenover, J.S. Effects of testosterone supplementation in the aging male. *J. Clin. Endocrinol. Metab.* 1992;75(4):1092–1098.

10. Kuipers, H., F.M. Peeze Binkhorst, F. Hartgens, et al. Muscle ultrastructure

after strength training with placebo or anabolic steroid. *Can. J. Appl. Physiol.* 1993;18(2): 189–196.

11. Almekinders, L.C. Anti-inflammatory treatment of muscular injuries in sport: An update of recent studies. *Sports Med.* 1999;28(6):282–288.

12. Beiner, J.M., P. Jokl. J. Cholewicki, et al. The effect of anabolic steroids and corticosteroids on healing of muscle contusion injury. *Am. J. Sports Med.* 1999;27(1):2–9.

13. Bakhshi, V., M. Elliott, A. Gentili, et al. Testosterone improves rehabilitation outcomes in ill older men. *J. Am. Geriatr. Soc.* 2000;48(5):550–553.

14. Evans, N.A., D.J. Bowrey, and G.R. Newman. Ultrastructural analysis of ruptured tendon from anabolic steroid users. *Injury* 1998;29(10):769–773.

15. Ferry, A., P. Noirez, C.L. Page, et al. Effects of anabolic/androgenic steroids on regenerating skeletal muscles in the rat. *Acta Physiol. Scand.* 1999;166(2):105–110.

16. Johansson, P., M. Hallberg, A. Kindlundh, et al. The effect of opiod peptides in the rat brain, after chronic treatment with the anabolic androgenic steroid, nandrolone decanoate. *Brain Res. Bull.* 2000;51(1):413–418.

17. Pasquariello, A., R. Di Toro, F. Nyberg, et al. Down-regulation of delta opioid receptor mRNNA by an anabolic steroid in neuronal hybrid cells. *Neuroreport* 2000;11(4):863–867.

18. Arvary, D., and H.G. Pope. Anabolic-androgenic steroids as a gateway to opioid dependence. *N. Engl. J. Med.* 2000;342(20):1532.

19. Tennant, F., D.L. Black, and R.O. Voy. Anabolic steroid dependence with opioid-like features. *N. Engl. J. Med.* 1988;319:578.

20. Frye, C.A., K.R. Van Keuren, P.N. Rao, et al. Analgesic effects of the neurosteriod 3-alpha-andrestanediol. *Brain Res.* 1996;709(1):1–9.

21. Giorgi, A., R.P. Weatherby, and P.W. Murphy. Muscular strength, body composition and health responses to the use of testosterone enanthate: A double blind study. *J. Sci. Med. Sport* 1999;2(4):341–355.

22. Snyder, P.J., H. Peachey, P. Hannoush, et al. Effect of testosterone treatment on body composition and muscle strength in men over 65 years of age. *J. Clin. Endocrinol. Metab.* 1999;84(8):2647–2653.

23. Lovejoy, J.C., G.A. Bray, C.S. Greeson, et al. Oral anabolic steroid treatment, but not parenteral androgen treatment, decreases abdominal fat in obese, older men. *Int. J. Obes. Relat. Metab. Disord.* 1995;19(9):614–624.

24. Simonson, E., W.C. Kerns, and N. Enzer. Effect of methyl testosterone treatment on muscular performance and the central nervous system of older men. *J. Clin. Endocrinol.* 1944;4:528–534.

25. Alen, M., K. Hakkinen, and P.V. Komi. Changes in neuromuscular performance and muscle fiber characteristics of elite power athletes self-administering androgenic and anabolic steroids. *Acta Physiol. Scand.* 1984;122(4):535–544.

26. Ariel, G., and W. Saville. Effect of anabolic steroids on reflex components. *J. Appl. Physiol.* 1972;32(6):795–797.

27. Blanco, C.E., P. Popper, and P. Micevych. *Neuroscience* 1997;78(3):873–882.

28. Madena-Pyrgaki, A., C. Pappas, A. Deligiannis, et al. Work capacity, contractile protein and quantitative electromyogram (EMG) changes following exercise or nandrolone decanoate treatment in experimentally induced muscle disuse atrophy in rats. *Acta Endocrinol.* (Copenh.) 1979;90(3):568–576.

29. Ferry, R.J., R.W. Cerri, and P. Cohen. Insulin-like growth factor binding proteins: New proteins, new functions. *Horm. Res.* 1999;51(2):53–67.

30. Hobbs, C.J., S.R. Plymate, C.J. Rosen, et al. Testosterone administration increases insulin-like growth factor-I levels in normal men. *J. Clin. Endocrinol. Metab.* 1993;77(3):776–779.

31. Zapf, J., M.Y. Donath, C. Schmid. [Spectrum of effectiveness of insulin-like growth factors]. *Schweiz. Med. Wochenschr.* 2000;130(6):190–195.

32. Hall, K., P. Bang, and K. Brismar. [Insulin-like growth factors. Future treatment in catabolism]? *Lakartidningen* 1995;92(26–27):2888–2671.

33. Binoux, M. The IGF system in metabolism regulation. *Diebete. Metab.* 1995;21(5):330–337.

34. Baxter, R.C. The insulin-like growth factors and their binding proteins. *Comp. Biochem. Physiol. B.* 1988;91(2):229–235.

35. Froesch, E.R., M. Hussain. Recombinant human insulin-like growth factor-I: A therapeutic challenge for diabetes mellitus. *Diabetologia* 1994;37(Suppl. 2):S179–185.

36. Taylor, W.N.: *Macho Medicine: A History of the Anabolic Steroid Epidemic.* Jefferson, N.C.: McFarland & Company, 1991, p.55.

37. Steroids in Amateur and Professional Sports — The Medical and Social Costs of Steroid Abuse. Hearings before the Committee on the Judiciary, United States Senate, 101st Congress, 1st Session (S. Hrg. 101–736). U.S. Government Printing Office, Washington, D.C., 1990.

Chapter 7

1. Editorial letter (authors not listed). Anabolic steroids: A dangerous breakfast of champions. *Am. Fam. Physician* 1988;38(2):99.

2. Hickson, R.C., K.L. Ball, and M.T. Falduto. Adverse effects of anabolic steroids. *Med. Toxicol. Adverse Drug Exp.* 1989;4(4):254–271.

3. Kibble, M.W., and M.B. Ross. Adverse effects of anabolic steroids in athletes. *Clin. Pharm.* 1987;6(9):686–692.

4. Editorial letter (authors not listed). Male infertility due to anabolic steroids. *Prescriere Int.* 1999;8(40):54.

5. Hughes, T.K., P.L. Rady, and E.M. Smith. Potential for the effects of anabolic steroid abuse in the immune and neuroendocrine axis. *J. Neuroimmunol.* 1998;83 (1–2):162–167.

6. Fiegel, G. [Drugs interacting with anabolic steroids]. *Clin. Ter.* 1991;136 (6):415–420.

7. Elford, J., G. Bolding, M. Maguire, et al. Do gay men discuss HIV risk reduction with their GP? *AIDS Care* 2000;12(3):287–290.

8. Hill, J.A., J.R. Suker, K. Sachs, et al. The athletic polydrug abuse phenomenon. *Am. J. Sports Med.* 1983;11(4):269–271.

9. Evans, N.A. Gym and tonic: A profile of 100 male steroid users. *Br. J. Sports Med.* 1997;31(1):54–58.

10. Meilman, P.W., R.K. Crase, C.A. Presley, et al. Beyond performance enhancement: Polypharmacy among collegiate uses of steroids. *J.Am. Coll. Health* 1995;44(3): 98–104.

11. DuRant, R.H., L.G. Escobedo, and G.W. Heath. Anabolic steroid use, strength training, and multiple drug use among adolescents in the United States. *Pediatrics* 1995;96(1 Pt. 1):23–28.

12. Arvary, D., and H.G. Pope. Anabolic-androgenic steroids as a gateway to opioid dependence. *N. Engl. J. Med.* 2000;342(20):1532.

13. Timby, N., A. Eriksson, and K. Bostrom. Gamma-hydroxybutyrate associated deaths. *Am. J. Med.* 2000;108(6):518–519.

14. Thiblin, I., O. Lindquist, and J. Rajs. Cause and manner of death among users of anabolic androgenic steroids. *J. Forensic Sci.* 2000;45(1):16–23.

15. Schneider, V., and E. Klug. [Doping — anabolic steroid abuse — careless homicide]. *Versicherungsmedizin* 1996;48(3):104–106.

16. Cannon, A. Steroid-using police cause brutality fears. *The Miami Herald* May 27, 1987, p.1.

17. Popping steroids and pumping lead. *Time* December 4, 1989, p.4.

18. Midgley, J.S., N. Heather, D. Best, et al. Risk behaviour for HIV and hepatitis infection among anabolic-androgenic steroid users. *AIDS Care* 2000;12(2):163–170.

19. Bolding, G., L. Sherr, M. Maguire, et al. HIV risk behaviours among gay men who use anabolic steroids. *Addiction* 1999;94(12):1829–1835.

20. Driessen, M., H. Muessingbrodt, H. Dilling, et al. Child sexual abuse associated with anabolic androgenic steroid use. *Am. J. Psychiatry* 1996;153(10):1369.

21. Uzych, L. Commentary on Leong GB and Silva J.A. A psychiatric-legal analysis of psychotic criminal defendents charged with murder. *J. Forensic Sci.* 1996; 41(2):187–188.

22. Middleman, A.B., A.H. Faulkner, E.R. Woods, et al. High-risk behaviors among high school students in Massachusetts who use anabolic steroids. *Pediatrics* 1995;96 (2 Pt. 1):268–272.

23. Tahmindjis, A.J. The use of anabolic steroids by athletes to increase body weight and strength. *Med. J. Aust.* 1976;1(26):991–993.

24. Street, C., J. Antonio, and D. Cudlipp. Androgen use by athletes: A reevaluation of the health risks. *Can. J. Appl. Physiol.* 1996;21(6):421.

25. Kennedy, M.C., and C. Lawrence. Anabolic steroid abuse and cardiac death. *Med. J. Aust.* 1993;158(5):346–348.

26. Lyngberg, K.K. [Myocardial infarction and death of a body builder after using anabolic steroids]. *Ugeskr. Laeger* 1991;153(8):587–588.

27. Luke, J.L., A. Farb, R. Virmani, et al. Sudden cardiac death during exercise in a weight lifter using anabolic androgenic steroids: Pathological and toxicological findings. *J. Forensic Sci.* 1990;35(6):1441–1447.

28. Hourigan, L.A., A.J. Rainbird, and M. Dooris. Intracoronary stenting for acute myocardial infarction (AMI) in a 24-year-old man using anabolic androgenic steroids. *Aust. N.Z.J. Med.* 1998;28(6):838–839.

29. Varriale, P., M. Mirzai-Tehrane, and A. Sedighi. Acute myocardial infarction associated with anabolic steroids in a young HIV-infected patient. *Pharmacotherapy* 1999;19(7):881–884.

30. Dickerman, R.D., F. Schaller, I. Prather, et al. Sudden cardiac death in a 20-year-old bodybuilder using anabolic steroids. *Cardiology* 1995;86(2):172–173.

31. Hausmann, R., S. Hammer, and P. Betz. Performance enhancing drugs (doping agents) and sudden death — a case report and review of the literature. *Int.J. Legal Med.* 1998;111(5):261–264.

32. Goldstein, D.R., T. Dobbs, B. Krull, et al. Clenbuterol and anabolic steroids: A previously unreported cause of myocardial infarction with normal coronary arteriograms. *South. Med. J.* 1998;91(8):780–784.

33. McNutt, R.A., G.S. Ferenchick, P.C. Kirlin, et al. Acute myocardial infarction in a 22-year-old world class weight lifter using anabolic steroids. *Am. J. Cardiol.* 1988;62(1):164.

34. Siekierzynska-Czarnecka, A., Z. Polowiec, M. Kulawinska, et al. [Death caused by pulmonary embolism in a body builder taking anabolic steroids]. *Wiad. Lek.* 1990;43(19–20):972–975.

35. Gaede, J.T., and T.J. Montine. Massive pulmonary embolus and anabolic steroid abuse. *JAMA* 1992;267(17):2328–2329.

36. Kledal, S., A.G. Clausen, and H. Guldager. [Fatal outcome with cerebral edema following abuse of anabolic steroids]. *Ugeskr. Laeger* 2000;162(15):2203–2204.

37. Moss-Newport, J. Anabolic steroid use and cerebellar hemorrhage. *Med. J. Aust.* 1993;158(11):794.

38. Schumacher, J., G. Muller, and K.F. Klotz. Large hepatic hematoma and intraabdominal hemorrhage associated with abuse of anabolic steroids. *N. Engl. J. Med.* 1999;340(14):1123–1124.

39. Thiblin, I., B. Runeson, and J. Rajs. Anabolic androgenic steroids and suicide. *Ann. Clin. Psychiatry* 1999;11(4):223–231.

40. Thiblin, I., O. Lindquist, and J. Rajs. Cause and manner of death among users of anabolic androgenic steroids. *J. Forensic. Sci.* 2000;45(1):16–23.

41. Melchert, R.B., and A.A. Welder. Cardiovascular effects of anabolic-androgenic steroids. *Med. Sci. Sports Exerc.* 1995;27(9):1252–1262.

42. Parssinen, M., U. Kujala, E. Vartiainen, et al. Increased premature mortality of competitive powerlifters suspected to have used agents. *Int. J. Sports Med.* 2000;21 (3):225–227.

43. Soe, K.L., M. Soe, and C.N. Gluud. [Liver pathology associated with anabolic androgenic steroids]. *Ugeskr. Laeger* 1994;156(17):2585–2588.

44. Young, G.P., P.S. Bhathal, J.R. Sullivan, et al. Fatal hepatic coma complicating oxymetholone therapy in multiple myeloma. *Aust. N. Z. Med.* 1977;7(1):47–51.

45. Nadell, J., and J. Kosek. Peliosis hepatis. Twelve cases associated with oral androgen therapy. *Arch. Pathol. Lab. Med.* 1977;101(8):405–410.

46. McDonald, E.C., and C.E. Speicher. Peliosis hepatis associated with administration of oxymetholone. *JAMA* 1978;240(3):243–244.

47. Kosaka, A., H. Takahashi, Y. Yajima, et al. Hepatocellular carcinoma associated with anabolic steroid therapy: A report of a case and review of the Japanese literature. *J. Gastroenterol.* 1996;31(3):450–454.

48. Falk, H., L.B. Thomas, H. Popper, et al. Hepatic angiosarcoma associated with androgenic-anabolic steroids. *Lancet* 1979;2(8152):1120–1123.

49. Daneshmend, T.K., and J.W. Bradfield. Hepatic angiosarcoma associated with androgenic-anabolic steroids. *Lancet* 1979;2(8154):1249.

50. Taxy, J.B. Peliosis: A morphologic curiosity becomes an iatrogenic problem. *Hum. Pathol.* 1978;9(3):331–334.

51. Goldman, B. Liver carcinoma in an athlete taking anabolic steroids. *J. Am. Osteopath. Assoc.* 1985;85(2):56.

52. Overly, W.L., J.A. Dankoff, B.K. Wang, et al. Androgens and heptocellular carcinoma in an athlete. *Ann. Intern. Med.* 1984;100(1):158–159.

53. Habscheid, W., U. Abele, and H.H. Dahm. [Severe cholestasis with kidney failure from anabolic steroids in a body builder]. *Dtsch. Med. Wochenschr.* 1999;124(36) 1029–1032.

54. Martorana, G., S. Concetti, F. Manferrari, et al. Anabolic steroid abuse and renal cell carcinoma. *J. Urol.* 1999;162(6):2089.

55. Froehner, M., R. Fischer, S. Leike, et al. *Cancer* 1999;86(8):1571–1575.

56. Roberts, J.T., and D.M. Essenhigh. Adenocarcinoma of prostate in 40-year-old body-builder. *Lancet* 1986;2(8509):742.

57. Mewis, C., I. Spyridopoulos, V. Kuhlkamp, et al. Manifestation of severe coronary heart disease after anabolic drug abuse. *Clin. Cardiol.* 1996;19(2):153–155.

58. Ferrera, P.C., D.L. Putnam, and V.P. Verdile. Anabolic steroid use as the possible precipitant of dilated cardiomyopathy. *Cardiology* 1997;88(2):218–220.

59. Nieminen, M.S., M.P. Ramo, M. Vittasalo, et al. Serious cardiovascular side effects of large doses of anabolic steroids in weight lifters. *Eur. Heart J.* 1996;17 (10):1576–1583.

60. Roeggia, M., G. Heinz, E. Werba, et al. Cardiac tamponade in a 21-year-old body builder with anabolica abuse. *Br. J. Clin. Pract.* 1996;50(7):411–412.

61. De Virgilio, C., R.J. Nelson, J. Milliken, et al. Ascending aortic dissection in weight lifters with cyctic medial degeneration. *Ann. Thorac Surg.* 1990;49(4):638–642.

62. Pettine, K.A. Association of anabolic steroids and avascular necrosis of femoral heads. *Am. J. Sports Med.* 1991;19(1):96–98.

63. Frankle, M.A. Association of anabolic steroids and avascular necrosis of femoral heads. *Am. J. Sports Med.* 1992;20(4):488.

64. Freeman, B.J., and G.D. Rooker. Spontaneous rupture of the anterior cruciate ligament after anabolic steroids. *Br. J. Sports Med.* 1995;29(4):274–275.

65. Sullivan, M.L., C.M. Martinez, and E.J. Gallagher. Atrial fibrillation and anabolic steroids. *J. Emerg. Med.* 1999;17(5):851–857.

66. Radis, C.D., and K.P. Callis. Systemic lupus erythematosus with membranous glomerulonephritis and transverse myelitis associated with anabolic steroid use. *Arthritis Rheum.* 1997;40(10):1899–1902.

67. Bahia, H., A. Platt, N.B. Hart, et al. Anabolic steroid accelerated multicompartment syndrome following trauma. *Br. J. Sports Med.* 2000;34(4):308–309.

68. Fiirgaard, B., and F.H. Madsen. Spinal epidural lipomatosis: Case report and review of the literature. *Scand. J. Med. Sci. Sports* 1997;7(6):354–357.

69. Mondelli, M., R. Cioni, and A. Federico. Rare mononeuropathies of the upper limb in bodybuilders. *Muscle Nerve* 1998;21(6):809–812.

70. Taylor, W.N. *Macho Medicine: A History of the Anabolic Steroid Epidemic.* Jefferson, N.C.: McFarland & Company, 1991, pp.55–56.

71. Urhaussen, A., and W. Kindermann. Sport-specific adaptations and differentiation of the athlete's heart. *Sports Med.* 1999;28(4):237–244.

72. Dickerman, R.D. Anabolic steroid-induced hepatotoxicity: is it overstated? *Clin. J. Sports Med.* 1999;9(1):34–39.

73. Ansell, J.E., C. Tiarks, and V.K. Fairchild. Coagulation abnormalities associated with the use of anabolic steroids. *Am.Heart J.* 125(2 Pt.1):367–371.

74. Palatini, P., F. Giada, G. Garavelli, et al. *J. Clin. Pharmacol.* 1996;36(12): 1132–1140.

75. Kiraly, C.L., Y. Collan, and M. Alen. Effect of testosterone and anabolic steroids on the size of sebaceous glands in power athletes. *Am. J. Dermatopathol.* 1987;9(6): 515–519.

76. Thompson, P.D., E.M. Cullinane, S.P. Sady, et al. Contrasting effects of testosterone and stanozolol on serum lipoprotein levels. *JAMA* 1989;261(8):1165–1168.

77. Hislop, M.S., B.D. Ratanjee, S.G. Soule, et al. Effects of anabolic-androgenic steroid use on gonadal testosterone suppression on serum leptin concentration in men. *Eur. J. Endocrinol.* 1999;141(1):40–46.

78. Kiraly, C.L., M. Alen, J. Korvola, et al. The effect of testosterone and anabolic steroids on the skin surface lipids and the population of Priopionibacteria acnes in young postpubertal men. *Acta Derm. Venereol.* 1988;68(1):21–26.

79. Nesterin, M.F., V.M. Budik, R.V. Narodetskaia, et al. [Effect of methandrostenolone on liver morphology and enzymatic activity]. *Farmakol. Toksikol.* 1980;43 (5):597–601.

80. Kuipers, H., J.A. Wijnen, F. Hartgens, et al. Influence of anabolic steroids on body composition, blood pressure, lipid profile and liver functions in body builders. *Int. J. Sports Med.* 1991;12(4):413–418.

81. Schurmeyer, T., U.A. Knuth, L. Belkien, et al. Reversible azoospermia induced by the anabolic steroid 19-nortestosterone. *Lancet* 1984;1(8374):417–420.

82. Deyssig, R., and W. Weissel. Ingestion of androgenic-anabolic steroids induces mild thyroidal impairment in male body builders. *J. Clin. Endocrinol. Metab.* 1993;76(4): 1069–1071.

83. Wemyss-Holden, S.A., F.C. Hamdy, and K.L. Hastie. Steroid abuse in athletes, prostatic enlargement and bladder outflow obstruction. *Br. J. Urol.* 1994;74(4):476–478.

84. Palatini, P., F. Giada, G. Garavelli, et al. Cardiovascular effects of anabolic steroids in weight-trained subjects. *J. Clin. Pharmacol.* 1996;36(12):1132–1140.

85. Dickerman, R.D., F. Schaller, N.Y. Zachariah, et al. Left ventricular size and function in elite bodybuilders using anabolic steroids. *Clin. J. Sports Med.* 1997;7(2): 90–93.

86. Ferenchick, G.S., S. Hirokawa, E.F. Mammen, et al. Anabolic-androgenic steroid abuse in weight lifters: Evidence for activation of the hemostatic system. *Am. J. Hematol.* 1995;49(4):282–288.

87. Hartgens, F., H. Kuipers, J.A. Wijnen, et al. Body composition, cardiovascular risk factors and liver function in long-term androgenic-anabolic steroids using bodybuilders three months after drug withdrawal. *Int. J. Sports Med.* 1996;17(6):429–433.

88. Ansell, J.E., C. Tiarks, and V.J. Fairchild. Coagulation abnormalities associated with the use of anabolic steroids. *Am. Heart J.* 1993;125(2 Pt.1):367–371.

89. Taylor, W.N. Super athletes made to order? *Psychology Today* 1985;19(5):62–66.

90. Hakkinen, K., and M. Alen. Physiological performance, serum hormones, enzymes and lipids of an elite power athlete during training with and without androgens and during prolonged training. *J. Sports Med.* 1986;26:92–100.

91. Holma, P. Effect of an anabolic steroid (Metandienone) on central and peripheral blood flow in well-trained male athletes. *Ann. Clin. Res.* 1977;9:215–221.

92. Lamb, D.R. Anabolic steroids in athletics: How well do they work and how dangerous are they? *Am. J. Sports Med.* 1984;12(1):31–38.

93. Strauss, R.H., M.T. Mariah, M.S. Liggett, et al. Anabolic steroid use and perceived effects in ten weight-trained women athletes. *JAMA* 1985;253(19):2871–2873.

94. Alen, M., M. Reinila, and R. Vihko. Response to serum hormones to androgen administration in power athletes. *Med. Sci. Sports Exerc.* 1985;17(3):354–359.

95. Martikainen, H., M. Alen, P. Rahkila, et al. Testicular responsiveness to human chorionic gonadotrophin during transient hypogonadotrophic hypogonadism induced by androgenic/anabolic steroids in power athletes. *J. Steroid Biochem.* 1986;25(1):109–112.

96. Webb. O.L., P.M. Laskarzewski, and C.J. Glueck. Severe depression of high-density lipoprotein cholesterol levels in weight lifters and body builders by self-administered exogenous testosterone and anabolic-androgenic steroids. *Metabolism* 1984;33(11): 971–975.

97. Taylor, W.N. Drug issues in sports medicine, Part 1: Steroid abuse and non-steroidal anti-inflammatory (NSAID) selection in athletic/active patients. *J. Neurol. Ortho. Med. Surg.* 1988;9(2):159–164.

98. Taylor, W.N. Synthetic anabolic-androgenic steroids: A plea for controlled substance status. *Phys. Sportsmed.* 1987;15(5):140–150.

99. Marshall, E. The drug of champions. *Science* 1988;242(4876):183–84.

100. Newman, S. Despite warnings, lure of steroids too strong for some Canadians. *CMAJ* 1994;151(6):844–846.

Chapter 8

1. Taylor, W.N. Are anabolic steroids for the long distance runner? (letter). *Annals Sports Med.* 1984;2(1):51–52.

2. _____. *Hormonal Manipulation: A New Era of Monstrous Athletes* Jefferson, N.C.: McFarland & Company, 1985.

3. _____. Super athletes made to order. *Psychology Today* 1985;(May):63–66.

4. _____. Effects and actions of human growth hormone. Presented at symposium on drugs in sports, American College of Sports Medicine Annual Meeting, San Diego, May 24, 1984.

5. _____. Synthetic anabolic-androgenic steroids: A plea for controlled substance status. *Physician Sportsmed.* 1987;15(5):140–150.

6. Anabolic Steroid Abuse. *FDA Drug Bulletin* 1987;17(3):27.

7. Taylor, W.N. Are anabolic steroids for the long distance runner? (letter). *Annals Sports Med.* 1984;2(1):51–52.

8. _____. Super athletes made to order. *Psychology Today* 1985;(May):63–66.

9. Sheridan, P.J. Androgen receptors in the brain: what are we measuring? *Endocrine Reviews* 1983;4(2):171–178.

10. Allee, W.C., N.C. Collias and C.Z. Lutherman. Modification of the social order of hens by the injection of testoterone propionate. *Physiol. Zoology* 1939;12(4): 412–440.

11. Buoissou, M.F., and V. Gaudioso. Effects of early androgen treatment on subsequent social behavior in heifers. *Horm. Behav.* 1982;16:132–146.

12. Simon, N.G., R.E. Whalen and M.P. Tate. Induction of male-typical aggression by androgens but not by estrogens in female adult mice. *Horm. Behav.* 1985;19: 204–212.

13. Van de Poll, N.E., D.E. Honge, F. van Oyen, et al. Failure to find sex differences in testosterone activated aggression in two strains of rats. *Horm. Behav.* 1981;15:94–105.

14. Kurischko, A., and M. Oettel. Androgen-dependent fighting behavior in male mice. *Endokrinologie* 1977;70:1–5.

15. Bouissou, M.G. Androgens, aggressive behavior and social relationships in higher mammals. *Horm. Behav.* 1983;18:43–61.

16. Zumpe, D., and R.P. Michael. Effects of testosterone on the behavior of male Cynomolgus monkeys (Macaca Fascicularis). *Horm. Behav.* 1985;19:165–177.

17. Steklis, H.D., G.L. Brammer, M.J. Raleigh, et al. Serum testosterone, male dominance, and aggression in captive groups of Vervet monkeys (Ceropithecus Aethiops Sabaeus). *Horm. Behav.* 1985;19:154–163.

18. Vest, S.A., and J.E. Howard. Clinical experiments with the use of male sex hormones. *J. Urol.* 1938;40:154.

19. Persky, H., K.D. Smith and G.K. Basu. Relation of psychological measures of aggression and hostility to testosterone production in man. *Psychosomatic Med.* 1971;33:265–277.

20. Kreuz, L.E., and R.M. Rose. Assessment of aggressive behavior and plasma testosterone in a young criminal population. *Psychosomatic Med.* 1972;34:321–332.

21. Ehrenkrants, J.E., E. Bliss, and M.H. Sheard. Plasma testosterone: Correlation with aggressive behavior and social dominance in man. *Psychosomatic Med.* 1974; 36:469–475.

22. Doering, C.H., H.K. Brodie, H.C. Kraemer, et al. Negative effect and plasma testosterone: a longitudinal human study. *Psychosomatic Med.* 1975;484–491.

23. Rada, R.T., D.R. Laws, and R. Kellner. Plasma testosterone levels in the rapist. *Psychosomatic Med.* 1976;38:257–266.

24. Dabbs, J.M., R.L. Frady, T.S. Carr, et al. Saliva testosterone and criminal violence in young adult prison inmates. *Psychosomatic Med.* 1987;49:174–182.

25. Oleweus, D., A. Mattsson, D. Schalling, et al. Testosterone, aggression, physical, and personality dimensions in normal adolescent males. *Psychosomatic Med.* 1980;42:253–269.

26. See references 1–4.

27. Taylor. Synthetic anabolic-androgenic steroids: A plea for controlled substance status. *Physician Sportsmed.* 1987;15(5):140–150.

28. Taylor, W.N., and A.B. Black. Pervasive anabolic steroid use among health club athletes. *Ann. Sports Med.* 1987;(3):158–161.

29. Taylor, W.N. Anabolic steroids: A plea for control. *Chiro. Sports Med.* 1987;1(2): 47–54.

30. _____. Unregulated synthetic anabolic-androgenic steroid self-use and human behavior. *Proc. Pan Am. Sports Med. Congress XII.* Bloomington, IN: Indiana University Press, 1987.

31. _____. Drug issues in sports medicine, Part 1: Steroid abuse and nonsteroidial anti-inflammatory (NSAID) selection in athletic/active patients. *J. Neurol. Ortho. Med. Surg.* 1988;9(2):159–164.

32. Pope, H.G., and D.L. Katz. Bodybuilders' psychosis. *Lancet* 1987;(April 11):863.

33. _____. Affective and psychotic symptoms associated with anabolic steroid use. *Am. J. Psychiatry* 1988; 145(4):487–490.

34. Taylor, W.N. Influences of synthetic anabolic/androgenic steroid self-use on human behavior. *J. Osteopathic Sports Med.* 1987; 1(2):19–25.

35. Pope, H.G., and D.L. Katz. Homicide and near-homicide by anabolic steroid users. *J. Clin. Psychiary* 1990;51(1):28–31.

36. Brower, J.K., F.C. Blow, T.P. Beresford, et al. Anabolic-androgenic steroid dependence. *J. Clin. Psychiatry* 1989;50(1):31–33.

37. Elofson, G., and S. Elofson. Steroids claimed our son's life. *Physician Sportsmed.* 1990;189(8):15–16.

38. Taylor. Are anabolic steroids for the long distance runner? (letter). *Annals Sports Med.* 1984;2(1):51–52.

39. See references 2 and 3.

40. Freinhar, J.P., and W. Alverez. Androgen-induced hypomania. *J.Clin. Psychiatry* 1985;46:354–355.

41. See references 1–5.

42. Barker, S. Oxymethalone and aggression. *Br. J. Psychiatry* 1987;151:564.
43. Taylor. Drug issues in sports medicine, Part 1: Steroid abuse and nonsteroidial anti-inflammatory (NSAID) selection in athletic/active patients. *J. Neurol. Ortho. Med. Surg.* 1988;9(2):159–164.
44. _____. Unregulated synthetic anabolic-androgenic steroid self-use and human behavior. *Proc. Pan Am. Sports Med. Congress XII.* Bloomington, IN: Indiana University Press, 1987.
45. Pope and Katz. Bodybuilders' psychosis. *Lancet* 1987;(April 11):863.
46. Kashkin, K.B., and H.D. Kleber. Hooked on hormones? An anabolic steroid addiction hypothesis. *J. Am. Med. Assoc.* 1989;262:3166–3170.
47. Choi, P.Y.L., A.C. Parrott, and D. Cowan. High-dose anabolic steroids in strength athletes: Effects upon hostility and aggression. *Hum. Psychopharmacol.* 1990;5: 349–356.
48. Lefavi, R.G., T.G. Reeve, and M.C. Newland. Relationship between anabolic steroid use and selected psychological parameters in male bodybuilders. *J. Sport Behav.* 1990;13:157–166.
49. Perry, P.J., W.R. Yates, and K.H. Andersen. Psychiatric symptoms associated with anabolic steroids: A controlled, retrospective study. *Ann. Clin. Psychiatry* 1990;2: 11–17.
50. Taylor, W.N. *Macho Medicine: A History of the Anabolic Steroid Epidemic.* Jefferson, N.C: McFarland & Company, 1991.
51. Uzych, L. Anabolic-androgenic steroids and psychiatric-related effects: A review. *Can. J. Psychiatry* 1992;37(1):23–28.
52. Isacsson, G., and U. Bergman. [Can anabolic steroids cause personality changes]? *Nord. Med.* 1993;108(6–7):180–181.
53. Schulte, H.M., M.J. Hall, and M. Boyer. Domestic violence associated with anabolic steroid abuse. *Am. J. Psychiatry* 1993;150(2):348.
54. Su, T.P., M. Pagliaro, P.J. Schmidt, et al. Neuropsychiatric effects of anabolic steroids in normal male volunteers. *J. Am. Med. Assoc.* 1993;269(21):2760–2764.
55. Burnett, K.F., and M.E. Kleiman. Psychological characteristics of adolescent steroid users. *Adolescence* 1994;29(113):81–89.
56. Choi, P.Y., and H.G. Pope. Violence toward women and illicit androgenic-anabolic steroid use. *Ann. Clin. Psychiatry* 1994;6(1):21–25.
57. Pope, H.G., and D.L. Katz. Psychiatric and medical effects of anabolic-androgenic steroid use: A controlled study of 160 athletes. *Arch. Gen. Psychiatry* 1994;51(5): 375–382.
58. Parrott, A.C., P.Y. Choi, and M. Davies. Anabolic steroid use by amateur athletes: Effects upon psychological mood states. *J. Sports Med. Phys. Fitness* 1994;34(3): 292–298.
59. Kouri, E.M., S.E. Lukas, H.G. Pope, et al. Increased aggressive responding male volunteers following the adminstration of gradually increasing doses of testosterone cypionate. *Drug Alcohol Depend.* 1995;40(1):73–79.
60. Nakatani, Y., and M. Udagawa. [Anabolic steroid abuse and mental disorder]. *Arukoru Kenkyuto Yakubutsu Ison.* 1995;5: 333–347.
61. Peet, M., and S. Peters. Drug-induced mania. *Drug Saf.* 1995;12(2):146–153.
62. Cooper, C.J., T.D. Noakes, T. Dunne, et al. A high prevalence of abnormal personality traits in chronic users of anabolic-androgen steroids. *Br. J. Sports Med.* 1996;30(3):246–250.
63. Corrigan, B. Anabolic steroids and the mind. *Med. J. Aust.* 1996;165(4): 222–226.
64. Dukarm, C.P., R.S. Byrd, P. Auinger, et al. Illicit substance use, gender, and the risk of violent behavior among adolescents. *Arch. Pediatr. Adolesc. Med.* 1996;150(8): 797–801.
65. Rubinow, D.R., and P.J. Schmidt. Androgens, brain, and behavior. *Am. J. Psychiatry* 1996;153(8):974–984.
66. Isacsson, G., M. Garle, E.B. Ljung, et al. Anabolic steroids and violent crime —

an epidemiological study at a jail in Stockholm, Sweden. *Compr. Psychiatry* 1998;39(4): 203–205.

67. Porcerelli, J.H., and B.A. Sandler. Anabolic-androgenic steroid abuse and psychopathology. *Psychiatr. Clin. North Am.* 1998;21(4):829–833.

68. Wilson-Fearon, C., and A.C. Parrott. Multiple drug use and dietary restraint in a Mr. Universe competitor: Psychobiological effects. *Percept. Mot. Skills* 1999;88(2): 579–580.

69. Thiblin, I., B. Runeson, and J. Rajs. Anabolic androgenic steroids and suicide. *Ann. Clin. Psychiatry* 1999;11(4):223–231.

70. Pope, H.G., E.M. Kouri, and J.I. Hudson. Effects of supraphysiologic doses of testosterone on mood and aggression in normal men: A randomized controlled trial. *Arch. Gen. Psychiatry* 2000; 57(2):133–140.

71. Thiblin, I., O. Linquist, and J. Rajs. Cause and manner of death among users of anabolic androgenic steroids. *J. Forensic Sci.* 2000;45(1):16–23.

72. Bahrke, M.S., C.E. Yesalis, and J.E. Wright. Psychological and behavioral effects of endogenous testosterone and anabolic-androgenic steroids: An update. *Sports Med.* 1996;22(6):367–390.

73. Street, C., J. Antonio, and D. Cudlipp. Androgen use by athletes: A reevaluation of the health risks. *Can.J. Appl. Physiol.* 1996;21(6):421–440.

74. Yates, W.R., P.J. Perry, J. MacIndoe, et al. Psychosexual effects of three doses of testosterone cycling in normal men. *Biol. Psychiatry* 1999;45(3):259–260.

75. Masonis, A.E.T., and M.P. McCarthy. Direct effects of the anabolic/androgenic steroids, stanozolol and 17 alpha-methyltestosterone, on benzodiazepine binding to the gamma-aminobutyric acid (a) receptor. *Neurosci. Lett.* 1995;189(1):35–38.

76. Masonis, A.E., and M.P. McCarthy. Effects of the androgenic/anabolic steroid stanzolol on GABAA receptor function: GABA-sinulated 36Cl-influx and [35S] TBPS binding. *J. Pharmacol. Exp. Ther.* 1996;279(1):186–193.

77. Frye, C.A., J.E. Duncan, M. Basham, et al. Behavioral effects of 3 alpha-androstanediol. II: Hypothalamic and preoptic area actions via a GABAergic mechanism. *Behav. Brain Res.* 1996;79:119–130.

78. Masonis, A.E., and M.P. McCarthy. Direct interactions of androgenic/anabolic steroids with the peripheral benzodiazepine receptor in rat brain: Implications for the psychological and physiological manifestations of androgenic/anabolic steroid abuse. *J. Steroid. Biochem. Mol. Biol.* 1996;58(5–6):551–555.

79. Bitran, D., R.J. Hilvers, C.A. Frye, et al. Chronic anabolic-androgenic steroid treatment affects brain GABA(A) receptor-gated chloride ion transport. *Life Sci.* 1996;58(7):573–583.

80. Tirassa, P., I. Thiblin, G. Agren, et al. High-dose anabolic androgenic steroids modulate concentrations of nerve growth factor and expression of its low affinity receptor (p75-NGFr) in male rat brain. *J. Neurosci. Res.* 1997;47(2):198–207.

81. Le Greves, P., W. Huang, P. Johansson, et al. Effects of an anabolic-androgenic steroid on the regulation of the NMDA receptor NR1, NR2A, and NR2B subunit mRNAs in brain regions of the male rat. *Neurosci. Lett.* 1997;226(1):61–64.

82. Thiblin, I., A. Finn, S.B. Ross, et al. *Br. J. Pharmacol.* 1999;126(6):1301–1306.

83. See references 76, 78, and 79.

84. Taylor. Super athletes made to order. *Psychology Today* 1985;(May):63–66.

85. See references 1–4.

86. Taylor. Effects and actions of human growth hormone. Presented at symposium on drugs in sports, American College of Sports Medicine Annual Meeting, San Diego, May 24, 1984.

87. The Steroid Trafficking Act of 1990. (see Appendix D, page 7).

88. Ibid, see reference 50.

89. Taylor, W.N. Drug issues in sports medicine, part 1. *J. Neurolgical & Orthopedic Med. Surg.* 1988;9(2):159–164.

90. _____. *Macho Medicine: A History of the Anabolic Steroid Epidemic.* Jefferson, N.C: McFarland & Company, 1991.

91. _____. Drug issues in sports medicine, part 1. *J. Neurolgical & Orthopedic Med. Surg.* 1988;9(2):159–164 and *Macho Medicine: A History of the Anabolic Steroid Epidemic*. Jefferson, N.C: McFarland & Company, 1991.

92. _____. *Hormonal Manipulation: A New Era of Monstrous Athletes* Jefferson, N.C.: McFarland & Company, 1985.

93. _____. *Macho Medicine: A History of the Anabolic Steroid Epidemic*. Jefferson, N.C: McFarland & Company, 1991.

94. _____. Drug issues in sports medicine, part 1. *J. Neurolgical & Orthopedic Med. Surg.* 1988;9(2):159–164

95. Pope, H.G., D.L Katz, and J.I. Hudson. Anorexia nervosa and "reverse anorexia" among 108 male bodybuilders. *Compr. Psychiatry* 1993;34(6):406–409.

96. Porcerelli, J.H., and B.A. Sandler. Narcissism and empathy in steroid users. *Am.J. Psychiatry* 1995;152(11):1672–1674.

97. Bloudin, A.G., and G.S. Goldfield. Body image and steroid use in male bodybuilders. *Int. J. Eat. Disord.* 1995; 18(2):159–165.

98. Schwerin, M.J., K.J. Corcoran, L. Fisher, et al. Social physique anxiety, body esteem, and social anxiety in bodybuilders and self-reported anabolic steroid users. *Addict. Behav.* 1996;21(1):1–8.

99. Wroblewska, A.M. Androgenic-anabolic steroids and body dysmorphia in young men. *J. Psychsom. Res.* 1997;42(3):225–234.

100. Gruber, A.J. and H.G. Pope. Psychiatric and medical effects of anabolic-androgenic steroid use in women. *Psychother. Psychosom.* 2000;69(1):19–26.

101. See references 2 and 4.

102. Taylor. *Hormonal Manipulation: A New Era of Monstrous Athletes* Jefferson, N.C.: McFarland & Company, 1985.

103. Yesalis, C.E., et al. Anabolic steroid use: Indications of habituation among adolescents. *J. Drug Educ.* 1989;19(2):103–116.

104. United States Department of Health and Human Services; Office of Inspector General. *Adolescent Steroid Use*. Washington, D.C., February 1991.

105. Boyea, S., et al. Ergogenic drug use among high school athletes: A three-year sequential study. Abstract presented at the annual meeting of the American College of Sports Medicine, May 1990.

106. United States Department of Health and Human Services; Office of Inspector General. *Adolescent Steroid Use*. Washington, D.C., February 1991.

107. Ibid.

108. Taylor. *Hormonal Manipulation: A New Era of Monstrous Athletes* Jefferson, N.C.: McFarland & Company, 1985.

109. Franklin, D. Stuck on steroids? *Hippocrates* 1990;(May/June):25–28.

110. Boyea, S., et al. Ergogenic drug use among high school athletes: A three-year sequential study. Abstract presented at the annual meeting of the American College of Sports Medicine, May 1990.

111. See references 1, 2, 4, 5.

112. Lamb, D.R. Anabolic steroids in athletics: How well do they work and how dangerous are they? *Am. J. Sports Med.* 1984;12(Jan.–Feb.):31–38.

113. Strauss, R.H., M.T. Liggett, and R.R. Lanese. Anabolic steroid use and perceived effects in ten weight-trained women athletes. *J.A.M.A.* 1985;253(May 17):2871–2873.

114. Hill, J.A., J.R. Suker, K. Sachs, et al. The athletic polydrug abuse phenomenon. A case study. *J. Am. Sports Med.* 1983;11(July–Aug.):269–271.

115. Burkett, L.N., and M.T. Falduto. Steroid use by athletes in a metropolitan area. *Phys. Sportsmed.* 1984;12(August):69–74.

116. Woolley, B.H., and D.W. Barnett. The use and misuse of drugs by athletes. *Houston Med. J.* 1986;2:29–35.

117. Taken from court exhibits. *US v James Bradshaw*; Case No. 86-6113, US District Court, Southern District of Florida, October 1986.

118. Boyea, S., et al. Ergogenic drug use among high school athletes: A three-year sequential study. Abstract presented at the annual meeting of the American College of Sports Medicine, May 1990.
119. Evans, N.A. Gym and tonic: A profile of 100 male steroid users. *Br. J. Sports Med.* 1997;31(1):54–58.
120. Meilman, P.W., R.K. Crace, C.A. Presley, et al. Beyond performance enhancement: Polypharmacy among collegiate users of steroids. *J. Am. Coll. Health* 1995;44 (3):98–104.
121. DuRant, R.H., L.G. Escobedo and G.W. Heath. Anabolic-steroid use, strength training, and multiple drug use among adolescents in the United States. *Pediatrics* 1995;96(1 Pt.1):23–28.
122. Middleman, A.B., and R.H. DuRant. Anabolic steroid use and associated health risk behaviours. *Sports Med.* 1996;21(4):251–255.
123. McBride, A.J., K. Williamson, and T. Petersen. Three cases of nalbuphine hydrochloride dependence associated with anabolic steroid use. *Br. J. Sports Med.* 1996;30 (1):69–70.
124. Wines, J.D., A.J. Gruber, H.G. Pope, et al. Nalbuphine hydrochloride dependence in anabolic steroid users. *Am. J. Addict.* 1999;8(2):161–164.
125. Wilson-Fearon, C., and A.C. Parrott. Multiple drug use and dietary restraint in a Mr. Universe competitor: Psychobiological effects. *Percept. Mot. Skills* 1999;88 (2):579–580.
126. Wroblewska. Androgenic-anabolic steroids and body dysmorphia in young men. *J. Psychsom. Res.* 1997;42(3):225–234.
127. Thiblin, et al. Cause and manner of death among users of anabolic androgenic steroids. *J. Forensic Sci.* 2000;45(1):16–23.
128. The Steroid Trafficking Act of 1990. 101st Congress 2nd Session, U.S. Senate, the Committee on the Judiciary, Report 101–433, Washington, D.C., August 30, 1990.

Chapter 9

1. Taylor, W.N. *Macho Medicine: A New Era of Monstrous Athletes.* Jefferson, N.C.: McFarland & Company, 1991.
2. de Kruif, P. *The Male Hormone.* New York: Harcourt, Brace and Company, 1945.
3. Ryan, A.J., Anabolic steroids: The myth dies hard. *Physician Sportsmed.* 1978;March:3.
4. Moxley, J.H. Drug abuse in athletes: Anabolic steroids and human growth hormone. AMA, Report of the Council on Scientific Affairs, Resolution 57, A-86, December 1986.
5. Cowart, V. Classifying steroids as controlled substances suggested to decrease athletes' supply, but enforcement could be a major problem. *JAMA.* 1987;257(22):3029.
6. Hearings before the Committee on the Judiciary, United States Senate, 101st Congress, 1st Session (S.Hrg.101–736). U.S. Government Printing Office, Washington, D.C., 1990.
7. Taylor. *Macho Medicine: A New Era of Monstrous Athletes.* Jefferson, N.C.: McFarland & Company, 1991.
8. American College of Sports Medicine: Position statement on the use and abuse of anabolic-androgenic steroids in sports. *Med. Sci. Sports* 1977;9:11–13.
9. American College of Sports Medicine: Position statement on the use of anabolic-androgenic steroids in sports, revised. *Sports Med. Bull.* 1984;19(3):13–18.
10. Taylor, W.N. *Anabolic Steroids and the Athlete.* Jefferson, N.C.: McFarland & Company, 1982.

11. _____. Effects and actions of human growth hormone. Presented at symposium on drugs in sports, American College of Sports Medicine annual meeting, San Diego, CA, May 24, 1984.
12. Haupt, H.A., and G.D. Rovere. Anabolic steroids: A review of the literature. *Am. J. Sports Med.* 1984;12(6):469–484.
13. Oakley, R. *Drugs, Society & Human Behavior.* St. Louis: C.V. Mosby Co., 1983.
14. Schmeckebier, L.F. *The bureau of prohibition.* Service Mongraph No. 57, Institute for Government Research, Brookings Institute, 1929.
15. Senate Committee on the Judiciary: *The illicit narcotic traffic.* Senate Report No. 1440, 84th Congress, 2nd Session, 1956.
16. Taylor. *Macho Medicine: A New Era of Monstrous Athletes.* Jefferson, N.C.: McFarland & Company, 1991.
17. Goldman, B. *Death in the Locker Room.* South Bend, IN: Icarus Press, 1985.
18. Depressant and stimulant drugs, Part 166, Title 21, *Code of Federal Regulations,* Washington, D.C., Food and Drug Administration, 1966.
19. Congressional Record, House of Representatives, House Bill H9170, September 24, 1970.
20. Ryan. Anabolic steroids: The myth dies hard. *Physician Sportsmed.* 1978; March:3.
21. Johnson, L.C., and J.P. O'Shea. Anabolic steroids: Effects on strength development. *Science* 1968;164:957–959.
22. Wright, J.E. *Anabolic Steroids in Sports.* Natick, MA: Sports Science Consultants, 1978.
23. American College of Sports Medicine: Position statement on the use of anabolic-androgenic steroids in sports, revised. *Sports Med. Bull.* 1984;19(3):13–18.
24. Ibid.
25. Taylor, W.N. The last word on steroids: Medicine can't ignore the issue. *Muscle & Fitness* 1984; February, 88+.
26. Taylor. Effects and actions of human growth hormone. Presented at symposium on drugs in sports, American College of Sports Medicine annual meeting, San Diego, CA, May 24, 1984.
27. _____. *Macho Medicine: A New Era of Monstrous Athletes.* Jefferson, N.C.: McFarland & Company, 1991.
28. _____. *Anabolic Steroids and the Athlete.* Jefferson, N.C.: McFarland & Company, 1982.
29. Fowler, W.M., G.W. Gardner, and G.H. Egstrom. Effect of an anabolic steroid on physical performance of young men. *J. Appl. Physiol.* 1965;20:1038–1040.
30. Ibid, see reference 21.
31. Casner, S.W., R.G. Early, and B.B. Carlson. Anabolic steroid effects on body composition in normal young men. *J. Sports. Med. Phys. Fitness* 1971;11:98–100.
32. Johnson, F.L., G. Fisher, L.H. Silvester, et al. Anabolic steroids: Effects on strength, body weight, oxygen uptake and spermatogenesis. *Med. Sci. Sports* 1972;4:43–45.
33. Fahey, T.D., and C.H. Brown. The effects of an anabolic steroid on strength, body composition and endurance of college males when accompanied by a weight training program. *Med. Sci. Sports* 1973;5:272–276.
34. Win-May, M., and M. May-tu. The effects of anabolic steroids on physical fitness. *J. Sports Med. Phys. Fitness* 1975;15:266–271.
35. Hervey, G.R., I. Hutchinson, A.V. Knibbs, et al. "Anabolic" effects of methandienone in men undergoing athletic training. *Lancet* 1976;2:699–702.
36. Ibid.
37. O'Shea, J.P., and W. Winkler. Biochemical and physical effects of an anabolic steroid in competitive swimmers and weight lifters. *Nutr. Rpts. Intern.*1970;2:351–362.
38. O'Shea, J.P. The effects of an anabolic steroid on dynamic strength levels of weight lifters. *Nutr. Rpts. Inter.* 1971;4:363–370.
39. Bowers, R.W., and J.P. Reardon. Effects of methandrostenolone (Dianabol) on strength development and aerobic capacity. *Med. Sci. Sports* 1972;4:54.

40. Ariel, G. The effect of anabolic steroid on skeletal muscle contractive force. *J. Sports Med. Phys. Fitness* 1973;13:187–190.
41. Ward, P. The effect of an anabolic steroid on strength and lean body mass. *Med. Sci. Sports* 1973;5:277–282.
42. Golding, L.A., J.E. Freydinjer, and S.S. Fisher. Weight, size, and strength—unchanged with steroids. *Physician & Sportsmed.* 1974;2:39–43.
43. Stanford, B.A., and R. Moffatt. Anabolic steroid: Effectiveness as an ergogenic aid to experienced weight trainers. *J. Sports Med. Phys. Fitness* 1974;14:191–197.
44. O'Shea, J.P. Biochemical evaluation of effects of stanozolol on adrenal, liver and muscle function in man. *Nutr. Rpts. Inter.* 1974;10:381–388.
45. Freed, D.L.J., and A.J. Banks. A double-blind crossover trial of methandieonone (Dianabol, Ciba) in moderate doses on highly trained experienced athletes. *Br. J. Sports Med.* 1975;9:78–81.
46. Haupt and Rovere. Anabolic steroids: A review of the literature. *Am. J. Sports Med.* 1984;12(6):469–484.
47. American College of Sports Medicine: Position statement on the use of anabolic-androgenic steroids in sports, revised. *Sports Med. Bull.* 1984;19(3):13–18.
48. Moxley. Drug abuse in athletes: Anabolic steroids and human growth hormone. AMA, Report of the Council on Scientific Affairs, Resolution 57, A-86, December 1986.
49. Cowart. Classifying steroids as controlled substances suggested to decrease athletes supply, but enforcement could be a major problem. *JAMA.* 1987;257(22):3029.
50. Ibid.
51. Ibid.
52. Ibid.
53. Ibid.
54. Langston, E.L. Statement of the American Medical Association to the Committee on the Judiciary, United States Senate, RE: Scheduling of anabolic steroids. April 3, 1989.
55. Yesalis, C.E., C.K. Barsukiewicz, A.N. Kopstein, et al. Trends in anabolic-androgenic steroid use among adolescents. *Arch. Pediatr. Adolesc. Med.* 1997;151(12): 1197–1206.
56. Radokovich, J., P. Broderick, and G. Pickell. Rate of anabolic-androgenic steroid use among students in junior high school. *J. Am. Board Fam. Pract.* 1993;6(4):341–345.
57. Tanner, S.M., D.W. Miller, and C. Alongi. Anabolic steroid use by adolescents: prevalence, motives, and knowledge of risks. *Clin. J. Sport Med.* 1995;5(2):108–115.
58. Scott, D.M., J.C. Wagner, and T.W. Barlow. Anabolic steroid use among adolescents in Nebraska schools. *Am. J. Health Syst. Pharm.* 1996;53(17):2068–2078.
59. Faigenbaum, A.D., L.D. Zaichkowsky, D.E. Gardner, et al. Anabolic steroid use by male and female students. *Pediatrics* 1998;101(5):E6.
60. Stilger, V.G., and C.E. Yesalis. Anabolic-androgenic steroid use among high school football players. *J. Community Health* 1999;24(2):131–145.
61. Haupt, H.A. Anabolic steroids and growth hormone. *Am. J. Sports Med.* 1993; 21(3):468–474.
62. Perko, M.A., J. Cowdery, M.Q. Wang, et al. Associations between academic performance of Division 1 college athletes and their perceptions of the effects of anabolic steroids. *Percept. Mot. Skills* 1995;80(1):284–286.
63. Radokovich, et al. Rate of anabolic-androgenic steroid use among students in junior high school. *J. Am. Board Fam. Pract.* 1993;6(4):341–345.
64. Anshel, M.H., and K.G. Russell. Examining athletes' attitudes toward using anabolic steroids and their knowledge of the possible effects. *J. Drug. Educ.* 1997;27 (2):121–145.
65. Goldberg, L., D. Elliot, G.N. Clarke, et al. Effects of a multidimensional anabolic steroid prevention intervention: The Adolescents Training and Learning to Avoid Steroids (ATLAS) program. *JAMA.* 1996;276(19):1555–1562.

66. Haupt. Anabolic steroids and growth hormone. *Am. J. Sports Med.* 1993;21(3): 468–474.

67. Lovstakken, K., L. Peterson, and A.L. Homer. Risk factors for anabolic steroid use in college students and the role of expectancy. *Addict. Behav.* 1999;24(3):425–430.

68. Scott, et al. Anabolic steroid use among adolescents in Nebraska schools. *Am. J. Health Syst. Pharm.* 1996;53(17):2068–2078.

69. Faigenbaum, et al. Anabolic steroid use by male and female students. *Pediatrics* 1998;101(5):E6.

70. Yesalis, C.E., N.J. Kennedy, A.N. Kopstein et al. Anabolic-androgenic steroid use in the United States. *JAMA.* 270(10):1271–1221.

Chapter 10

1. Taylor, W.N. *Hormonal Manipulation: A New Era of Monstrous Athletes.* Jefferson, NC: McFarland & Company, 1985.

2. _____. Super athletes made to order. *Psychology Today* 1985;(May):63–66.

3. _____. Synthetic HGH should be classified as a controlled substance to prevent abuse. *Genetic Engineering News*, 1986;6:4.

4. _____. Synthetic human growth hormone: A call for federal control. *Physician Sportsmed.* 1988;16(3):189–192.

5. _____. Gigantic athletes: The dilemma of human growth hormone. *Futurist* 1985;(August):8–12.

6. _____. Will synthetic human growth hormone become the peril of genetic engineering? *Ann. Sports Med.* 1986;2:197–199.

7. _____. *Anabole Steroide im Leistungssport.* Arnsberg: Auflage Novagenics Verlag, 1990.

8. Moxley, J.H. Drug abuse in athletes: Anabolic steroids and human growth hormone. AMA, Report of the Council on Scientific Affairs, Resolution 57, A-86, December 1986.

9. Illicit Diversion and Abuse of Human Growth Hormone. Hearings before the Subcommitee on Health and the Environment, U.S. House of Representatives, 100th Congress, First Session. Washington, D.C: U.S. Government Printing Office, 1987.

10. Sullivan, R., and S. Song. Are drugs winning the Games? *Time*, Sept. 11, 2000, pp. 90–92.

11. Franke, W.W., and B. Beredonk. Hormonal doping and androgenization of athletes: A secret program of the German Democratic Republic government. *Clin. Chem.* 1997;43(7):1262–1279.

12. Laure, P. [Doping: epidemiological studies]. *Presse. Med.* 2000;29(24): 1365–1372.

13. Mottram, D.R. Banned drugs in sport: Does the International Olympic Committee (IOC) list need updating? *Sports Med.* 1999;27(1):1–10.

14. Cecchi, R., and L. Cipolloni. Comparative analysis of European legislation on doping. *Med. Law* 1995;14(7–8):571–579.

15. Taylor, W.N. *Macho Medicine: A History of the Anabolic Steroid Epidemic.* Jefferson, N.C.: McFarland & Company, p.96, 1991.

16. Kin, C.A. Coming soon to the "genetic supermarket" near you. *Stanford Law Rev.* 1996;48(6):1573–1604.

17. Ibid.

18. Savine, R., and P.H. Sonksen. Is the somatopause an indication for growth hormone replacement? *J. Endocrinol. Invest.* 1999;22(5 Suppl):142–149.

19. Bradley, C.A., and T.M. Sodeman. Human growth hormone: Its use and abuse. *Clin. Lab. Med.* 1990;10(3):473–477.

20. Kreck, C. S., Bingel, E. Heberlein, et al. [Social medicine aspects of growth hormone treatment in children]. *Versicherungsmedizin* 1999;51(4):186–193.

21. Kicman, A.T., R.V. Brooks, and D.A. Cowan. Human chorionic gonadotrophin and sport. *Br. H. Sports Med.* 1991;25(2):73–80.

22. Cowan, D.A., A.T. Kicman, C.J. Walker, et al. Effect of administration of human chorionic gonadotrophin on criteria used to assess testosterone administration in athletes. *J. Endocrinol.* 1991;131(1):147–154.

23. Delbeke, F.T., P. Van Eenoo, and P. De Backer. Detection of human chorionic gonadotrophin misuse in sports. *Int. J. Sports Med.* 1998;287–290.

24. Kicman, A.T., and D.A. Cowan. Peptide hormones and sports: Misuse and detection. *Br. Med. Bull.* 1992;48(3):496–517.

25. Bower, K.J. Withdrawal from anabolic steroids. *Curr. Ther. Endocrinol. Metab.* 1994;5:291–296.

26. Robyn, C., M. L'Hermite, R. Lecercq, et al. Effects of testosterone and gonadotrophin responses to synthetic LH and FSH releasing hormone (LRH) in normal men. *Acta Endocrinol.* (Copenh.) 1976;83(4):692–699.

27. Katz, M., B.L. Pimstone, P.J. Carr, et al. Plasma gonadotropin and gonadotropin-releasing hormone levels after intranasal administration of gonadotropin releasing hormone. *J. Clin. Endocrinol. Metab.* 1976;43(1):215–221.

28. Laszi, F., J. Julesz, G. Bartfai, et al. Serum FSH and LH levels in men after administration of a long-acting LH-RH preparation. *Acta Med. Acad. Sci. Hung.* 1982; 39(3–4):125–131.

29. de Kretser, D.M., H.G. Burger, B. Hudson, et al. The pituitary-testicular response to luteinizing hormone releasing hormone administration to normal men. *Aust. N.Z.J. Med.* 1975;5(3):227–230.

30. Jaramillo Jaramillo, C., V. Perez-Ingante, Marcia Lopez, et al. Serum LH, FSH and testosterone response to the administration of a new LH-RH analog, D-Trp6-LH-RH, in normal men. *Int. J. Fertil.* 1977;22(2):77–84.

31. Baumann, G. Growth hormone heterogeneity: Genes, isohormones, variants, and binding proteins. *Endocr. Rev.* 1991;12(4):424–449.

32. Charrier, J., and J. Martal. Growth hormones: Polymorphism (minireview). *Reprod. Nutr. Dev.* 1988;28(4A):857–887.

33. G. Baumann. Metabolism of growth hormone (GH) and different molecular forms of GH in biological fluids. *Horm. Res.* 1991;36(Suppl.1):5–10.

34. Tchelet, A., A. Gertler, E. Sakal, et al. Selective modification of human growth hormone by site-directed mutagenesis: Implications for the diversity of biological actions. *Horm. Res.* 1994;41(Suppl. 2):103–112.

35. Pontiroli, A.E. Peptide hormones: Review of the current and emerging uses by nasal delivery. *Adv. Drug Deliv. Rev.* 1998;29(1–2):81–87.

36. Cameron, C.M., J.L. Kostyo, V. Kumar, et al. Trypsin-resistant forms of human growth hormone have diabetogenic and insulin-like activities. *Biochim. Biophys. Acta* 1985;841(3):254–260.

37. Chen, W.Y., N.Y. Chen, J. Yun, et al. Amino acid residues in the third alpha-helix of growth hormone involved in growth promoting activity. *Mol. Endocrinol.* 1995;9(3):292–302.

38. Tchelet, A., T. Vogel, D. Helman, et al. Selective modification at the N-terminal region of human growth hormone that shows antagonistic activity. *Mol. Cell. Endocrinol.* 1997;130(1–2):141–152.

39. Vittone, J., M.R. Blackman, J. Whitehead-Busby, et al. Effects of single nightly injections of growth hormone-releasing hormone (GHRH 1-29) in healthy adults. *Metabolism* 1977;46(1):89–96.

40. Harris, A.S. Review: Clinical opportunities proved by the nasal administration of peptides. *J. Drug Target* 1993;1(2):101–116.

41. Svensson, J.A., and B. Bengtsson. Clinical and experimental effects of growth hormone secretagogues on various organ systems. *Horm. Res.* 1999;51(Suppl. 3):16–20.

42. Chapman, I.M., M.A. Bach, E. Van Cauter, et al. Stimulation of the growth hormone (GH)-insulin-like growth factor I axis by daily oral administration of a GH secretagogue (MK-677) in healthy elderly subjects. *J. Clin. Endocrinol. Metab.* 1996;81 (12):4249–4257.

43. Arvat, E., L. Di Vito, B. Maccogno, et al. Effects of GHRP-2 and hexarelin, two GH-releasing peptides, on GH, prolactin, ACTH and cortisol levels in man: Comparison with the effects of GHRH, TRH and hCRH. *Peptides* 1997;18(6):885–891.

44. Ghigo, E., E. Arvat, L. Gianotti, et al. Growth hormone-releasing activity of hexarelin, a new synthetic hexapeptide, after intravenous, subcutaneous, intranasal, and oral administration in man. *J. Clin. Endocrinol. Metab.* 1994;78(3):693–698.

45. Arvat, E., L. Di Vito, F. Lanfranco, et al. Tyr-Ala-Hexarelin, synthetic octapeptide, possesses the same endocrine activities as Hexarelin and GHRP-2 in humans. *J. Endocrinol. Invest.* 1999;22(2):91–97.

46. Aoli, J.A., B.J. Gertz, M.L. Hartman, et al. Neuroendocrine responses to a novel growth hormone secretagogue, L-692,429, in healthy older adults. *J. Clin. Endocrinol. Metab.* 1994;79(4):943–949.

47. Bellone, J., L. Ghizzoni, G. Aimaretti, et al. Growth hormone-releasing effect of oral growth hormone-releasing peptide 6 (GHRP-6) administration in children with short stature. *Eur. J. Endocrinol.* 1995;133(4):425–429.

48. Gertz, B.J., J.S. Barrett, R. Eisenhandler, et al. Growth hormone response in man to L-692,429, a novel nonpeptide mimic of growth hormone-releasing peptide-6. *J. Clin. Endocrinol. Metab.* 1993;77(5):1393–1397.

49. Korbonits, M., and A.B. Grossman. Growth hormone releasing peptides (GHRP) and their analogues. *Orv. Hetil.* 1996;137(45):2503–2509.

50. Camanni, F., E. Ghigo, F. Arvat. Growth hormone-releasing peptides and their analogs. *Front. Neuroendocrinol.* 1999;19(1):47–72.

51. Deghenghi, R. The development of "impervious peptides" as growth hormone secretagogues. *Acta Paediatr. Suppl.* 1997;423:85–87.

52. Sartorio, A., A. Conti, S. Ferrero, et al. GH responsiveness to repeated GHRH or hexarelin administration in normal adults. *J. Endocrinol. Invest.* 1995;18(9):718–722.

53. Massoud, A.F., P.C. Hindmarsh, and C.G. Brook. Hexarelin-induced growth hormone, cortisol, and prolactin release: A dose-response study. *J. Clin. Endocrinol. Metab.* 1996;81(12):4338–4341.

54. Bowers, C.Y., G.A. Reynolds, D. Durham, et al. Growth hormone (GH)-releasing peptide stimulates GH release in normal men and acts synergistically with GH-releasing hormone. *J. Clin. Endocrinol. Metab.* 1990;70(4):975–82.

55. Loche, S., A. Colao, M. Cappa, et al. Acute administration of hexarelin stimulates GH secretion during the day and night. *Clin. Endocrionol.* (Oxf.) 1997;46(3): 275–279.

56. Ghigo, E., E. Arvat, and F. Camanni. Orally active growth hormone secretagogues: state of the art and clinical perspectives. *Ann. Med.* 1998;30(2):159–168.

57. Maccario, M. E. Arvat, M. Procopio, et al. Metabolic modulation of the growth hormone-releasing activity of hexarelin in man. *Metabolism* 1995;44(1):134–138.

58. De Marinis, L., A. Mancini, D. Valle, et al. Role of food intake in the modulation of hexarelin-induced growth hormone release in normal human subjects. *Horm. Metab. Res.* 2000;32(4):152–156.

59. Massoud, A.F., P.C. Hindmarsh, and G.C. Brook. Hexarelin induced growth hormone release is influenced by exogenous growth hormone. *Clin. Endocrinol.* (Oxf.) 1995;43(5):617–621.

60. Cappa, M., S. Setzu, S. Bernardini, et al. Exogenous growth hormone administration does not inhibit the growth hormone response to hexarelin in normal men. *J. Endocrionol. Invest.* 1995;18(10):762–766.

61. Eakman, G.D., J.S. Dallas, S.W. Ponder, et al. The effects of testosterone and dihydrotestosterone on hypothalamic regulation of growth hormone secretion. *J. Clin. Endocrinol. Metab.* 1996;81(3):1217–1223.

62. Loche, S., P. Cambiasco, D. Carta, et al. The growth hormone-releasing activity of hexarelin, a new synthetic hexapeptide, in short normal and obese children and in hypopituitary subjects. *J. Clin. Endocrinol. Metab.* 1995;80(2):674–678.

63. Loche, S., A. Colao, M. Cappa, et al. The growth hormone response to hexarelin in children: Reproducibility and effect of sex steroids. *J. Clin. Endocrinol. Metab.* 1997;82(3):861–864.

64. Argente, J., L.M. Garcia-Sergura, J. Pozo, et al. Growth hormone-releasing peptides: Clinical and basic aspects. *Horm. Res.* 1996;46(4–5):155–159.

65. Bellone, J., G. Aimaretti, E. Bartolotta, et al. Growth hormone-releasing activity of hexarelin, a new synthetic hexapeptide, before and after puberty. *J. Clin. Endocrinol. Metab.* 1995;80(4):1090–1094.

66. Hatton, J., M.S. Luer, and R.P. Rapp. Growth factors in nutritional support. *Pharacotherapy* 1993;13(1):17–27.

67. Johansson, A.G., E. Lindh, W.F. Blum, et al. Effects of growth hormone and insulin-like growth factor I in men with idiopathic osteoporosis. *J. Clin. Endocrinol. Metab.* 1996;81(1):44–48.

68. Mauras, N., and M.W. Haymond. Metabolic effects of recombinant human insulin-like growth factor-I in humans: Comparison with recombinant human growth hormone. *Pediatr. Nephrol.* 1996;10(3):318–323.

69. Backeljauw, P.F., and L.E. Underwood. Prolonged treatment with recombinant insulin-like growth factor-1 in children with growth hormone insensitivity syndrome — a clinical research center study. GHIS Collaborative Group. *J. Clin. Endocrinol. Metab.* 1996;81(9):3312–3317.

70. Kupfer, S.R., L.E. Underwood, R.C. Baxter, et al. Enhancement of the anabolic effects of growth hormone and insulin-like growth factor I by use of both agents simultaneously. *J. Clin. Invest.* 1993;91(2):391–396.

71. Mauras, N., K.O. O'Brien, S. Welch, et al. Insulin-like growth factor I and growth hormone (GH) treatment in GH-deficient humans: Differential effects on protein, glucose, lipid, and calcium metabolism. *J. Clin. Endocrinol. Metab.* 2000;85(4): 1686–1694.

72. Wilson, M.E. Administration of IGF-I affects the GH axis and adolescent growth in normal monkeys. *J. Endocrinol.* 1997;153(2):327–335.

73. Russell-Jones, D.L. Hormone abuse in sport. *Growth Horm. IGF Res.* 1999; 9(Suppl. A):63–65.

74. Jarvis, C.A. Tour de Farce. *Br. J. Sports. Med.* 1999;33(2):142–143.

75. Pell, J.M., and R. Aston. Active immunization with a synthetic peptide region of growth hormone: increased lean tissue growth. *J. Endocrinol.* 1991;131(1):R1-4.

76. Anwer, K., M. Shi, M.F. French, et al. Systemic effect of human growth hormone after intramuscular injection of a single dose of a muscle-specific gene medicine. *Hum. Gene Ther.* 1998;9(5):659–670.

77. MacColl, G.S., F.J. Novo, N.J. Marshall, et al. Optimisation of growth hormone production by muscle cells using plasmid DNA. *J. Endocrinol.* 2000;165(2): 329–336.

78. Taylor, W.N. Effects and actions of human growth hormone. Presented at symposium on drugs in sports, American College of Sports Medicine annual meeting, San Diego, May 24, 1984.

79. Crist, D.M., G.T. Peake, P.A. Egan, et al. Body composition response to exogenous GH during training in highly conditioned athletes. *J. Appl. Physiol.* 1988;65(2):579–584.

80. Crist, D.M., G.T. Peake, R.B. Loftfield, et al. Supplemental growth hormone alters body composition, muscle protein metabolism and serum lipids in fit adults: Characterization of dose-dependent and response-recovery effects. *Mech. Ageing Dev.* 1991; 58(2–3):191–205.

81. Deyssig, R., H. Frisch, W.F. Blum, et al. Effect of growth hormone treatment on hormonal parameters, body composition and strength in athletes. *Acta Endocrinol.* (Copenh.) 1993;128(4):313–318.

82. Karila, T., H. Koistinen, M. Seppala, et al. Growth hormone induced increase in serum IGFBP-3 level is reversed by anabolic steroids in substance abusing power athlete. *Clin. Endocrinol.* (Oxf.) 1998;49(4):459–463.

83. Giorgi, A., R.P. Weatherby, and P.W. Murphy. Muscular strength, body composition and health responses to the use of testosterone enanthate: a double blind study. *J. Sci. Med. Sport* 1999;2(4):341–355.

84. Yarasheski, K.E., J.A. Campbell, K. Smith, et al. Effect of growth hormone and resistance exercise on muscle growth in young men. *Am J. Physiol.* 1992;262 (3 pt. 1): E261–267.

85. Rosen, C.J. Growth hormone and aging. *Endocrine* 2000;12(2):197–201.

86. Gibney, J., J.D. Wallace, T. Spinks, et al. The effects of 10 years of recombinant human growth hormone (GH) in adult GH-deficient patients. *J. Clin. Endocriol. Metab.* 1999;84(8):2596–2602.

87. Wallymahmed, M.E., P. Foy, D. Shaw, et al. Quality of life, body composition and muscle strength in adult growth hormone deficiency: The influence of growth hormone replacement therapy for up to 3 years. *Clin. Endocrinol.* (Oxf.) 1997;47(4): 439–446.

88. Jorgensen, J.O., N. Vahl, T.B. Hansen, et al. Growth hormone versus placebo treatment for one year in growth hormone deficient adults: Increase in exercise capacity and normalization of body composition. *Clin. Endocrinol.* (Oxf.) 1996;45(6):681–688.

89. Al-Shoumer, K.A., B. Page, E. Thomas, et al. Effects of four years' treatment with biosynthetic human growth hormone (GH) on body composition in GH-deficient hypopituitary adults. *Eur. J. Endocrinol.* 1996;135(5):559–567.

90. Rodrigeuz-Arnao, J. Jabbar, K. Fulcher, et al. Effects of growth hormone replacement on physical performance and body composition in GH deficient adults. *Clin. Endocrinol.* (Oxf.) 1999;51(1):53–60.

91. Cuneo, R.C., S. Judd, J.D. Wallace, et al. The Australian Multicenter Trial of Growth Hormone (GH) Treatment in GH-Deficient Adults. *J. Clin. Endocrinol.* 1998;83 (1):107–116.

92. Carroll, P.V., R. Littlewood, A.J. Weissberger, et al. The effects of two doses of replacement growth hormone on the biochemical, body composition and psychological profiles of growth hormone-deficient adults. *Eur. J. Endocrinol.* 1997;137(2):146–153.

93. Whitehead, H.M., C. Boreham, E.M. McIlrath, et al. Growth hormone treatment of adults with growth hormone deficiency: Results of a 13-month placebo controlled cross-over study. *J. Clin. Endocrinol.* (Oxf.) 1992;36(1):45–52.

94. Papadakis, M.A., D. Grady, D. Black, et al. Growth hormone replacement in healthy older men improves body composition but not functional ability. *Ann. Int. Med.* 1996;124(8):708–716.

95. Woodhouse, L.J., S.L. Asa, S.G. Thomas, et al. Measures of submaximal aerobic performance evaluate and predict functional response to growth hormone (GH) treatment in GH-deficient adults. *J. Clin. Endocrinol Metab.* 1999;84(12):4570–4577.

96. Chung, Y.S., H.C. Lee, S.K. Hwang, et al.Growth hormone replacement therapy in adults with growth hormone deficiency; thrice weekly low dose administration. *J. Korean Med. Sci.* 1994;9(2):169–178.

97. Cuneo, R.C., F. Salomon, C.M. Wiles, et al. Growth hormone treatment in growth hormone-deficient adults. I. Effects on muscle mass and strength. *J. Appl. Physiol.* 1991;70(2):688–694.

98. _____. Growth hormone treatment in growth-hormone-deficient adults. II. Effects on exercise performance. *J. Appl. Physiol.* 1991;70(2):695–700.

99. Jorgenson, J.O., L. Thuesen, J. Muller, et al. Three years of growth hormone treatment in growth hormone-deficient adults: Near normalization of body composition and physical performance. *Eur. J. Endocrinol.* 1994;130(3):224–228.

100. Cuttica, C.M., L. Castoldi, G.P. Gorrini, et al. Effects of six-month administration of recombinant human growth hormone to healthy elderly subjects. *Aging* (Milano) 1997;9(3):193–197.

101. Taaffe, D.R., L. Pruitt, J. Reim, et al. Effect of recombinant human growth hormone on the muscle strength response to resistance exercise in elderly men. *J. Clin. Endocrinol. Metab.* 1994;79(5):1361–1366.
102. Welle, S., C. Thornton, M. Statt, et al. Growth hormone increases muscle mass and strength but does not rejuvenate myofibrillar protein synthesis in health subjects over 60 years old. *J. Clin. Endocrinol. Metab.* 1996;81(9):3239–3243.
103. Salomon, F., R.C. Cuneo, R. Hesp, et al. The effects of treatment with recombinant human growth hormone on body composition and metabolism in adults with growth hormone deficiency. *N. Engl. J. Med.* 1989;321(26):1797–1803.
104. Jorgensen, J.O., N. Moller, T. Wolthers, et al. Fuel metabolism in growth hormone-deficient adults. *Metabolism* 44(10 Suppl. 4):103–107.
105. Nam, S.Y., and C. Marcus. Growth hormone and adipocyte function in obesity. *Horm. Res.* 2000;53(Suppl. S1):87–97.
106. Ho, K.K., A.J. O'Sullivan, and D.M. Hoffman. Metabolic actions of growth hormone in man. *Endocr. J.* 1996;43(Suppl.):S57–63.
107. Morales, A., J.P. Heaton, and C.C Carson. Andropause: A misnomer for a true clinical entity. *J. Urol.* 2000;163(3):705–712.
108. Savine, R., and P. Sonksen. Growth hormone — hormone replacement for somatopause? *Horm. Res.* 2000;53(Suppl. S3):37–41.
109. Umpleby, A.M., and D.L. Russell-Jones. The hormonal control of protein metabolism. *Baillieres Clin. Endocrinol. Metab.* 1996;10(4):551–570.
110. Haupt, H.A. Anabolic steroids and growth hormone. *Am. J. Sports Med.* 1993;21(3):468–474.
111. Spalding, B.J. Black-market biotechnology: Athletes abuse EPO and HGH. *Biotechnology* 1991;9(11):1050.
112. Deyssig, R. and H. Frisch. Self-administration of cadaveric growth hormone in power athletes. *Lancet* 1993;341(8847):768–769.
113. Davies, J.S., C.L. Morgan, C.J. Currie, et al. Growth hormone use by body builders. *Br. J. Sports Med.* 1997;31(4):352–353.
114. Pierard-Franchimont, C., F. Henry, J.M. Crielaard, et al. Mechanical properties of skin in recombinant human growth factor abusers among adult bodybuilders. *Dermatology* 1996;192(4):389–392.
115. Frisch, H. Growth hormone and body composition in athletes. *J. Endocrinol. Invest.* 1999; 22(5 Suppl.):106–109.
116. Laudo Pardos, C., V. Puigdevall Gallego, and M.J. del Rio Mayor. [Hormonal substances used as ergogenic agents]. *Med. Clin.* (Barc.) 1999;112(2):67–73.
117. Sturmi, J.E., and D.J. Diorio. Anabolic agents. *Clin. Sports Med.* 1998;17(2): 261–282.
118. Knopp, W.D., T.W. Wang, B.R. Bach, et al. Ergogenic drugs in sports. *Clin. Sports Med.* 1997;16(3):375–392.
119. Barinaga, M. Biotech patents. Genentech, UC settle suit for $200 million. *Science* 1999;286(5445):1655.
120. Taylor, W.N. Drug issues in sports medicine, Part II. Growth hormone abuse and anti-hypertensive drug selection in athletic/athletic patients. *J. Neurol. Orthoped. Med. Surg.* 1988;9(2):165–169.
121. _____. Personal communications from self-users of growth hormone.
122. Ramirez, O.T., and R. Quintero. Pharmaceutical biotechnology emerges in Mexico. *Nat. Biotechnol.*1999;17(1):934.
123. Bamberger, M., and D. Yeager. Over the edge. *Sports Illustrated*, April 14, 1997, pp.61–70.
124. Taylor, W.N. Personal communications with athletes.
125. _____. Gigantic athletes: The dilemma of human growth hormone. *Futurist* 1985;(August):8–12.
126. _____. Super athletes made to order. *Psychology Today* 1985;(May):63–66.

127. _____. Hormonal Manipulation: A New Era of Monstrous Athletes. Jefferson, N.C.: McFarland & Company, 1985, 66–67.

128. Smals, A.E., G.F. Pieters, A.G. Smals, et al. Sex difference in growth hormone response to growth hormone-releasing hormone between pubertal tall girls and boys. *Acta Endocrinol.* (Copenh.) 1987;116(2):161–164.

129. Tauber, M., C. Pienkowski, and P. Rochiccioli. Growth hormone secretion in children and adolescents with familial tall stature. *Eur. J. Pediatr.* 153(5):311–316.

130. Ibid.

131. Martha, P.M., A.D. Rogol, J.D. Veldhuis, et al. A longitudinal assessment of hormonal and physical alterations during normal puberty in boys. III. The neuroendocrine growth hormone axis during late puberty. *J. Clin. Endocrinol. Metab.* 1996–81(11):4068–4074.

132. Bellone, J., S. Bellone, G. Aimaretti, et al. The negative GH auto-feedback in childhood: Effects of rhGH and/or GHRH on the somatotroph response to GHRH or hexarelin, a peptidyl GH secretagogue, in children. *J. Endocrinol. Invest.* 2000;23 (3):158–162.

133. Butenandt, A., and G. Hanisch. Uber Testoseron, Umwandlund des Dehyroandrosterons in Androstendiol und Testosterone; ein Weg zur Dartselllun des Testosterones aus Cholesterin. *Stschr. F. Physiol. Chem.* 1935;237:89.

134. Hitler's final days recalled by physician. *Am. Med. News* 1985; October 11, p. 14.

135. Taylor, W.N. Oral and written testimony provided on April 8, 1987. *Illicit Diversion and Abuse of Human Growth Hormone.* Hearings before the Subcommittee on Health and the Environment, House of Representatives, 100th Congress, First Session. Washington, D.C.: U.S. Government Printing Office, 1987.

Chapter 11

1. Laure, P. [Doping: epidemiological studies]. *Presse. Med.* 2000;29(24): 1365–1372.

2. Mottram, D.R. Banned drugs in sport. Does the International Olympic Committee (IOC) list need updating? *Sports Med.* 1999;27(1):1–10.

3. Personal communications with Robert O. Voy, M.D., chief medical officer and director of Sports Medicine for the United States Olympic Committee, May 1984.

4. Taylor, W.N. "Prescribing for the Competitive Athlete." In: *Winter Sports Medicine* Eds: Casey, J.C., C. Foster, and E.G. Hixon. Philadelphia: F.A. Davis Company, 1990, pp.92–101.

5. Taylor, W.N. *Macho Medicine: A History of the Anabolic Steroid Epidemic.* Jefferson, N.C.: McFarland & Company, 1991.

6. Bergman, R., and R.E. Leach. The use and abuse of anabolic steroids in Olympic-caliber athletes. *Clin. Orthop.* 1985;198:169–172.

7. Schanazer, W., and M. Donike. Metabolism of boldenone in man: Gas chromatographic/mass spectrometric identification of urinary excreted metabolites and determination of excretion rates. *Biol. Mass. Spectrom.* 1992;21:3–16.

8. Taylor, W.N. *Hormonal Manipulation: A New Era of Monstrous Athletes.* Jefferson, N.C.: McFarland & Company, 1985.

9. Catlin, D.H., C.K. Hutton, and S.H. Starcevic. Issues in detecting abuse of xenobiotic anabolic steroids and testosterone by analysis of athletes' urine. *Clin. Chem.* 1997;43(7):1286.

10. Ibid.

11. Personal comments made to the author by Donald H. Catlin, M.D. in his laboratory at UCLA in June 1984.

12. Bamberger, M., and D. Yaeger. Over the edge: Aware that drug testing is a sham, athletes seem to rely more than ever on banned performance enhancers. *Sports Illustrated* April 14, 1997:66.
13. Ibid., 62, 66.
14. Ibid., 62.
15. Ibid.
16. Bowers, L.D. Athletic drug testing. *Clin. Sports Med.* 1998;17(2):299–318.
17. Kicman, A.T., D.A. Cowan, L. Myhre, et al. Effects of sports drug tests on ingesting meat from steroid (methenolone)-treated animals. *Clin. Chem.* 1994;40(11 Pt.1):2084–2087.
18. Arneth, W. [Hormones in animal production — a health risk for the consumer]? *Z. Gesamte. Inn. Med.* 1992;47(2):45–47.
19. Peters, A.R. Endocrine manipulation — toxicological frontiers. *J. Reprod. Fertil. Suppl.* 1992;45:193–201.
20. Snow, D.H. Anabolic steroids. *Vet. Clin. North Am. Equine Pract.* 1993;9(3): 563–576.
21. Daeseleire, E.A.I., A.D. Guesquiere, and C.H. Peteghem. Multiresidue analysis of anabolic agents in muscle tissues and urine of cattle by GD-MS. *J. Chromatogr. Sci.* 1992;30:409–414.
22. Debruyckere, G., R.E. Sagher, and C. Van Peteghem. Clostebol-positive urine after consumption of cantaminated meat. *Clin. Chem.* 1992;38:1869–1873.
23. Bjorkhem, I., and H. Ek. Detection and quanitation of 19-norandrosterone in urine by isotope dilution-mass spectrometry. *J. Steroid Biochem.* 1982;17:447–451.
24. Schanazer and Donike. Metabolism of boldenone in man: Gas chromatographic/mass spectrometric identification of urinary excreted metabolites and determination of excretion rates. *Biol. Mass. Spectrom.* 1992;21:3–16.
25. Schanzer, W., G. Opfermann and M. Donike. Metabolism of stanozolol: Identification and synthesis of urinary metabolites. *J. Steroid Biochem.* 1990;36:153–174.
26. van der Vies, J. Pharmacokinetics of anabolic steroids. *Wien Med. Wochenschr.* 1993;143(14–15):366–368.
27. Schanzer, W., P. Delahaut, H. Geyer, et al. Long-term detection and identification of metandienone and stanozolol abuse in athletes by gas chromatography-high-resolution mass spectometry. *J. Chromatogr. B.* 1996;687:93–108.
28. Schanzer, W., H. Geyer, A. Gotzmann, et al. Endogenous production and excretion of boldenone, an androgenic anabolic steroid. In: Donike, M., H. Geyer, A. Gostzmann, et al., eds. *Proc., 12th Cologne workshop on dope analysis. April 10–15, 1994.* Edition Sport, Koln: Sport und Buch Strauss, 1995:199–211.
29. Donike, M., K.R. Barwald, K.Klostermann, et al. Nachweis von exogenem Testeron [Detection of exogenous testosterone]. In: Heck, H., W. Hollmann, H. Liesen, et al. eds. *Sport: Leistung und Gesundheit, Kongrressbd.* Dtsch. Sportarztekonggress. Koln: Deutscher Arzte-Verlag, 1983:293–298.
30. Catlin, et al. Issues in detecting abuse of xenobiotic anabolic steroids and testosterone by analysis of athletes' urine. *Clin. Chem.* 1997;43(7):1280–1288.
31. Kicman, A.T., R.V. Brooks, S.C. Collyer, et al. Criteria to indicate testosterone administration. *Br. J. Sports Med.* 1990;24:253–264.
32. Carlstrom, K., E. Palonek, M. Garle, et al. Detection of testosterone by increased ratio between serum concentrations of testosterone and 17-alpha-hydroxyprogesterone. *Clin. Chem.* 1992;38:1779–1784.
33. Perry, P.J., J.H. MacIndoe, W.R. Yates, et al. Detection of anabolic steroid administration: Ratio of urinary testosterone to epitestosterone vs the ratio of urinary testosterone to luteinizing hormone. *Clin. Chem.* 1997;43(5):731–735.
34. Deslypere, J.P., P.W. Wiers, A. Sayed, et al. Urinary excretion of androgen metabolites, comparison with excretion of radioactive metabolites after injection of [4-C14] testosterone: Influence of age. *Acta Endocrinol.* (Copenh.) 1981;96:265–272.

35. Raynaud, E., M. Audran, J.F. Brun, et al. False-positive cases in detection of testosterone doping. *Lancet* 1992;340:1468–1469.

36. Garle, M., R. Ocka, E. Palonek, et al. Increased urinary testosterone/epitestosterone ratios found in Swedish athletes in connection with a national control program evaluation of 28 cases. *J. Chromatogr. B.* 1996;687:55–59.

37. Dehennin, L. Detection of simultaneous self-administration of testosterone and epitestosterone in healthy men. *Clin. Chem.* 1994;40:106–109.

38. Becchi, M., R. Aguilera, Y. Farizon, et al. Gas chromatography/combustion/isotope-ratio mass spectrometry analysis of urinary steroids to detect misuse of testosterone in sport. *Rapid Commun. Mass Spectrom.* 1994;8:304–308.

39. Aguilera, R., M. Becchi, H. Casablanca, et al. Improved method of detection of testosterone abuse by gas chromatography/combustion/isotope ratio mass spectrometry analysis of urinary steroids. *J. Mass Spectrom.* 1996;31:169–176.

40. Schanzer, et al. Endogenous production and excretion of boldenone, an androgenic anabolic steroid. In: Donike, M., H. Geyer, A. Gostzmann, et al., eds. *Proc., 12th Cologne workshop on dope analysis. April 10–15, 1994.* Edition Sport, Koln: Sport und Buch Strauss, 1995:199–211.

41. Korenman, S.G., H. Wilson and M.B. Lipsett. Isolation of 17-alpha-hydroxyandrost-4-en-3-one (epitestosterone) from human urine. *J. Biol. Chem.* 1964;239: 1004–1006.

42. Dehennin, L., and A.M. Mosumotos. Long-term administration of testosterone enanthate to normal men; alterations of the urinary profile of androgen metabolites potentially for detection of testosterone misuse in sport. *J. Steroid Biochem.* 1993;44: 179–89.

43. Catlin, D.H., B. Salehian, T. Boghosian, et al. Changes in urinary testosterone and epitestosterone after sublingual testosterone cyclodextrin administration. [Abstract]. *Clin. Res.* 1993;42:74A.

44. Deslypere, et al. Urinary excretion of androgen metabolites, comparison with excretion of radioactive metabolites after injection of [4-C14] testosterone: Influence of age. *Acta Endocrinol.* (Copenh.) 1981;96:265–272.

45. Bergman and Leach. The use and abuse of anabolic steroids in Olympic-caliber athletes. *Clin. Orthop.* 1985;198:169–172.

46. Wolthers, B.G., and G.P. Kraan. Clinical applications of gas chromatography and gas chromatography-mass spectrometry of steroids. *J. Chromatogr. A.* 1999;843(1–2): 247–274.

47. Augilera, R., D.H. Catlin, M.Becchi, et al. Screening urine for exogenous testosterone by isotope ratio mass spectrometric analysis of one pregnanediol and two androstanediols. *J. Chromatogr. B. Biomed. Sci. Appl.* 1999;727(1–2):95–105.

48. Hold, K.M., C.R. Borges, D.G. Wilkins, et al. Detection of nandrolone, testosterone, and their esters in rat and human hair samples. *J. Anal. Toxicol.* 1999;23(6): 416–423.

49. Giaillard, Y., F. Vayssette, A. Balland, et al. Gas chromatographic-tandem mass spectrometric determination of anabolic steroids and their esters in hair: Application in doping control and meat quality control. *J. Chromatogr. B. Biomed. Sci. Appl.* 1999;735(2): 189–205.

50. Segura, J., S. Pichini, S.H. Peng, et al. Hair analysis and detectability of single dose administration of androgenic steroid esters. *Forensic Sci. Int.* 2000;107(1–3): 347–359.

51. Saugy, M., C. Cardis, C. Schweier, et al. Detection of human growth hormone doping in urine: Out of competition tests are necessary. *J. Chromatogr. B. Biomed. Appl.* 1996;687(1):201–211.

52. Abramson, F.P., B.L. Osborn, and Y. Teffera. Isotopic differences in human growth hormone preparations. *Anal. Chem.* 1996;68(11):1971–2.

53. Birkeland, K.I., and P. Hemmersbach. The future of doping control in athletes. Issues related to blood sampling. *Sports Med.* 1999;28(1):25–33.

54. Birkeland, K.I., M. Donike, A. Ljunqvist, et al. Blood sampling in doping control: First experiences from regular testing in athletes. *Int. J. Sports Med.*1997;18(1):8–12.

55. Cayla, J.L., and A. Duvallet. [Screening for exogenous erythropoietin. *Presse. Med.* 1999;28(18):992–996.

56. Bidlingmaier, M., Z. Wu, C.J. Strasburger, et al. Test method: GH. *Baillieres Best Pract. Res. Clin. Endocrinol. Metab.* 2000;1(99–109.

57. Kickman, A.T., J.P. Miell, J.D. Teale, et al. Serum IGF-I and IGF binding proteins 2 and 3 as potential markers of doping with human GH. *Clin. Endocrinol.* (Oxf.) 1997;47(2):43–50.

58. Wallace, J.D., R.C. Cuneo, R. Baxter, et al. Responses of the growth hormone (GH) and insulin-like growth factor axis to exercise, GH administration, and GH withdrawal in trained adult males: A potential test for GH abuse in sport. *J. Clin. Endocrinol. Metab.* 1999;84(10):3591–3601.

59. Uralets, V.P., and P.A. Gillette. Over-the-counter delta5 anabolic steroids 5-androsen 3.17-dione, 5-androsten-3beta, 17beta-diol; dehydroepiandrosterone; and 19-nor-5-androsterone-3,17 dione: excretion studies in men. *J. Anal. Toxicol.* 2000;24(3): 188–193.

60. Taylor. *Hormonal Manipulation: A New Era of Monstrous Athletes.* Jefferson, N.C.: McFarland & Company, 1985.

Chapter 12

1. Taylor, W.N. *Macho Medicine: A New Era of Monstrous Athletes.* Jefferson, NC: McFarland & Company, 1991.

2. _____. *Anabolic Steroids and the Athlete.* Jefferson, NC: McFarland & Company, 1982.

3. _____. *Macho Medicine: A New Era of Monstrous Athletes.* Jefferson, NC: McFarland & Company, 1991.

4. de Kruif, P. *The Male Hormone.* New York: Harcourt, Brace and Company, 1945.

5. Ibid.

6. Taylor, W.N. *Osteoporosis: Medical Blunders and Treatment Strategies.* Jefferson, NC: McFarland & Company, 1996.

7. Newerla, G.J. The history of the discovery and isolation of the male hormone. *New England J. Med.* 1943:228(2): 39–47.

8. NIH Panel Issues Statement on Osteoporosis Prevention, Diagnosis, and Treatment. Bethesda, MD. March 29, 2000.

9. Weil, A. The history of internal secretions. *M.Life* 1925;32:73–97.

10. *The Works of Aristotle,* translated by A. Thompson, vol. 4, book 9. London: Oxford Univ. Press, 1910.

11. *The Extant Works of Aretaeus, the Capadocuean. On Gonorrhea.* Translated by F. Adams. London: Syndenham Society, 1954, p. 346.

12. Rolleston, H. *The Endocrine Organs in Health and Disease: With a historical overview.* London: Oxford Univ. Press, 1936, p. 390.

13. Willis,T. *Cerebri Anatome: Cui Accessit Nervorum Descripto et Asus.* London: J. Flesher, 1664, p. 456.

14. Hunter, J. *A Treatise of the Blood, Inflammation, and Gunshot Wounds.* London: Nicol, 1974, p. 224.

15. Berthold, A.A. Transplantation der Hoden. *Arch. f. Anat. Physiol, u. Wissensch. Med.* 1848;42–46.

16. Brown-Sequard, C. E. Du role physiologique et therapeutique d'un suc extrait de testicules d'animaux d'apres nombre de faits observes ches l'homme. *Arch. de Physiol.* 1889; 1:739–746. Brown-Sequard, C.E. Experience domonstrant is puissance dynamogenique ches l'homme d'un liquide extrait de testicules d'animaux. *Arch. de Physiol.* 1889; 1:651–658.

17. de Kruif. *The Male Hormone.* New York: Harcourt, Brace and Company, 1945.
18. Newerla. The history of the discovery and isolation of the male hormone. *New England J. Med.* 1943:228(2): 39–47.
19. Salomon, F., R.C. Cuneo, R. Hesp, et al. The effects of treatment with recombinant human growth hormone on body composition and metabolism in adults with growth hormone deficiency. *New England J. Med.* 1989; 321(26): 1797–1803.
20. McGee, L.C. The effect of injection of a lipoid fraction of bull testicle in capons. *Proc. Inst. Med.* 1927;6:242.
21. Salomon, et al. The effects of treatment with recombinant human growth hormone on body composition and metabolism in adults with growth hormone deficiency. *New England J. Med.* 1989; 321(26): 1797–1803.
22. Gallagher, T. F., and F. C. Koch. The testicular hormone. *J.Biol.Chem.* 1929;84: 495.
23. David, K., E. Dingemanse, and J. Freud. Uber krystallinisches mannliches Hormon aus Hoden (Testosteron), wirksamer als aus Hard oder aus Cholesterin bereitetes Androsteron. *Ztschr. f. Physiol. Chem.* 1935;233–281.
24. Ruzicka, L., A. Wettstein, and H. Kaegi. Sexualhormone VIII Darstellung von Testosteron unter Anwedung gemischter ester. *Hevl. Chim. Acta.* 1935;18:1478. Butenandt, A., and G. Hanisch. Uber Testosteron; ein Weg zur Darstellun des Testosterons aus Cholesterin. *Ztschr. f. Physiol. Chem.* 1935;237:89.
25. de Kruif. *The Male Hormone.* New York: Harcourt, Brace and Company, 1945.
26. Newerla. The history of the discovery and isolation of the male hormone. *New England J. Med.* 1943:228(2): 39–47.
27. Taylor. *Macho Medicine: A New Era of Monstrous Athletes.* Jefferson, NC: McFarland & Company, 1991.
28. Hitler's final days recalled by physician. *Am. Med. News* 1985;October 11: 14+.
29. Mocquot, M., and R. Moricard. *Bull. Sco. d'obsst. et. gyne.* 1936; 25:787–792.
30. Margiel, E., and E. Zwilling. *Polska gaz. lek.* 1936; 15:815–820.
31. Butenandt, A. *Naturwiss* 1936;24:15–19.
32. Robson, J.M. *Proc. Soc. Exper. Biol. & Med.* 1936;35:49–53.
33. Leipner, S. *Dermat. Wchnschr.* 1936;103:914–920.
34. Laqueur, E., K. David, E. Dengemanse et al. *Ztschr. fl. physiol. Chem.* 1936;233: 281–289.
35. Zuckerman, S., and R. Greene. *Lancet* 1936;2:1433–4.
36. Salmon, U. J. *Proc. Soc. Exper. Biol. & Med.* 1937;37:488–495.
37. Zuckerman, S. *Lancet* 1937;233:676–679.
38. Koch, F.C. *Physiol Rev.* 1937;17:153–159.
39. Kochakian, C.D. Excretion of male hormones. *Endocrinology* 1937;21:60–67.
40. Hamilton, J.B. Treatment of sexual underdevelopment with synthetic male hormone substance. *Endocrinology* 1937;21:649–654.
41. Hamilton, J.B., and G. Hubert. Photographic nature of tanning of human skin as shown by studies of male hormone therapy. *Science* 1938;38:481–487.
42. Barahal, H.S. Testosterone in male involutional melancholia. *Psychiatric Quarterly* 1938;12:743–749.
43. Dix, V.W. *Brit. Med. J.* 1938;2:362–363.
44. Cary, F. S. *Illinois Med. J.* 1938;73:486–491.
45. Kurzrok, L., C.H. Birnberg, and S. Livingston. The treatment of female menopause with male sex hormone. *Endocrinology* 1939;24:347–350.
46. Edwards, E.A., J.B. Hamilton, and S.Q. Duntley. Testosterone propionate as a therapeutic agent in patients with organic disease of the peripheral vessels. *N. Engl. J. Med.* 1939;220:865–869.
47. Lafitte, A., and G. Huret. Desquilbre ovarian et dematoses; action therapeutique de Phormone male dans certaines varietes de psoriasis et d'eczrewas. *Presse. Med.* 1939;47:472–477.

48. Reichert, T. The treatment of juvenile acne, pruritis senilis and senile eczema with testosterone propionate. *Schweiz. med. Wchnschr.* 1939;51:119–123.

49. Bolend, R. *Southern Med. J.* 1939;42:154–159.

50. Day, R.V. *J. Urol.* 1939;41:210–215.

51. Hamilton, J.B. Significance of sex hormones in tanning of the skin of women. *Proc.Soc.Exp. Biol. Med.* 1939;40:502–503.

52. Kurzrok, L., C.H. Birnberg, and S. Livingston. The treatment of female menopause with male sex hormone. *Endocrinology* 1939;24:347–350.

53. Mazer, C., and M. Mazer. The treatment of dysfunctional uterine bleeding with testosterone propionate. *Endocrinology* 1939;24(5):599–602.

54. Albright, F., E. Bloomberg, and P.H. Smith. Postmenopausal osteoporosis. *Trans. Assoc. Am. Phys.* 1940;55:1940.

55. Council on Pharmacy and Chemistry, A.M.A.: The present status of testosterone propionate: Three brands, Perandren, Oreton and Neo-Hombreol not acceptable for N.N.R. *JAMA* 1939;112:1449.

56. "Food and Drug Administration (FDA)." *The World Book Encyclopedia*, 1966, p.303.

57. Oakley, R. *Drugs, Society & Human Behavior.* St. Louis: C.V. Mosby Co., 1983.

58. Ibid.

59. Curtis, J.M., and E. Witt. Sex Hormones: Activities of the Food and Drug Adminstration in the field of sex hormones, *J. Clin. Endocrinol.* 1941;1:363–365.

60. Ibid.

Chapter 13

1. Fruehan, A.E. and T. F. Frawley. Current status of anabolic steroids. *JAMA* 1963;184(7):527-532.

2. Johnson, B.E., B. Lucasey, R.G. Robinson, et al. Contributing diagnosis in osteoporosis: The value of a complete medical evaluation. *Arch. Intern. Med.* 1989; 149:1069-1072.

3. Laan, R. F., W. C. Bujis, L.J. Erning, et al. Differential effects of glucocorticoids on cortical and appendicular and cortical vertebral bone mineral content. *Calcif. Tissue Int.* 1993;52:5-9.

4. Khosla, S., E.G. Lufkin, S.F. Hodgston, et al. Epidemiology and clinical features of osteoporosis in young individuals. *Bone* 1994; 551-555.

5. Lukert, B.P. Glucocorticoid-induced osteoporosis. *Southern Med. J.* 1992;85: 2548-2551.

6. Walsh, L.J., C.A. Wong, M. Pringle, et al. Use of oral corticosteroids in the community and the prevention of secondary osteoporosis; a cross sectional study. *Brit. Med. J.* 1996;313:344-346.

7. Peat, I.D., S. Healy, D.M. Reid, et al. Steroid induced osteoporosis: An opportunity for prevention? *Ann. Rheum. Dis.* 1995;54:66-68.

8. Bell, R., A. Carr, and P. Thompson. Managing corticosteroid induced osteoporosis in medical outpatients. *J. Royal Coll. Physicians Lond.* 1997;31:158-161.

9. LoCascio, V., E. Bonucci and B. Imhimbo, et al. Bone loss in response to long-term glucocorticoid therapy. *Bone Miner.* 1990;8:39-51.

10. Reid, I. R. and A. B. Grey. Corticosteroid osteoporosis. *Baillieres Clin. Rheumatol.* 1993;7:573-587.

11. Picado, C., and M. Luengo. Corticosteroid-induced bone loss: Prevention and management. *Drug Saf.* 1996;15(5):347-359.

12. Olbricht, T., and G. Beneker. Glucocorticoid-induced osteoporosis: Pathogenesis, prevention and treatment, with special regard to rheumatic diseases. *J. Intern. Med.*1993;234(3):237-244.

13. Delany, A.M., Y. Dong, and E. Canalis. Mechanisms of glucocorticoid action in bone cells. *J. Cell. Biochem.* 1994;56:295-302.

14. Swolin, D., C. Brantsing, C. Matejka, et al. Cortisol decreases IGF-1 mRNA levels in human osteoblast cells. *J. Endocrinol.* 1996;149:397-403.

15. Suzuki, Y., Y. Ichikawa, E. Saito, et al. Importance of increased urinary calcium excretion in the development of secondary hyperparathyroidism of patients under glucocorticoid therapy. *Metabolism* 1983;32:151-156.

16. Cosman, F., J. Nieves, J. Herbert, et al. High dose glucocorticoids in multiple sclerosis patients exert direct effects on the kidney and skeleton. *J. Bone Miner. Res.* 1994; 9:1097-1105.

17. Gennari, C. Differential effects of glucocorticoids on calcium absorption and bone mass. *Br. J. Rheumatol.* 1993;32(Suppl. 2):11-14.

18. Reid, I.R., and H.K. Ibbertson. Evidence of decreased tubular resorption of calcium in glucocorticoid-treated patients. *Horm. Res.* 1987;27: 200-204.

19. Brandli, D.W., G. Golde, M. Greenwald, et al. Corticosteroid-induced osteoporosis: A cross sectional-study. *Steroids* 1991;56:518-523.

20. Chappard, D., E. Legrand, M.F. Basle, et al. Altered trabecular architecture induced by corticosteroids: A bone histomorphometric study. *J. Bone Miner. Res.* 1996;11:676-685.

21. Erlichman, N., and T.V. Holohan. Bone densitometry: Patients receiving prolonged steroid therapy. *Health Technol. Assess.* 1996;9:i-vi,1-31.

22. Lukert, B.P., and L. G. Raisz. Glucocorticoid-induced osteoporosis: Pathogenesis and management. *Ann. Intern. Med.*1990;112:352-364.

23. Brochner-Mortensen, K., S. Gjorup, and J.H. Thaysen. The metabolic effect of new anabolic 19-nor-steroids: Metabolic studies on patients with chronic rheumatoid arthritis during combined therapy with Prednisone and anabolic steroid. *Acta Med. Scand.* 1959;165(3): 197-205.

24. Ibid.

25. Package insert for Dianabol, Ciba Laboratories, New York, 1959.

26. Parsons, L., and S.C. Sommers. *Gynecology*. Philadelphia and London, W.B. Saunders Company, 1962, p. 1056.

27. Williams, R.H. *Textbook of Endocrinology*. Philadelphia and London, W.B. Saunders Company, 1962, p. 500.

28. Beeson, P.B., and W. McDermott. *Textbook of Medicine*. Philadelphia and London, W.B. Saunders Company, 1963, p. 1501.

29. revised package insert for Winstrol, Winthrop Laboratories, New York, 1965.

30. Goodman, L.S., and A. Gilman. *The Pharmacological Basis of Therapeutics.* Toronto and London, Macmillan, 1970, p.1576.

31. Krusen, F. H. *Physical Medicine and Rehabilitation*. Philadelphia, London, and Toronto, W.B. Saunders, 1971, p. 563.

32. Revised package insert for Winstrol, Winthrop Laboratories, New York, 1971.

33. Revised package insert for Dianabol, Ciba Laboratories, New York, 1980.

34. Woodard, D. Letter to the editor, Treating of osteoporosis. *New Engl. J. Med.* 1984;312(10):647.

35. American College of Sports Medicine: Position statement on the use and abuse of anabolic-androgenic steroids in sports. *Med. Sci. Sports* 1977;9:11-13.

36. *The Physicians' Desk Reference*, Montvale, NJ, Medical Economics Company, 1976.

37. Harrison, T.R. *Principles of Internal Medicine*, New York, McGraw-Hill, Inc., 1977, p. 2032.

38. Lockefeer, J.H. [Revision consensus osteoporosis]. *Ned Tijdschr. Geneeskd.* 1992; 136(25):1204-1206.

39. Adami, S., V. Fossaluzza, R. Rossini, et al. The prevention of corticosteroid-induced osteoporosis with nandrolone decanoate. *Bone Miner.* 1991;15:73-81.

40. Adami, S., and M. Rossini. Anabolic steroids in corticosteroid-induced osteoporosis. *Wien. Med. Wochenschr.* 1993;143(14-15):395-397.

41. Adachi, J.D., W.G. Bensen and A.B. Hodsman. Corticosteroid-induced osteoporosis. *Semin. Arthritis Rheum.* 1993;22(6):375-384.

42. Renier, J.C., I. Quere, J. Tonon, et al. [Outcome of osteoporosis in Cushing disease. Presentation of a severe form in adults treated with nandrolone. Very favorable course with a 32-years follow-up]. *Rev. Rhum. Ed. Fr.* 1994;61(6-7):513-520.

43. Geusens, P. Nandrolone decanoate: Pharmacological properties and therapeutic use in osteoporosis. *Clin. Rheumatol.* 1995;14(suppl.3):32-3.

44. Reid, I.R., D.J., Wattie, M.C. Evans, et al. Testosterone therapy in glucocorticoid-treated men. *Arch. Intern. Med.* 1996;156(11):1173-1177.

45. Picado, C., and M. Luengo. Corticosteroid-induced bone loss: Prevention and management. *Drug Saf.* 1996;15(5):347-359.

46. Zaqqa, D., and R.D. Jackson. Diagnosis and treatment of glucocorticoid-induced osteoporosis. *Cleveland Clin. J. Med.* 1999;66(4):221-230.

47. Eyre, D.R. Bone biomarkers as tools in osteoporosis management. *Spine* 1997;22(24 Suppl.):17S-24S.

48. Chestnut, C.H., J. L. Ivey, H.E. Gruber, et al. Stanozolol in post-menopausal osteoporosis: Therapeutic efficacy and possible mechanism of action. *Metab. Clin. Exp.* 1983;32:571-580.

49. Ekenstam, E., G. Stalenheim, and R. Hallgren. The acute effect of high dose corticosteroid treatment on serum osteocalcin. *Metab. Clin. Exp.* 1988;37:141-144.

50. Raisz, L.G., B. Wiita, A. Artis, et al. Comparison of the effects of estrogen alone and estrogen plus androgen on biochemical markers of bone formation and resorption in postmenopausal women. *J. Clin. Endocrinol. Metab.* 1996;81(1):37-43.

51. Couch, M., F.E. Preston, R.G. Malia, et al. Changes in plasma osteocalcin concentrations following treatment with stanozolol. *Clin. Chim. Acta* 1986;158:43-47.

52. Ibid.

53. Adami, S., V. Fossaluzza, R. Suppi, et al. The low osteocalcin levels of glucocorticoid-treated patients can be brought to normal by nandrolone decanoate administration. In: Christiansen, C., J.S. Johansen, and B.J. Riis, eds. *Osteoporosis 1987*. Copenhagen: Osteopress ApS, 1987, pp. 1039–1049.

54. Vaishnav, R., J.N. Beresford, J.A. Gallagher, et al. Effects of the anabolic steroid stanozolol on cells derived from human bone. *Clin. Sci.* 1988;74:455-460.

55. Beneton, M.N.C., A.J.P. Yates, S. Rogers, et al. Stanozolol stimulates remodeling of trabecular bone and net formation of bone at the endocortical surface. *Clin. Sci.*1991;81:543-549.

56. Ibid.

57. Pfeilschifter, J., C. Scheidt-Nave, G. Leidig-Bruckner, et al. Relationship between circulating insulin-like growth factor components and sex hormones in a population-based sample of 50- to 80-year-old men and women. *J. Clin. Endocrinol. Metab.* 1996;81(7):2534-2540.

58. Hobbs, C.J., S.R. Plymate, C.J. Rosen, et al. Testosterone administration increases insulin-like growth factor-1 levels in normal men. *J. Clin. Endocrinol. Metab.* 1993;77(3):776-779.

59. Judd, H.C., J.E. Judd, W.E. Lucas, et al. Endocrine function of the post-menopausal ovary: Concentrations of androgens and estrogens in ovaries and peripheral vein blood. *J. Clin. Endocrinol. Metab.* 1974;1020.

60. Longcope, C. Adrenal and gonadal androgen secretion in normal females. *J. Clin. Endocrinol. Metab.* 1986;15:213.

61. Judd, H.L., and S.S.C. Chen. Serum androstenedione and testosterone levels during the menstrual cycle. *J. Clin. Endocrinol. Metab.* 1973;36:475-481.

62. Frock, J., and J. Money. Sexuality and the menopause. *Psycholther. Psychosom.* 1992;57:29-33.

63. Steinberg, K.K., L.W. Freni-Titulaer, E.G. De Puey, et al. Sex steroids and bone density in perimenopausal women. *J. Clin. Endocrinol. Metab.* 1989;69:533-539.

64. Hallstron, T. Sexuality in the climacteric. *Clin. Obstet. Gynecol.* 1977;4:227-239.

65. Longcope, C., C. Franz, C. Morello, et al. Steroid and gonadotrophin levels in women during the peri-menopausal years. *Maturitas* 1986;8:189-196.

66. Zumoff, B., G.W. Strain, L.K. Miller, et al. Twenty-four hour mean plasma testosterone concentration declines with age in normal premenopausal women. *J. Clin. Endocrinol. Metab.* 1995;80:3537-3545.

67. Rannevik, G., S. Jeppsson, O. Johnell, et al. A longitudinal study of the peri-menopausal transition: Altered profiles of steroid and pituitary hormones, SHBG and bone mineral density. *Maturitas* 1995;21:103-113.

68. Procope. B. Studies on the urinary excretion, biological effects and origin of estrogens in postmenopausal women. *Acta Endocrinol.* (Copenh). 1969;135:1-86.

69. Greenblatt, R.B. Androgenic therapy in women. *J. Clin. Endo. Metab.* 1942;2: 65-66.

70. Berlind, M. Oral administration of methyl testosterone in gynecology. *J. Clin. Endo.* 1941;991.

71. Goldman, A. Androgen therapy in women. *J. Clin. Endo.* 1942; 2:750.

72. Salmon, U.J., and S.H. Geist. Effect of androgens upon libido in women. *J. Clin. Endocrionol Metab.* 1943;3:235-238.

73. Harrison, T.J. *Principles of Internal Medicine* New York: McGraw-Hill, 1977, p. 612.

74. Greenblatt, R.B. The use of androgens in the menopause and other genetic disorders. *Obstet. Gynecol. N. America* 1987;14(1):251.

75. Taylor, W.N. *Osteoporosis: Medical Blunders and Treatment Strategies*. Jefferson, N.C.: McFarland & Company, 1996.

76. Taylor, W.N., and C. Alanis. Triple sex steroid replacement therapy for osteoporosis after surgical menopause. *J. Neurol. Orthop. Med. Surg.* 1992; 13:16-19.

77. Szucs, J., C. Horvath, E. Kollin, et al. [Treatment of postmenopausal osteoporosis with low doses of calcitonin and a calcitonin-anabolic combination]. *Orv. Hetil.* 1992;133(23):1414-1418.

78. Hassager, C., and C. Christiansen. Epidemiology, biochemistry and some results with treatment of postmenopausal osteoporosis. *Wein. Med. Wochenscher.* 1993;143 (14-15):389-391.

79. Need, A.G., T.C. Durbridge, and B.E. Nordin. Anabolic steroids in postmenopausal osteoporosis. *Wien. Med. Wochenschr.* 1993;143(14-15):392-395.

80. Passeri, M., M. Pedrazzoni, G. Pioli, et al. Effects of nandrolone decanoate on bone mass in established osteoporosis. *Maturitas* 1993;17(3):211-219.

81. Taylor, W.N., C. Alanis, and D.J. Wigley. Oral cyclical stanozolol and daily micronized 17-beta estradiol combination therapy for postmenopausal osteoporosis: *J. Neurol. Orthop. Med. Surg.* 1994;15:25-30.

82. Lyritis, G.P., C. Androulakis, B. Magiasis, et al. Effect of nandrolone decanoate and 1-alpha-hydroxy-calciferol on patients with vertebral osteoporotic collapse. A double-blind clinical trial. *Bone Miner.* 1994;27(4):209-217.

83. Erdtsieck, R.J., H.A. Pols, C. van Kuijk, et al. Course of bone mass during and after hormonal replacement therapy with and without addition of nandrolone decanoate. *J. Bone Miner. Res.* 1994;9(2):277-283.

84. Watts, N.B., M. Notelovitgs, M.C. Timmons, et al. Comparison of oral estrogens and estrogens plus androgen on bone mineral density, menopausal symptoms, and lipid-lipoprotein profiles in surgical menopause. *Obstet. Gynecol.* 1995; 85(4):529-537.

85. Adachi, J.D. Current treatment options for osteoporosis. *J. Rheumatol. Suppl.* 1996;45:11-14.

86. Flicker, L., J.L. Hopper, R.G. Larkins, et al. Nandrolone decanoate and intranasal calcitonin as therapy in established osteoporosis. *Osteoporos. Int.* 1997;7(1):29-35.

87. Phillips, E. and C. Bauman. Safety surveillance of esterified estrogens-methyltestosterone (Estratest and Estratest HS) replacement therapy in the United States. *Clin. Ther.* 1997;19(5): 1070-1084.

88. Barrett-Connor, E., R. Young, M. Notelovitz, et al. A two-year, double-blind comparison of estrogen-androgen and conjugated estrogens in surgically menopausal women: Effects on bone mineral density, symptoms and lipid profiles. *J. Reprod. Med.* 1999;44(12):1012-1020.

89. Harrison, T.R. *Principles of Internal Medicine.* New York: McGraw-Hill, 1977, p. 1961.

90. Hamdy, R.C. , S.W. Moore, K. E. Whalen, et al. Nandrolone decanoate for men with osteoporosis. *Am. J. Ther.* 1998;5(2):89-95.

91. Turner, H.H. The clinical use of synthetic male sex hormone. *Endocrinol.* 1939;24(6):763-773.

92. Thomas, H.B., and R.T. Hill. Testosterone propionate and the male climacteric. *Endocrinol.* 1941;26:953-954.

93. Goldman, S.F., and M.J. Markham. Clinical use of testosterone in the male climacteric. *J. Clin. Endo.* 1942;2:237-242.

94. Samuels, L.T., A.F. Austin, F. Henschel, et al. Influence of methyl testosterone on muscular work and creatine metabolism in normal young men. *J. Clin. Endo.* 1942;2:649-654.

95. Davidoff, E., and G.L Goodstone. Use of testosterone propionate in treatment of involutional psychosis in the male. *Arch. Neuro. Psych.* 1942;48:811-817.

96. Danziger, L., and H.R. Blank. Androgen therapy in agitated depressions in the male. *Med. Ann. Dist. Columbia* 1942;11(5):181-183.

97. Robie, T.R. Psycho-endocrinotherapy in personality disorders of eunuchoidism. *Dis. Nervous Sys.* 1943;4:42-46.

98. Werner, A.A. The male climacteric: Additional observations of thirty-seven patients. *J. Urology* 1943;49:872-882.

99. Lamar, C.P. Clinical endocrinology of the male with special reference to the male climacteric. *J. Florida Med. Assoc.* 1940;26(8):398-404.

100. Cowley, G. Testosterone and other hormone treatments offer attention: Aging men. *Newsweek*, September 16, 1996, pp. 66-75.

101. Lacayo, R. Are you man enough? *Time*, April 24, 2000, pp. 58–64.

102. Tan, R.S. Managing the andropause in aging men. *Clin. Geratrics* 1999;7(8):63-8.

103. Burns-Cox, N., and C. Gingell. The andropause: Fact or fiction? *Postgrad. Med. J.* 1997;73:553-556.

104. Jenkins, T. Male menopause: Myth or monster? *Vibrant Life* 1995;1(6):12-13.

105. Vermuellen, A., R. Rubens and L. Verdnock. Testosterone secretion and metabolism in male senescence. *J. Clin. Endocrinol.* 1972;34(4):730-745.

106. Gray, A. Age, disease and changing sex hormones in middle-aged men: Results of the Massachusetts Male Aging Study. *J. Clin. Endocrinol. Metab.* 1991;73(5):1016-1025.

107. Ibid.

108. Vermeulen, A. Androgens and male senescence. In: Nieschlag, E. and H.M., eds. *Testosterone: Action, Deficiency, Substitution.* Berlin: Springer Verlag, 1990; 261-273.

109. Nieschlag, E. Reproductive function in young fathers and grandfathers. *J. Clin. Endocrinolol. Metab.* 1982;55:676-681.

110. Abasi, A.A. Low circulating levels of insulin-like growth factors and testosterone in chronically institutionalized elderly men. *J. Am. Geriatr. Soc.* 1993;41(9):975-982.

111. Kenney, R.A. In: *Physiology of Aging* 2nd ed. Chicago: Year Book Medical Publishers, 1989.

112. Tan, R.S., and P. Phillip. Attitudes of older males toward the andropause. *Am. Geriatr. Soc.* 1998;46(9):S74.

113. Hamilton, J.B. Treatment of sexual underdevelopment with synthetic male hormone substance. *Endocrinol.* 1937;21:649-654.

114. Eidelsberg, J., and E. A. Ornstein. Observations on the continued use of male sex hormone over long periods of time. *Endocrinol.* 1949;26:46-53.

115. Escamilla, R., and H. Lisser. Testosterone therapy in eunuchoids: Clinical comparison of parenteral implantation, and oral administration of testosterone compounds in male eunuchoidism. *J. Clin. Endocrinol.* 1941;1(8):633-642.

116. McCullagh, E.P., and L.A. Lewis. Carbohydrate metabolism of patients treated with methyl testosterone. *J. Clin. Endocrinol.* 1942;2:507-510.

117. Pullen, R.L., J.A. Wilson, E.C. Hamblen, et al. Clinical reviews in andrologic endocrinology: II. Treatment of androgenic failure. *J. Clin. Endocrinol.* 1942;2:655-663.

118. Keynon, A.T., K. Knowlton, G. Lotwin, et al. Comparison of metabolic effects of testosterone propionate with those of chorionic gonadotrophin. *J. Clin. Endocrinol.* 1942;2:685-689.

119. Nagelberg, S.B., L. Laue, D.L. Loriaux, et al. Cerebrovascular accident associated with testosterone therapy in a 21-year-old hypogonadal man. *New Engl. J. Med.* 1986;314(10):649-650.

120. Masters, W.H., and D.T. Magallon. Androgen administration in the postmenopausal woman. *J. Clin. Endocrinol.* 1950;10:348-358.

121. Glass, S.J. The advantages of combined estrogen-androgen therapy in the menopause. *J. Clin. Endocrinol.* 1950;10:1611-1617.

122. Greenblatt, R.B., W.E. Barfield, J.F. Garner, et al. Evaluation of an estrogen, androgen, estrogen-androgen combination, and a placebo in the treatment of the menopause. *J. Clin. Endocrinol.* 1950;10:1547-1558.

123. Henneman P.H., and S. Wallach. The use of androgens and estrogens and their metabolic effects: A review of prolonged use of estrogens and androgens in postmenopausal and senile osteoporosis. *Arch. Int. Med.* 1957;100:715-723.

124. Parsons, L., and S.C. Sommers. *Gynecology* Philadelphia and London, W.B Saunders Company, 1962, p. 1056.

125. Sherwin, B.B., and M.M. Gelfand. Sex steroids and affect in the surgical menopause: A double-blind, cross-over study. *Psychoneuroendocrinol.* 1985;10(3):325-335.

126. Foster, G.V., H.A. Zacur and J.A. Rock. Hot flashes in postmenopausal women ameliorated by danazol. *Fertility Sterility* 1985;43(3):401-404.

127. Sherwin, B.B., and M.M. Gelfand. Differential symptom response to parenteral estrogen and/or androgen administration in the surgical menopause. *Am. J. Obstet. Gynecol.* 1985;151(2):153–160.

128. _____. Effects of parenteral administration of estrogen and androgen on plasma hormone levels and hot flushes in the surgical menopause. *Am. J. Obstet. Gynecol.* 1984; 148:552–556.

129. _____. The role of androgen in the maintenance of sexual functioning in oophorectomized women. *Psychosom. Med.* 1987;49:397-402.

130. Burger, H.G., J. Hailes, M. Menelaus, et al. The management of persistent symptoms with estradiol-testosterone implants: Clinical, lipid and hormonal results. *Maturitas* 1984;6:351-358.

131. Burger, H.G., J. Hailes, J. Nelson, et al. Effect of combined implants of estradiol and testosterone on libido in postmenopausal women. *Br. Med. J.* 1987;294:936-937.

132. Warnock, J.K., J.C. Bundren and D.W. Morris. Female hypoactive sexual desire disorder due to androgen deficiency: Clinical and psychometric issues. *Psychopharmacol. Bull.* 1997;33(4):761-766.

133. Sarrel, P., B. Dobay, and B. Wiita. Estrogen and estrogen-androgen replacement in postmenopausal women dissatisfied with estrogen-only therapy: Sexual behavior and neuroendocrine responses. *J. Reprod. Med.* 1998;43(10):847-856.

134. Jubelirer, S.J. The management of menopausal symptoms in women with breast cancer. *W.V. Med J.* 1995;91(2):54-56.

135. Lindsay, R., D. McKhart and A. Kraszewski. Prospective double-blind trial of synthetic steroid (Org OD 14) for preventing postmenopausal osteoporosis. *Br. Med. J.* 1980;May 17: 1207-1209.

136. Hannover, N., K.B. Bjarnason, H. Haarbo, et al. Tibolone: Prevention of bone loss in late postmenopausal women. *J. Clin. Endocrionol. Metab.* 1996;81(7):2419–2422.

137. Riggs, B.L. Editorial: Tibolone as an alternative to estrogen for the prevention of postmenopausal osteoporosis in selected postmenopausal women. *J. Clin. Endocrinol. Metab.* 1196;81(7):2417-2418.

138. Palacios, S., C. Menendez, A.R. Jurado, et al. Changes in sex behavior after menopause: Effects of tibolone. *Maturitas* 1995;22(2):155-161.

139. Lyritis, G.P., S. Darpathios, K. Basdekis, et al. Prevention of post-oophorectomy bone loss with tibolone. *Maturitas* 1995;22(3):247-253.

140. Lindsay, P.C., R.W. Shaw, H.J. Bennink, et al. The effect of add-back treatment with tibolone (Livial) on patients treated with the gonadotropin-releasing hormone agonist triptorelin (Decapeptyl). *Fertil. Steril.* 1996;65(2):342–348.

141. Berning, B., C.V. Kuijk, J.W. Kuiper, et al. Effects of two doses of tibolone on trabecular and cortical bone loss in early postmenopausal women: A two-year randomized, placebo-controlled study. *Bone* 1996;19(4):395-399.

142. Bjarnason, N.H., K. Bjarnason, J. Haarbo, et al. Tibolone: Prevention of bone loss in late postmenopausal women. *J. Clin. Endocrionol. Metab.* 1996;81(7):2419–2422.

143. Argyroudis, E.M., G. Iatrakis, A. Kourkoubas, et al. Tibolone in the treatment of psychosomatic symptoms in menopause. *Clin. Exp. Obstet. Gynecol.* 1997;24(3): 167-168.

144. Nathorst-Boos, J., and M. Hammar. Effect of sexual life — a comparison between tibolone and a continuous estradiol-noresthisterone acetate regimen. *Maturitas* 1997;26(1):15-20.

145. Botsis, D., D. Kassanos, D. Kalogirou, et al. Vaginal ultrasound of the endometrium in postmenopausal women with symptoms of urogenital atrophy on low-dose estrogen or tibolone treatment: A comparison. *Maturitas* 1997;26(1):57-62.

146. Genazzani, A. D., O. Gamba, L. Nappi, et al. Modulatory effects of a synthetic steroid (tibolone) and estradiol on spontaneous and GHRH-induced GH secretion in postmenopausal osteoporosis. *Maturitas* 1997;28(1):27-33.

147. Studd, J., I. Arnala, P.M. Kicovic, et al. A randomized study of tibolone on bone mineral density in osteoporotic postmenopausal women with previous fractures. *Obstet. Gynecol.* 1998;92(4 Pt 1):574-579.

148. Albertazzi, P., R. Di Micco, and E. Zanardi. Tribolone: A review. *Maturitas* 1998;30(3):295-305.

149. Hammar, M., S Christau, J. Nathorst-Boos, et al. A double-blind, randomized trial comparing the effects of tibolone and continuous combined hormone replacement therapy in postmenopausal women with menopausal symptoms. *Br. J. Obstet. Gynaecol.* 1998;105(8):904-911.

150. Ross, L.A., E.M. Alder, E.H. Cawood, et al. Psychological effects of hormone replacement therapy: A comparison of tibolone and sequential estrogen therapy. *J. Psychosom. Obstet. Gynaecol.* 1999;20(2):88-96.

151. Castelo-Branco, C., E. Casals, F. Figueras, et al. Two-year prospective and comparative study on the effects of tibolone on lipid pattern, behavior of apolipoproteins AI and B. *Menopause* 1999;6(2):92-97.

152. Taylor and Alanis. Triple sex steroid replacement therapy for osteoporosis after surgical menopause. *J. Neurol. Orthop. Med. Surg.* 1992; 13:16-19

153. Taylor, et al. Oral cyclical stanozolol and daily micronized 17-beta estradiol combination therapy for postmenopausal osteoporosis: *J. Neurol. Orthop. Med. Surg.* 1994;15:25-30.

154. Edwards, E.A., J.B. Hamilton, and S.Q. Duntley. Testosterone propionate as a therapeutic agent in patients with organic disease of the peripheral vessels: A preliminary report. *New Engl. J. Med.* 1939;220:865-870.

155. Bonnell, R.W. , C.P. Prichett, and T.E. Rardin. Treatment of angina pectoris and coronary artery disease with sex hormones. *Ohio State Med. J.* 1940;37(6):554-556.

156. Lesser, M.A. The treatment of angina pectoris with testosterone propionate. *N. Engl. J. Med.* 1942;226(2):54.

157. Hamm, L. Testosterone propionate in the treatment of angina pectoris. *J. Clin. Endocrinol.* 1942;2:325-328.

158. Lesser, M.A. The treatment of angina pectoris with testosterone propionate: Further observations. *N. Engl. J. Med.* 1943:228(6):185-188.

159. _____. Testosterone propionate therapy in one hundred cases of angina pectoris. *J. Clin. Endocrinol.* 1946;6:549-557.

160. Levine, S.A., and W.B. Likoff. The therapeutic value of testosterone propionate in angina pectoris. *N. Engl. J. Med.* 1943;229:770-772.

161. Walker, T.C. The use of testosterone propionate and estrogenic substance in the treatment of essential hypertension, angina pectoris and peripheral vascular disease. *J. Clin. Endocrinol.* 1942;2:560-568.

162. McGavack, T.H. Angina-like pain; a manifestation of the male climacterium. *J. Clin. Endocrinol.* 1943;3:71-80.

163. Opit, L. The treatment of angina pectoris and essential hypertension by testosterone propionate. *Med. J. Australia* 1943;1:546.

164. _____. The treatment of angina pectoris and peripheral vascular disease by testosterone propionate. *Med. J. Australia* 1943;2:173.

165. Sigler, L.H. and J. Tulgan. Treatment of angina pectoris by testosterone. *New York State J. Med.* 1943;43:1424-1428.

166. Strong, G.F., and A. W. Wallace. Treatment of angina pectoris and peripheral vascular disease with sex hormones. *Canad. Med. Assoc. J.* 1944;50:30-33.

167. Waldman, S. The treatment of angina pectoris with testosterone propionate. *J. Clin. Endocrinol.* 1945;5:305-371.

168. Deslypere, J.P., and A. Vermeulen. Aging and tissue androgens. *J. Clin. Endocrinol. Metab.* 1981;53:430-436.

169. Deslypere, J.P., A. Sayad, L. Verdonc, et al. Androgen concentrations in sexual and non-sexual skins as well as in striated muscle in man. *J. Steroid. Biochem.* 1980;13:1455-1460.

170. Deslypere, J.P., and A. Vermeulen. Influence of age on steroid concentrations in skin and striated muscle in women and in cardiac muscle and lung tissue in men. *J. Clin. Endocrinol. Metab.* 1985;61:648-653.

171. Shapiro, H., J. Christianna, and W.H. Frishman. Testosterone and other anabolic steroids as cardiovascular drugs. *Am. J. Ther.* 1999;6(3):167-174.

172. Chekanov, V.S., G.V. Tchekanov, M. A. Rieder, et al. Force enhancement of skeletal muscle used for dynamic cardiomyoplasty and as a skeletal muscle ventricle. *ASAIO J.* 1995;41(3):M499-507.

173. Blunt, R.J., and J.M. Porter. Raynaud syndrome. *Sem. Arthritis Rheum.* 1981;10(4):282-308.

174. *The Physicians' Desk Reference,* 1980.

175. Lowe, G.D. Anabolic steroids and fibrinolysis. *Wilen. Med. Wochenschr.* 1993;143(14-15):385-385.

176. Kirsner, R.S., W.H. Eaglstein, and M.H. Katz, et al. Stanozolol causes rapid pain relief and healing of cutaneous ulcers caused by cryofibrinogenemia. *J. Am. Acad. Dermatol.* 1993;28(1):71-74.

177. Williamson, A.E., L.A. Cone, and G.S. Huard. Spontaneous necrosis of the skin associated with cryofibrinogenemia, cyroglobulinemia, and homocystinuria. *Ann. Vasc. Surg.* 1996;10(4):365-369.

178. "Osteoporosis Clues May Lie in Space." (Symposium of the National Aeronautics and Space Administration Space Biomedical Research Institute, sponsored by Baylor College of Medicine) *Medical World News* 1986; March 10:104-107.

179. Hargens, A. R., and D.E. Watenpaugh. Cardiovascular adaptation to spaceflight. *Med. Sci. Sports Exerc.* 1996;28(8):982.

180. Baldwin, K.M. Effect of spaceflight on the functional, biochemical, and metabolic properties of skeletal muscle. *Med. Sci. Sports. Exerc.* 1996;28(8):983-987.

181. Tipton, C.M., J.E. Greenleaf, and C.G.R. Jackson. Neuroendocrine and immune system responses with spaceflights. *Med. Sci. Sports. Exerc.* 1996;28(8):988-998.

182. Tipton, C.M., and A. Hargens. Physiological adaptations and countermeasures associated with long-duration spaceflights. *Med. Sci. Sports. Exerc.* 1996;28(8):974-976.

183. Covertino, V.A. Exercise as a countermeasure for physiological adaptation to prolonged spaceflight. *Med. Sci. Sports Exerc.* 1996;28(8):999-1014.

184. Baldwin. Effect of spaceflight on the functional, biochemical, and metabolic properties of skeletal muscle. *Med. Sci. Sports. Exerc.* 1996;28(8):987.

185. Albright, F., E. Parson, and E. Bloomberg. Cushing's syndrome interpreted as hyperadrenocoticism leading to hypergluconeogenesis: Results of treatment with testosterone propionate. *J. Clin. Endocrinol.* 1941;1(5):375-384.

186. Jones, R., E.P McCullagh, D.R. MuCullagh, et al. Methy testosterone. IV. Observations on the hypermetabolism induced by methyltestosterone. *J. Clin Endocrinol.* 1941;1(8):656-663.

187. Reifenstein, E.C. The protein anabolic activity of steroid compounds in man. Supplement to the minutes of the First Meeting of the Conference on Bone and Wound Healing. Josiah Macy, Jr. Foundation, September 11-12, 1942.

188. Werner, S.C., and R. West. Nitrogen retention, creatinuria and other effects of the treatment of Simmond's disease with methyl testosterone. *J. Clin. Invest.* 1943;22 (3):163-189.

189. Kochakian, C.D., and S.H. Bassett. Presentation paper at the 4th Conference on Bone and Wound Healing. Josiah Macy, Jr., Foundation, 1943, p.165.

190. Talbot, N.B., A.M. Butler, and E.A. MacLachlan. Effect of testosterone and allied compounds on mineral, nitrogen and carbohydrate metabolism in a girl with Addison's disease. *J. Clin. Invest.* 1943;22(4):583-594.

191. Kenyon, A.T., K. Knowlton, I. Sandiford, et al. The metabolic effects of testosterone proprionate in Addison's disease. *J. Clin. Endocrinol.* 1943:3(3):131-136.

192. Bassett, S.H., E.H. Keutmann, and C.D. Kochakian. Effect of injections of testosterone propionate on male subjects with nephrotic syndrome. *J. Clin. Endocrinol.* 1943;3(7):400-404.

193. Kinsell, L.W., S. Hertz, and E.C. Reifenstein. Effect of testosterone compounds upon nitrogen balance and creatine excretion in patients with thyrotoxicosis. *J. Clin. Invest.* 1944;23(6):880-890.

194. Simonson, E., W.M. Kearns, and N. Enzer. Effect of methyl testosterone on the muscular performance and central nervous system of older men. *J. Clin. Endocrinol.* 1944;4:528-534.

195. Hoagland, C.L., R.E. Shank, and H. Gilder. Effect of testosterone propionate and methyl testosterone on creatinuria in progressive muscular dystrophy. *Proc. Soc. Exp. Biol. Med.* 1944;55:49-51.

196. Abels, J.C., N.F Young, and H.C. Taylor. Effects of testosterone and of testosterone propionate on protein formation in man. *J. Clin. Endocrinol.* 1944;4:198-201.

197. Butler, A.M., N.B. Talbot, E.A. MacLachlan, et al. Effect of testosterone propionate on losses incident to inadequate dietary intake. *J. Clin. Endocrinol.* 1945;5(8):327-336.

198. Abbot, W.E., J.W. Hirshfield, H.H. Williams, et al. Metabolic alterations following thermal burns. VI. The effect of altering the nitrogen and caloric intake or of admistering testosterone propionate on the nitrogen balance. *Surgery* 1946;20:284.

199. Wilkins, L. and W. Fleischmann. The influence of various androgenic steroids on nitrogen balance and growth. *J. Clin. Endocrinol.* 1946(6):383-401.

200. Shelton, E.K., and A.E. Vardon. The use of methyl testosterone in the treatment of premature infants. *J. Clin. Endocrinol.* 1946;6:812-816.

201. Shelton, E.K., A.E. Vardon, and J.S. Mark. Experimental use of testosterone compounds in premature infants. *J. Clin. Endocrinol.* 1947;7:708-713.

202. Reid, L.C., A.B. Clark, and H.A. Rusk. Newer concepts of protein metabolism in relation to acute phases of disease or injury and to convalescence and rehabilitation. *Postgrad. Med.*1956;19:206-215.

203. Watson, R.N., M.H. Bradley, R. Callahan, et al. A six-month evaluation of an anabolic drug, norethandrolone, in underweight patients. *Am. J. Med.* 1959;26:236-242.

204. Smith, C., and P.C. Johnson. Anabolic effect of 19-nortestosterone phenylpropionate in underweight geriatric women. *Am. J. Geriat. Soc.* 1961;9:304-311.

205. Weston, R.E. Studies on the anabolic effects of Nilevar in patients with chronic congestive heart failure. Proceedings of a conference on the clinical use of anabolic agents. Searle Research Laboratories, Chicago, April 9, 1956, p. 6.

206. Beal, J.M., H. Gilder, D.L. Weeks et al. The effects of anabolic hormones in surgical patients. Proceedings of conference on the clinical use of anabolic agents, p. 23. Searle Research Laboratories, Chicago, April 9, 1956.

207. Abbott, W.E. , S. Levey, H. Krieger, et al. The effect of 19-nor-testosterone cyclopentylpropionate on nitrogen balance and body weight in postoperative patients. *S. Forum* 1956;7:80-86.

208. Peden, J.C., M.C. Maxwell, and A. Ohin. Anabolic effect of a new synthetic steroid on nitrogen metabolism after operation. *Arch. Surg.* 1957;75:625-629.

209. Webb, W.R., and H.S. Howard. Metabolic observations on effect of varied caloric and protein intake on anabolic effects of nor iso-androsterone (Nivelar) following pulmonary resections, abstracted. *Am. J. Med.* 1959;27:331.

210. Bradshaw, J.S., W.E. Abbott, and S. Levey. Use of anabolic steroids in surgical patients. *Am. J. Surg.* 1960;99:600-607.

211. Neuhauser, M., J. Bergstrom, L. Chao, et al. Urinary excretion of 3-methylhistidine as an index of muscle protein catabolism in postoperative trauma: The effect of parenteral nutrition. *Metabolism* 1980; 29(12):1206-1213.

212. Lukaski, H.C., J. Mendez, E.R. Buskirk, et al. A comparison of methods of assessment of body composition including neutron activation analysis of total body nitrogen. *Metabolism* 1981;30(8):777-782.

213. Bilmazes, C., R. Uauy, L.N. Haverberg, et al. Muscle protein breakdown rates in humans based on N-methylhistidine (3-methylhistidine) content of mixed proteins in skeletal muscle and urinary output of N-methylhistidine. *Metabolism* 1978;27(5):525-530.

214. Lukaski, H., and J. Mendez. Relationship between fat-free weight and urinary 3-methylhistidine excretion in man. *Metabolism* 1980; 29(8):758–761.

215. Lewis, L., M. Hahn, and J.R. Kirkpatrick. Anabolic steroid administration during nutritional support: A therapeutic controversy. *J. Parenteral Enteral Nutrition* 1981;5(1):64-66.

216. Forbes, G.B. The effect of anabolic steroids on lean body mass: The dose response curve. *Metabolism* 1985;34(6):571-573.

217. "Large research effort" in sports is planned by the Arthritis Institute, *NIH Week* 1987;7(April 13):1-2.

218. Taylor, W.N. "Sportsmedicine Forum." *Physician Sports Med.* 1987;15(11):36.

219. Schols, A.M., P.B. Soeters, R. Mostert, et al. Physiologic effects of nutritional support and anabolic steroids in patients with chronic obstructive pulmonary disease: A placebo-controlled randomized trial. *Am. J. Respir. Crit. Care Med.* 1995;152(4 Pt 1):1268-1274.

220. Casaburi, R. Skeletal muscle function in COPD. *Chest* 2000;117(5 Suppl.1): 267S-271S.

221. Schols, A.M. Nutrition in chronic obstructive pulmonary disease. *Curr. Opin. Pulm. Med.* 2000;6(2):110-115.

222. Ferreira, I.M., I.T. Verreschi, L.E. Nery, et al. The influence of 6 months of oral anabolic steroids on body mass and respiratory muscles in undernourished COPD patients. *Chest* 1998;114(1):19-28.

223. Spungen, A.M., D.R. Grimm, M. Strakhan, et al. Treatment with an anabolic agent is associated with improved respiratory function in persons with tetraplegia: A pilot study. *Mt. Siani J. Med.* 1999;66(3):201-205.

224. Bauman, W.A., and A.M. Spungen. Metabolic changes in persons after spinal cord injury. *Phys. Med. Rehabil. Clin. N. Am.* 2000;11(1):109-140.

225. Shapiro, J., J. Christiana, and W.H. Frishman. Testosterone and other anabolic steroids as cardiovascular drugs. *Am. J. Ther.* 1999;6(3):167-74.

226. Mendenhall, C.L., T.E. Moritz, G.A. Roselle, et al. A study of oral nutritional support with oxandrolone in malnourished patients with alcoholic hepatitis: Results of a Department of Veterans Affairs Cooperative Study. *Hepatology* 1993;17(4):564-575.

227. Alexander, L.R., A.M. Spungen, M.H. Liu, et al. Resting metabolic rate in subjects with paraplegia: The effect of bed sores. *Arch. Phys. Med. Rehab.* 1995;76:819-822.

228. Demling, R., and L. De Santi. Closure of the "non-healing wound" corresponds with correction of weight loss using the anabolic agent oxandrolone. *Ostomy Wound Manag.* 1998;44:58-68.

229. Ohonovskyi, V.K., M.D. Podilchak, A.S. Matskiv, et al. [Treatment of purulent and necrotic lesions of the lower extremities in patients with diabetes mellitus]. *Klin. Khir.* 1993;9-10:37-40.

230. Shizgal, H.M. Anabolic steroids and total parenteral nutrition. *Wien. Med. Wochenschr.* 1993;143(14-15):375-380.

231. Buyukgebiz, A. and I. Kovanlikaya. Oxandrolone therapy in skeletal dysplasia. *Turk. J. Pediatr.* 1993;35(3):189-196.

232. Beiner, J.M., P. Jokl, J. Cholewicki, et al. The effect of anabolic steroids and corticosteroids on healing of muscle contusion injury. *Am. J. Sports Med.* 1999;27(1):2-9.

233. Fenichel, G., A. Pestronk, J. Florence, et al. A beneficial effect of oxandrolone in the treatment of Duchenne muscular distrophy: A pilot study. *Neurology* 1997;48 (5):1225-1226.

234. Tawil, R. Outlook for therapy in muscular dystrophies. *Semin. Neurol.* 1999;19(1):81-86.

235. Demling, R.H., and L. DeSanti. Oxandrolone, an anabolic steroid, significantly increases the rate of weight gain in the recovery phase after major burns. *J. Trauma* 1997;43(1):47-51.

236. Demling, R.H. Comparison of the anabolic effects and complications of human growth hormone and the testosterone anlog, oxandrolone, after severe burn injury. *Burns* 1999;25(3):215-221.

237. Demling, R.H., and D.P. Orgill. The anticatabolic and wound healing effects of the testosterone analog oxandrolone after severe burn injury. *J. Crit. Care* 2000;15(1):12-17.

238. Morton, R., O. Gleason, and W. Yates. Psychiatric effects of anabolic steroids after burn injuries. *Psychomatics* 2000;41(1):66-68.

239. Demling, R.H., and L. DeSanti. Oxandrolone, an anabolic steroid, significantly increases the rate of weight gain in the recovery phase after major burns. *J. Trauma* 1997;43(1):47-51.

240. Tchekmedyian, N.S., C. Halpern, and J. Ashley, et al. Nutrition in advanced cancer: Anorexia as an outcome variable and target of therapy. *J. Parenter. Enteral. Nutr.* 1992;19(6):88S-92S.

241. Bakhshi, V., M. Elliott, A. Gentili, et al. Testosterone improves rehabilitation outcomes of ill older men. *J. Am. Geriatr. Soc.* 2000;48(5):550-553.

242. Mader, J.T., M.E. Shirtliff, S. Bergquist, et al. Bone and joint infections in the elderly: Practical treatment guidelines. *Drugs Aging* 2000;16(1):67-80.

243. Rosenthal, N. Clinical observations on osteoporosis and myleofibrosis. *Arch. Intern. Med.* 1943;71:793-813.

244. Erf, L.A., and P.A. Herbut. Primary and secondary myleofibrosis: A clinical and pathological study of thirteen cases of fibrosis of the bone marrow. *Ann. Intern. Med.* 1944;21:863-889.

245. Kennedy, B.J. Effect of androgenic hormone in myleofibrosis. *JAMA* 1962;182: 116-119.

246. Gardner, F.H., and D.G. Nathan. Androgens and erythropoiesis. III. Further evaluation of testosterone treatment of myleofibrosis. *N. Engl. J. Med.* 1966;274:420-426.
247. West, W.O. The treatment of bone marrow failure with massive androgen therapy. *Ohio State Med. J.* 1965;61:347-355.
248. Hartman, R.C., D.E. Jenkins, L.C. McKee, et al. Paroxysmal nocturnal hemoglobinuria: Clinical and laboratory studies relating to iron metabolism and therapy with androgen and iron. *Medicine* (Baltimore) 1966;45:331-363.
249. Boada, J.J., and A.M. Frumin. Erythrokinetics in sickle cell anemia after Durabolin therapy. *Clin. Res.* 1962;10:196.
250. Lundh, B., and F.H. Gardner. The hematological response to androgens in sickle cell anemia. *Scand. J. Haematol.* 1970;7:389-397.
251. DeGowin, R.L., A.R. Levender, M. Forland, et al. Erythropoiesis and erythropoietin in patients with chronic renal failure treated with hemodialysis and testosterone. *Arch. Int. Med.* 1970;72:913-918.
252. Richardson, J.R., and M.B. Weinstein. Erythropoietic response of dialyzed patients to testosterone administration. *Arch. Intern. Med.* 1970;72:919-926.
253. Shaldon, S., K.M. Koch, and R. Opermann. Testosterone therapy for anemia in maintenance dialysis. *Br. Med. J.*1971;3:212-215.
254. Parker, J.P., G.J. Beirne, N.J. Desai, et al. Androgen-induced increase in red cell 2,3-disphosphoglycerate. *N. Engl. J. Med.* 1972;287:381-838.
255. Duarte, L., R.L. Sandoval, F.E. Squivel, et al. Androstane therapy of aplastic anemia. *Acta Haematol.* 1972;47:140-145.
256. Daiber, A., L. Herve, I. Con, et al. Treatment of aplastic anemia with nandrolone decanoate. *Blood* 1970;36:748-753.
257. Silink, S.J., and B.G. Firkin. An analysis of hypoplastic anemia with special reference to the use of oymetholone ("Adroyd") in its therapy. *Aus. Ann. Med.* 1968;17: 224-235.
258. Allen, D.M., M.H. Fire, T.F. Necheles, et al. Oxymetholone therapy in aplastic anemia. *Blood* 1968;32:83-89.
259. Sanches-Medal, L., A. Gomez-Leal, and L. Duarte-Zapata. Anabolic therapy in aplastic anemia. *Blood* 1966;28:979.
260. Sanchez-Medal, L., and J. Pizzuto. Effects of oxymetholone in refractory anemia. *Arch. Intern. Med.* 1964;113:721-729.
261. Khahl, M., and A.H. Isbrachim. The treatment of aplastic anemia with anabolic steroids. *Acta Paediatr.* 1962;51:201-208.
262. Martins, J.K. Use of nandrolone phenylpropionate in refractory anemias. *Curr. Ther. Res.* 1961;3:513-519.
263. Chang, J.C., B. Slutzker, and N. Lindsay. Remission of pure red cell aplasia following oxymetholone therapy. *Am. J. Med.* 1978;275(3):345-351.
264. Wallel, E., N. Cambier, M.T. Caulier, et al. Androgen therapy in myelodysplastic syndromes with thrombocytopenia: A report of 20 cases. *Br. J. Haematol.* 1994;87(1):205-208.
265. Katayama, Y., K. Kojima, E. Omoto, et al. Androgen therapy in combination with granulocyte colony-simulating factor and erythropoietin in a patient with refractory anemia. *Int. J. Hematol.* 1996;65(1):89-92.
266. Jockenhove, F., E. Vogel, W. Reinhardt, et al. Effects of various androgen substitution therapy on erythropoiesis. *Eur. J. Med. Res.* 1997;2(7):293-298.
267. Teruel, J.L., R. Marcen, J. Navarro-Antolin, et al. Androgen versus erythropoietin for the treatment of anemia in hemodialyzed patients: A prospective study. *J. Am. Soc. Nephrol.* Jan. 7, 1996; (1):140-144.
268. Wemyss-Holden, S.A., F.C. Hamdy, and K.J. Hastie. Steroid abuse in athletes, a prostatic enlargement and bladder outflow obstruction — is there a relationship? *Br. J. Urol.* 1994;74(4):476-478.
269. Evans, W.J. What is sarcopenia? *J. Gerontol. A. Biol. Med. Sci.* 1995;50(Sec No.):5-8.

270. Baumgartner, R.N., K.M. Koehler, D. Gallagher, et al. Epidemiology of sarcopenia among the elderly in New Mexico. *Am. J. Epidemiol.* 1998;147(8):755-763.

271. Roubenoff, R. The pathophysiology of wasting in the elderly. *J. Nutr.* 1999;129(1S Suppl.):256S-259S.

272. Frichkencht, R. Effect of training on muscle strength and motor function in the elderly. *Reprod. Nutr. Dev.* 1998;38(2):167-174.

273. Melton, L.J., S. Khosla, C.S. Crowson, et al. *J. Am. Geriatr.* 2000;48(6):625-630.

274. Dutta, C. Significance of sarcopenia in the elderly. *J. Nutr.* 1997;127 (5Suppl.):992S-993S.

275. Lamberts, S.W., A.W. van de Beld, and A.J. van der Lely. The endocrinology of aging. *Science* 1997;278(5337):419-424.

276. Baumgartner, R.N., D.L. Waters, D. Gallagher, et al. Predictors of skeletal muscle mass in elderly men and women. *Mech. Ageing Dev.* 1999;107(2):123-136.

277. Short, K.R., and K.S. Nair. Mechanisms of sarcopenia and aging. *J. Endocrinol. Invest.* 1999;(5 Suppl.):95-105.

278. Hoffman, D.M., R. Pallasser, M. Duncan, et al. How is whole body protein turnover perturbed in growth hormone-deficient adults? *J. Clin. Endocrinol. Metab.* 1998;83(12):4344-4349.

279. Proctor, D.N., R. Balogopal, and K.S. Nair. Age-related sarcopenia in humans is associated with reduced rates of specific muscle proteins. *J. Nutr.* 1998;128 (2 Suppl.):351S-355S.

280. Dutta, C., and E.C. Hadley. The significance of sarcopenia in old age. *J. Gerontol. A. Biol. Sci. Med. Sci.* 1995;50(Spec. No.):1-4.

281. Fielding, R.A. The role of progressive resistance training and nutrition in the preservation of lean body mass in the elderly. *J. Am. Coll. Nutr.* 1995;14(6):587-594.

282. Evans, W.J. Reversing sarcopenia: How weight training can build strength and vitality. *Geriatrics* 1996;51(5):51-53.

283. Evans, W. Functional and metabolic consequences of sarcopenia. *J. Nutr.* 1997;127(5 Suppl.):998-1003S.

284. Bross, R., M. Havanbakht, and S. Bhasin. Anabolic interventions for aging-associated sarcopenia. *J. Clin. Endocrinol. Metab.* 1999;84(10):3420.

285. Creutzberg, E.C., and A.M. Schols. Anabolic steroids. *Curr. Opin. Clin. Nutr. Metab. Care* 1999;2(3):243-253.

286. Cohen, P., I. Ocrant, P.J. Fielder, et al. Insulin-like growth factors (IGFs): Implications for aging. *Psychoneuroendocrinology* 1992;17(4):335-342.

287. Bross, R., R. Casaburi, T.W. Storer, et al. Androgen effects on body composition and muscle function: Implication for the use of androgens as anabolic agents in sarcopenia states. *Baillieres Clin. Endocrinol. Metab.* 1998;12(3):365-378.

288. Savine, R., and P. Sonksen. Growth hormone — Hormone replacement for the somatopause? *Horm. Res.* 2000;53(Suppl. S3):37-41.

289. Tenover, J.S. Effects of testosterone supplementation in the aging male. *J. Clin. Endocrinol. Metab.* 1992;75(4):1092-1098.

290. Snyder, P.J., H. Peachey, P. Hannoush, et al. Effect of testosterone treatment on body composition and muscle strength in men over 65 years of age. *J. Clin. Endocrinol. Metab.* 1999;84(8):2647-2653.

291. Ghigo, E., E. Arvat, and F. Camanni. Orally active growth hormone secretagogues: State of the art and clinical perspectives. *Ann. Med.* 1998;30(2):159-168.

292. Camanni, F., E. Ghigo, and E. Arvat. Growth hormone-releasing peptides and their analogs. *Front. Neuroendocrinol.* 1998;19(1):47-72.

293. Kupfer, S.R., L.E. Underwood, R.C. Baxter, et al. Enhancement of the anabolic effects of growth hormone and insulin-like growth factor I by use of both agents simultaneously. *J. Clin. Invest.* 1993;91(2):391-396.

294. Taafee, D.R., L. Pruitt, J. Reim, et al. Effect of recombinant human growth hormone on the muscle strength to resistance exercise in elderly men. *J. Clin. Endocrinol. Metab.* 1994;79(5):1361-1366.

295. Welle, S., C. Thornton, M. Statt, et al. Growth hormone increases muscle mass and strength but does not rejuvenate myofibrillar protein synthesis in healthy subjects over 60 years old. *J. Clin. Endocrinol. Metab.* 1996;81(9):3239-3243.

296. Sheffield-Moore, M. Androgens and the control of skeletal muscle protein synthesis. *Ann. Med.* 2000;32(3):181-186.

297. Bross, R., T. Storer, and S. Bhasin. Aging and muscle loss. *Trends Endocrinol. Metab.* 1999;10(5):194-198.

298. Nemechek, P.M., B. Polksy, and M.S. Gottlieb. Treatment guidelines for HIV-associated wasting. *Mayo Clin. Proc.* 2000;75(4):386-394.

299. Strawford, A., T. Barbieri, R. Neese, et al. Effects of nandrolone decanoate therapy in borderline hypogonadal men with HIV-associated weight loss. *J. Acquir. Immune Defic. Syndr. Human. Retrovirol.* 1999;20(2):137-146.

300. Van Loan, M.D., A. Strawford, M. Jacob, et al. Monitoring changes in fat-free mass in HIV-positive men with hypotestosteronemia and AIDS wasting syndrome treated with gonadal hormone replacement therapy. *AIDS* 1999;13(2):241-248.

301. Romeyn, M., and N. Gunn. Resistance exercise and oxandrolone for men with HIV-related weight loss. *JAMA* 2000;284(2):176.

302. Bhasin, S., T.W. Storer, M. Javanbakht, et al. Testosterone replacement and resistance exercise in HIV-infected men with weight loss and low testosterone levels. *JAMA* 2000;283(6):763-770.

303. Sattler, F.R., S.V. Jaque, E.T. Schroeder, et al. Effects of pharmacological doses of nandrolone decanoate and progressive resistance training in immunodeficient patients infected with human immunodeficiency virus. *J. Clin. Endocrinol. Metab.* 1999;84(4):1268-1276.

304. Hirschfeld, S. Use of human recombinant growth hormone and human recombinant insulin-like growth factor-I in patients with human immunodeficiency virus infection. *Horm. Res.* 1996;46(4-5):215-221.

305. Ferrando, S.J., J.G. Rabkin, L. Poretsky. Dehydroepiandrosterone sulfate (DHEAS) and testosterone: Relation to HIV illness stage and progression over one year. *J. Acquir. Immune. Defic. Syndr.* 1999;22(2):146-154.

306. Segal, D.M., M. Perez, and P. Shapshak. Oxandrolone, used for treatment of wasting disease in HIV-1 infected patients, does not diminish the antiviral activity of deoxynucleoside analogues in lymphocyte and macrophage cell cultures. *J. Acquir. Immune Defic. Syndr. Hum. Retrovirol.* 1999;20(3):215-219.

307. Rabkin, J.G., C.J. Wagner, and R. Rabkin. A double-blind, placebo-controlled trial of testosterone therapy for HIV-positive men with hypogonadal symptoms. *Arch. Gen. Psychiatry* 2000;57(2):141-147.

308. Abbaticola, M.M. A team approach to the treatment of AIDS wasting. *J. Assoc. Nurses AIDS Care* 2000;11(1):45-56.

309. Kugelmass, N. Androgenic arrest of familial enuresis in 75 children. *J. Clin. Endocrinol.* 1946;6:823-825.

310. Hotchkiss, K.S. Effects of massive doses of testosterone propionate upon spermatogenesis. *J. Clin. Endocrinol.* 1944;4:117-120.

311. Mazer, C., and M. Mazer. The treatment of dysfunctional uterine bleeding with testosterone propionate. *Endocrinology* 1939;24(5):599-602.

312. Freed, S.C. Therapeutic use of testosterone in aqueous suspension. *J. Clin. Endocrinol.* 1946;6:571-574.

313. Small, M., C.D. Forbes, and A.C. MacCuish. Metabolic effects of stanozolol in Type II diabetes melllitus. *Horm. Metabol. Res.* 1986;18:647-648.

314. Woolf, P.D., R. W. Hamill, J.V. McDonald, et al. Transient hypogonadotrophic hypogonadism caused by critical illness. *J. Clin. Endocrinol. Metab.* 1985;60(3):444-540.

315. Falabella, A.F. American Academy of Dermatology 1998 Awards for Young

Investigators in Dermatology. The anabolic steroid stanozolol upregulates collagen synthesis through the action of transforming growth factor-beta1. *J. Am. Acad. Dermatol.* 1998;39(2 Pt 1):272-273.

316. Falabella, V., A.S. Greenberg, L. Zhou, et al. Stimulation of collage synthesis by the anabolic steroid stanozolol. *J. Invest. Dermatol.* 1998;111(6):1193-1197.

317. Helfman, T., and V. Falanga. Stanozolol as a novel therapeutic agent in dermatology. *J. Am. Acad. Dermatol.* 1995;33(2 Pt.1):254-258.

318. Elnicki, D.M. Hereditary angioedema. *South. Med. J.* 1992;85(11):1084-1090.

319. Muto, M., H. Furumoto, A. Ohmura, et al. Successful treatment of vitiligo with sex steroid-thryoid hormone mixture. *J. Dermatol.* 1995;22(10):770-772.

320. Lovejoy, J.C., G.A. Bray, C.S. Greeson, et al. Oral anabolic steroid treatment, but not parenteral androgen treatment, decreases abdominal fat in obese, older men. *Int. J. Obes. Relat. Metab. Disord.* 1995;19(9):614-624.

321. Lovejoy, J.C., G.A. Bray, M.O. Bourgeois, et al. Exogenous androgens influence body composition and regional body fat distribution in obese postmenopausal women — a clinical research center study. *J. Clin. Endocrinol. Metab.* 1996;81(6):2198-2203.

322. Crowne, E.C., W.H. Wallace, C. Moore, et al. Effect of low dose oxandrolone and testosterone treatment on the pituitary-testicular and GH axes in bonds with constitutional delay of growth and puberty. *Clin. Endocrinol.* (Oxf.) 1997;46(2):209-216.

323. Ingle, J.N., D.I. Twito, D.J. Schaid, et al. Randomized clinical trial of tamoxifen alone or combined with fluoxymesterone in postmenopausal women with metastatic breast cancer. *J. Clin. Oncol.* 1988;6(5):825-831.

324. Kellokumpu-Lehtinen, P., R. Huovinen, and R. Johansson. Hormonal treatment of advanced breast cancer: A randomized trial of tamoxifen versus nandrolone decanoate. *Cancer* 1987;60(10):2376-2381.

325. Ingle, J.N., D.I. Twitto, D.J. Schaid, et al. Combination hormonal therapy with tamoxifen plus fluoxymesterone versus tamoxifen alone in postmenopausal women with metastatic breast cancer: An updated analysis. *Cancer* 1991;67(4):886-891.

326. Swain, S.M., S.M. Steinberg, C. Bagley, et al. Tamoxifen and fluoxymesterone versus tamoxifen and danazol in metastatic breast cancer — a randomized study. *Breast Cancer Res. Treat.* 1988;12(1):51-57.

327. Pain, J.A., S.S. Wickrenesinghe, and J.W. Bradbeer. Combined tamoxifen and anabolic steroid as primary treatment for breast carcinoma in the elderly. *Eur. J. Surg. Oncol.* 1990;16(3):225-228.

328. Sledge, G.W., P. Hu, G. Falkson, et al. Comparison of chemotherapy with chemohormonal therapy as first-line therapy for metastatic, hormone-sensitive breast cancer: An Eastern Cooperative Oncology Group study. *J. Clin. Oncol.* 2000;18(2):262-266.

329. Wilmore, D.W. Impediments to the successful use of anabolic agents in clinical care. *J. Parenter. Enteral. Nutr.* 1999;23(6 Suppl.):S210-213.

Chapter 14

1. "The Four-Minute Mile." *Encyclopaedia Britannica.* London:William Benton, Publisher. 1965;22:342.

2. Vandenberghe, K., M. Goris, P. Van Hecke, et al. Long-term creatine intake is beneficial to muscle performance during resistance training. *J. Appl. Physiol.* 1997; 83(6):2055–2063.

3. Volek, J.S., N.D. Duncan, S.A. Mazzetti, et al. No effect of heavy resistance training and creatine supplement on blood lipids. *Int. J. Sport Nutr. Exerc. Metab.* 2000; 10(2):144–156.

4. Becque, M.D., J.D. Lochmann, and D.R. Melrose. Effects of oral creatine supplementation on muscular strength and body compositon. *Med. Sci. Sports Exerc.* 2000;32(3):654–658.

5. Kreider, R.B., M. Ferreira, M. Wilson, et al. Effects of creatine supplementation on body composition, strength, and sprint performance. *Med. Sci. Sports Exerc.* 1998;30(1):73–82.

6. Mihic, S., MacDonald, J.R., S. Mckenzie, et al. Acute creatine loading increases fat-free mass, but does not affect blood pressure, plasma creatinine, or CK activity in men and women. *Med. Sci. Sports Exerc.* 2000;32(2):291–296.

7. Volek, J.S., N.D. Duncan, S.A. Mazzetti, et al. Performance and muscle fiber adaptations to creatine supplementation and heavy resistance training. *Med. Sci. Sports Exerc.* 1999;31(8):1147–1156.

8. R.B. Kreider, R. Klesges, and K. Harmon. Effects of ingesting supplements designed to promote lean tissue accretion on body composition during resistance training. *Int. J. Sport Nutr.* 1996;6(3):234–246.

9. Nissen, S., R. Sharp, M. Ray, et al. Effect of leucine metabolite beta-hydroxy-beta-methylbutyrate on muscle metabolism during resistance-exercise training. *J. Appl. Physiol.* 1996;81(5):2095–2104.

10. Clark, R.H., G. Feleke, M. Din, et al. Nutritional treatment for acquired immunodeficiency virus-associated wasting using beta-hydroxy beta-methybutyrate, glutamine, and arginine: A randomized, double-blind, placebo-controlled study. *J. Parenter. Enteral. Nutr.* 2000;24(3):133–139.

11. Panton, L.B., J.A. Rathmacher, S. Baier, et al. Nutritional supplementation of the leucine metabolite beta-hydroxy-beta-methylbutyrate (hmb) during resistance training (1). *Nutrition* 2000;16(9):734–739.

12. Gadzhieva, R.M., S. N. Portugalov, V.V. Paniushkin, et al. [A comparative study of the anabolic action of ecdysten, leveton and Prime Plus, preparations of plant origin]. 1995;58(5):46–48.

13. Azizov, A.P., R.D. Seifulla, I.A. Andudinova, et al. [The effect of the antioxidants elton and leveton on the physical work capacity of athletes.] *Eksp. Klin. Farmakol.* 1998; 61(1):60–62.

14. Elam, R.P., D.H. Hardin, R.A. Sutton, et al. Effects of arginine and ornithine on strength, lean body mass and urinary hydroxyproline in adult males. *J. Sports Med. Phys. Fitness* 1989;29(1):52–56.

15. Vanderberghe, K., M. Goris, P. Van Hecke, et al. Long-term creatine is beneficial to muscle performance during strength training. *J. Appl. Physiol.* 1997;83(6): 2055–2063.

16. Demant, T.W., and E.C. Rhodes. Effects of creatine supplementation on exercise performance. *Sports Med.* 1999;28(1):49–60.

17. Silber, M.L. Scientific facts behind creatine monohydrate as sport nutrition supplement. *J. Sports Med. Phys. Fitness* 1999;39(3):179–188.

18. Ibid.

19. LaBotz, M., and B.W. Smith. Creatine supplement use in an NCAA Division I athletic program. *Clin. J. Sports Med.* 1999;9(3):167–169.

20. I.K. Smith. Crazy for creatine. *Time*, June 12, 2000, p. 93.

21. Benzi, G. Is there a rationale for the use of creatine either as a nutritional supplementation or drug administration in humans participating in a sports? *Pharmacol. Res.* 2000;41(3):255–264.

22. Kraemer, W.J., and J.S. Volek. Creatine supplementation: Its role in human performance. *Clin. Sports Med.* 1999;18(3):651–666.

23. Stout, J., J. Eckerson, K. Ebersole, et al. Effect of creatine loading on neuromuscular fatigue threshold. *J. Appl. Physiol.* 2000;88(1):109–112.

24. Casey, A., and P.L. Greenhaff. Does dietary creatine supplementation play a role in skeletal muscle metabolism and performance? *Am. J. Clin. Nutr.* 2000;72(2Suppl): 607S–617S.

25. Kreider, et al. Effects of creatine supplementation on body composition, strength, and sprint performance. *Med. Sci. Sports Exerc.* 1998;30(1):73–82.

26. Theodorou, A.S., C.B. Cooke, R.F. King, et al. The effect of longer-term cre-

atine supplementation on elite swimming performance after an acute creatine loading. *J. Sports. Sci.* 1999;17(11):853–859.

27. Leenders, N.M., D.R. Lamb, and T.E. Nelson. Creatine supplementation and swimming performance. *Int. J. Sport Nutr.* 1999;9(3):251–262.

28. Mujika, I., S. Padilla, J. Ibanez, et al. Creatine supplementation and sprint performance in soccer players. *Med. Sci. Sports Exerc.* 2000;32(2):518–525.

29. Kamber, M., Koster, M., R. Kreis, et al. Creatine supplementation — part I: Performance, clinical chemistry, and muscle volume. *Med. Sci. Sports Exerc.* 1999;31 (12):1763–1769.

30. McNaughton, L.R., B. Dalton, and J. Tarr. Effects of creatine supplementation on high-intensity exercise performance in elite performers. *Eur. J. Appl. Physiol. Occup. Physiol.* 1998;78(3):236–240.

31. Jones, A.M., T. Atter, and K.P. Georg. Oral creatine supplementation improves multiple sprint performance in elite ice-hockey players. *J. Sports Med. Phys. Fitness* 1999;39(3):189–196.

32. Terjung, R.L., P. Clarkson, E.R. Eichner, et al. American College of Sports Medicine roundtable. The physiological and health effects of oral creatine supplementation. *Med. Sci. Sports Exerc.* 2000;32(3):706–717.

33. Demant, T.W., and E. C. Rhodes. Effects of creatine supplementation on exercise performance. *Sports Med.* 1999;28(1):49–60.

34. Poortmans, J.R., and M. Francaux. Long-term oral creatine supplementation does not impair renal function in healthy adults. *Med. Sci. Sports. Exerc.* 1999;31(8): 1108–1110.

35. Slater, G.J., and D. Jenkins. Beta-hydroxy-beta-methylbutyrate (HMB) supplementation and the promotion of muscle growth and strength. *Sports Med.* 2000; 30(2):105–116.

36. Kreider, R.B. Dietary supplements and the promotion of muscle growth with resistance exercise. *Sports Med.* 1999;27(2):97–110.

37. Nissen, S., R.L. Sharp, L. Panton, et al. Beta-hydroxy-beta-methylbutyrate (HMB) supplementation in humans is safe and may decrease cardiovascular risk factors. *J. Nutr.* 2000;130(8):1937–1945.

38. Van Koevering, M.T., H.G. Dolezal, D.R. Gill, et al. Effects of beta-hydroxy-beta-methylbutyrate on performance and carcass quality of feedlot steers. *J. Anim. Sci.* 1994;72(8):1927–1935.

39. Slater, G.J., P.A. Logan, T. Boston, et al. Beta-hydroxy beta-methylbutyrate (HMB) supplementation does not influence the urinary testosterone:epitestosterone ratio in healthy males. *J. Sci. Med. Sport* 2000;3(1):79–83.

40. Cauffield, J.S., and H.J. Forbes. Dietary supplements used in the treatment of depression, anxiety, and sleep disorders. *Lippincotts Prim. Care Pract.* 1999;3(3): 290–304.

41. Tode, T., Y. Kikuchi, and J. Hirata, et al. Effect of Korean red ginseng on psychological functions in patients with severe climacteric syndromes. *Int. J. Gynaecol. Obstet.* 1999;67(3):169–174.

42. Salvati, G., G. Genovesi, L. Marcellini, et al. Effects of Panax ginseng C.A. Meyer saponins on male fertility. *Panminerva Med.* 1996;38(4):249–254.

43. Lambert, M.I., J. A. Hefer, R.P. Millar, et al. Failure of commercial oral amino acid supplements to increase serum growth hormone concentrations in male bodybuilders. *Int. J. Sports. Nutr.* 1993;3(3):298–305.

44. Fogelholm, G.M., H.K. Naveri, K.T. Kiilavuori, et al. Low-dose amino acid supplementation: No effects on serum human growth hormone and insulin in male weightlifters. *Int. J. Sport Nutr.* 1993;3(3):290–297.

45. Mero, A., H. Pitkanen, S.S. Oja, et al. Leucine supplementation and serum amino acids, testosterone, cortisol and growth hormone in male power athletes during training. *J. Sports Med.* 1997;37(2):137–145.

46. Marcell, T.J., D.R. Taafe, S.A. Hawkins, et al. Oral arginine does not stimulate basal or augment exercise-induced GH secretion in either young or old adults. *J. Gerontol. A. Biol. Sci. Med. Sci.* 1999;54(8):M395–399.

47. Elam, R.P., D.H. Hardin, R.A. Sutton, et al. Effects of arginine and ornithine on strength, lean body mass, and urinary hydroxyproline in adult males. *J. Sports Med. Phys. Fitness* 1989;29(1):52–56.

48. Di Luigi, L., L. Guidetti, F. Pigozzi, et al. Acute amino acids supplementation enhances responsiveness in athletes. *Med. Sci. Sports Exerc.* 1999;31(12):1748–1754.

49. MacLean, D.A., and T.E. Graham. Branched-chain amino acid supplementation augments plasma ammonia responses during exercise in humans. *J. Appl. Physiol.* 1993;74(6):2711–2717.

50. Ghigo, E., E. Arvat, G. Rizzi, et al. Arginine enhances the growth hormone-releasing activity of a synthetic hexapeptide (GHRP-6) in elderly but not in young subjects after oral administration. *J. Endocrinol. Invest.* 1994;17(3):157–162.

51. Platell, C., S.E. Kong, R. McCauley, et al. Branched-chain amino acids. *J. Gastroenterol. Hepatol.* 2000;15(7):706–717.

52. Metzl, J.D. Strength training and nutritional supplement use in adolescents. *Curr. Opin. Pedeiatr.* 1999;11(4):292–296.

53. Ibid.

54. Lissoni, P., G. Rovelli, L. Giani, et al. Endocrine effects of two pineal hormones other than melatonin in health volunteers: 5-methoxytryptophol and 5-methoxytryptamine. *Recenti Prog. Med.* 1998;89(4):183–185.

55. Valcavi, R., M. Zini, G.J. Maestroni, et al. Melatonin stimulates growth hormone secretion through pathways other than the growth hormone-releasing hormone. *Clin. Endocrinol.* (Oxf.) 1993;39(2):193–199.

56. Forsling, M.L., M.J. Wheeler, and A.J. Williams. The effect of melatonin adminstration on pituitary hormone secretion in man. *Clin. Endocrinol.* (Oxf.) 1999;51 (5):637–642.

57. Van Cauter, E., L. Plat, M.B. Scharf, et al. Simultaneous stimulation of slow-release sleep and growth hormone secretion by gamma-hydroxybutyrate in normal young men. *J. Clin. Invest.* 1997;100(3):745–753.

58. Galloway, G.P, S.L. Fredrick, F.E. Staggers, et al. Gamma-hydroxybutyrate: An emerging drug of abuse that causes physical dependence. *Addiction* 1997;92(1):89–96.

59. Louagie, H.K., A.G. Verstraete, C.J. De Soete, et al. A sudden awakening from a near coma after combined intake of gamma-hydroxybutyric acid (GHB) and ethanol. *J. Toxicol. Clin. Toxicol.* 1997;35(6):591–594.

60. Williams, H., R. Taylor, and M. Roberts. Gamma-hydroxybutyrate (GHB): A new drug of misuse. *Ir. Med. J.* 1998;91(2):56–57.

61. Kam, P.C., and F.F. Yoong. Gamma-hydroxybutyric acid: An emerging recreational drug. *Anaesthesia* 1998;53(12):1195–1198.

62. Smith, K.M. Drugs used in acquaintance rape. *J. Am. Pharm. Assoc.* 1999;39(4): 519–525.

63. Davis, L.G. Fatalities attributed to GHB and related compounds. *South. Med. J.* 1999;92(10):1037.

64. Craig, K., H.F. Gomez, J.L. McManus, et al. Severe gamma-hydroxybutyrate withdrawal: A case report and literature review. *J. Emerg. Med.* 2000;18(1):65–70.

65. Schwartz, R.H., R. Mitleer, and M.A. LeBeau. Drug-facilitated sexual assault ("date rape"). *South. Med. J.* 2000;93(6):558–561.

66. Takahara, J., S. Yunoki, W. Yadushiji, et al. Stimulatory effects of gamma-hydroxybutyric acid on growth hormone and prolactin release in humans. *J. Clin. Endocrinol. Metab.* 1977;1014–1017.

67. Steele, M.T., and W.A. Watson. Acute poisoning from gamma hydroxybutyrate (GHB). *Mo. Med.* 1995;92(7):354–357.

68. Friedman, J., R. Weslake, and M. Furman. "Grievous bodily harm:" Gamma hydroxybutyrate abuse leading to a Wernike-Korsakoff syndrome. *Neurology* 1996;46 (2):469–471.

69. Timby, N., A. Eriksson, and K. Bostrom. Gamma-hydroxybutyrate associated deaths. *Am. J. Med.* 2000;108(6):518–519.

70. Addolorato, G., E. Castelli, G.F. Stefanini, et al. An open multicentric study evaluating 4-hydroxybutyric acid sodium salt in the medium-term treatment of 179 alcohol dependent subjects. GHB Study Group. *Alcohol Alcohol.* 1996;31(4):341–345.

71. Ferrara, S.D., S. Zotti, L. Tedeschi, et al. Pharmacokinetics of gamma-hydroxybutyric acid in alcohol dependent patients after single and repeated oral doses. *Br. J. Clin. Pharmacol.* 1992;34(3):231–235.

72. Gallimberti, L., G. Canton, N. Gentile, et al. Gamma-hydroxybutyric acid for treatment of alcohol withdrawal syndrome. Lancet 1989;2(8666):787–789.

73. Bant, T., and M. Hojo. The central action of gamma-butyrolactone and gamma-hydroxybutyrate. II. The effect of GHB and related agents on the cortical dendritic responses. *Jpn. J. Pharmacol.* 1969;19(1):89–101.

74. Gerra, G., R. Caccavari, B. Fontanesi, et al. Naloxone and metergoline effects on growth hormone response to gamma-hydroxybutyric acid. *Int. Clin. Psychopharmacol.* 1995;10(4):245–250.

75. Rosen, M.I., H. R. Pearsall, S.W. Woods, et al. Effects of gamma-hydroxybutyric acid (GHB) in opioid-dependent patients. *J. Subst. Abuse Treat.* 1997;14(2): 149–154.

76. Ferrara, S.D., R. Giorgetti, S. Zancaner, et al. Effects of single dose of gamma-hydroxybutyric acid and lorazepam on psychomotor performance and subjective feelings in healthy volunteers. *Eur. J. Clin. Pharmacol.* 1999;54(11):821–827.

77. Addolorato, G., G. Balducci, E. Capristo, et al. Gamma-hydroxybutyric acid (GHB) in the treatment of alcohol withdrawal syndrome: A randomized comparative study versus benzodiazepine. *Alcohol. Clin, Exp. Res.* 1999;23(10):1596–1604.

78. Hunderup, M.C., and A.J. Jorgensen. [Poisoning with gamma-hydroxybutyrate. Cases reported in connection with "cultural festivals" in August 1999 in Kolding]. *Ugeskr. Laeger* 1999;161(50):6939–6940.

79. Addolorato, G., M. Cibin, F. Caputo, et al. Gamma-hydroxybutyric acid in the treatment of alcoholism: Dosage fractioning utility in non-responder alcoholic patients. *Drug Alcohol Depend.* 1998;53(1):7–10.

80. Fisker, S., S. Neilsen, L. Ebdrup, et al. The role of nitric oxide in L-arginine-stimulated growth hormone release. *J. Endocrinol. Invest.* 1999;22(5 Suppl.):89–93.

81. Rigamonti, A.E., S.G. Cella, N. Marazzi, et al. Nitric oxide modulation of the growth-hormone-releasing activity of Hexarelin in young and old dogs. *Metabolism* 1999;48(2):176–182.

82. Pinilla, L., M. Tena-Sempere, E. Aguilar, et al. Nitric oxide stimulates growth hormone secretion in vitro through a calcium- and cyclic guanosine monophosphate-independent mechanism. *Horm. Res.* 1999;51(5):242–247.

83. Atz, A.M., and D.L. Wessel. Sildenafil ameliorates effects of inhaled nitric oxide withdrawal. *Anesthesiology* 1999;91(1):307–310.

84. Pinilla, L., D. Gonzalez, M. Tena-Sempere, et al. Nitric oxide (NO) stimulates gonadotropin secretion in vitro through a calcium-dependent, cGMP-independent mechanism. *Neuroendocrinology* 1998;68(3):180–186.

85. Cuttica, C.M., M. Giusti, L. Bocca, et al. Nitric oxide modulates in vivo and in vitro growth hormone release in acromegaly. *Neuroendocrinology* 1997;66(6): 426–431.

86. Moretto, M., F.J. Lopez, and A. Negro-Vilar. Nitric oxide regulates luteinizing hormone-releasing secretion. *Endocrinology* 1993;133(5):2399–2402.

87. Pinilla, L., M. Tena-Sempere, D. Gonzalez, et al. The role of nitric oxide in the control of basal and LHRH-stimulated LH secretion. *J. Endocrinol. Invest.* 1999;22(5): 340–348.

88. Hurford, W.E. The biologic basis for inhaled nitric oxide. *Respir. Care Clin. N. Am.* 1997;3(3):357–369.

89. Durand, F., P. Mucci, L. Safont, et al. Effects of nitric oxide inhalation on pulmonary gas exchange during exercise in highly trained athletes. *Acta Physiol. Scand.* 1999;165(2):169–176.

90. Rich, J.D., B.P. Dickinson, N.A. Merriman, et al. Insulin use by bodybuilders. *JAMA* 1998;279(20):1613.

91. Konrad, C., G. Schupfer, M. Wietlisbach, et al. [Insulin as an anabolic: Hypoglycemia in the bodybuilding world]. *Anasthesiol. Intensivmed. Notfallmed. Schmerzther.* 1998;33(7):461–463.

Chapter 15

1. Akst, D. *Wonder Boy: Barry Minkow — The Kid Who Swindled Wall Street*, New York: Charles Scribner's Sons, 1990.

2. Elofson, G., and S. Elofson. Steroids claimed our son's life. *Physician Sportsmed.* 1990; 18(8):15-16.

3. Taylor, W.N. Gigantic athletes: The dilemma of human growth hormone. *Futurist* 1985;(August): 8-12.

Chapter 16

1. Fields, L., W.R. Lange, N.A. Kreiter, et al. A national survey of drug testing policies for college athletes. *Med. Sci. Sports Exerc.* 1994;26(6):682–686.

2. Sator, M.O., P. Franz, C. Egarter, et al. Effects of tibolone on auditory brainstem responses in postmenopausal women — a randomized, double-blind, placebo-controlled trial. *Fertil. Steril.* 1999;72(5):885–888.

3. Hervey, G.R., I. Hutchinson, A.V. Knibbs, et al. "Anabolic" effects of methandienone in men undergoing athletic training. *Lancet* 1976;2(7988):699–700.

4. Uralets, V.P., and P.A. Gillette. Over-the-counter delta5 anabolic steroids 5-androsen-3,17-dione; 5-androsten-3beta, 17beta-diol; dehydroepiandrosterone; and 19-nor-5-androsten-3,17-dione: Excretion studies in men. *J. Anal. Toxicol.* 2000;24(3): 188–193.

5. Lovstakken, K., L. Peterson, and A.L Homer. Risk factors for anabolic steroid use in college students and the role of expectancy. *Addict. Behav.* 1999;24(3):425430.

6. Pope, H.G. and D.L. Katz. Psychiatric and medical effects of anabolic-androgenic steroid use: A controlled study of 160 athletes. *Arch. Gen. Psychiatry* 1994;51(5): 375–782.

7. Su, T.P., M. Pagliaro, P.J. Schmidt, et al. Neuropsychiatric effects of anabolic steroids in male normal volunteers. *JAMA* 1993;269(21):2760–2764.

8. Kelly J.P., and B. E. Leonard. Models and responses in depression and aggression. *Biochem. Soc. Trans.* 1998;26(1):6165.

9. Bjork, J.M, D.M. Dougherty, and F.G. Moeller. A positive correlation between self-ratings of depression and laboratory-measured aggression. *Psychiatry Res.* 1997;69(1): 3338.

10. Riley, W.T., F.A. Treiber, and M.G. Woods. Anger and hostility in depression. *J. Nerv.Ment. Dis.* 1989;177(11):668–674.

11. Carstens, S., and I. Andersen. [Intranasal glucagon in the treatment of hypoglycemia: A therapeutic possibility in the future]. *Ugeskr. Laeger* 1994;156(30):4339–4342.

12. Perry, H.M. Risk of Creutzfeldt-Jakob disease in bodybuilders. *Br. Med. J.* 1993;307(6907):803.

13. Long, S.F., M.C. Wilson, K.J Sufka, et al. The effects of cocaine and nandrolone co-administration on aggression in male rats. *Prog. Neuropsychopharmacol. Biol. Psychiatry* 1996;20(5):839–856.

14. Evans, N.A., D.J. Bowery, and G.R. Newman. Ultrastructure analysis of ruptured tendon from anabolic steroid users. *Injury* 1998;29(10):769–773.

15. Orchard, J.W., and J.P. Best. Test violent offenders for anabolic steroid use. *Med. J. Aust.* 1994;161(3):232.

16. Laudat, A., J. Guechot, and A.M. Palluel. Seminal androgen concentration and residual sperm cytoplasm. *Clin. Chim. Acta* 1998;276(1):1118.

17. Foreman, M.I., and I. Clanachan. The percutaneous penetration of nandrolone decanoate. *Br. J. Dermatol.* 1975;93(1):4752.

18. Dey, D.C., N. Ahmed, A. Quasem, et al. Effect of anabolic steroid on the development and treatment of rickets in rats. *Bangladesh Med. Res. Counc. Bull.* 1978;4(1):3237.

19. Cole, T.J. Secular trends in growth. *Proc. Nutr. Soc.* 2000;59(2):317–324.

20. Itil, T.M., S.T. Michael, M. Shapiro, et al. The effects of mesterolone, a male sex hormone in depressed patients (a double blind controlled study). *Methods Find. Exp. Clin. Pharmacol.* 1984;6(6):331–337.

21. Weisbel, L., M. Follenius, and G. Brandenberger. [Biologic rhythms: Their changes in night-shift workers]. *Presse. Med.*1999;28(5):252–258.

22. Beaufrere, B. Can growth hormone counteract the effects of glucocorticoids on protein metabolism? *Acta Paediatr. Suppl.*1999;88(428):97–99.

23. Tomten, S.E., J. A. Falch, K.I. Birkeland, et al. Bone mineral density and menstrual irregularities: A comparative study on cortical and trabecular bone structures in runners with alleged normal eating behavior. *Int. J. Sports Med.* 1998;19(2):92–97.

24. Fine, R.N., E.K. Sullivan, and A. Tejani. The impact of recombinant human growth hormone treatment on final adult height. *Pediatr. Nephrol.* 2000;14(7):679–681.

Index

About the Author

William N. Taylor, M.D., has been an anabolic steroid researcher for more than two decades. He has published several articles for both the scientific and lay press. Dr. Taylor has four previous books that deal with the use and abuse of anabolic steroids and growth hormones: *Anabolic Steroids and the Athlete* (1982), *Hormonal Manipulation: A New Era of Monstrous Athletes* (1985), *Macho Medicine: A History of the Anabolic Steroid Epidemic* (1991), and *Osteoporosis: Medical Blunders and Treatment Strategies* (1996), all published by McFarland.

Dr. Taylor's educational background includes a B.S. in chemistry from the University of West Florida (1975), an M.S. in chemical and polymer engineering from the University of Tennessee (1976), and an M.D. from the University of Miami School of Medicine (1981), where he was inducted into the national Alpha Omega Alpha Honor Medical Society. He completed a flexible internship in the Pensacola Educational Program (1982).

Dr. Taylor became a Fellow in the American College of Sports Medicine in 1985. He was selected as a physician crew chief for the United States Olympic Committee's Drug Control/Education Program during the quadrennial 1984–1988. He was an early voice in the effort to have anabolic steroids reclassified as controlled substances under federal law.

4096